The American Utopian Adventure

FRANCES WRIGHT: *FREE ENQUIRER*

Frances Wright at 40.

Frances Wright
Free Enquirer: The
Study of a Temperament

By A. J. G. PERKINS *and*
THERESA WOLFSON

ILLUSTRATED

PORCUPINE PRESS, INC.
Philadelphia 1972

Library of Congress Cataloging in Publication Data

Perkins, Alice J   G
   Frances Wright, free enquirer.

  (The American utopian adventure)
  Bibliography: p.
  1. D'Arusmont, Mme. Frances (Wright) 1795-1852.
I. Wolfson, Theresa, 1897-   joint author.
HQ1413.D2P4 1972   301.24'2'0924 [B]   79-187457
ISBN 0-87991-008-9

First edition 1939 (New York: Harper & Brothers, Publishers, 1939)

Reprinted 1972 by PORCUPINE PRESS, INC., 1317 Filbert St., Philadelphia, Pa. 19107

Manufactured in the United States of America

CONTENTS

ILLUSTRATIONS

PART ONE

CHAPTER I

The Making of a Rebel

How far does the challenge and menace of a world in chaos affect the awakening consciousness of a newborn child?

Frances Wright was born on September 6th, 1795, two years after those September massacres which heralded in the first French republic and plunged all Europe into war. Her birthplace was the busy, prosperous old trading city of Dundee at the mouth of the river Tay. A grim huddle of stone, old houses so closely interlocking, so darkly overhanging its narrow streets and stinking wynds and closes, that one wonders how the people who were condemned to pass their lives there were able to bear it.

But bear it they did in great numbers, for old Dundee was overcrowded by the shifting population that is always attracted to any important seaport. What better breeding place could be found for the new ideas of liberty, equality, fraternity, which were playing such havoc among old, established institutions across the English Channel?

One is not surprised to read in the records of the town, that a riotous mob, excited by demagogic leaders, actually planted a Liberty Tree under the shadow of the old town Cross, in imitation and celebration of the French fete of July 14th. The tree, indeed, was promptly uprooted by soldiers called out by the city magistracy, but there were rumors that it still lived, replanted secretly in a garden owned by a revolutionary sympathizer.

As for young James Wright, father of Frances, family tradition has it that for the whole first year of his marriage, up to the birth of his eldest child, a son, he was under police surveillance. He was more than suspected of a dangerous sympathy with the tendencies expressed by Thomas Paine in his famous tract, *The Rights of Man*, published in 1791. He had, in fact, been one of those who contributed to the expenses of a cheap reprint of that work to bring it within the

3

means of the very poor. He was also suspected of connection with the famous meeting of the Friends of the People, in Edinburgh, which resulted in the trial and punishment of two young men. Thomas Muir, a student of Glasgow College, and Thomas Fysse Palmer, a young Unitarian minister of Dundee were both transported to Botany Bay and died in consequence of their sufferings there. The story goes that James Wright saved himself and his friends from further persecution by taking a small boat one dark night and rowing out alone into the center of the river with all the compromising papers in his possession; "dangerous documents," so we read in the Dundee records, "which he committed to the keeping of the Tay."

The Wrights were tradesmen, linen merchants of Dundee. The great man of the family was a certain Alexander, town councillor in 1724. But James Wright's mother was a sister of James Milne, professor of moral philosophy in Glasgow College, and the boy himself received a better education than that common among tradesmen, even Scots tradesmen, of the late eighteenth century. He was sent to the best schools of Perth and Edinburgh, and afterwards to Trinity College, Dublin. He had the further advantage of some months' travel on the Continent. Even after he had settled down with his uncle Alexander in the linen trade, he still retained tastes and habits above his station. His collection of rare coins and trade tokens such as were common between business men in the old days when other forms of small currency were insufficient, may be seen today among other collections of the same kind in the British Museum.

And his wife, Camilla Campbell, daughter of General Duncan Campbell (one of the Campbells of Inverary and very proud and conscious of the fact) would seem also to have come of a class accustomed to consider itself as on a distinctly higher social level than either tradesmen or college professors. An article appearing in the *Gentleman's Magazine* shortly after her death tells us that she was a woman of unusual beauty and angelic goodness, with great sensibility, a high sense of propriety, generosity, frankness, integrity of principle and independence of mind. She was not yet twenty when she entered upon this new life so full of contrasts—and not always agreeable contrasts—to everything she was accustomed to. No great loss of material ease and comfort perhaps, for these were oftener found in the households of prosperous tradespeople than in the homes of the Scots nobility of that day. The Wrights, for instance, are said to have had their own especial table linen, interwoven with the family name.

But there was often, too, a lack of ceremony amounting even to un-couthness, in the homes of the Scottish industrial class, which must have made the young wife's relations with her husband's numerous kinsfolk a matter of tact and patience. There is a letter of hers, how-ever, written to her husband on the fourth anniversary of their mar-riage, while she herself was on a visit to her father and sister in Eng-land, which proves that she was happy and not only happy but proud, and satisfied with her surroundings.

Frances Wright was at this time a baby less than two years old with an elder brother hardly more than a year older. She had been brought by her parents to be shown off to her grandfather and young aunt. But James had gone back to Dundee with the baby and its nurse, leaving his wife for the first time, perhaps, since their marriage, to complete her visit alone.

Ripon, April 11th, 1796.

On this happy day, my dearest James, I am sure you will expect that I should write you a few lines, as we are separated from each other. I need not say how much more rejoiced I should be to have your dear self here, but when I think how tenderly you are employed in caring for our beloved children, I less regret your absence, though it is on the day I regard as the most valued of my life.

Yours, with Dick's scrawl came on Friday last. [Dick was the eldest child, the three-year old] Many thanks to you for it. I was very anxious to hear you had got home safe, and the infants with Nursey were so well. I hope that little Fan will feel no bad effects from the weaning and cutting her first teeth, which I was much afraid of—Dick having been so ill.

Not one word am I saying about the good people here, who have been so attentive to me since I came. Town and Country have all been here with the kindest invitations. I have been out very little since I came on account of Dad being called to Wakefield on the death of an officer, the man who came so drunk into the coach when you was here with Fan.

Dad drove me yesterday to Fountain Abbey with which I am much delighted. In the evening, though it was Sunday, we went to a musical party and a supper at the Honorable Mr. Hobart's. He has been married for some time to a sweet little woman, they have five children, and are as domestic as ourselves, for which I admire them.

My father got a letter from Mr. Watson [head of the Dun-dee Grammar school and Camilla's uncle by marriage], in which he mentioned the children being down there. I beg Nursey will be careful not to let them be in that part of the town any more. I am so afraid of the chin cough or measles. God bless you.

The postscript is from the father-in-law, General Campbell.

My dear James
    Though I am hurried to death in writing my Infant of a nephew's accounts for last quarter to send the paymaster, I break off to say that by the Lord I will drink your health and your good-for-nothing wife's on this day, in as full a bumper as I can convey to my Receiver, and will not forget Richard nor Fan. May you all live and be as happy, as I can, from my heart, wish you. I send many returns of this day. On her approaching Natal day I will repeat the wish and Bumper also. God bless you. Cam and Fan are both plaguing me, yet believe me, I am
                    Yours affectionately
                                        D. C.

As might have been guessed from that sentence in Camilla's letter which contained the command to "Nursey" that the children should not be taken to the crowded center of the town, the house in which James Wright had set up housekeeping after his marriage was somewhat removed from that part of Old Dundee which harbored the great mass of its inhabitants. Miln Building, the Nethergate, is the name usually given for her birthplace. The original building, however, was pulled down very shortly after the Wrights left it; but the houses built on the same site are more than a hundred years old and are probably very much on the same plan as those which they have replaced.

From the windows at the back of these old houses in the Nethergate, the ebb and flow of the tides of the North Sea could be clearly felt and seen. For many years, until the waters of the Tay were caught and confined into their modern tidal basins, people could and did bathe in the sea from their gardens. A right of way through these same gardens led to the open country, with its scattered farms, its gently rolling hills and its purple heather. And within the house there was a normal family life, in the wholesome companionship of an elder brother and a baby sister, a young father and mother happy in their three children, happy in each other. Perhaps if this fortunate state of things could have continued even a few years longer, that side of Frances Wright's character which gave her such unhappiness even in the midst of really great achievement, which thwarted her best endeavor for the benefit of society, which betrayed her finally into a bitter and lonely old age, would have remained in safe proportion, or, perhaps never have developed at all.

But these last years of the eighteenth century were not a propitious time for happy family life in the home of a Dundee tradesman.

The first result of war with France had been a sudden prosperity. Trade flourished while the army was hurriedly prepared for its campaign in the Low Countries. Domestic manufacture reaped a golden harvest, when the foreign sources of supply were cut off, or rendered uncertain by enemy movements the other side of the English Channel. But Pitt's policy of lending money to his allies soon drained the country of gold. The suspension of specie payments with the resulting inflation of paper, the fluctuation of values and the instability of individual profit and loss, is part of the history of the time.

Some time in the year 1797 James Wright's affairs were so involved that he was reduced to the desperate expedient of putting all his real estate into the hands of his uncle and two other Dundee tradesmen, to save it from his creditors. And almost at the same moment the heavier shadow of his wife's failing health fell upon him. She died in Feb. 1798, when Frances was only a little over two years old, leaving to this child at least, a blank of loneliness and emptiness which all her later life she tried in vain to fill. The death of her father followed some two months later, only a week after the fifth anniversary of his marriage. From that time on, all the responsibility for the up-bringing of the three orphan children fell to the Campbell side of the family.

The boy Richard, his father's heir, but heir, most probably to little else but difficulties and debts, was placed with the family of Watson cousins, children of Duncan Campbell's elder sister. They had deserted the Campbell tradition of military service and set themselves up in a firm of cotton importers, Messrs. Watson & Wighton, in Glasgow. The boy did not see his sisters again for more than eight years, but he seems to have been very happy with his Watson kinfolk. He was especially attached to his cousin Betsy, who presided over the household after Mrs. Watson died, and whom he learned to call mother.

The two little girls, however, were taken at once to England and spent the rest of their childhood and early youth with their grand-father and young aunt, Frances Campbell. From all one knows of this maternal grandfather, he seems to have been a very characteristic example of the smart soldier of his day, rather a mental lightweight, possessed of a measure of swagger and good looks which enabled him to marry, as he did, a woman of excellent social position and family connections, with a very considerable personal fortune. His wife, Elisabeth Friend, daughter of a dean of Canterbury Cathedral, was on her mother's side a Robinson, of Rokeby, Yorkshire. Mrs. Montagu, the bluestocking, was her aunt, and Barron Rokeby, Bishop of Armagh and Primate of all Ireland, famous for his pride, his passion for building, and his immaculate white lawn sleeves, was her great-uncle.

Thus it happened that, left orphans at an early age, little Frances and Camilla Wright were heiresses in a small way. They were wards in chancery for their share of their grandmother's fortune, by which court they had also been placed under the personal guardianship of their young aunt, their mother's only sister.

Their first stopping place seems to have been in London, but in 1806 Miss Campbell set up her own establishment near the charming Devonshire village of Dawlish, where she proceeded to devote herself wholeheartedly to the up-bringing of her two little nieces, on the same rigid lines which had directed her own education, with all the advantages and disadvantages of a class tradition against which the storms of the French Revolution had beaten in vain.

Unfortunately, Fanny was too much the product of her age and generation to submit easily to these new surroundings. She herself tells in later writing, how quickly she perceived the inconsistencies and absurdities of the world about her. The sight of the unnumbered poor in London, for instance, the wretched women, the starving children who came sometimes to beg at the door of her grandfather's carriage during their daily drives, excited her pity even while still very young.

"Why are those people so poor?" she asked.

"Because they are too lazy to work," answered General Campbell.

"But you don't work, Grandfather."

"Certainly not," replied the General. "I could not associate with the rich if I worked. It is a shame for a rich man to work. Some are born rich and some are born poor. The Scriptures say, 'The poor you shall have always with you.' God intended that there should be poor and that there should be rich."

She pursued him further with questions as to how he came to be born one of the fortunate rich.

"I inherited it from my father and he from his father, and so on for many generations."

And when she continued to express her sense of the unfairness of such an arrangement, her grandfather put an end to the conversation. "You must not indulge in thoughts like these. They will prevent you from being admitted into good society. You are fitting yourself to associate with the canaille of the streets."

It was the same with her teachers when she pressed them too hard with searching questions. See the following passage in her autobiography, written quaintly in the third person:

> "Being checked on one occasion by a shrewd and deep mathematician and physician who observed that her question was dangerous, she replied, 'Can Truth be dangerous?' 'It is thought so,' was the answer. She learned on this occasion two things, the one that truth had still to be found, the other, that men were afraid of it."

When Fanny was about fourteen and her brother Richard a year and a half older, the family was temporarily reunited during a visit of the latter to his grandfather and aunt on his way to the war as a cadet in the service of the Great East India Company.

A bundle of letters from Richard Wright to his cousin and adopted mother, Miss Betsy Watson, gives a simpler and more genial impression of the persons and circumstances surrounding his sisters than any of Fanny's memories of that same period.

> I arrived here on Sunday about eight o'clock and found your brother in bed at the London Coffee House. When I opened the door of his bed room he did not know me for some time and was quite surprised when I told him I had come by the mail.
>
> He got up and breakfasted and carried me to my grandfather, General Campbell. At first sight of him I was quite surprised to see such a young-looking man, for I was expecting to see a man of eighty, quite crippled and crooked, but I saw quite the contrary, and he just answers to the description you gave me of him.
>
> At two o'clock on Sunday, we went to Hyde Park and

walked there for two hours, and we saw about two or three thousand carriages, and I suppose about one thousand gentlemen riding on horseback. I was quite astonished to see such grand sights, and your brother laughed at me for I could do nothing but stare at everything and so attentively that I was like to be rode over every minute. The livery servants here of the principal noblemen, have all got epaulets and cocked hats and when you see them upon the streets you would take them for officers in the army.

On Wednesday we went to the India House and they would not pass me as I had not yet a proper certificate of my age, and my grandfather had to write all the way to Dundee, and if it does not arrive before Wednesday next I cannot be passed for a fortnight, which is a long time considering the shortness of the time I have to be here and besides that, we have to go to Devonshire to see Miss Campbell and my sisters, and when I do see them (as I am wishing very much to see them) I will give you a particular description of them and what kind of a house they have got etc.

When I was walking yesterday upon the streets with my grandfather, he did nothing else but say at every step he took, "How do ye do, my Lord, or General," etc. I said to him that he knew nobody but lords and generals. He said, "You are very right for I know nothing but Lords and Generals and a parcel of such like devils." He tells me he does not dine alone a day in a week. He is going out today and we were out yesterday at Mr. Kerr's M. P., who to be sure had a grand dinner, and ten or twelve different sorts of wines. The ladies here drink as long as the gentlemen, till they depart to the parlor, which is sometimes at a late hour. . . . It is a pity but what I was a lady for I could give you a fine description how the ladies dress here, but you cannot see them in the street for they are never out of their coaches from morning till night.

I have one wonder to tell you and it is the greatest of them all. It was the Queen and the Princesses. I never saw such an ugly looking woman as the queen is, and as for the princesses their faces are so fat that you would think that they were blown up with a pair of bellows.

We were at the House of Commons last night and we are going to the Opera tonight.

P. S. I am happy to tell you that Miss Campbell is to advance the £500 (for my commission).

The next letter is from Dawlish.

12th. June, 1809.

I arrived here on Saturday after a very fatiguing journey from London and found my aunt and sisters all in good health and waiting with great anxiety about my arrival and they got up at four o'clock in the morning and every knock at the door they said they were sure that it was my Grandfather and me. I was very much surprised at the first sight of Fanny. She was so tall that I took her for my aunt. Miss Campbell is a much younger and prettier woman than I expected to see. She is 5 feet 7 inches in height, and every bit as thick as you are. Fanny is as tall as you are, but very thin indeed but she is as pretty as Mary Hutchinson [The name is underlined several times in his letter] which I really did not expect to see.

My sisters and I are going away to take a six miles ride. The horses are at the door. Miss Campbell lives in great style.

The next letter is from Portsmouth, from which place the expedition was to sail.

July 5th. . . .

I was very sorry to part with my aunt and dear sisters. If ever you come to London you must go and see them for they are very anxious to see you. . . . I have got all my things ready and just going aboard, and my grandfather is in such a devil of a hurry to get me on board that I am afraid I won't be able to fill this sheet. . . . This place is crowded with soldiers going on the expedition.

He had time, however, for a hurried scrawl to his sister Fanny, of which only the following fragment has been preserved:

I enclose you a small quantity of my mother's hair and my own hair (it was cut off when I was very young). I believe you have got some of our mother's hair already, but accept this, although there is but a small quantity of it. I am just going on board.

The expedition was attacked by the French after it left Madeira and Richard Wright was one of the first shot in the engagement.

But before this letter could reach England, General Campbell had also died very unexpectedly. His last informal will was addressed to his daughter in extreme agitation in the expectation of a sudden and violent death. He left everything he possessed when he died, some two hundred pounds, or a little more, in South Sea stock to his grandson Richard Robinson Wright, with last words to his dearest daughter and his dear grandchildren. "Angels forever guard you and them. When I am in heaven, if indeed I may hope to go thither, I think my fondest employment will be to look down and watch over you all and my few friends. Yours with a bleeding and affectionate heart and your ever loving fond Father, Duncan Campbell."

The loss of a grandfather whom she neither loved nor respected made so little impression on his eldest grandchild that she never even mentions it in any later reference to her youth. But the death of her only brother, so unexpectedly restored to her after years of separation, was quite another matter. It was the last blow in a series of disasters which made her gradually come to think of herself as one marked by fate itself for special calamity.

A handful of early verses preserved by her with other records of the past give glimpses of a nature morbidly self-involved, an exaggerated belief in herself as a being extraordinarily endowed with unusual gifts of genius which must set her forever apart from the common world, and a haunting fear that she might die young before these great gifts could find expression.

But all this intense inner life was protected and concealed from her antipathetic surroundings by a profound *farouche* reserve.

Note her own account of her introduction to the existence of a great free young country in the Western Hemisphere with a history which roused in her a very passion of enthusiasm. Writing, as she was accustomed, in the third person, she said:

> While still a very young girl, she found by chance among some old books tumbled together in a chest in her aunt's library, a copy of Botta's *Istoria della Rivoluzione Americana,* the only work on a subject so politically heterodox which had found a place in the aristocratical libraries which surrounded her youth. From that moment she awoke, as it were, to a new existence. Life was full of promise, the world a theatre of interesting observation and useful exertion. There existed a country consecrated to freedom, and in which man might awake to the full knowledge and full exercise of his powers. To see that country was, now at the age of 16, her fixed but

secret determination. For not to a living being did she communicate her intention. She had absolutely devoured the
Italian Historian and was in the full tide of ecstasy when a
sudden apprehension seized her. Was the whole thing a
romance? What had become of the country and the nation?
She had never heard of either. A panic terror seized upon
her. She flew to examine every atlas in the library. The first
was not of recent date and showed no trace of the United
States. She opened with trembling hands another and another. At length she saw "United States" marked along the
Atlantic littoral of North America. Still, after all, was the
story she had read a true one? She now sought carefully
among the more modern authors in the library, and found
Belsham's *History of George III*. Its perusal quieted her ap-
prehensions. Her heroes were true men and her land of
promise had a local habitation and a name.

It could not have been many weeks afterwards that, on
visiting a British Admiral in whose house she was familiar,
she found the veteran, who had retired, blind and infirm from
the service but full of zeal for it and his country, in a state
of great agitation. To her inquiries, he replied that she came
like his good angel to throw oil upon the troubled waters
and that much he had need of consolation, for those wicked
rebels were at their old work again.

"What rebels, my dear sir?"

"Ah, my child! Those impudent rebels of our American
colonies. It is an old story of which you know nothing. And
the less everybody know the better, but they are picking up
our ships again all over the ocean." And then came such a
storm of passion and honest vexation from the worthy veteran
that her curiosity was silenced in sympathy and she passed
some hours in diverting his attention from a subject which she
burned to investigate.

From that day forward while all around her were engrossed in the news of the day [it was the very crisis of the
Napoleonic Wars when the French at last were beginning to
give ground before the victorious allies] her thoughts dwelt
with unceasing interest, frequent alarm, and unsatisfied curiosity on the fate and history of the young nation upon whose
short but gallant war of defence, the papers of the day
scarcely vouchsafed an intelligible notice, and the sound of
whose name never greeted her ears nor passed her lips. . .

Her own declaration of independence took place some two years after the Peace of Paris, when she was still under age. Whether her own and her sister's sudden departure from their aunt's home was an act of open rebellion on their part or whether it was actually a flight from unusual violence and oppression one has no means of knowing beyond a letter written by Fanny to her aunt some six years after the quarrel, in reply to one from Miss Campbell to her niece on the anniversary of her fortieth birthday.

Miss Campbell's letter no longer exists. It had been found by Fanny's only daughter, Sylva, in a box of her mother's papers after her mother's death, and is described by her as unexceptionable in its tone and "affectionate at every point." So much cannot be said of Fanny's reply, so carefully composed, so measured in its bitterness that one can only hope that it was never sent.

> I now sit down, madame, to address to you a letter which it was as little my desire as my intention to have written, had you not yourself called me to do so.
>
> First let me say that I write as leisurely as coolly. You, Madame, are the last person in the world to whom I should write without weighing my words as well as my sentiments. The forbearance with which I have hitherto addressed you might well, if you thought—and how could you not think—on all the crying wrongs that from my first infancy I have received from your hands?—excite your amazement.
>
> It might also, I think, have awakened your gratitude.
>
> If I should now seem to show you less of that indulgence which has hitherto led me to pass over in silence what I had thought must have been anguish to you to remember, you will admit that I have sufficiently evinced that I do it with much reluctance, that I have been very slow to assume the tone of the injured or the accuser, and very willing to forget as well as to forgive. It is you yourself, Madame, who now after a lapse of six years, force me to turn my thoughts backwards to the days of my suffering infancy and youth, and to conjure up before me in your person the image of an enemy and an oppressor.
>
> I spare you, Madame, a review of the days of my childhood, days that wrung such a drop of blood from my heart—and have left me in the sad experience of life and of the nature of my fellow creatures, which, under your tuition, I,

at that early age acquired, tokens of bitterness that I shall carry with me to the grave.

I will refer to later injuries not less cruel in her who inflicted them, if less felt by those who were the object of them.

I was eighteen and my sister seventeen when you consented to release us from violence and insult by a removal from your roof to that of your friends. But how did you do this? Not by throwing us into an asylum of friendship whose kindness might have cheered the hearts you had broken, not even driving us into peaceful though cheerless solitude.

You looked at the children of a sister, just entering into life unprotected, unfriended—and you threw them, or did what you could to throw them, not merely on a wide and reckless world, but on one prepared for prejudice and suspicion. By hints conveyed by word and letters, to nearly all who had felt for us esteem or friendship, or even had so much as heard our name—by misrepresentation or absolute falsehoods, you accounted for the circumstances of our separation from you our Aunt and legal guardian, and thus shielded your own character by endeavors to blast ours.

The letter concludes in a tone of feigned surprise that Miss Campbell could ever have thought it possible to reinstate herself, as a justly offended but forgiving relative with the nieces she had so deeply injured. "It is beyond your power to irritate me. I had thought it also beyond your power to astonish me. I have now expressed leisurely and calmly the contempt with which your conduct has inspired me. I have done it for the last time."

Strange that the very violence and bitterness of this arraignment makes one hesitate to take it at its face value! One can find no evidence that Miss Campbell's conduct towards her two young wards ever excited either question or unfavorable comment among her own friends and neighbors at Dawlish. She lived to the advanced age of ninety, loved and respected by the very people who had every opportunity of knowing the worst as well as the best of her treatment of her sister's children and the real cause for their sudden departure from under her charge.

As to the outward and visible signs of the education she inflicted upon her young kinswomen without their consent, and seemingly against their will, one has the following conclusion of no less biased and prejudiced a person than Fanny's own great-uncle on her father's side, Professor Milne of Glasgow College, with whom the two sisters made their home after their escape from their aunt's authority.

> When I see my two nieces, girls of whom I may be justly vain, well principled, well informed, elegantly accomplished, fit to take their places among society of any rank, and to be received in it with esteem and respect, when I compare them with what in all likelihood they would have been, had their education been carried on under the direction of any other connection they have ever had since the death of their amiable mother, I am compelled to forget much or all that I have ever looked on with blame in their Aunt's conduct towards them and to believe that to her, their debt can never be overpaid. . . .

In the face of such contrary evidence the case between Miss Campbell and her two nieces must remain forever undecided, or decided in the usual human way with the blame equally distributed on both sides.

This uncle whose home became their place of refuge after the sisters' flight from their aunt, had also been the friend and guardian of their father when he too had been left an orphan at an early age. He was well known and highly respected in his position of professor of moral philosophy on the faculty of Glasgow College. At the time his two great-nieces came to live with him, his wife and five grown-up children were all alive and some of them still living at home. Narrow circumstances. Narrow quarters. A very great change from the formal ample style of living to which the two young girls had been accustomed during the years they spent with their aunt, where, as Fanny takes pains to tell one, they had never even learned to dress themselves without the help of a maid.

An even greater contrast to the aristocratic traditions and Tory orthodoxy of her aunt's friends and neighbors among the county families of Devonshire and Somerset was presented by the busy, noisy, dirty city of Glasgow whose standards and customs were set by the families of respectable business men and manufacturers, Whigs in politics, Calvinists in faith and doctrine, staunch members of the Established Church of Scotland.

And there in the midst of this teeming city life, within a stone's throw of its most miserable slums was the ancient site of Glasgow College, old dark buildings of a most somber aspect, low towers and curtains of monastic architecture, built round two narrow, stone-paved quadrangles, the larger one of these being given over to the families of the resident professors, the other to the business of the college proper. These two quadrangles were connected by a vaulted passage-way. Beyond to the eastward, also approached by an arched passage, stretched the college gardens, of considerable extent, a rich back-ground of lawns and trees and walks along the banks of the river haunted by the memory of Reid, Adam Smith, and other worthies of the college in its palmy days.

One of the first acts of Fanny's new freedom was the request for an introduction to the college library where she was allowed to browse as she pleased.

According to her own account, printed years afterwards in the columns of a Dundee newspaper, the first use she made of this in-estimable privilege was to search the library for books about the United States. Quoting further from this newspaper article:

> She found it possible to procure the peculiar information which she had coveted and had not been able to procure in the aristocratical libraries of her childhood; first as to the early colonial history and character of the primitive settlers of the United States and second as to the then actual condi-tion and point of progress of the American population. Under the last of these heads she could obtain little information, but, after some search she was enabled, in connection with the first, to obtain the most varied and ample records, in the library of the University. Upon explaining the nature of the documents she wished to procure, to the librarian, Professor Muirhead, he led her to a remote and little frequented com-partment of the library, and pointing around it, filled as it was with volumes and pamphlets from floor to ceiling, ob-served that she would find there all that had ever appeared in print respecting the American Colonies, adding that "if she was curious in the same she might select and study the records at her leisure as they were seldom consulted."

Out of this mass of dull, dusty, often out-dated information, Fanny was able to extract a world of information which was to stand her in good stead in the years to come.

But her new opportunities for free inquiry did not confine them-selves to dead books. There were still men of scholarship and ability among the college professors whom Fanny and her sister were to meet in their uncle's parlor. The Scottish School of Philosophy, so-called, was at the height of its influence. Its chief luminary, Dugald Stewart, had studied under Reid in his youth and did not die till 1828. Much discussion must have gone on in Fanny's presence over the laws of mind and matter, the true relation between morality, virtue, and human happiness, the compromise that can be made between a materialistic and rationalistic point of view and the belief in the Christian miracles.

The result was a rapid and complete abandonment of those dreamy emotional religious convictions to which by her own confession she had turned for help and comfort at moments of crisis during her unhappy childhood.

Not so much an abandonment, one may say, as a conversion, for she threw much more passion and devotion into her new philosophy of life than she had ever expended on the paralyzing orthodoxy of the Church of England in which she had been so carefully brought up under her aunt's direction.

It was during a long visit to Miss Janet Millar, an unmarried sister of her aunt, Mrs. Milne, that she first managed to give these new opinions literary shape. Miss Millar lived alone on a small estate called Millheugh, near the little town of Hamilton some thirty miles away from Glasgow in the Clyde Valley. It was a lovely spot, in wildly picturesque surroundings, which had come to the Millars through their mother, a connection of the great landholding family of Hamilton, from whom the town itself derived its name.

There, as Fanny tells us herself some years later, "without any settled plan or ambition to do more than enliven a few winter evenings of some friends in the country" the girl wrote a little tract in the style of Plato's *Dialogues*, whose spirit, however, was not Platonic but rather an exaltation of the Epicurean philosophy.

Her ignorance of Greek and Latin prevented her from pursuing her research on the subject of this old Greek sage, back to its original sources. But Bayle's *Classical Dictionary*, either in its original French or in translation, was easily accessible, even in some of the private libraries by which she was surrounded. From this monumental work she could obtain all and more than all she needed in the production of her own little tract. But the result which she obtained was something more than a mere clever compilation of the main tenets of the Epicurean philosophy dressed up in literary form. It has all the warmth and charm of a genuine spiritual experience. It is, in fact, the first instance of that unusual capacity she had of absorbing herself body and soul into the very life and thought of any being whom she had for the moment accepted as entirely worthy of admiration. She liked to think of herself and hear other people call her "the Philosopher," and she seems to have really tried to submit her naturally disputatious mind and her violent uncompromising temper to the example of the gentle Epicurus.

But the hard work necessary for the production of *A Few Days in Athens*, the name under which her tract finally appeared in print, did not prevent her from entering on a new field of literary activity of quite a different kind.

One of the great events of her stay in Glasgow was John Kemble's visit to that city, just before his retirement from the stage. She went to see him act in his great role of Coriolanus. During the next few days, in a sustained burst of mental excitement, she composed and completed a three-act drama in Shakespearean blank verse which she called *Altorf*, after the hero of an imaginary incident in the old struggle of the Swiss against the encroachments of Austria.

Then followed weeks of futile efforts to get her play read and judged by Kemble himself, or failing this to put it into the hands of the new manager of his theater in London, Mr. Harris. After a long period of agonizing suspense, her manuscript was returned to the name and address she had assumed for this purpose,

> Mr. Hill
> Archdeacon Cameron's College
> Glasgow,

without a word or sign that it had been read by anyone.

One often laughs in later years at the real anguish such an experience may inflict on a young man or woman at the outset of a literary career, but Frances Wright never learned to laugh, never outgrew the pain and bitterness of this first serious rebuff. She managed, however, to assuage her wounded pride by insisting that her failure of recognition lay at least partially in her choice of theme, peculiarly unacceptable to theatrical managers whose business it was to entertain a world given over to the blackest kind of political reaction. She was gradually comforted to feel herself one of that small brave minority content to suffer in silence rather than prostitute their talents by joining in the general conspiracy of those in power to "keep the truth from the multitude."

In her efforts to get her manuscript into Kemble's hands and back again without sacrificing her anonymity, she had been greatly helped by her cousin and devoted friend, James Watson. He was a captain in a marching regiment with no other resources for supporting a wife than his very scanty pay as an officer in the king's army. This had not prevented him, however, from falling in love with his handsome English cousin. Even if he had been able to support her in anything like the way she was accustomed to, she was under age and could not marry without the consent of her aunt, her sole legal guardian, with power, as her Uncle Milne hastened to tell her, which was "sufficiently great to occasion very serious inconvenience and evil to the ward that acts in contempt of it."

The cousins had, therefore, to be content with a long engagement, and during her lover's frequent absences, Fanny had plenty of time to indulge those melancholy and solitary moods which so often darkened and disturbed even the most prosperous and peaceful periods of her life.

But the very year Fanny herself had reached the age of twenty-one and could do as she pleased in the future conduct of her life, the two cousins suddenly decided that they had been mistaken in their feeling for one another and parted by mutual consent.

One cannot believe that this first brief love affair played an important part in her emotional life at this period of her development. It is aptly described in the following passage of a letter received by Fanny from the wise old friend, Mrs. Craig Millar, in whom alone she confided the secrets of her heart. "His feeling for you was a very ordinary mixture of admiration and self-love gratified by your attachment. You yourself acknowledge that your imagination invested him with its own coloring. You see in yourself an incapacity or weakness of the passionate side of your nature when you have not given it a fair trial."

But the place left empty by her lover was more than filled by the splendid shadow of the poet Byron. It is hardly possible that under her aunt's careful tutelage Fanny had ever been allowed to read Byron. But after she went to Glasgow in November 1816, came the publication of the third canto of *Childe Harold*, and from that time he became for Fanny, as for so many others of her generation (a generation born too late for the promise of the French Revolution, destined to wear out its youth in the dead stagnation of the aftermath) the extreme expression of all she had ever thought and suffered in a world which seemed to have gone altogether wrong—a kindred spirit, a twin soul. Indeed in a far-off way she was right in recognizing certain intimate resemblances between his nature and hers. There was the same morbid egotism, the same pleasure in defying public opinion, the same tendency to consider oneself a being set apart from infancy for special misfortune, the same restless vanity under the same cloak of contemptuous indifference. On the other hand, though she lacked the authentic spark of genius which made all things permissible to the elder poet, in faith, in earnestness, in an almost sacrificial capacity for self-dedication to the highest ends, Fanny actually stood on higher ground than he.

In her first effort to follow her new leader, however, she managed to achieve only a very poor imitation of the passionate pilgrim singing his way across the battlefields and ruined cities of Europe, in a long didactic poem which never saw the light except in short extracts used by her as captions for chapters in more successful works.

"Thoughts of a Recluse," for that is the name she gave to her work, was, as might have been expected, second-rate, and highly imitative in its form, but none the less, as she herself describes it in its introduction, "the offspring of a warm heart and a young and ardent mind which has turned with disgust from life even at its entrance, and having tried by its own standards the feelings and actions of men and found them wanting, has made the mistake of passing from condemnation of the error to resentment against the agent, with much indignation against the persecutors of liberty, or its betrayers which all-calming, all-convincing time has chastened and subsequent reflection corrected."

For even in her native Scotland in the midst of all that natural beauty and gallant tradition, she was obliged to witness new evidence of that essential wrongness of human society which had already stirred her to indignant protest at the sight of the beggars gathering round her grandfather's carriage in London streets. It was the time of the depopulation of the Highlands by the great landlords, who were turning their estates into game preserves. Fanny herself saw an emigrant vessel clear out of the Clyde, loaded with peasant folk thus deprived of their farms.

"It had on board," she tells us, "among other exiles, a grandmother with, I think, seven grandchildren. These seemingly helpless people were bound not for Canada but for the States. . . . I have heard from residents in the north of Scotland, tales that might have melted other hearts than those of dreaming poets—of tender youth and feeble age, passing the winter's night with no other canopy but the heavens, of some expiring under the united ills of hunger, cold, and despair."

It was then and there, as she tells us many years later, that "she pronounced to herself a solemn oath, to wear ever in her heart the cause of the poor and the helpless; and to aid in all she could in redressing the grievous wrongs which seemed to prevail in society. She, not unfrequently, recalls the engagement then taken and feels that she has done her best to fulfil it."

While still in the throes of her struggle to bring life and fire to her first long poem, Fanny made a new friend, a woman in her late forties, whose wise comment on the broken engagement has been already quoted in this chapter.

This was Mrs. Craig Millar, widow of the favorite brother of Mrs. Milne and Miss Janet Millar of Millheugh. Her husband had been the friend and fellow conspirator of Fanny's own father during those dark days when sympathy with the ideals of the French Revolution was considered a crime punishable with fine, imprisonment or exile by the ruling classes of England.

From all one knows about Mrs. Millar through her long and intimate correspondence with Frances Wright, she seems to have been a woman of excellent mind, good education and a great deal of saving humor. She had seen a good deal of the world, first as the daughter of a distinguished physician and thinker, Dr. William Cullem of Edinburgh, in the days when Edinburgh led the world as a center of brilliant and learned society; then as the wife of a political exile in Philadelphia and New York during the later years of Washington's administration. For some time now she had been living in the utmost seclusion in narrow circumstances with an unmarried sister, Miss Margaret Cullem, in Whitburn, a tiny seaside place near Newcastle.

Fanny and she met and were attracted to each other during one of Mrs. Millar's infrequent visits to her two sisters-in-law in Scotland. The older woman especially was swept off her feet into a very passion of admiring affection for the younger, which had in it sometimes even a touch of awe. Indeed, in the first flush of her rather unusual beauty, Fanny was a person peculiarly capable of exciting both the one and the other of these two feelings.

The description of her personal appearance at this time shows her as a woman with a commanding presence; exceptionally tall, with a rather massive head covered with light brown hair in clustering curls, set forward on a beautiful neck and shoulders. Her eyes were especially handsome, of a deep blue, with a sort of prophetic earnestness in their gaze which gave her a certain likeness to a Roman sybil. Add to this an extraordinary gift of expression, a lofty idealism tempered with Byronic melancholy, and the picture is clear in the words of her adoring friend. "I now view you, my dear Fanny, with your youth, talents, independence, and impassioned temperament, afloat on a full if dangerous sea, with streamers flying and sails set."

Mrs. Millar often returned to this simile of a ship under full sail, or a bird on shining pinions moving swiftly and irresistibly to the goal of its desire, to describe her impressions of Fanny Wright at this moment of her career. There was often too, a tone of half-concealed apprehension as if she saw something difficult and dangerous under all that appearance of youthful confidence and energy, something which did not necessarily mean a safe journey to an assured and certain port.

For a while, at the height of their sentimental attachment for each other, these two women seem to have followed the custom of the time and addressed each other in private by high-sounding names. An ode in Fanny's best style, found among her papers at her death, is dedicated to "Marcella" and signed "Malvina." But as their affection deepened and strengthened in closer acquaintanceship, these fantastic names were gradually dropped and replaced by others better suited to their new relation. For Fanny, at least, this new affection came to replace all the lost treasure of a mother's love which she had so poignantly missed during her unhappy childhood, while she herself fell easily enough into the position of a child, the dearly loved and specially cherished child of a tender mother.

It was to have an even greater influence in her life, however, as the last link in the chain which had been gradually drawing her steps away from the familiar circumstances of her native land to the country which had excited "the first yearnings of her young affections" while still an unwilling prisoner under her aunt's authority.

Mrs. Millar had spent two years in America with her young husband before his tragic death from sunstroke. She was still in touch with friends who had been kind to her in those days, and every reference to her experiences there roused anew all Fanny's early longing to see with her own eyes the land of her dreams.

In the spring of 1818 both Frances and Camilla became of age, free from those restrictions on their movements which they had suffered hitherto as wards in chancery. By this time, also, Fanny's health had begun to be seriously affected by the winter climate of Scotland. Frequent colds and coughs seemed to hint at a settled weakness of the lungs.

It was during a long visit which both sisters paid to their new friends at Whitburn that she suddenly conceived and carried out all the necessary preliminaries of a trip to America.

In a newspaper article which appeared many years later in a Scots newspaper written in the third person but inspired directly by her, she explains it all as follows:

> Her real motives for the voyage were disguised from all but one gifted female friend and Professor Milne. The former who had accompanied her husband to the U. S. in his flight from persecution in 1794, supplied the few letters she was willing to take. The latter to whom she only communicated her intended voyage at the very moment of its execution, and after her passage to New York and that of her sister had actually been secured, came to see her embark at Liverpool with her young companion for a distant country in whom she knew not a living soul!
>
> When he gently reproached her on account of her singular reserve on the subject of a voyage so startling to all her friends and painful to him, and asked the reason of the preference she gave to America, over Italy or Greece which he had already recommended to her attention as more in harmony with her early studies, she asked, in reply, if a new country inhabited by free men was not more worthy to attract curiosity than countries in ruins inhabited by slaves? "The sight of Italy, dear uncle, prostrated under the leaden sceptre, would break my heart!"
>
> The generous and enlightened friend received her explanations with sympathetic kindness, observing that she was the child of her father and must have inherited her views and principles in her blood.

Another and even more illuminating glimpse into her state of mind at this important crisis of her life is given by a manuscript poem found among her papers at her death but never published, dedicated to Byron's *Childe Harold*.

To Harold

The ship rides free, the sails are to the wind.
To other scenes, to other worlds I fly.
I leave no home, and yet I gaze behind,
I leave no loves yet clouded is my eye.

But not with tears. I do not weep nor groan,
For I have grieved, joyed, trusted, loved the last;
A blighted, blasted wretch, I stand alone,
A blank the future, madness all the past.

We ne'er have met, we never may meet, yet oft
My spirit is with thine and converse holds.
We ne'er have met and ne'er may meet, but soft!
Time's sealed record strange secrets may unfold.

We ne'er have met, we ne'er may meet, yet if
The wild waves spare, I pledge me by this sign
I will return, nor move my shattered skiff,
Till it have sought and found and hailed thine.

Strange is the course I run, and far the goal.
I sweep th' arena and no eye beholds,
Yet soon with daring hand and fearless soul
I seize the crown that Fame there distant holds.

Then when the herd I loathe and I despise,
The dastard herd that made and mocked my pain
Shall turn on one they spurned, admiring eyes,—
Then, Harold, thou shalt hear from me again.

Nor home nor loves nor country, yet I throw
A long deep gaze upon the world behind;
It holdeth one, it holdeth one I know
With heart as waste—as deep, and proud a mind.

Start—but 'tis truth. There is a soul on earth,
Twin-born, the same, the counterpart of thine;
As strange, as proud, as lonely from its birth—
With powers as vast. Harold, that soul is mine!

CHAPTER II

A New Discovery of America

FRANCES and Camilla Wright made their first trip to America in the American-owned packet ship *Amity*, with a Yankee crew and captain. They set sail from Liverpool on August 2nd, 1818 and arrived the beginning of September after a voyage of thirty days. In spite of fair weather and favoring winds the younger of the two sisters was very seasick most of the time. Fanny, however, was not disabled either by sickness or nervous fears. Her first letter to Mrs. Millar from New York describes the voyage as a delightful experience.

> Our fellow passengers were cheerful, obliging, and con-versable. The ship was excellent, her captain a weather-beaten veteran, a kindhearted as well as experienced sailor who looked, not merely after the safety of his ship but the comfort of every living being on board her. I observed much and often the quietness as well as the matchless activity of the crew. No scolding on the part of the captain nor sulky looks on that of the men. The ship was indeed well named the *Amity*, for I never heard a dispute on board her save indeed one night when I was the unwilling auditor of an argument in the adjoining cabin which gradually waxed to a wrangle between a young Scotchman, firm in the belief of grace and predestination, an older Englishman, as firm in the non-belief of both articles, and an American who without agreeing with either seemed to keep peace between both. In this good office he probably succeeded as, in the middle of a nicely drawn distinction on the part of the Englishman, between foreknow-ing and foredecreeing, I fell asleep and waked to no other noise than the creaking of timber and lashing of the waves.

Her description of their arrival is especially charming.

It was not without emotion that, on the evening of the 30th day from that on which we had cleared out of the Mersey, we heard the cry of "Land!" and straining our eyes, in the direction of the setting sun, saw the heights of Neversink slowly rise from the waters, opposing a black screen to the crimson glories of the evening sky. You will but too well remember the striking position of New York. [She is writing of course to Mrs. Millar.] The magnificent bay, whose broad and silver waters, sprinkled with islands, are so finely closed by the heights of the Narrows, which, jutting forward with a fine sweeping bend, give a circular form to the immense basin which receives the waters of the Hudson—this bay is grand and beautiful as when you admired it some twenty years since, only it is, perhaps, more thickly studded with silver-winged vessels from the light sharp-keeled boat through all the varieties of shape and size to the proud three-masted ship, setting and lowering its sails to or from the thousand ports of distant Europe or yet more distant Asia.

Everything in the neighborhood of this city exhibits the appearance of life and cheerfulness. The purity of the air, the brilliancy of the unspotted heavens, the crowd of moving vessels shooting in various directions up and down and across the bay, the forest of masts crowded round the quays and wharfs at the entrance of the East River. There is something in all this—in the very air you breathe, and the fair and moving scene that you rest your eye upon, which exhilarates the spirits and makes you in a good humor with life and your fellow creatures. We approached these shores under a fervid sun but the air, though of a higher temperature than I had ever experienced, was so entirely free of vapor that I thought it was for the first time in my life that I had drawn a clear breath. I was no longer sensible of any weakness of the lungs, nor have I as yet been reminded of this infirmity.

While our ship slowly moved through the still waters, pointing her course to the city, numberless little boats, well manned with active rowers darted from the distant shores, and moored alongside our lazy vessel . . . These boats had something picturesque as well as foreign in their appearance. Built unusually long and sharp in the keel, they shot through the bright waters with a celerity that almost startled the eye. Their rowers, tall and slender, but of uncommon nerve and agility, were all cleanly dressed in the light clothing suited to a warm climate, their large white shirt collars unbuttoned and thrown back on their shoulders, and light hats of straw or cane with broad brims shading their sunburnt faces. These faces were uncommonly intelligent. Piercing grey eyes, glancing from beneath even and projecting brows, features generally regular and complexions which, burned to a deep brown, were somewhat strangely contrasted with the delicate whiteness of the clothing . . . They all spoke good English with a good voice and accent. I had before observed the same of the crew of the *Amity*.

Approaching the city at sunset, I shall not soon forget the impression which its gay appearance made upon me. . . . Immediately in our front, the Battery with its little fort and its public walks, diversified with trees, impending over the water, numberless well-dressed figures gliding through the foliage, or standing to admire our nearing vessel. In the background the neatly painted houses receding into the distance, the spirey tops of the poplars, peering above the roofs and marking the line of the streets [trees she disliked, as she insists], a tree that has no one good quality to recommend it, for the rapidity of its growth cannot be accounted one, since we can only observe upon it in the words of the old proverb that "ill weeds grow apace." One is the more disposed to quarrel with this vile stranger from the uncommon beauty of the native trees. The city, gradually enlarging from the Battery as from the apex of a triangle, the eye followed, on one side, the broad channel of the Hudson, and the picturesque shores of Jersey, on the other, the more winding waters of the East River, its quays and warehouses scarce discernible through the forest of masts that were crowded as far as the eye could reach. Behind us stretched the broad expanse of the bay whose islets, crowned with turreted forts, their colors streaming from their flag staffs, seemed to slumber on the still and glowing waters. [Part of the defense of New York harbor thrown up during the War of 1812, and not yet dismantled.]

When our ship neared the quays, there was some bustle occasioned by the moving crowd of vessels that intervened between us and the shore, and many active tars sprang from the yards and rigging of the surrounding ships to assist in clearing our passage . . . And when we finally touched the land there was no lack of good offices from the citizens of the quay. One laid planks to assist the passengers in their descent from the vessel, another lent a hand to stay their unsteady feet, while some busied themselves in taking charge of their bundles and portmanteaus. There was in the look and air of these men, though clad in working jackets, something which told that they were rendering civilities, not services, and that a kind "thank ye" was all that should be rendered in return.

Arriving at a boarding house that had been recommended to us, we were very kindly welcomed by a sprightly intelligent young woman, the sister of the more staid and elderly matron of the house. The heat continued with little abatement after sunset, and every window and door of the house was open. While seated refreshing ourselves with tea and fruit and conversing with our lively hostess, a sound which had filled our ears from the first moment that we left behind us the bustle of the wharfs, now completely fixed our attention. "Tic-a-te-tic, tic-a-te-tic," was cried as it were, by a thousand voices. "Pray thee, what is this noise?" I asked. "Noise? I hear none," said the lady. I insisted that there certainly was a noise and to my ears a most uncommon one. Our good-humored hostess listened again. "I hear nothing, unless it be the catty-dids." I have since had one of these insects in my hand. In size it is larger than the ordinary grasshopper and in color a much more vivid green. It is perfectly harmless and altogether a most delicate creature. This whimsical cry with the shorter note of the little tree frog, the chirp of crickets, and the whiz and boom of a thousand other flying creatures creates, at this season to the ear of the stranger, a noise truly astounding.

Another thing astounding to the young Wrights in this new city was the price they had to pay for the simplest and barest kind of living. One reads, for instance, in one of Mrs. Millar's earliest letters:

We are extremely grieved to hear of the discomforts to which you are exposed respecting lodgings, servants, and expenses in general and lament that you will have to pay so dearly merely to see America. I don't see how you will contrive to live with the enormous expense of New York. We know you have no vanity and can be very economical but we fear your unavoidable expenses may plunge you into difficulties, and difficulties once begun, accumulate in an increasing ratio. But however bad the servants may be, I don't think you ought to send for C. You would have all your expense of bringing her out and then she would certainly marry in a few months.

On this point at least, Frances seems to have taken her old friend's advice and engaged a woman obtained on the spot for the domestic service which she found necessary during the year she spent in New York. "The native American," she remarks later out of the intimate experience thus acquired, "when she can be obtained, makes a valuable domestic . . . The foreigner, however, must be careful not to rub their pride. No American will receive an insulting word. A common mode of resenting an imperious order is to quit the house without waiting or even asking for a reckoning."

They also changed their first boardinghouse near the Battery for another at the head of Broadway, less expensive and pleasanter in every way for two young unprotected females.

It is interesting to hear what Frances has to say about this peculiarly American institution.

> The social mode of living here, adopted in hotels and boarding-houses offers great advantages to foreigners, who may be desirous of mixing easily with the natives and of observing the tone of the national manners. During the few days that we have lived in this house, we have met with a greater variety of individuals from all parts of the Union than we could have done in as many months by visiting in half the private houses of the city. Families from the eastern states and gentlemen from the south and west have successively appeared and departed, and left with us many invitations to their various dwellings.

But it was not only at the boardinghouse table that she learned to know Americans. She talked continually with people of the working classes, wherever they were to be found. As, for instance, the sailors on board the *Amity* whom she found a pleasant contrast to the dour Scots fisherfolk on the beaches near her uncle's summer home at Fairlie. Then there was the mason going to his work; the woman coming home from market with her basket of provisions; the small shopkeeper; the farmer whom she met by chance on a river steamboat. It was from such as these that she received a mass of information about the politics, the customs, and the laws of the country, of which she was to make good use in the future.

The city itself continued to delight her, with its broad sidewalks, its pleasant opulent and easy appearance, even in its poorest quarters such a contrast to London and Glasgow. "No dark alleys," she tells us, "whose confined and noisome atmosphere marks the presence of a dense and suffering population; no hovels in whose ruined garrets, or dank and gloomy cellars crowd the wretched victims of vice and disease, whom penury drives to despair, ere she opens to them the grave."

On the other hand she was forced to admit the absence of any public building worth noticing, except the City Hall, but the city possessed what was much better, she insisted, "streets of private dwellings, often elegant and always comfortable."

She also made excursions outside the city, into Long Island and New Jersey, in which last-named state she found the country especially lovely with its low hills sinking into extensive valleys watered by clear streams, its neat white dwellings, usually low and broad-roofed, shaded by projecting piazzas and very generally by enormous weeping willows. "These exotics," she tells us, "seem to take wonderfully to the soil and climate and are much cultivated in the more immediate neighborhood of houses, as well on account of their rapid growth as from the massiveness of their foliage, and from their being the earliest trees to bud, and the latest to cast their leaves." She also found some very lovely though few "lordly dwellings" scattered along the shores of Manhattan Island.

One of her most charming bits of description is the account of the spot where Mrs. Millar had spent some time during her exile in America.

We turned down the little lane, wild and rocky as when you traversed it, and reached the gate just as the sun was sinking behind the heights of the Jersey shore. I thought that you had gazed on the same object from the same spot. I cannot describe how dreary and sad, how fraught with painful recollections the scene was to me. . . . You know the spot, but it doubtless lives in your memory as inhabited by kind friends, and breathing within and without, warmth, comfort, beauty, and hospitality. We found it desolate and deserted, the house without a tenant, gradually falling into disrepair, the fences broken down, the trees and shrubs all growing wild, while the thick falling leaves that strewed the ground, and rustled beneath our feet, the season, the keen searching air of a November evening, even the hour, pressed on the heart the conviction of the slenderness of that link which holds us to this changing world, to its good or ill, its joys and sorrows.

She had found the summer climate of New York glorious in spite of its great and unaccustomed heat. "The resplendent sun shining on for days and weeks, the air so pure, so light, so genial," waked her, so she tells us, to a new existence. And, like every other visitor to this country the brilliant colors of our autumn foliage filled her with amazement. She was amazed by the hues "assumed by nature at the first touch of frost," from the dwarf sumac with its berries and leaves of vivid crimson, up to the towering forest trees, with their branches in extreme and whimsical contrasts of gold, red, green, orange, russet, through all their varieties of shade.

But as for the American winter! All she can say in its favor is, "Those whom it likes may like it." And she did not feel herself one of the favored few. For in those days she was still very sensitive to cold weather, constantly confined to the house by a series of coughs and colds. She never got over her amazement at the way American women, especially the young girls could "flutter along through the biting air in dresses more suited to an Italian winter than to one which approaches nearer to that of Norway," without serious damage to their health. "Broadway, the chosen resort of the young and gay in these cold bright mornings," she tells one, "seems one moving cloud of painted butterflies."

In that crowd of pretty fluttering "butterflies" these two tall handsome girls, with their sober English clothes, their solid footwear, and their general air of good breeding and good social position, could not have passed unnoticed, even before it was generally known who they were.

Among the letters provided by their faithful friend Mrs. Craig Millar was a letter of introduction to a gentleman who was peculiarly able to present them to the best the city had to offer.

Mr. Charles Wilkes was to a rather unusual extent, even in that city of strangers, a citizen of the world. He had come to New York with his father, Israel Wilkes, an elder brother of the notorious John Wilkes of Westminster, shortly after the close of the American Revolution. He is described by one who knew him then as an humble, unassuming young Englishman, in the employment of the newly established Bank of New York. From these small beginnings, however, he had worked his way up through all the minor offices, and at the time of Fanny's first visit to New York he was one of the bank's most trusted officials. A man in his early sixties, living with his large family of grown-up sons and daughters on a charming estate in old Greenwich village; a man of many friends, the kindest, most hospitable of beings, he was liked and respected by his adopted countrymen in spite of his persistent loyalty to the land of his birth. For he remained a British subject to the end of his life, dressing in the old English fashion for gentlemen of his class at home—blue coat, buff waistcoat and long hair; keeping up constant communication with his Wilkes kindred in London, and making frequent visits to Europe, especially after the marriage of his eldest daughter Charlotte to Francis Jeffrey, famous editor of the *Edinburgh Review.*

He was an old friend of Mrs. Millar's ever since the days of that lady's exile in America, when he had been exceedingly kind to her and her young husband. He was the person to whom she would naturally turn for the same kindly offices in behalf of her "beloved children," in a like situation. The result was a very real and lasting friendship between the whole Wilkes family and the two young Scots women. Fanny especially seems to have taken one of her sudden fancies to Charles Wilkes himself, flattering him to the top of his bent, making him the special object of her affectionate regard and respect, while he on his part fell a ready victim to her dominant personality, in spite of his natural antipathy for exactly those ideals and tendencies which made the United States a land of such glorious promise to enthusiasts like Frances Wright. For in politics Mr. Wilkes was a conservative, one of the not inconsiderable group who wished to preserve his adopted country in the best liberal tradition of Europe, always a little anxious and wistful when it seemed inclined to kick over the traces and make a new way for itself in the manner of democratic states.

With such introductions Frances and Camilla Wright had every opportunity of seeing the best of New York society as it existed in the first decades of the last century. But though still young enough and handsome enough to enjoy it, Fanny, at least, seems to have preferred to comment on the frivolous amusements of young people in the new world, as one far, far, above and beyond the possibility of sharing innocent pleasure. She laughs a little at the readiness of young unmarried men and women to run twenty miles through the biting air of winter for an impromptu party at the house of some friend. "All is in moment set astir," she continues, "carpets up, music playing, and youths and maidens mingling in the mazy dance, French dances, usually, chiefly quadrilles, which are certainly prettier to look at than the interminable country dances one sees at home. A pretty scene for a half hour or so, but any one who has survived the buoyant spirits of youth will then find it better to walk home again!"

She was generous in her praise of the sweetness and beauty of the American girls but was inclined to laugh at the young men.

> They do not in general appear to me to equal in grace their young companions nor indeed in general ease of manner and address. In accosting a stranger, they often assume a solemnity of countenance that is at first rather appalling. They seem to look as if waiting until you should "open your mouth in wisdom," or as if gathering their strength to open theirs in the same manner. I have more than once upon such an occasion hastened to collect my startled wits, expecting to be posed and shamed by some profound inquiry into the history of the past, or the probable events of the future. I could ill convey to you the sudden relief I had then experienced on hearing some query upon the news of the day, or as to my general opinion of Lord Byron's poetry.

Thus already she betrays her impatience of the ordinary give and take of general social intercourse, and describes her hermit tasks rather amusingly in a letter to her uncle Milne who had asked her to tell him something about "herself."

> About me, Frances Wright, spinster, familiarly Fanny, more and most familiarly Fan! What an odd fancy! My dear uncle, that is just the only subject I have no story upon. Anything else, and it please you, I have a ready wit. I will write you of a carrot, or a turnip or a potato, of any vegetable, in short but the vegetable "self!"
>
> Now just reflect and you will be satisfied that my outs and ins would make no figure in history, and for this very reason that I neither go out nor come in except it be now and then for a walk by way of exercise, or for a morning call by way of civility (very seldom this) or for an evening visit (this seldomer still) upon compulsion. Yes, upon compulsion, Camilla usually previous to such exertion on my part, hold-

ing a sermon of three hours and a quarter, to hasten the last word of which, I strike my colors and yield to the enemy. "Very true, my dear, very true, I'll go, I'll go." And then?— Why and then I go. Well and then? Oh, and then I am usually very stupid, though there are some people kind enough to think me so-so, and even sometimes vastly agreeable. But this I mention to prove to you the good humor and politeness of the people of this city rather than my own facetiousness.

But her dislike of fashionable society did not prevent her from forming an intimate friendship with William Theobald Wolfe Tone, the son and only surviving child of the Irish rebel of that name. He had come to America with his mother and stepfather, the only place where he could be sure of a welcome as the son of a man who had been tried and condemned as a traitor to his country for his share in the French expedition against the coast of Ireland (which had ended so disastrously at Bantry Bay). The only trade he knew was that of a soldier, and he was on his way to Washington in the hope of getting a commission in the United States Army, if such a thing were possible for a man not yet a citizen of the United States, when chance and Mrs. Craig Millar threw him together with Fanny Wright.

Mrs. Millar had met the widow of Wolfe Tone when both were exiles in a foreign land—at the time of the persecutions of 1794. She had known Mary Tone's present husband, Thomas Wilson, and his more distinguished brother, Christopher North, of *Blackwood's Magazine*, ever since she was a girl in Edinburgh. She was delighted to hear of the meeting of these old friends and her beloved Fanny in New York, but then a little later much disturbed by the latter's enthusiastic reception of the young man. One finds her writing anxiously:

"Your account of 'Young Sidney' shows me how interesting he is becoming to you. I tremble for the consequences."

But as it turned out, she need not have troubled. This new friendship which began so hotly was to run its course without permanent effect on either Fanny or her young Sidney. For, as it happened, Wolfe Tone was neither a hero nor a martyr but a charming and rather pathetic young Irishman, broken in health, disappointed in his hopes for future distinction in Europe, with that queer fatalistic attitude towards life in general, found so often in those destined for an early death.

For a while, at least, he seems to have found it pleasant to be carried by the warm stream of Fanny's flattering appreciation, to let himself drift along wherever she chose to take him, to lend himself to any special use she liked to make of him while his own immediate plans for the future were left to take care of themselves.

She made him the confidant of her hopes and plans for a dramatic success in the United States. She read her play aloud to a tiny selected audience in which he was the chief critic.

In spite of the advice and entreaties of Mrs. Craig Millar whom she had made the confidante of her new designs, she had insisted on taking the whole bundle of her manuscript plays with her to America, with the hope that the theatrical managers in a free country like the United States would be glad to produce them for the very reasons which prevented their success in the old rotting civilizations of Europe.

What was it like—this play which Fanny so passionately hoped and believed was to make her everlasting fame as a dramatic writer?

It would be unfair to judge it by any strict standard of modern criticism. But it would be equally unfair to dismiss it altogether as utterly wanting in dramatic power and human appeal. And, read aloud in a lovely voice by an exceptionally good-looking young woman, at a time when the freshness and daring of its handling was much more apparent than it would be today, it might easily have sounded better than it was, to a susceptible young Irishman like Wolfe Tone. Its plot was founded on an imaginary incident in the Swiss Wars of Independence already celebrated in Schiller's drama of William Tell. A truly republican play, as its American critics continued to insist in all their notices upon it! The influence of Byron is also evident in the character of the hero, Eberard von Altorf, leader of the Swiss revolutionists. Gloomy, sensitive, and repellent in ordinary human society, Altorf has been forced into a marriage of political expediency, with the sister of one of the rebel chieftains, Giovanna, a creature of almost impossible moral perfection, whom he does not and cannot love.

The plot turns on the efforts of Rosina, daughter of his country's enemy, Count Rosenberg, to whom he had been betrothed before his defection to the rebels, to restore him to his first allegiance. She follows him to the rebel camp. They are discovered together with results which make him an unwilling deserter from the patriot ranks. This apparent treachery draws down upon him the curse of his aged father and a final denouemen t of suicide or death for all the principal characters except the injured wife.

The whole story is treated with a warmth and freshness of feeling not a little shocking to those prudish souls who knew the author as a young unmarried woman, who had already surprised them by her disregard for those minor conventions which continued to hedge round her age and sex even in free America.

American men had already won their reputation for subservience to their wives, mothers, and daughters in their own domestic sphere, but it was a different matter when it came to admitting these to the free use of their powers in any other field of human activity. In fact American men of the early nineteenth century so little liked a female blue-stocking, that James Madison's second election to the presidency was actually imperiled by the masculine prejudice against his charming and strong-minded wife.

It is safe to conclude, therefore, that if Fanny had not been willing to keep her authorship of *Altorf* a complete secret, if she had not resigned herself to letting someone like Wolfe Tone act as the connecting link between her and the actors of the New York theaters, she could never have succeeded in getting her masterpiece before the American public.

Theater-going was not the fashion in the circles to which she had been introduced by Charles Wilkes. For that gentleman's private opinion on the subject, turn to one of his own letters to Mrs. Millar.

> Nothing can be, as far as I can judge, more degraded than our stage. The only passport to success here seems to be success in London and I am very confident that the public taste here is to the full as much vitiated as it is with you. I have but very little acquaintance with the Manager of our theatre, who to say the truth, is a person with whom I could not associate and whose taste and talents of every kind are, I should think below mediocrity. He would be incapable of judging of works such as you describe and incapable of relishing them even if he understood them. Nor do I think he has any advisors who would do any better.

As a matter of fact, however, there was and always had been from very early times a large theater-going audience in New York. How could it have been otherwise in that city, then as always a city of strangers, of lonely people living in hotels and boardinghouses, birds of passage, well-to-do foreigners with the habits of European capitals still upon them?

Long before Frances Wright appeared on the scene, the old Park Theatre was a going concern. The building was constructed after the best European models, with four tiers of boxes rising in a semicircle between the pit and the gallery and four private boxes with a room to retire to on the stage. It was extremely well lighted by ten glass chandeliers suspended from gilt iron brackets projecting from the first story; and resplendent with blue and white paneling, gold ornaments and crimson festoons over every box.

New York also possessed its own stock and star company, whose manager, Edmund Simpson, was by no means the poor ignorant creature described in Mr. Wilkes' letter. Born in England and originally intended for a mercantile life, he had run away from home to go on the stage, where he soon became a very creditable success. He came to New York in 1809 as actor manager of the Park Theatre, from Dublin, where he had been acting acceptably for some years. In his own profession he was generally recognized as a spirited director, an excellent fellow, of unblemished morals, with a good face and figure, especially for the parts he usually played, the dashing young man in light society; or a devoted husband.

Much the same kind of thing might be said about most of the actors and actresses who played with him at the Park Theatre. They too were almost without exception, British by birth, and had made their reputation in the course of engagements with good English companies in the London or Dublin theaters.

The majority of the plays presented to American audiences were also of British authorship. But to these must be added numerous Continental successes, both French and German, which had been translated and modified to suit the taste of an audience even then more cosmopolitan than the ordinary theater-going crowds in London. And the repertoire of the Park Theatre included besides, some thirty original works, including plots drawn from local subjects, such as the tragedy of *André*, by William Dunlap, one of the former owners of the old Park.

It was easy enough for Wolfe Tone to find his way into the enchanted regions behind the footlights from which Frances Wright was so hopelessly excluded by age and sex, and social position. The manager of the Park Theatre was not an Irishman, but he had lived long enough in Dublin to feel the glamour of the name of Ireland's most cherished martyr, and the same may be said of those of the troop who had been with Simpson in Dublin. This much in his favor the young Irishman had from the beginning. But how he managed to persuade whoever it was who had the final word in such matters, to take the risk of presenting a play like *Altorf* on an American stage, must remain forever a mystery.

A play which had never been produced on any stage in Europe, written without any of the essential technique of theatrical management, in a style too, which required a great tragic actor to give it its proper effect! A play by a perfectly unknown writer!

Perhaps the deciding voice in the matter was that of young James Wallack, the elder Wallack as one is now accustomed to call him in memory of his more famous son, Lester. Wallack was one of the group of English actors and actresses brought over by Simpson in anticipation of an exceptionally brilliant season in the theaters of New York and Philadelphia during the winter of 1818-1819. He appeared in New York for a star engagement at the Park Theatre on February 10th. His favorite parts were heavy tragedy, his voice and face being considered by his admirers as even better than Charles Kemble's for such roles.

The character of Altorf was both heavy and tragic and may have caught his fancy as furnishing an opportunity for his particular kind of talent in a new role. He was billed to appear as the hero on February 19th, 1819. Simpson himself took the part of de Rheinthal, Altorf's brother-in-law. Mrs. Barnes, late of His Majesty's Theatre Royal, Drury Lane, played Rosina, the frail heroine of the play. The other parts were easily distributed.

Friendly influences were evidently at work to attract a representative audience on the first night. . . . Advance notices obviously intended to create a favorable impression before the event appeared in several of the New York papers. "The tragedy of Altorf had never been performed on any theatre." Its representation on the stage of the Park Theatre presented an opportunity to an American audience, the first in many years, of deciding on the merits of a new play, on its first appearance. "A full attendance and success on this occasion might encourage the manager as well as the author, to make further and similar efforts, etc., etc."

The great night arrived just as New York was digging itself out from under a deep fall of snow; the new rules put into effect that same winter for the regulation of hackney coaches at the theater were fairly successful in preventing the usual quarrels and confusion outside public places of amusement, between the ill-mannered drivers of public conveyances and the coachmen of the few private carriages of which the city then boasted. The newspapers tell us that the old "Park" was filled with a representative audience, not only the usual theater-going crowd who could always be depended on to see their favorite actor in a new role, but a large contingent of the Irish element who had already begun to make their home in New York, drawn by their old affection for the name of Wolfe Tone. For in his effort to keep the real name and sex of the author a secret, Tone himself was by many persons believed to have written the whole play as well as the prologue which appears over his name in all printed copies of *Altorf* still in existence. The presence of Mr. Charles Wilkes, with his whole family, in one of the stage boxes, and the Cadwallader Coldens, and other members of New York's most exclusive society, in prominent places in the audience, made the occasion something of a social event. It is thus described in next day's *Evening Post*: "Expectations were gratified. There was a greater share of applause than we have ever before witnessed. At every fall of the curtain between the acts, peals of approbation resounded through the House, and at the end of the play loud cries of 'Bravo! Author! Altorf!' were heard from boxes, pit and gallery, and were only stopped on Mrs. Barnes appearing to speak the prologue, which we could not distinctly hear."

At the call for "Author!" the eyes of the few who were in the secret must inevitably have turned to the stage box where Fanny sat with her sister Camilla, side by side with Mr. and Mrs. Wilson, and accompanied by young Wolfe Tone. What she actually thought and felt at the moment, is faintly reflected in Mrs. Millar's next letter.

> Joy, joy, to you, our beloved Fanny. How shall I tell you what we have felt, the tremendous anxiety with which we perused your pages, or the burst of delight and exultation with which we read your triumph. Great indeed, was your kindness in giving us so minute an account. Although we thought you entitled to every success, yet the realization of it gives us infinite pleasure. What an extraordinary situation was the moment in which you left the House. What a moment when, on the Curse being pronounced at the last scene, you turned to Tone and exclaimed, "Good God! Is it possible that I . . . etc., etc." How much do I envy Camilla and the Wilsons during that whole evening! If you were dis-

turbed by seeing the piece murdered, you have the consolation of being convinced what it will prove elsewhere with
full justice done to it.

But, as it turned out, that first evening was the high-water mark of
Fanny's success. As bad luck would have it, the great popular hero
of the hour, General Jackson, chose this particular moment for a visit
to New York. For two days the city was in the throes of celebration,
banquets, illuminations, a special entertainment at the Park Theatre.
On this occasion the play, *Pizzaro*, supposed to be better suited to the
tastes of the Conqueror of the Seminole Indians, and the Raider of
the Spanish territory of Florida, was substituted for *Altorf*, originally
billed for that evening.

Fanny's play was, indeed, revived after the departure of General
Jackson, and received two more presentations during Wallack's engagement, the receipts from the last being dedicated to the author.
But the attendance was disappointing and the results, financially
speaking, a failure.

The secret of the authorship of the play had been very badly kept
by her talkative old friend, Mr. Charles Wilkes. Among her own
friends at least, it did not survive that first evening in the Park Theatre.

"I need hardly tell you my regret . . ." writes Mrs. Millar. "Indeed
it is not easy for me to say whether I was most grieved at the discovery or surprised at the manner in which it took place. If you had
really made the proper impression on Mr. Wilkes he must have acted
differently. His family must have been very blamable to give any hint
of it to Mr. Colden or others. We can only hope that you will succeed
in raising contrary reports so as to prevent full disclosure and particularly to prevent its travelling to this side of the water . . ."

But an article in the New York *Columbian* made the disclosure almost obligatory. Some contributor to the editorial page of this newspaper insisted that no one but an American could have written the
play for the excellent reason that there was no dramatist in England
at this day capable of producing such a work.

Shall it be that we import forever our literature, our opinions and our fashions from England? Our country is daily
becoming more illustrious in arms and in the acts of government. It is time for the Muse of literature to try her flight to
America and we trust that she will be cheered in her progress

by every American heart . . . We advance this opinion without waiting for the fiat of an English audience or an English review, and we are sure that it will be confirmed by all those of our countrymen who dare to think for themselves.

Fanny's friends among that bitter remnant left from the Irish Rebellion of '98, notably that old companion and fellow conspirator of the elder Wolfe Tone, Dr. McNevin, at once seized upon this theory of newborn American genius in the hopes of "nettling the English," for whom any praise of their former colonists must always be disagreeable. But Fanny herself put an end to all further discussion of the matter by offering her play under her own name to Mathew Carey, head of the famous Philadelphia publishing house whose name appears on so many first editions of American classics. It appeared early in May, 1819, in a small octavo, paper-covered edition of which a copy is still to be found among the rare books of the New York Public Library.

After the title page with the name of the author and the date when the play was first acted in New York, comes an affectionate dedication to Mrs. Craig Millar, which that lady must have read with mingled feelings, gratification for this new proof of Fanny's attachment, mixed with very real regret at finding all her advice about certain too expressive passages in the manuscript utterly disregarded.

Then comes a preface, even more disturbing to Fanny's wise old friend, for obvious reasons.

> I cannot offer this tragedy with my name affixed to it, to the people of America, without saying a few words that may in some degree express my sense of the generous manner in which the play has been received by the inhabitants of this city. Whatever may be its success hereafter, I shall never forget that as the work of a nameless author it was accepted by the theatre of New York and received with applause by an American audience. In publishing it under my name perhaps I am a second time putting to the proof the generosity of the American public. A stranger, a foreigner, a young and unknown woman, my name can draw no attention to the title page and give no weight to the work itself. Yet I do not so wrong the people of this country as to apprehend that it will influence them unfavorably. Should it occur to them that they are perusing the work of a foreigner, it will perhaps

also occur to them that that foreigner has sought their country uninvited, from a sincere admiration of the government, a heartfelt love of its freedom, a generous pride and sympathy for its rising greatness.

The rest of the preface is taken up with Fanny's suggestions for a new school of dramatic writing and representation in the United States.

Here is the country where Truth may lift her Voice without fear, where the words of Freedom may not only be read in the closet but heard from the stage. England pretends to an unshackled press but there is not a stage in England from which the dramatist might breathe the sentiments of enlightened patriotism. In America alone might such a stage be formed, a stage that should be like that of Greece, a school of virtue; where all that is noble in sentiment, generous and heroic in action should speak to the hearts of a free people and inspire each rising generation with all the better and nobler feelings of human nature.

Her slaps and fleers at the decline of legitimate tragedy in England was no doubt pleasant writing for a person who could never forget the uncourteous treatment of her play at the hands of Kemble's manager, Mr. Harris, but for any one like Fanny, still passionately anxious for favorable recognition in her own land, they might better have been left unsaid. The preface concludes with the graceful admission that she at least was far from supposing herself the person to form such a theater as her imagination had conceived, but, in her own words:

If I might only hope by my example to encourage other and more gifted minds to employ their powers in this work, and thus to effect and complete what I could only imagine, I shall feel that I have not wholly laboured in vain and merit perhaps to leave my name in remembrance with the people of this great country which in its infancy, has brought the art of government to perfection and is destined I would fondly hope, in its mature age, to foster and advance every other art and be at once the land of liberty and of genius.

The effect of this performance upon Mrs. Millar is best described by her own letter on the subject.

I have seen *Altorf* and felt much affected by the precious little paragraphs written on its title page. I read your play again with deep interest and admiration, although my opinion of the Curse is unaltered—and formed the same conclusions which I hold, I wished to hear what others whose judgment I could respect, would think before I should write fully to you. I have been in Edinburgh for ten days. I heard much while there though I cannot in honor tell you from whom, Fanny! It is from the tender, anxious heart of a mother I speak, so forgive it. A mother will tell you things no other human being will. And as "unknown-to-be" your mother, I can hear things you cannot.

The objection of your name being fixed to *Altorf* even in America, I find still more strongly the opinion of people here than even my own. The Preface too, though all true and good is considered as injurious to your success. It is in a tone of confidence that would excite a feeling of opposition to a young Shakespeare. "And where is the use of it?" say they. Say it when you have once won publicity—your meed of praise from lettered nations, and that tribute sanctioned by years. The world will consider your age, your sex, and they will rebel against being taken by storm. If you answer that you despise them, then do not address them at all. Publish your works, act them, but do not give them a character yourself, leave them to speak for you to posterity. You will say I am harsh and too plain. My dear, dear and loved Fanny, I feel myself compelled by miserable anxiety and affection and honor to tell you what I know those you would respect think . . . Fame will be yours but do not, by appearing to demand and court it, subject your fair fame to the dirty bespattering of a world you despise.

There is also a line that I would implore you to change wholly. It is Page 43, line 8. "The burning kisses we have mixed together." Pardon my saying this is not in character with your pure and delicate and tender Rosina, and from a young female author, will be thought improper and more than improper.

It is not likely that Fanny ever admitted the wisdom of this last suggestion but there is ample evidence that she was already beginning to suffer just such consequences as her old friend feared and predicted from that freedom and facility in depicting passionate love already noticed in the description of her play. One hears through

Eliza Wilkes, niece of Charles, that Miss Wright's play had offended many persons by its politics and morals. Once people got it into their heads to talk this way, there was no limit to what they might believe and suspect about a young unmarried woman in Fanny's position, a young woman who had already rather shocked public opinion by her indifference to social convention in many ways, who had allowed herself to be seen more frequently than was strictly prudent all the past winter in the company of an engaging young man like Wolfe Tone.

It was fortunate that Mr. Charles Wilkes never ceased to be her staunch admirer and faithful friend. Her play, he insisted, showed genius and talents very wonderful in so young a woman, and his belief in her moral integrity remained unshaken.

"We are glad he has shown such a just confidence in you," says Mrs. Millar. "Perhaps this confidence has been strengthened by a letter of Margaret's to Mr. Jeffrey, which I have no doubt Mr. Jeffrey would repeat to him."

Wolfe Tone too, seems to have simplified the situation by disappearing out of her life as suddenly as he had entered it. The next time one hears of him is at Washington urging his claims to a commission in the United States Army, and from the moment they parted in New York, there is no evidence that he and Fanny ever met again. Did anything happen to interrupt a friendship which had begun so propitiously in mutual admiration and a common interest in Fanny's play? It must have been largely for her sake that he had lingered at her side all that winter instead of proceeding immediately to Washington about his own business. She owed him a debt of gratitude for his many and invaluable services in bringing *Altorf* to the notice of the managers of the Park Theatre. He had been largely instrumental in the play's final success. His name had appeared on the prologue. He had shared the experiences of that first night when the house cried, "Author! Author!" and looked towards the box where Fanny and he had sat enthroned together.

Then suddenly all mention of his name ceases from the record of Fanny's life till he reappears for a moment as a sneering critic of her book on America, a man who wraps himself in unfriendly silence whenever her name is mentioned.

The rest of his short life was spent in America where he succeeded in getting his commission as lieutenant of artillery in the United States Army. He married a Miss Sampson, daughter of one of his father's old companions in the Irish Rebellion, and died in his early thirties, of the same disease which had carried off his brothers and sisters, leaving two little daughters but no son to carry on his name in his adopted country.

Even before his exit from the scene of Fanny's first success, she had begun to suffer the inevitable reaction from that mood of high confidence in which she had penned her preface—as if all the world were already at her feet. Her letters to Mrs. Millar became fuller and fuller of Byronic contempt of the whole human race, herself included, and human success as well as human failure. She despised it all!

One good result of her premature publication of *Altorf* did, however, actually accrue to her. She made enough money by it to enable her to resume her original plan of seeing America, at least as much of it as was possible for two young women of moderate means, traveling alone in the hot months of an unusually hot summer.

In letters to Mrs. Millar describing her trip (which later became Chapters IX to XVI of her book on America) one finds a pleasant relief from the struggles of baffled genius which had absorbed her heart and mind during those last days of her stay in New York.

One need not follow her too closely in her journey up the Hudson and then by stage over rougher and rougher roads up the valley of the Mohawk River, across the state to Lewiston on the Niagara River at its junction with Lake Ontario. All the foreign travelers who wrote about this country during the first thirty years of the last century have followed and described the same route.

But there is a freshness and gaiety about her descriptions, a discriminating appreciation of the strangeness as well as the beauty of the new country through which she was passing, a liking for its people, a sympathy in the whole great drama of a people's conquest of primeval wilderness, which give her narrative a quality and distinction lacking in other books on the same subject.

"What is there in life more pleasing," she exclaims at the beginning of the long exhausting trip across the western country, "than to set forward on a journey with a light heart, a fine sun in the heavens above you, and the earth breathing freshness and fragrance after the summer rain." She nearly broke her own and her faithful sister's neck while scrambling about the Falls of the Genesee. "A young man who the next day became our fellow traveller, told me that he had observed the earth crumble beneath our weight and strike the water below, that his blood had run cold for many minutes after we had left our dangerous position."

She leaves an unearthly description of a log cabin on a clearing of the wilderness.

> During the summer nights it often presents a very singular appearance. It is not unusual, when the hot months set in, to clear away the mud which stops the interstices between the logs as they are raised horizontally upon each other, so as to allow a free passage to the external air. In the darkness of the forest, the light streaming through these crevices gives to the cabin the appearance of being either illuminated or on fire. . . . The cotter's evening light is interesting everywhere but doubly so when it shines in a world of solitude such as this.

On the other hand, the physical evils that the first occupiers of this soil had to endure, the ravages of malarial fever in those regions transversed by the Great Western Road before it reaches Lewiston filled her soul with passionate pity. She was told that the fever was the result of the rapid settling of the country, the destruction of trees:

> The collection of the waters from the creeks and the swamp, brought by the action of a powerful sun to a state of putrefaction. I could not pass one of these reservoirs of disease without a sickness of heart, and this was not a little increased when a young farmer was assisted by his father into the wagon, seemingly in the last stage of decline. As I placed the poor creature in the seat least uneasy of the comfortless vehicle and arranged a buffalo skin with the addition of a great coat behind his back, he told me he was recovering from the intermitting fever and going to seek change of air at the house of a neighbor twenty miles distant.

The moon was up and the chills of an autumnal night had succeeded a day of summer heat when the sisters entered the frontier village of Lewiston.

> Alighting at a little tavern we found the only public apartment sufficiently occupied and accordingly made bold to enter a small room which by the cheering blaze of an oak fire, we discovered to be the kitchen, and for the time being the peculiar residence of the family of the house. The arrival of the coach had thrown all into confusion. The busy matron, nursing an infant with one arm and cooking with the other,

seemed working out of strength and almost out of temper. A tribe of young urchins, kept from their rest by the unusual stir, were lying half-asleep, some on the floor and some upon a bed which filled a third of the apartment. We were suffered to establish ourselves by the fire, and having relieved the troubled hostess from her chief encumbrance, she recovered good humor and presently prepared our supper. While rocking the infant, it was with pleasure that I observed its healthy cheeks and those of the drowsy imps scattered around. It was unnecessary to be told that we were now on healthy ground. In the night when all was still, I heard the first rumbling of the cataract.

But it was not only the Falls of Niagara which made this part of her journey especially interesting to Frances Wright. All along the shore of Lake Erie and Lake Ontario and the Niagara River were battle fields of the War of 1812. That war had first roused her and made her conscious of herself as a thinking, independent being, detached from, and often antagonistic to, the thoughts and convictions of those about her. It was quite to be expected, therefore, that she should absorb everything she could see or hear about the war, and usually in a distinctly anti-British spirit. "Would to heaven," she exclaims in commenting on the Massacre of the River Raisin, "that we could find—not an excuse, for that were impossible—but some palliation of the horrors perpetrated on that spot!" And she cannot speak severely enough about the conduct of the British general in command on that occasion.

Indeed her strongly anti-British attitude in everything relating to this highly controversial moment in the history of Great Britain and the United States was undoubtedly one of the reasons for the torrent of abuse which greeted her book of *Views of America* from her English audience.

Was it some faint apprehension of her own future life work which made her look so longingly towards the vast hinterland beyond Lake Erie?

"We felt no small desire to strike south from Erie to Pittsburg and view with our own eyes the growing wonders of the western territory, but our plans were already arranged, etc., etc."

One need not follow her with any great detail as she made her return journey, along the north shore of Lake Ontario. It was probably more to save money that she chose the land route in one of those breakneck, springless, two-wheeled cablike vehicles which were all the French habitants had to offer the unhappy traveler, instead of one of the Lake steamboats (so much more comfortable but also more expensive).

As a result of days of scorching heat followed by nights of winter chill and fog, she seems to have had a touch of the prevailing Lake fever, which continued to hang about her during her brief visit to Montreal and shortened her stay in Canada.

"The icy winds of the equinox and some remaining weakness (from my illness) scolding me into prudence, we sacrifice our visit to Quebec and strike south to the States." So she explained her change of plan in a letter to Mrs. Millar, dated October, 1819.

But New York was still in quarantine after one of its recurring epidemics of yellow fever and she seems to have spent most of the autumn after her return from Canada in the country near New Brunswick, in the house of an old friend and fellow countryman of Charles Wilkes, named John Garnett. Garnett, like Wilkes, was one of that not inconsiderable number of Englishmen who seem only to have waited till the conclusion of peace between Great Britain and her erstwhile colonies to come and settle in America. He had bought a large estate on the banks of the lovely Raritan River, including a beautiful house, one of the most exquisite examples of later colonial architecture in New Jersey. It still stands with very little change from the time when John Garnett first came to live there. The same beautiful French wall paper which he imported from the factory of Dufour, in Paris, still decorates its halls: a view of the Seine on the ground floor, and Hindustan scenery on the floor above. A circular drive, shaded by handsome trees, and curving close to the steep grassy banks of the river gave and still gives the main approach to the house. At the back one still can see the remains of John Garnett's formal garden.

Fortunately both house and grounds have been preserved from the destruction which has overtaken so many remnants of a past age, by a deed of perpetual possession conferred to the city of New Brunswick by their last owner, Anthony Dey, under the name of Buccleuch Mansion and Park.

The family of the Garnetts when Fanny first became acquainted with them consisted of Garnett himself, a man of more than middle age, a wife, a son, and two unmarried daughters. At first she was more fascinated with the character and accomplishments of the head of the family than with either of her two contemporaries, Harriet and Julia. "Never was a mind more rich in treasures, never a heart more overflowing with benevolence," according to a later description of this new friend. "The scientist Lavater has chosen the very type of his countenance for the portrait of benevolence as it appears in his book on physiognomy. Never was a soul more ardent in the love of liberty and of all that is good and great." For, as often happened among men grounded in the last years of the eighteenth century, the proprietor of the White House was also a warm adherent of the liberal philosophy of the French Encyclopedists, and almost as confident as Fanny herself of the ultimate success of the American experiment. He was also a member of numbers of learned societies, with a local reputation for profound knowledge in mathematics and astronomy. Some of his sane, wise comments on the new world about him were to find a place among Fanny's own "Views" of America. Her friendship for him was broken by his death, which was sudden and quite unexpected, the result of a stroke of apoplexy which came in his sleep only a few days after she had said good-by to him when she sailed for Europe. His wife and daughters were to play an important part subsequently in the lives of the two sisters until their names finally disappear from the record.

Her last winter in the United States was divided between New Brunswick and Philadelphia, and in the latter city she had her final triumph—her *succès d'estime*—with an American audience, when her play *Altorf* was produced in the Arch Street Theatre with the American actor, Cooper, in the principal role.

As a matter of fact, Cooper was an American by choice, having been born an Englishman, son of a prominent physician of Harrow-on-the-Hill. He had made his first and greatest reputation in this country, to say nothing of a fortune from the American stage, and had married into one of the old-established families of New York State.

His wife was a beauty and a wit, as well as an heiress. His lavish hospitality, his love of fine horses, good company, good eating and deep drinking, made him something of a social lion in New York. As a young actor he had been remarkable for his extraordinary beauty in every particular which most counted on the stage, and at forty-four, the age he had reached when Fanny first came in contact with him, he was still very handsome and still at the zenith of his own profession. However, as he spent his money as fast as he made it, he had but lately sold his handsome town house on the corner of Broadway and Leonard Street and was living rather soberly with his wife and growing family in Philadelphia when not engaged in star parts in one or another of the principal cities of the United States.

This time there was no intermediary between Fanny and the actor and management of her play. To her and to her alone belongs the credit of persuading a man of Cooper's importance in the history of the American stage that her play was worth his notice.

One finds her also making a favorable impression on that competent authority on plays and actors in this country at the beginning of the nineteenth century, old William Dunlap. The following passage in his diaries refers to her thus:

"Arrived in Bristol, Penn. October 19th. Cooper in Philadelphia. See 2 young Scotch women, Misses Wright. The eldest 21 [*sic*]. Author of *Altorf* played at New York last year and now to be played in Phila. Cooper to play Altorf. He reads the play and I find much to praise."

Further notice of the first and only night of *Altorf* in Philadelphia is found in an unsigned letter which appeared in Duane's famous newspaper, the *Aurora*, some ten days after the event, January 14th. From this one gathers that the character of the old father, Erlach, was taken by Mr. Wood, the actor-manager of the Chestnut Street Theatre, and Rosina was played by Mrs. Wood, who rather fancied herself in tragic parts, though it was hinted that she kept her position in the company because she was the wife of her husband. Mrs. Entwistle, an actress of real parts and great popularity both in Philadelphia and New York, played Giovanna to Wallack's de Rheinthal. Cooper, of course, appeared as the hero, Altorf, and called forth reiterated applause from an enthusiastic audience. The letter goes on to praise the play to the skies, on the same lines followed by earlier critics. A real republican piece for a republican people. A first performance by a young lady. Great merit. Sentiments dignified, style always clear, sometimes highly nervous, elegant and pathetic. But the character and conduct of Giovanna were pronounced by hyper-critics as unnatural, and the curse of Erlach, came in for the usual disapproval.

No reason is ever offered either by Fanny or anyone else why, if the play was given at all, it did not receive a longer run; but her book

on America dwells with delight on the outside appearance of Philadelphia.

> I never walked the streets of any city with so much satisfac-
> tion. It has not, indeed, the commanding position of New
> York, which gives to that city an air of beauty and grandeur
> very imposing to a stranger, but it has more of the appearance
> of a finished and long-established metropolis. I am not sure
> that the streets have not too many right angles and straight
> lines to be altogether pleasing to the eye, but they have so
> much the air of cheerfulness, cleanliness, and comfort, that it
> would be quite absurd to find fault with them. The side pave-
> ments are regularly washed every morning by the domestics
> of each house, a piece of out-door housewifery, by the way,
> which must be somewhat mischievous to the ladies' thin
> slippers, but which adds much to the fair appearance, and,
> I doubt not, to the good health of the city.

The only exception to all this beauty and cleanliness was the river
front.

> Instead of leaving a sloping bank of verdure rising grad-
> ually from the river, which would have left the city to the
> view of its magnificent waters as well as to wholesome and
> refreshing breezes, it is choked up with wharfs and ugly
> ruinous buildings, the nest of infection during the heats of
> summer. . . . The crowd of ugly buildings and altogether
> the negligence of this confused corner of the city forms a
> strange contrast to the regular beauty which opens to the eye
> the moment you emerge from it.

The last event of this first visit to America was a trip to Washington
in April, just a month before her return to her own country.

The moment for this visit was ill chosen, if Fanny had wished to
see the Sixteenth Congress at its best. All the finest talent and loftiest
rhetoric of its members had been exhausted in those fierce debates
upon the Missouri Compromise Bill, passed and out of the way by
the beginning of March. And when Fanny and her sister arrived in
Washington, there was nothing more exciting going on than a debate
on the tariff, one of those preliminary skirmishes of the battle for
high protection which was to result seven years later in the Tariff
of Abominations which nearly disrupted the Union.

But the impression made on her by the Speaker of the House, Henry Clay, already well on the road to fame as "the great compromiser" was beyond her highest expectation, she tells us later. Apparently great confusion attended the final taking of the vote but "his sonorous voice quelled the tempest instantaneously, and produced a silence so profound that the drop of a pin might be heard upon the floor." Mr. Clay told someone afterwards, "that since he had presided in the House he had never but once seen it equally agitated."

She was presented to President Monroe, and wrote:

> I meant to rise, or rather I afterwards felt I ought to have risen. But when suddenly introduced to me by a senator, with the simple air of a private gentleman, and the calmness of a sage, he opened conversation, my recollection for a moment left me, and I fixed my eyes upon the venerable character before me with silent emotion, which he, quietly continuing his discourse, seemed unconscious of having excited, and thus relieved me from the awkwardness of framing an apology for my absence of formality.

She and her sister sailed from New York to Liverpool on the 10th of May, 1820. She had not written the great poem which was to be a pendant piece to Byron's *Childe Harold*. She had not succeeded in her plan for founding a new school of American drama on the lines suggested by her own play of *Altorf*. But she had collected a mass of impressions and convictions, and practical information about the people and the government of the country in which she had spent the last two and a half years, which was to take final form in her book, *Views of Society and Manners in America in a series of letters from that country during the years, 1818, 1819, and 1820, by an Englishwoman*. Such was the wordy title of the book which lifted her all at once from obscurity to some measure of the fame for which her soul thirsted. It had a surprisingly large sale on both sides of the Atlantic. It was translated into several European languages. It was praised to the skies, or cast into the depths of contemptuous disapproval as the opinions of the reader varied from radical Whig to extreme Tory, and it holds even now a creditable position among the early books of travel in this country.

CHAPTER III

The Friend of Lafayette

Yes, I have left you, regions of the sun.
Land of the free, I've bade thee my farewell;
The reckless gale our proud ship driveth on,
And thou art sunk beneath the billows' swell.

Shame on the wretch can tread thy sacred shore
And feel no generous thoughts expand his mind!
Can speak thy name, and think thy story o'er,
Nor bless thee in the name of all mankind.

But hark! What clamor makes the battling wind!
Ocean and Heaven mix in wild uproar.
The raging deep in mountains rolls behind.
And storm and tempest point our track before.

Farewell! Farewell! kindly I'll think on thee,
Land of the West! And so may'st thou retain
In some warm hearts kind memory of me,
A cheerless Pilgrim on life's stormy main.

FANNY's book on America was finished early in the spring of 1821. A new friend, Thomas Thornely of Liverpool, had already found her a publisher, Longman's, Rees, Hurst, & Co. of Paternoster Row, London, who had also handled the poetry of Moore and Campbell and could be trusted not to be too much shocked by the liberal tone of the "Views" to which her new work was dedicated.

A large part of the book was taken bodily from her correspondence with Mrs. Craig Millar, but it was never Fanny's intention to produce merely a lively description of travel on the lines already made popular by such female writers as Lady Morgan. Two-thirds of her book were frankly educational, learned disquisitions on the laws and underlying principles of the Federal Union and Government of the American States, the history of their establishment, the development of their political parties, all with a view to proving what a great and free people could accomplish by a representative democracy.

No one knew better than Fanny how unpopular these "Views" of hers on the American experiment would be with a large and influential group of conservatively minded people in both England and America. The dedication of her book to her good old Tory friend, Mr. Charles Wilkes, was almost in the form of an apology.

> My dear friend, although I am uncertain how far the sentiments contained in this little volume may be in unison with yours, I cannot resist that impulse of the heart which induces me to inscribe its pages to you. . . . Where in the following letters, I may have expressed opinions at variance with yours, I am persuaded that you will view them with candour, and that notwithstanding the defects you may find in this little work, you will pardon my seizing this opportunity of openly expressing the high respect I feel for your character and my grateful remembrance of the many proofs of friendship with which you have honored me.

But she was surprised, though she ought not to have been, by a very cool notice in the *North American Review*, just beginning a new lease of life under the brilliant management of a young Unitarian minister, Edward Everett. For she did not realize how deeply she had offended conservative opinion in New England by her sharp criticism of the Federalist party during the War of 1812.

The article in question regrets, "her extraordinary warmth against a class of our citizens of which she knows no harm, whose capital was not favored with a visit from her." It was a pity too, it remarks, "that she had not been sufficiently well-informed about a great political party to avoid the vulgar error of spelling the name 'Federal' instead of 'Federalist.'"

The extreme of vituperative violence against her is to be found, of course, in Lockhart's Tory review, the Quarterly Review, which sums up her book as:

> An impudent attempt to foist into public notice under a spurious title, namely that of an Englishwoman, a most ridiculous and extravagant panegyric on the government and

people of the United States, accompanied by the grossest and most detestable calumnies against this country that folly and malignity ever invented. An Englishwoman with the proper spirit and feeling attached to that proud title would blush to be thought the author of such a work. We will not, we can not believe that one so lost to shame exists among us, and are rather disposed, therefore, to attribute it to one of those wretched hirelings who under the assumed name of travellers etc. supply the radical press.

The *Literary Gazette* follows suit with the confident assertion that the book was written by no Englishwoman or Englishman but was the production of a red-hot American deeply imbued with bitter feelings against the mother country.

All this was exactly what she herself had expected and rather welcomed under the circumstances. But she never got over her annoyance at the unfriendly silence of Lord Jeffrey's *Edinburgh Review*, the one great liberal magazine of the time, from which she might have expected favorable notice. One reason she did not get it may be divined from a letter of Camilla Wright to her young cousin James Milne describing a visit both sisters made to Edinburgh the winter just before the publication of Fanny's book.

> Whitburn, Sunderland
> Feb. 6th, 1821

Though my last communication to you was dated from Avon Bank I will not fatigue both you and myself by a minute account of our perigrinations in the land of our fathers previous to our settling ourselves for the winter in this little village. [Whitburn] Suffice it to say that during our three weeks sojourning in the modern Athens, we had the satisfaction of frequently meeting with Mr. Jeffrey, that great little man, who sets himself, and is set by others, at the head of all that is great in literature and politics in that city. I, for my part thought him a flippant, conceited, though amusing little man, who is spoilt by the adulation of the minor satellites that move in his orbit, who seem to consider him as the source of their light and life, who, in common with many others, have raised him to a height that men with less assumption but possessing far greater talents and ability have failed to attain.

From our intimate acquaintance with his wife's relations

THE FRIEND OF LAFAYETTE 57
in New York, they united in showing us much attention, for
which, from the above Phillipic you will judge I make but
a poor return—but public men are free game, though my
love and respect for his father-in-law, Mr. Wilkes, will certainly induce me to be more guarded in the expression of
opinion to people in general.

Lord Jeffrey has often been described by his contemporaries as a
man of such diminutive stature that he might almost be called a dwarf,
while his aversion to exaggerated statement of any kind was one of
his most noted characteristics. One is afraid, therefore, that when
once brought face to face with a woman like Fanny, with her gift
for ready expression, her thirst for admiration, her physical presence,
especially her height, the temptation to give this dominating and impressive personality a timely snub would have been irresistible. But
whatever the reason, the *Edinburgh Review* never broke its insulting
silence to her book, in spite of the efforts of old friends like Mrs.
Millar to enlist Jeffrey's editorial eloquence in its service.

From other sources, however, Fanny soon began to receive letters
and messages full of flattering appreciation. Note especially the following from Charles Maclaran, the editor of that well-known Whig
newspaper, the *Scotsman*.

Your book fell into my hands on my return from London,
and of the pleasure which it gave me, you may judge by
the following circumstances. I read the whole on a Sunday
and going out at night, met a friend who knew how I had
been employed who asked me how I liked the work of which
he knew nothing. My answer was, "I have read and wept,
and wept and read." Perhaps this is not to be attributed to
the merits of the book, great as they are. Had you expended
three times the eloquence upon any other theme it would
have not moved me so much. But in the fortunes of America
I have long felt an interest amounting to enthusiasm. I had
fondly hoped that her admirable political institution would
raise the character of her people in virtue, energy, and dignity
above the level of society in Europe where human nature
toils on in darkness and sorrow under a load of evils which
renders the work of reformation a disheartening and almost
hopeless task.

I have read almost everything written upon the United
States for some years and must confess that after taking

pains to inform myself, my hopes as to the future moral
greatness of the Americans were founded rather upon a general confidence in the principles of human nature, than upon
anything which the existing state of society exhibited. It was
therefore with the greater pleasure that I found what I
wished to be true, yet was afraid to rely upon, so amply
confirmed by the result of your experience and observation. . . .

My sentiments, I believe, are not singular, and my nature
is not softer than that of other people, so from me you may
judge, not absolutely of all your readers but of a good many.

The same letter contains an illuminating comment on the article
in the *North American Review*. "It no doubt displays considerable
talent and industry but its principles are borrowed from the *London
Quarterly*, the organ of government by influence and corruption,
coercive and restrictive laws, every abomination practiced by the old
governments of Europe."

The same delighted acceptance of the book as a much needed ref-
utation of current opinions about the United States appears in an
unsigned French letter found among Fanny's papers. *"Ceci me rapelle
un ouvrage d'un grand merite. Les* Lettres sur l'Amerique *sont un
service essential rendu à la liberté. L'auteur refute indirectement toutes
les preventions, toutes les calomnies que quelques écrivains anglais,
(a gagè, ou plutot à pension) ont répandu sur les États Unis. Elle les
fait aimés. Elle montre les fruits excellents qui naissent d'une constitution libre, et il n'y a point d'exaggeration, point d'enthusiasme factise.
On n'est point tenté de dire 'c'est trop beau pour être cru.'"*

The great high priest of the Utilitarian philosophy, Jeremy Bentham,
also read her book and wrote immediately asking her to visit him
next time she came to London. This was a favor not usually granted
to women, not even Madame de Staël. "Tell Bentham," she is reported
as saying on her arrival in London, "that I will see nobody till I have
seen him." And his reply, "I am sorry, for in that case she will see
nobody."

He lived alone, retired from the world, in Queen's Square Place,
Westminster, in quaint surroundings which he was pleased to call his
"Hermitage"; an old house in a large garden shaded by age-old trees
and containing other buildings, notably the house which had shel-
tered Milton during the latter part of his life.

For many years he had been engaged in a philosophical enquiry into Man and the State, on the principle that institutions must be judged by their utility and by that alone. He believed that human motives were rooted in self-interest, which it was the task of education and legislation to enlighten. Each man's enlightened self-interest working through a very wide franchise, must result in the creation of a government whose interests, unlike those of a governing aristocracy, would be in harmony with those of the majority of people.

It was by the sheer logical application of that challenging, fascinating, yet strangely unlovely method of thought still known today as Utilitarianism that he had adopted the United States as his ideal of useful government. He was never tired of comparing its cheap and honest machinery with the corruption and extravagance at home. He was always anxious to meet and talk to anyone who could give him any practical information as to how things were really going in that country, and it was one of his quaint habits to send such a person some note or letter like the one we quote below, expressing his desire in this matter.

> During your stay in London my Hermitage such as it is, is at your service, and you will be expected in it. I am a single man, turned of seventy, but as far from melancholy as a man need be. Hour of dinner six; tea between nine and ten; bed a quarter before eleven. Dinner and tea in company. Breakfast my guests, whoever they are, have in their rooms and at their own hour and by themselves, etc., etc.

Other quaint personal habits of his have been made familiar to us by frequent description: his childlike simplicity, good health and vivacity, his Quaker-like brown coat, white worsted stockings and floating white locks, his trotting walk as he took his daily exercise in St. James' Park or round and round the paths of his own garden. One knows about his favorite stick, Dapple, his sacred teapot, Dick, his love for cats and mice and flowers, his foolish vanities and affectations which did not for a moment detract from the actual weight and substance of the man. The monumental mass of manuscript which kept a whole staff of secretaries and editors busy for years after his death and is not even yet fully classified and formulated, bear evidence of his extraordinary energy of mind, his inexhaustible mental curiosity.

A strange friendship for one who had already found a twin soul

in the romantic poet, Lord Byron! Byron was anything but a Utilitarian. One is told that, when confronted with Bentham's famous
Table of the "Springs of Action" sent him as a guide to his intercourse
with the Greek patriots in their war for independence, he had burst
into ribald laughter. Such cut and dried analysis of the human pas-
sions must have seemed exquisitely ridiculous to a man like the poet
who knew them so well at first hand.

But there was a hard dry side in Fanny's own nature which prevented her from being a consistent Romantic even in the most romantic
moment of her youth. She responded instinctively to the hard dry
reasoning of Bentham's system and did not feel its limitations in
imagination, or in real understanding of human nature, because of
those very limitations in herself.

She also quickly discovered the essential likeness between Bentham's theory of enlightened selfishness, and the Epicurean doctrine
that the desire for pleasure and the avoidance of pain are the underlying motives beneath all human action. This was a doctrine which
Fanny herself had already acknowledged during those winter evenings at Millheugh when she read aloud her own tract on Epicurus to
an admiring audience of friends and cousins.

We may smile at the innocent flattery of Mrs. Millar's letter addressed to her at Queen's Square Place and dated September, 1821.

"I was delighted with your account of Bentham. The two philosophers actually sleeping together in the same house! How little would
one of them, on leaving Whitburn, have believed they would be so
nearly in the situation of Diogenes!"

Bentham's opinion of Fanny appears in an old letter which she
preserved to the end of her life. Who wouldn't?

"The strongest sweetest mind that ever cased in a human body."

But her book on America was to have more important and far-
reaching results in her own life than the approval of a distinguished
philosopher like Jeremy Bentham.

She was still at Whitburn, with her sister and her old friend Mrs.
Millar, making plans for a winter on the Continent, when she was
flattered and delighted to receive a letter in that cryptic handwriting
with which she was soon to become so poignantly familiar—her first
letter from General Lafayette.

Lafayette was, at this time, about sixty-seven years old, a widower,
living for the greater part of the year in a sort of patriarchal state,

surrounded by children and grandchildren, on his country estate of La Grange.

The château with its surrounding acres, lying some forty miles to the southeast of Paris in the pleasant and fertile valley of the River Yères, had been saved from the confiscations of the French Revolution by the energy and foresight of Madame de Lafayette, whose property it originally was. It became the family refuge after Lafayette had returned from his Austrian prison at Olmütz in 1808, and there he remained in a sort of voluntary exile, until the fall of Napoleon, with whose imperial ambitions he had little or no sympathy.

Under the Bourbon Restoration, however, after the bestowal of that measure of popular government known in history as *La Charte*, Lafayette had again emerged to take a prominent part in public affairs. In 1818 he had been elected to the Chamber of Deputies, as liberal member from the department of La Sarthe, and instantly became a thorn in the side of the extreme reactionaries in Parliament who could never forgive him for his share in the events which brought about the deaths of Louis XVI and Marie Antoinette.

He was a thorn too, in the side of many of his own family who, even while adoring him for his personal qualities, could not feel any sympathy with his fanatical devotion to the idea~ and ideals of 1789.

A speech delivered in the Chamber of Deputies on June 4th of that same year had excited a passionate fury of resentment among the adherents to the old order who made the Conservative majority in the House.

"He thinks he is still on his white horse," cried one of these in taunting reminder of that one unfortunate incident of his life when he had let the mob from Paris enter the palace at Versailles and penetrate the very bedroom of the Queen.

"Have you read," wrote his sister-in-law, Madame de Montagu, to Mlle. de Rovera, "the speech of my brother-in-law in the Chambre des Députés and his eulogy of the Revolution? I am indignant with it. I see him however, and no one suspects my feeling, for in our family relations he is always perfect and full of the best advice, but his blindness and his moral frenzy for liberty are a cross I have to bear."

Another glimpse of him at this period of his life we get in the Souvenirs of the Duke de Broglie, son-in-law of Madame de Staël, an old friend though of a later generation, a moderate in politics and a member of the House of Peers.

One had to love M. de Lafayette, for the man himself, which was an easy matter, but one got nothing by being one of his real friends. For he made no difference between an honorable man and a *vaurien*, between a man of intellectual value and a fool. The whole world fell for him into two classes, those who did and those who did not say to him what he said to himself. He was a prince surrounded by people who flattered and robbed him. All that splendid fortune, nobly gained and nobly dedicated, was wasted among adventurers and spies. One gained nothing either, by taking him for a leader, because he was always ready to engage himself in any kind of enterprise, at the first appeal of the first comer, exactly like a gentleman of the good old times, who fought for the mere joy of conflict, the pleasure of danger and the desire to oblige a friend.

Thanks to a portrait of him by Ary Scheffer which appeared in the Paris Salon of 1822, we know exactly how he looked at this particular moment of his life: a very fine gentleman, fashionably dressed in a voluminous overcoat, with high collar and elaborate cuffs, thrown back to reveal a dark waistcoat and long loose trousers, and "Standing as though out walking," so he describes his position to this same sister-in-law, "my cane and hat in hand like this." "And your other hand?" asks his sister anxiously, having been told by some mischievous gossiper that the picture represented him flourishing a charter of liberties.

"It is in my pocket," he replied, "which is better, dear sister, than to have it in the pocket of others."

The face of the portrait still retains the features of the youthful Lafayette, long nose, retreating forehead and chin, small wide-open slightly staring eyes, made so familiar to us by unnumbered busts and statues set up by a grateful country to commemorate his services at the time of the American Revolution. But with the passing years it had become incredibly old and ugly, and though still the face of an invincible idealist, it was also that of a man whom new times and new necessities had turned into a credulous schemer and conspirator.

For opposition to the Bourbon Restoration was not confined to the Chamber of Deputies. Bonapartists and Republicans alike, besides taking their share in the daily debates of the Chamber, kept themselves closely in touch with a secret revolutionary society composed for the most part of young men, who called themselves *Carbonari*, in imitation of the Italian society of the same name. These were actively though secretly engaged in sowing disaffection in the French Army, hoping by revolts and mutinies among the soldiers and under-officers to terrorize the existing government into a more liberal policy, or even to overthrow it.

For example, side by side with the speech of June 4th, delivered by General Lafayette from the tribune of the Chamber of Deputies, one must place his unproved but too probable connection with a very nearly successful attempt to blow up the famous old fortress of Vincennes, in the outskirts of Paris. The discovery of the plot in time to prevent it, the trial and conviction of a whole host of lesser conspirators, while the men higher up went unpunished, were among the unpleasant incidents of that same summer.

This very human, very faulty, but peculiarly lovable being, who had assumed heroic shape for Fanny long ago while she was still a girl under her aunt's roof at Dawlish, was now to become the object of her idolatrous devotion, her guide and friend through some of the strangest adventures of her strange and adventurous life.

His letter complimenting her on her book has not been preserved, but it also evidently contained the suggestion of a meeting between these two lovers of Free America as soon as possible after her arrival in Paris.

The following vivid account of their first meeting from Fanny's pen is found in the Bentham collection of familiar correspondence.

Having passed a day in Paris I set out for La Grange (about 40 English miles from hence). Imagine my dismay on finding that General Lafayette had crossed me on the road, having been summoned on business to Paris. His family (which comprises three generations, sons and daughters, with their wives, husbands, and children, to the number in all of 19) received me with every possible demonstration of respect and regard, but were in despair at the absence of the General as I was in the same.

I determined to return next day to meet him here in Paris, which I did. You will say again, "Giddy goose! Why did you set off for La Grange without having written beforehand?" There are reasons for everything, Great Philosopher. I had found a letter in Paris notifying me of the approach of some English friends who were coming to see all the sights of this gay city in the short space of ten days. Civility, therefore, constraining for this brief period, my stay in Paris, I was obliged to seize the only day that remained to me before their arrival, for my journey into the country.

Returning late at night, I sent a note early the following morning to General Lafayette, who soon answered it in person. Our meeting was scarcely without tears (at least on my side) and whether it was that this venerable friend of human liberty saw in me what recalled to him some of the most pleasing recollections of his youth (I mean those connected with America) or whether he was touched by the sensibility which appeared at that moment in me, he evidently shared my emotion.

He remained about an hour, and promised to return in the evening. (He was engaged to dine with Benjamin Constant.) My sister and all the rest of the family escorted our English friends to Beaujour, a sort of French Vauxhall, while I remained to receive General Lafayette.

We held an earnest tête-à-tête, until after midnight. The main subject of our discourse was America, although we wandered into many episodes and digressions. The enthusiasm and heart affection with which he spoke of our Utopia, the high respect he expressed for the character of its people, the ardent love of liberty which breathed through all his discourse, found, I need not say, an answering note of sympathy in me.

He told me he had been particularly interested by my allusion to the history of the American Revolution. "You made me live those days over again." In speaking of the Revolutionary Army, he exclaimed, "We were an army of brothers. We had all things in common, our pleasures, our pains, our money, and our poverty." At another time, he observed, "No historian could render justice to the virtue of that army, no words could paint their fortitude, their disinterested and sublime patriotism." He observed also upon the simple manners, warm hospitality, and pure morals of the American nation. "You have only rendered justice to them," he added smiling. "Truly they are the best and happiest people in the world."

From that moment Fanny and the General were friends in thought, word and deed. "*Ah, quelle pournée pour moi que celle de hier!*" says she, writing to him the next morning. "*Que je suis heureuse et fière de votre amitié et de cette adoption qui unit mon sort au votre pour la vie! J'en suis digne, mon ami, j'en suis digne. Mon cœur me le dit. Je m'estime plus depuis que je vous aie connu. Il faut bien que je vale quelque chose ayant su attirer votre amitié et votre confiance."*

A long visit of both sisters to La Grange served to reinforce the favorable impressions of that first meeting between Frances and her paternal friend. That crenelated and medieval structure whose moated walls and five pointed towers were as familiar to American youth of the early nineteenth century as Mount Vernon itself, was to become a second home during all the months and years of the sisters' stay in France. La Grange, at the time Fanny first came to know it, was something more than the stately home of a noble hospitable family. It had become a sort of shrine where those ideals which had given such haunting beauty to the early days of the French Revolution were still preserved for worship, where the General himself was loved and adored as one adores a god or a principle. Indeed the worship and flattery poured upon him by friends, family, everyone, in fact, by whom he was most closely surrounded, might have turned the head of a stronger man than he.

First in that list of worshipers came the ladies of his household, his two daughters, Madame Charles de la Tour Maubourg and Madame Louis de Lasteyrie, and his daughter-in-law, Madame George de Lafayette, by birth de Tracy. It was they who received and made welcome with that ineffable French courtesy which can conceal such infinite reserves beneath its smooth suave surface, any and every guest whom the General's indiscriminate hospitality precipitated upon them for weeks and months at a time.

The daily life of the castle seems to have been conducted according to a somewhat rigid routine, described in the unpublished letter of an American lady, written at about this time.

We rise not very early. About 10:30 the breakfast bell rings and on the stairs all the family meet, the children of every size who the sound of the bell draws from their different rooms. On the breakfast table of large dimension, is spread a dinner! Soups, roast mutton, tea, coffee, toast, and butter are handed round.

After breakfast we walk, or if wet, read aloud, or talk, till 12 when the mothers retire with their daughters into their various rooms and we pass into ours. At 5:30, dinner bell, after which we stroll about the grounds till lighted lamps find us in the salon, reading aloud, English or French.

There are also charming accounts of pleasant afternoons when the children had all gone back to their own quarters, and the elders gathered on the lawn which stretched away towards the pleasance on the other side of the moat, where in the shade of two fine trees one could watch the arrival of new guests, from Paris or America, at the castle entrance. On such occasions General Lafayette was often induced to talk of his own extraordinarily varied past, falling involuntarily into "a special tone of voice, slow and carefully modulated, which gave even to his lightest and most casual anecdote something of the emphasis and veracity of history."

The General had his private quarters—his study and library—in the highest apartment of one of the five round towers of the château. Here Fanny spent long hours alone with him. Here hung her portrait, painted especially for him, as we learn from frequent reference in the Lafayette correspondence, by Ary Scheffer, a favored visitor at La Grange and busy at the same time with the General's own portrait. And the room directly beneath him, where she could hear his footsteps on the floor above her, came soon to be considered as Fanny's own whenever she stayed at La Grange.

This daily intercourse was hardly interrupted when both families were settled for the winter in Paris, in spite of distance between Fanny's new abode on the Rive Gauche and the General's apartments in the Rue D'Anjou, that new fashionable region which had come into existence since the Revolution, known in the common talk of the day, as the "Quartier Brilliant."

Before their first meeting with Lafayette, Frances and Camilla had already arranged to join forces for the winter with the family of John Garnett of New Brunswick. Garnett himself, one may remember, had died in his sleep a few days after Fanny had said good-by to him on her departure for England. There was no will; so his beautiful house and most of his possessions were sold at auction the following summer, and with what fortune was left them after the debacle, his widow and two daughters left America to pass the rest of their lives in Europe. When Fanny and her sister returned to Paris from La Grange, they were already established on the edge of the Faubourg St. Germain in an old house which had once been part of a convent, with windows overlooking the convent garden, where black-robed nuns came and went at the sound of the chapel bell. The little street in which the convent stood connected the two main arteries of the old quarter of the Luxembourg, the Rue de Sèvres and the Rue Vaugirard, and is known today as the Rue de l'Abbé Gregoire. In Fanny's time it was called the Rue St. Maur. House and convent still remain untouched by time, behind the high blank wall which hides them from sight of the everyday world.

A network of narrow tortuous streets lay between the Rue St. Maur and the General's quarters on the other side of the Seine, but neither distance nor difficulty could prevent the carriage of General Lafayette, drawn by his two white-nosed horses, from making its way halfway across Paris two or three times a week to leave a little note like the following, for his new friend.

Mardi Matin. . . . Je ne pourrais pas avoir le plaisir de vous voir aujourd'hui, ma bien chère amie, grand motif de plus pour regretter La Grange, où j'avais pris la douce habitude de passer la journée avec les deux excellentes et aimables soeurs. Ma matinée à la Chambre n'en a été que plus ennuiente. J'espère vous voir demain matin. Bon jour et milles amitiés de

LF.

Very often, however, the carriage contained the General himself, coming to spend hours in the little room which had once been a nun's cell and now was Fanny's study. He was deeply interested in the French translation of her *Views on America,* of which she was then correcting the proof. He comforted her in her rages over the obstinacy and stupidity of her French translator, a certain M. Parisot, ex-officer of the French Marines, who was not as amenable to her suggestions as she thought proper.

It was Lafayette, no doubt, who inspired the flattering notice of this book when it finally appeared in French, early that same winter, written by one of the editors of the liberal sheet, the *Constitutionnel,* Monsieur Etienne, personal friend and fellow deputy of Lafayette.

Voyage aux Etats Unis traduit par J. T. Parisot, officier de Marine eliminé en 1815, printed by Bechet ainé and for sale by the Editor (Parisot), 57 Quai des Augustins, and by Arthur Bertrand, Rue de Hautefeuille.

This young English woman endowed with all the charms of beauty, belonging to a family both rich and well considered . . . has written like a man of letters, travelled like a savant, observed like a moralist, reflected like a philosopher, and reasoned like a publicist, while still hardly more than twenty years old. Serious books have been her playthings since childhood; the methods of government, exercised her earliest intelligence. She adored liberty at the age when a young woman usually makes her sacrifices to Love, and not finding it sufficiently beautiful or sufficiently pure in her native country, she crossed vast seas in order to find it freed at last from every false disguise, and having found it, to render to it the worship of a fervent and impassioned heart. Mademoiselle Wright is this young author, charming and grave, etc., etc.

Indeed, from all accounts that first winter in Paris was one of the most brilliant and stimulating periods of Fanny's life. Lafayette never did anything kind by halves. He saw to it that his friends and family were her friends. His old uncle the Comte de Segur invited her to some of his most delightful dinner parties and evening receptions. She was in intimate relation with both the Lasteyries, Count Louis, the husband of Virginie de Lafayette, and Charles, the last a man of just the type in which Fanny particularly delighted, widely interested in all the new inventions which might improve the condition of the working classes. His wife, a niece of the great Mirabeau, continued to be a faithful friend to Fanny when the other great ladies of Lafayette's immediate family began to be unkind.

One finds also frequent reference to many of Lafayette's fellow deputies. Admission to the visitors' gallery in the Chamber could be obtained only through cards, the gift of a member.

Here is a note which accompanied a whole handful of such cards for all the family at the Convent:

> Monday Morning
> I arrived too late last night, dear ladies, to be admitted at your door, when I came to bring the tickets which I now leave for you. One must come "en bonnet ou en cheveux," that is to say, dressed as when one goes to dinner "en ville." It is essential to arrive early. My servant Bastien will wait for you at the entrance of the Pavillon de l'Horloge, porte lateral de droite. Farewell, dear ladies. Receive the assurance of my tender attachment.

After this first introduction there were numerous visits to the Chamber, even when nothing particular was going on, and Lafayette was not expected to speak, for to quote her own words, "How could I ever be bored in a place where you are! Anyway, I am always content to find myself face to face with the Left Wing, no matter what one is talking about." For Fanny soon became almost as well informed as her "paternal friend" in the politics of the Bourbon Restoration as well as the various personal characteristics of the various ministers who succeeded one another in power that winter.

It was some time, however, before she had any knowledge or suspicion of her admired friend in his second and secret role as aider and abettor of the revolutionary society of the French *Carbonari*.

The widespread activities of this society were carried on by local units protected from the introduction of police spies, and from each other by an elaborate system of secret forms and pass words. Its Supreme Lodge, or Vente Suprême which served as a clearing house for its scattered activities and directed its policies, had its seat in Paris. And here, one is informed by dependable historians of the Bourbon Restoration, General Lafayette as well as several of the most prominent members of the Left Wing were frequently found in intimate conversation with its ruling spirits. Here also might be found more than one of those agreeable acquaintances Fanny had made during her first long visit to La Grange. Ary Scheffer, that charming young man with his sensitive artist's face and lofty forehead shaded by Byronic waves of soft brown hair, his gentle dreamy manners, was a *Carbonaro*, as well as his two brothers, Henri and Arnold, and their friends the two Thierrys, later to become among the most distinguished of French historians.

In the Supreme Vente at Paris was hatched one after another of those conspiracies against the Bourbon government which went up like rockets during all the first winter of Fanny's stay in France. All of them were destined, however, to come fizzling down, duds, bringing only ruin and desolation for everyone engaged in them.

The first of these was the so-called plot of Belfort, named from the garrison town on the edge of the Rhine Valley which had been chosen by the *Carbonari* as the meeting place for the mutinous troops of all that region from Strasbourg to Colmar, where Lafayette himself was to take command and set up a Provisional government in company with two other prominent members of the Left Wing.

Two letters from Fanny to her paternal friend dated December 27th and December 29th, the very week set for the outbreak, and directed to Lafayette at La Grange where she confidently believed him to be in peaceful intercourse with his family at that particular moment, are ample evidence of her complete ignorance of the approaching explosion at Belfort.

I like to think of you at La Grange, my excellent friend, although it deprives me of your society. You have need of a few days repose after all your fatigues in this city. I am indeed unreasonable enough to lament that I do not pass them with you and to envy those who enjoy the good that is denied me. I am anxious to hear how you made out on your journey, and how you found all the dear inmates of the château. What sweet hours I have passed in those walls! I must pass many more there and—(receive the threat from a prophetic one!) *shall* pass many more there. Hitherto my life has had so little pleasure in it that I am sure there must be now much good in store for me, and for all those connected with me. Much, therefore, for you, my excellent friend!

Saturday Night—Paris—(December 29th)
I have nothing to say that can be new to my best friend and yet I feel disposed to write. Time at present hangs heavy on my hands and on my heart, and it seems as if the burden could alone be lightened by discoursing with a friend. I mean not, however, to call your attention from important matters to my idle words. Throw them aside till you have some moments of leisure, or perhaps of weariness, then possibly they may serve to banish anxious thoughts. The prattle of a child has sometimes done as much for a wise man. You know I am your child, the child of your affections, the child of your adoption. You have given me this title and I shall never part with it. To possess this title was the highest of my wishes, to deserve it, my proudest ambition. And in truth, my excellent friend, I feel that I do deserve it by the reverence that I bear to your virtue, by my sympathy in all your sentiments, in all your undertakings, in all your pleasures, and all your pains, by the devotedness of my affection, the feelings of my confidence; by all this and more than this I feel that I merit the friendship and parental fondness of the best and greatest man that lives. Write to me, my friend, my father. One word will suffice, but let me have that word soon and often.

The news of the day is a conspiracy and insurrection at

Saumur, or some town resembling the name. The Funds are
falling, and disturbances are talked of in some of the Austrian dominions. The Turks are putting to death and torture
all the Greeks of Constantinople. No whispers, in short, but
of strife and commotion.

This is a strange world! May the efforts of the good and
wise improve it, and when we shut our eyes upon it, may we
open them upon another! Vale F. W.

The publicity which followed the discovery of the plot of Belfort
put an end to Fanny's detachment from the world of secret conspiracy
which absorbed so much of the General's life at the moment of her
closest intimacy with him. It would be a mistake to conclude that
Lafayette himself was ever in personal danger of either death or imprisonment for his well-authenticated connection with *Carbonari*
activities at this time.

The inviolability of a deputy was much to the fore at this particular
moment of French history. And even without this protection, the
ministry of Louis XVIII had enough political sense to realize that
Lafayette in liberty and conspiring was not nearly so great a threat
to the reputation of the Bourbon monarchy either at home or abroad,
as Lafayette a martyr to government oppression in prison.

But he never lost his sense of responsibility for the hard fate of
those lesser victims of conspiracy, captains, sergeants, civilian sympa-
thizers who had been caught in the dragnet of the Bourbon police.
He was reckless in his connivance with their attempts to escape from
prison before their trial, and generous in his efforts to ameliorate their
condition when they found themselves penniless and without resources in a foreign land.

London was full of such unfortunates, not only Frenchmen, but
the wreckage thrown up by the sea from all those other unsuccessful
revolutions which had been disturbing the peace of Europe ever
since the fall of Napoleon and the final restoration of autocracy after
the Battle of Waterloo. It was during a ten weeks' visit to London,
through the months of February, March, and April, that Frances
Wright was able to make herself particularly useful to her beloved
old friend, as a link between him and such objects of his secret
bounty.

It happened by great good luck that Fanny had made all her plans
for this visit to London, long before there was any special and secret
reason for it.

Longman was going to bring out another edition of her book on America and she wished to take advantage of this opportunity to correct some errors which she had discovered in the original manuscript. She also proposed to amplify certain references to the Continental Army of the American Revolution to please her old friend, General Lafayette. And Lafayette himself had suggested that she should submit her little tract on Epicurus for publication at the same time. She hoped to get one of her plays acted in a London theater with the famous actor, Macready, in the principal part.

Her letters to Lafayette during this ten weeks' visit to London give a vivid impression of all these varied interests. His to her during this same period are no longer available but they evidently came regularly twice a week in the portfolio of the French Ambassador and his affection and dependence on her in this and all emergencies are clearly reflected in her replies.

She begins with a scrawl written immediately after her arrival in London and dated from the house of her old philosopher in Queen's Square Place.

> I trust the storm which held your Fanny in some jeopardy throughout Saturday did not extend to Paris or you may have felt some anxiety. The storm was tremendous and fully established the omnipotence of steam. The wind veered ahead as we cleared the harbor of Calais at 9.00 P.M., but in spite of its fury we were off Dover by 6.00 in the evening. To approach the land was, however, impossible and so we ran up to Ramsgate and were taken off in boats, sick, wet and weary, in storm and darkness, as forlorn wights as ever landed from the bark of Charon. We reached London last night and this morning I began business by visiting bankers, lawyers, and making appointments to meet others.

Such is the guarded language in which she usually informed her paternal friend concerning the very delicate and secret business she had undertaken in his behalf. As for instance in the following long letter a little later:

> Feb. 7th. I have been all day talking about house rents, powers of attorney, and heaven knows what, with heaven knows who, and heaven knows where. I trust, however, I shall soon see my friend's affairs arranged. I have, as yet, attended little to my own. Next week I hope to be free to

set about them. I have a copy of the second edition of our book, Views of Society and Manners, by me, but have scarcely looked into it. I think, however, that our corrections have been properly made.

I read over again and again that passage in your last letter and always with moistened eyes.

As long as my eyes can see they will see you beside me.

Yes, I will be the ministering spirit of your latter days. I am generous enough to feel a melancholy pleasure in the thought that in the common order of Nature it will be I not you who must drink the cup of bitterness which comes with personal bereavement. But alas, alas! why must it always come to me?

February 9th gives a detailed account of service in his behalf.

I took this morning a hasty breakfast, and set off in search of your friend. You may believe that I do not lose an instant in executing a commission of yours. He had left London some time since for Lisbon where he had directed his letters to be forwarded. I turned away and had retraced a fourth of my steps when I recollected that you might desire his address and turned back to ascertain it. "Poste Restante, Lisbonne." I have thought it wiser to return your letter than to forward it to Lisbon since you say that it contains introductions which can be of no use to him there. I have been casting about in my mind what were best to do with it, and had almost decided upon sending it to the porte feuille of the Portuguese minister when it occurred to me that it may contain what you would not like to entrust to the poste restante of Lisbon. Nor can it go more expeditiously from here than from Paris. Indeed it cannot go as expeditiously, the English mail to Portugal going only once a fortnight and by sea. All things duly weighed in the balance, therefore, I return it to you. I hope I do right. [And here comes a half page of mysterious reference to "friends of the cause" in Paris and Lisbon, written in a kind of cypher which makes it quite impossible to translate.]

Among other performances, I have paid this day no less than three visits to the War Office. What to do there? you will say. Not to inquire into the army expenses, nor to sue for a commission but only to see a gentleman upon the subject "of my friend's business." An old "saw" has it that the third time brings luck, and so I found it, for I found my man.

I dare say you marvel sometimes at my independent way of walking through the world just as if nature had made me of your sex instead of poor Eve's. Trust me, my beloved friend, the mind has no sex but what habit and education give it, and I, who was thrown in infancy upon the world like a wreck upon the waters, have learned as well to struggle with the elements as any child of Adam's.

But after walking far and wide in this over-grown city, I find myself alone at the fireplace in the house of my good old Socrates (Jeremy Bentham) privileged to sit down in an arm chair and feel myself tired, too tired to do anything useful and, therefore, it is that I am talking nonsense to you. I wish I had your second letter. I know there is one on the road. Methinks I would have one every day, and had I the arranging of the mails and portfolios, it should be so. But you will have no time to listen to this idle chattering . . .

She had no difficulty in placing her tract on Epicurus with Longman, under its present name, *A Few Days in Athens*. There is a copy of this first English edition in the Library of the British Museum, a slender octavo volume, beautifully printed on fine paper with wide margins and an impressive title page and a short dedication to Jeremy Bentham.

Her first intention had been to dedicate the book to Lafayette but, as it was the only one of her works in any way suited to the taste and calling of her Good Socrates she explained most regretfully to Lafayette that, "I feel I must sacrifice the pleasure of placing your name on the title page and inscribe it to my old Philosopher. I know he will be sensible to this little tribute of respect, and the more so as he will know that his name will not dispose the English public more favorably to the work.

"Our good old friend carries his years as bravely as ever, except that he is more deaf. This infirmity is a greater trouble to me than it appears to be to him. You remember the difficulty I find in raising my voice. An hour's conversation with my Socrates leaves me more fatigued than does a walk of six miles. . . ."

This work once through the press she could have returned to France with an easy mind and a good conscience if she had not in the meantime managed to entangle herself in the schemes of that inveterate plotter and schemer in the sacred cause of liberty, General Guglielmo Pepe, hero of the unsuccessful *Carbonari* Revolution in the Kingdom of Naples and Sicily the preceding year.

For months after his defeat at Rieti, Pepe had led the life of a hunted exile in the fastnesses of the Abruzzi until he was able to make his way across the Mediterranean and Spain to England. But, like so many Italian political exiles of that time, having lost all hope of bettering conditions at home, he remained deeply interested in the cause of free institutions wherever he saw them threatened.

His present deep interest was Spain where a recent military revolt under a gallant soldier named Riego, had reduced a shockingly bad king, Ferdinand VII, to comparative impotence, and set up a desperate attempt at a liberal constitutional government—one of those ill-fated adventures from which that unhappy people have suffered so often.

Pepe had passed through Spain on his way to England, and found many friends among the Liberal Constitutional leaders in and out of the new government at Madrid. He was eager to enlist liberals in Europe on their side, in his own way, which was always the way of secret conspiracy against established government organizations. He longed to get in touch with the *Carbonari* movement in France, and especially with the man who, in the world of secret conspiracy at least, was believed to be their leader. France, however, was especially closed to a man who had so lately been in rebellion against the King of Naples and Sicily who happened also to be the father of the widowed Duchess of Berri, mother of the infant heir to the French crown.

But the young Milanese, Count Pisa, who had accompanied Pepe in his wanderings ever since the defeat at Rieti was prepared to take the chance of evading the Bourbon secret police. The difficulties and dangers of such an undertaking, however, would be very much lessened by a personal letter to General Lafayette.

And here Fanny comes upon the scene. As it happened, the very house where Pepe had been most hospitably received and made at home after his arrival in England was also the second home of Fanny during her visit to London.

One may be a little surprised to learn that this house, No. 16 Keppel Street, Bloomsbury, was the home of a highly respectable barrister with rooms in Lincoln's Inn, Mr. Thomas Trollope; and of his lively wife, best remembered today as the author of that amusing book, *Do-*

mestic Manners of the Americans, and mother of the famous novelist, young Thomas, then but a child of six years old.

An amusing account of the family at this time is found in the *Reminiscences* of the eldest son, T. Adolphus Trollope, written in his old age.

"I see myself alone in the back drawing room of No. 16," he tells us, "in which room the family breakfast takes place probably to avoid the necessity of lighting another fire in the dining room below at 7.00 A.M. . . . My parents had not yet come down to breakfast nor had the tea urn been brought in by the footman. Nota bene. My father was a poor man and his establishment altogether on a modest footing. But it never would have occurred to him or my mother that they could get on without a man in livery."

Tom Trollope goes on to give one a list of the most frequent visitors to the household. Dr. Nott, prebendary of Winchester Cathedral; Miss Gabell, eldest daughter of the headmaster of Winchester College; Lady Dyer, widow of the philanthropist, General Sir Thomas Dyer—pillars of society, so it sounds at first reading—and one begins to wonder how a convinced radical and political innovator like Fanny Wright could have found a place in such circles.

Mrs. Trollope in her lively youth, however, was far from being the perfect example of an orthodox conservative-minded English matron she became in her later years, and the people who came and went in Keppel Street were frequently the same as those Fanny met in the Hermitage.

One turns again to T. Adolphus Trollope for the following amusing glimpse of General Pepe. "A remarkably handsome man but not a brilliant or amusing companion. His sobriquet among the ladies of the family was '*Gâteau de Plomb!*' But none the less was he highly and genuinely respected among them. . . . He had a simple, dignified, placid manner of enunciating the most astounding platitudes, and replying to the laughter they sometimes produced by a calm and gentle smile."

Fanny's first impression of Pepe can be guessed by her hurried request to Lafayette to send her forthwith "another copy of the French translation of 'Views of Society and Manners in America.' I want General Pepe to read it," she says, "as I think it might give him ideas upon some subjects of which he understands little, and which it were well he understood much. A fine, warm-hearted patriot but a very crude legislator. It is not every country that is blessed with a Lafayette . . . His creed, however, is a good one as to the outline, and the filling up may be mended, though I doubt if the head be as deep as the heart is warm.

"You are the only person in the world who is always right on such matters. Oh! would to heaven we could multiply you by twelve and then by the square of twelve and then by the cube of the square of twelve, and then spread you abroad among the nations of the earth."

But in spite of all this appearance of political ineptitude, Pepe knew exactly what he wanted and how to get it from the very people who were only too inclined to regard him as an amiable ineffective bore.

Note the following extract from a letter from Fanny to General Lafayette late in February:

"I have promised Major Cartwright an introduction to you for Count Pisa, Pepe's aide-de-camp, about to set off by the way of Paris. I will write more of him when I have seen him which will be to-morrow evening."

She also introduced him to the family at the Convent in the Rue St. Maur, where the young Italian was received and made much of by Julia and Harriet Garnett almost as warmly sympathetic with the cause of liberalism in Europe as Fanny and Camilla Wright. Many letters which could not be trusted even to the portfolio of the British and French Ambassadors which had so far preserved Fanny's correspondence with her "paternal friend" from police interference, went unchallenged in packets from the Convent to the house in Keppel Street.

One of these precious missives sent for even safer keeping by a private hand, was returned to Fanny because the name of the super-scription was so blotted that it could not be read. "I have reclaimed the letter," she tells Lafayette, "from the gentleman who promised to take it, and now send it by my usual channel. Give it to Pisa and say that he will hear again soon. Tell him that in future he had better give his letters for London to you to be forwarded to Camilla."

This passage is noteworthy as one of the few in which Pisa is spoken of openly by his real name. She is far more apt to refer to him under a sobriquet which she herself had invented, but which soon came to be used more frequently than his own, in circles where too free a use of proper names might result in inconvenience to their owners. "Pylades," faithful friend and companion of Orestes! The

very name shows how little he meant to her in comparison with another member of that group of foreign exiles whom she had learned
to know in London. The real name of the real hero, in Fanny's mind
and heart at least, remains a mystery. He might have been Count
Porro, mentioned once casually in her letters, but all that is certain
about him is that his Christian name was Eugene and that very
shortly after his first meeting with her he came to hold a place of
paramount importance in Fanny's life.

One finds her pouring out her heart about this new friend, this
dear brother, in letter after letter to her faithful confidant, General
Lafayette.

> My new friend . . . is sitting beside me at this moment
> writing a letter to Paris, which he wishes me to send by the
> portfolio of the Ministry. Here it is! He is gone! Oh, I am very
> much interested in him more than is reasonable.

> March 15th. Your letters of the 7th and the 11th reached me
> last night, my most excellent friend. The presence of a party
> of friends and strangers did not restrain me from opening
> them. Our new friend, who was in his room, opened his ears
> no less eagerly than did I my eyes. . . . He has a noble soul
> and a sweet nature . . . but I see in him a sanguineness of
> temper and a contempt of danger which makes me appre-
> hensive lest he should some day run upon the enemy's spear
> too hastily. I would, however, that men of this character were
> more numerous among your countrymen, and in the world
> at large. The game cannot now be won by longheaded calcu-
> lations. We want hands of steel and heads of flame. But all
> countries are richer in these than this dull England. My
> Socrates has just been all but cursing it. Truly it makes the
> blood boil as one walks among a nation grinded to the earth
> with oppression until it be too spiritless even to groan beneath
> the burden.

> Men here hug their chains, with you they shake them, the
> despised Spaniards break them. Nothing is talked of here
> but the state of the treasury and the profligate expenditures
> of government. The calculation of pounds, shillings and
> pence, a calculation which should have begun a half century
> ago, leaves the English people no thought for the great cause
> of European liberty which will be lost or won before they find
> out that it has been made a question. Our friend [Eugene]

always begs me to tender to you the assurance of his highest consideration and esteem. Your name is often in his mouth, as it must be in that of all noble men. I say "our friend" because I can never have a friend that is not yours, and because he entertains for you every possible sentiment of esteem and high consideration. Tell Count Pisa that his letter arrived in course of post and has given much pleasure. I think only of you and France. When shall I be restored to both?

Only a few days now and I shall be talking to you in France, telling you all the secrets of a heart which, believe me, will never want to have anything to hide from the best friend that ever existed. What goodness, what adorable goodness is yours to me, Oh, my friend, my father, my brother! Believe me, no new friendship, however dear it may be, is capable of replacing this sentiment, at the same time so tender and so reverent that you have permitted me to consecrate to you.

I know when I place myself again at your feet, you will be merciful to your young friend, if she has had the misfortune to inspire passionate feeling in a soul of flame, and to be at the same time incapable of remaining insensible to its virtues, to its misfortunes, to its great qualities combined with so much "noblesse," so much virile beauty. But I confess to you with the same frankness that the first feeling of my heart is for you, this feeling which is at the same time a filial affection and a confident and perfect friendship, respect, admiration, adoration and everything else that is of the most tender and of the most devoted. . .

I really think my departure is fixed for next Saturday. It is possible, however, that tomorrow's post will let me get off several days earlier. Believe me, it is no longer a "faiblesse de coeur" which holds me here all these days, though I cannot say that I am quite exempt from such weakness. How could I part from a being so noble in all respects, at such a moment, perhaps forever, without anguish of heart?

I have suffered greatly since my arrival in London, and it is only upon your breast that I can pour out my heart. How fortunate I am after all, to have such a friend in whom I can confide all my thoughts, and who finds me worthy of a like confidence.

I won't look too far into the future. You know that I am not a coward, even for my friends, and it costs more to have courage for them than for oneself. I do not want to hinder them in anything, but how is it possible to remain a spectator to their combats, to their dangers! Your own position, my good friend, occasions me a host of disquieting thoughts, but I must take an interest inferior only to that which I feel in you, in this second friend, so unfortunate, so adventurous and des- tined—but who can foretell his destiny?

He is very anxious about Pylades from whom he has not yet received any news.

I have this moment received the letter from him I was waiting for. He cannot let me go before Saturday. He will spend tomorrow with me, when we will arrange everything.

In this desperate word, "everything," she no doubt included all those last promises and assurances so necessary for two people who had been drawn together irresistibly by the same fate which now seemed about to part them for ever.

But, in fact, they did meet once again under the strangest, one might almost say portentous circumstances.

The story goes that General Pepe had volunteered for a special mission of advice and encouragement to the hard-pressed Liberal Government of Spain. But before he could set out on his journey by British steamboat for Lisbon, he must receive a packet of letters from Lafayette in Paris, which were to serve as his credentials with the Spanish Cortes at Madrid. Just how compromising the contents of this packet would be for those involved in these secret negotiations may be imagined if one can believe Pepe when he tells us that it contained letters from General Lafayette to various members of the Cortes, in which he advised these to recognize the new South Ameri- can republics of Colombia and Mexico, in return for fantastic promises of money, fleets, and armies from these republics, in case of French intervention to restore Ferdinand VII to his old autocratic power. There were also hints that some part of that Spanish-American money had actually been collected and was only waiting for a word from the Spanish ministry to be transported to Madrid by way of the Pyrenees, with suggestions that the French *Carbonari* could make good use of some of this to destroy the morale of the French Army already being collected along the frontier in preparation for a descent into Spain, the following year.

Count Pisa had already offered to carry the money from Paris to an unnamed French general in command at the frontier who could be trusted to place it at the best advantage.

It was obvious that such compromising documents could not be confided to any of the usual methods of secret correspondence between Paris and London.

"It was finally arranged," says Pepe, "that I should go to Dover, where Miss Wright and her sister Camilla who lived in Paris, should come and bring me the papers. These two ladies, animated with the most ardent patriotism, having arrived at Dover, gave me great hope of a change of government in France, and after having given me the letters of Lafayette, returned from Dover to Paris, while I resumed my voyage to Lisbon."

The only time Fanny herself mentions this adventure is indirectly in the following poem with the title, "From Stella to Eugene with her picture."

> When standing on the sea-beat shore
> And listening to its lengthening roar
> Steals not her form thine eyes before
> > Whose heart is thine?
>
> Or if the distant uplands please
> And softer murmurings of the trees,
> Comes not her voice upon the breeze
> > Whose heart is thine?
>
> And when this speechless form you view
> Ah! Think of her who thinks on you,
> And to her memory be true
> > Whose heart is thine.
>
> Though few may be her youthful charms
> She knows not jealousy's alarms
> 'Tis she alone can fill thy arms
> > Whose heart is thine.
>
> She does not fear that other fair
> Of finer form or nobler air
> Will steal the place that she holds there
> > Whose heart is thine.
>
> And if here gazing, you should sigh
> For cheek more fair, more lustered eye,
> Then shall these words the want supply
> > The heart is thine.

On his way back from Dover, Pepe had the unpleasant experience of seeing his papers searched by the English police. Only by calling upon the names of Sir Francis Burnett and others of his influential radical friends could he persuade these investigators to desist before they reached those compromising documents so lately committed to his care by Fanny and her sister. The rest of his journey to Lisbon was carried out in perfect safety.

Eugene had apparently been left in London for some weeks after the departure of his chief for Lisbon, during which time he and Fanny kept in constant touch through letters. He seems to have got into some mysterious trouble about money if one can believe the following anguished note from Fanny to Lafayette.

> I send you a letter, my beloved friend, which has grieved me more than surprised me. I see well all the difficulties which surround our poor friend, not only disappointed hopes and projects, but the air of having promised what he cannot perform. To a certain degree his word will seem passed and broken.
>
> Weigh the matter well, my dear friend, and think if it be impossible that I should supply at least in part what others refuse. The proposal may seem wild, but I assure you it is not made without reflection . . .
>
> I shall now go to Laffitte's to see what loose money I have in his hands that I may send a draft on Monday. I have little hopes of its being of any real service but at least it will prove to him that there is in this world some sincerity in friendship . . .

Her lover, however, seems to have been enough of a gentleman to return the money, for the reason set forth in the following from Fanny to Lafayette.

> Our friend refuses the bill sent by his sister, which gives her much pain. "The sum," says he, "could only serve for my own necessities and I do not need it. For the same reason I have refused 500 francs from a friend here."

> Our poor merchant [The use of common business terms to conceal less legitimate activities was a favorite subterfuge of those who suspected their letters might fall into the hands

of the police] leaves London without having done much in the way of trade. But he still continues to act the philosopher, for merchants must do that, as well as politicians, or they would cut their throats the first gloomy Saturday, in the manner of Tortoni, driven mad for lack of ice. [Referring to a legend about the death of a famous confectioner of Paris under the Restoration.] Our merchant writes, "I do not see why it is that the baseness, the feebleness and the worthlessness of men never discourage me. Men are what they are and always will be, and one must learn to work with men as they are and not as they ought to be."

If Tortoni had reasoned the same, touching the seasons, he might be walking in the Champs Élysées upon earth instead of in hell.

All record of Fanny's lover ceases after he joined his chief in Spain. Fanny's last reference to him is a poem found among her papers after her death.

> And art thou faithless? Ah, Eugene
> Thou smitest on a bruised heart
> One that so oft betrayed hath been
> Thou shouldest have spared it this last smart.
>
> We met. Thou hadst an Angel's air.
> I looked into thy beaming eye.
> I thought that all was candor there,
> And love and fond fidelity.
>
> I heard thy prayer, I gave my troth,
> I held thee to my bleeding heart.
> Thou sawest its wounds and wept for ruth,
> Then turned—and stung it like the rest.
>
> Yet go! I breathe nor plaint nor prayer.
> I have not strength nor heart to do it.
> I wish not e'en in my despair
> That thou shouldst live, my love, to rue it.
>
> I chide thee not, I wish thee blest,
> Pray that thy sun be clouded never.
> Pray too, that on thy new Love's breast
> Thy head may sleep in peace forever.

I know she smiles and speaks thee fair,
With words more burning far than mine.
But oh! false Traitor, oh, beware!
Oaths are weak chains. Remember thine!

CHAPTER IV

Snares and Pitfalls

THE wounds inflicted on Fanny's heart by her unfaithful lover were no harder to bear for a person of her exalted interests than the spectacle of what was going on on the other side of the Pyrenees during those disastrous years of 1823-1824.

The liberal cause in Spain was being done to death by friends and foes alike. The doctrinaire idealists, both the ministry and Cortes, were utterly incapable of directing or subduing the furious activities of the radical elements in the party which continued to sow dissensions in the liberal ranks and prevent any united front against the common enemy.

A rebellion of the peasant population of the northern provinces instigated by their priests against the government had already embroiled the unfortunate country in an embittered civil war.

Intervention had been decided upon at the meeting of the sovereigns of the Holy Alliance in Verona the preceding autumn. The ministers of Louis XVIII were only too ready to undertake the task, if for no other reason than the salutary effect a few successful foreign military victories might have on the morale of the army which had been shown to be so dangerously impaired by *Carbonari* propaganda. Twenty thousand picked troops were sent across the border under the command of the Duke of Angoulême, the eldest son of the king's brother, and heir to the throne on the deaths of his uncle and father.

A few inveterate conspirators like General Lafayette did, indeed, continue to play with the idea of spreading disaffection among the soldiers and under-officers of this army of invasion.

According to Lafayette's own story told with his usual charming garrulity in a conversation between himself and the banker, Nolte, during his visit to New Orleans some two years later, two regiments were actually on the point of mutiny during a short delay on their way to Spain at Toulouse. "The matter was quieted, however," says Lafayette, "and kept as still as possible. But all was ready as I know by my private correspondence with some of the officers. All that was wanting to make a revolution succeed was money. I went to Laffitte, but he was full of doubts and only dallied with the matter. Then I offered to do it without his help. Said I, 'On the first interview that you and I have without witnesses, just put a million francs in bank notes on the mantel shelf which I will pocket unseen by you. Then leave the rest to me.' Laffitte still fought shy of it, deliberated, hesitated, and at last declared he would have nothing to do with it."

But one is inclined to believe that even a million francs contributed to the cause of French Carbonarism at that moment would have had little or no effect on the final outcome of the war.

A few, a very few small scattered groups of French *Carbonari* and French refugees already under sentence from their government for earlier adventures of the same kind, took their way towards Spain in advance of the regular armies. Wearing their old imperial uniforms and drawn up in battle array under the glorious old tricolor, on the Spanish side of the Bidassoa they made a last desperate appeal to their former comrades in arms to rally to the cause of human freedom. In vain! The French Army as a whole was perfectly loyal to its commanders of the French Expedition into Spain. They did not blench when confronted with that devoted little band of French refugees and political exiles. They fired when they were told, "three charges of grape, one of shot and a volley of musquetry, putting the whole band to flight and killing four officers and seven privates."

Their advance across Spain was a triumphal progress.

No effort was made by the threatened government to defend Madrid. Ministers and Cortes chose the safer policy of flight to the fortified peninsula of Cadiz, taking the king with them, now openly a prisoner since he refused to leave Madrid except by force. The only laurels won by the army of invasion were at the siege and capture of the Trocadero, one of the outlying forts which protected the city.

The short-lived Palais of the Trocadero in Paris was built to commemorate the capitulation of this Spanish fortress which brought the Liberal Government to its knees.

"You have seen the newspapers," writes Lafayette to Fanny when the news reached Paris, "with their account of the arrival of the miserable Ferdinand at French Headquarters, the occupation of the city by our army, the Arc de Triomphe!

"They are even thinking of perching the Duke of Angoulême beside the statue of Napoleon on the Column of the Place Vendôme. But in spite of all this, liberty is not going to perish from the earth, not even from this old rotten Europe. The present moment, however, will not be very easy to live through."

As might have been expected he spent his money like water in his efforts to ease the hard fate of friends caught in the maelstrom of Spanish defeat and the horrible aftermath: death, exile or imprisonment for everyone remotely connected with the late government who had the bad luck to fall into Ferdinand's hands on that monarch's restoration to absolute authority.

Count Pisa was one of those unfortunates who were fated to pay by long imprisonment for their generous service to the late government. A fund was raised among his friends to improve his condition in his miserable dungeon, to which Fanny contributed with her usual reckless generosity. After more than two years in prison, Pisa did manage to make his escape in time to die fighting for Greek Independence in 1825. But Pepe survived to play a gallant part some years later in the revolt of Venice against its Austrian masters which still remains one of the high spots in the history of the Italian Risorgimento.

The ruin of those liberal hopes in Spain with which both Fanny and Lafayette were so intimately connected, served only to strengthen the peculiar friendship which had so long united them. At the same time, however, the cordial relations which had hitherto existed between the two young Scots women and Lafayette's immediate family seem to have undergone a mysterious change.

For some unexplained reason neither Fanny nor Camilla was invited to make their usual long visit at La Grange before the family assembled in Paris for the winter. No lessening of the General's affection for his "fille adoptive" or his desire to have her near him is found in the letters which passed between them during this same period. Note the following extract from a letter from Lafayette at La Grange to Fanny in Paris dated November 17th, 1823.

> The two Scheffers are leaving after dinner, my beloved Fanny. I cannot let pass this occasion for sending you two words. . . .
>
> I took a long walk this morning. I need no arm to lean on, except my dear Fanny's, but one of the grooms went with me and took my instructions by the way. The little round fountain

has become very pretty. The little stream that feeds it is running nicely. Black [Fanny's dog who had been left behind at La Grange after his mistress's last visit there] had the fine idea today of taking a bath in the basin of the fountain. He came back delighted with his adventure, but he always has the look as if he were asking me something. I know what it is as well as if we were talking together, etc., etc."

Then follows a page full of intimate comment on the political situation as to one on whose sympathy he could count for all the anxieties and distresses by which her mind as well as his were so painfully invaded. He concluded in words which appear so often in his correspondence with his "beloved Fanny." "I have only one word to say to you and even that word is unnecessary. Your heart will tell you what it is. A thousand tender messages to those who have the happiness to possess you. I embrace you, dear Fanny, with all my heart."

But in spite of all he could do about it, the moment was approaching when Lafayette's older friends and family decided that the friendship between him and this young Scotch woman, a stranger and alien in their midst, had lasted long enough. It is more than likely that Fanny's own dominant characteristics contributed not a little to this result. The very intensity of her own feelings and opinions, her blindness to anyone else's point of view when it did not coincide with her own, made her enemies among the very persons whom anyone in her very vulnerable position ought to have been careful to retain as her friends.

But there were also an increasing number of persons who for various reasons were really anxious to hurt her. "Mischief-makers and busy-bodies work of whom I knew little or nothing. Meddling politicians jealous of my supposed influence, who had asserted to the son that nothing was done or said without my approbation and that his father was held in leading strings! Silly and ill-natured women, who supposed intentions of another nature, and the Lord knows what. All this operating upon little minds and petty jealousies! etc., etc." Her own explanations of the situation in a later letter to Mrs. Craig Millar.

And just at the moment when everything was tending to an open break with Lafayette's family and intimate friends came the question of his visit to America.

The first invitation from President Monroe was received in Novem-

Frances Wright at 32 in the costume adopted
by the New Harmony Community in 1826.

Nashoba, from a drawing of A. Hervieu, the young Frenchman whom Frances Wright brought back with her from Europe in 1827 to teach drawing in her model plantation school.

Anonymous pencil drawing of Frances Wright and her husband shortly after their marriage. Aged respectively 40 and 56.

Paris 11 Octobre 1835. –

Monsieur

J'ai des nouvelles de mon mari; elles promettent mal. pour la rencontre dont vous étiez convenu ensemble. Le tems des vacances lui a fait manquer presque toutes les personnes avec lesquelles il avoit à faire ce qui l'a obligé d'aller plus loin qu'il ne projetait et qui ne lui permet guère d'avance de déterminer le jour auquel il pourra se trouver a Blois. Pressé par le tems il sera sans doute obligé de revenir en toute hâte à Paris. pour d'autres affaires qui exigent également sa présence. Je sais qu'il sera bien contrarié d'avoir manqué à plusieurs reprises de passer quelques jours avec vous.

Je vous prie Monsieur de présenter mes souvenirs affectueux a Madame. Ma petite Sylva est encore a la campagne.; si elle était a mes côtés elle ne manquerait pas de me parler de ses jeunes amies.

Respect et estime.

W. P. Dammont.

Autograph letter by Frances Wright.

Sylva D'Arusmont as a child of 5.

Phiquepal D'Arusmont
at the time of his divorce from his wife.

ber of 1823, while Lafayette was still a member of the Chamber of
Deputies, one good reason at least why it should seem impossible of
acceptance. But he lost his seat in the February elections, lost also
his inviolability as a deputy, and at once began to feel the animosity
of a government which had always hated him but had so far been
restrained from showing its real unfriendliness by the power of his
great name.

The double role he had played as deputy and conspirator, its signal
lack of success in all he had been most anxious to accomplish, the
crushing defeat of the Liberal cause not only in Spain but in France,
his own defeat at the polls, all this had contributed to diminish his
own hitherto persistent prestige. A defeated, discredited, and financially embarrassed old man!

It was at this moment when his skies looked darkest that the invitation to America, repeated with even more flattering insistence
(at the beginning of the year), brought him a new lease on everything he valued most in life, or so it no doubt seemed to him. His
age, his infirmities, his lack of money even to pay his debts at home,
to say nothing of the expenses of a long and costly journey, all this
and more besides must have been urged in affectionate objection to
the American adventure by each and every member of his large and
devoted family. Fanny, however, from the first, took the opposite
point of view, and had already made up her mind that, if her paternal
friend decided to make the visit to America, she would go with him.
There was an insuperable conflict between her and the family of
Lafayette.

That their father should set out on a journey which must from its
very object and circumstances be attended with the widest publicity,
accompanied by an unmarried woman, young enough to be his daughter and old enough to be his wife, but in actual fact holding to him
neither of these two relations, was a spectacle that a proud old French
family like that of the Lafayettes could not contemplate without dismay. It was not only natural, therefore; it was inevitable that the
kindly tolerance with which they had accepted their father's latest
pet should be replaced by feelings so actively unfriendly that no
surface habit of hospitality could entirely conceal them. This painful
change was seen and deplored by Fanny's friend and well-wisher,
Madame Charles de Lasteyrie, during a visit she paid at La Grange
in company with the two sisters. "I assure you," one reads in a letter
of hers written a little later to Fanny herself, "that when I was in

the house, my remark was to my husband, 'if I experienced anywhere, even for one hour what I saw them endure for one week, I would have left the house in an instant.'"

Fanny herself, however, seems to have been extraordinarily slow in recognizing the ruthless purpose which lay beneath the changed attitude of the ladies at La Grange. Her eyes were suddenly opened to her own danger by a letter from Julia Garnett on a visit to friends in London, horrified by the scandalous stories she heard on all sides about her adored friend and General Lafayette.

In time to come Fanny learned to care less than nothing about what the world thought and said about her, as long as she herself was convinced of the purity of her intentions. But at twenty-eight she still retained enough sensitiveness to public opinion to be deeply moved, even a little distracted by this sudden discovery of what both friends and foes were really thinking and saying about her on both sides of the Channel. Her first reaction to it seems to have been flight back to her own country and her own friends. But she could find no reassurance during the week she spent in London, for strangely enough the scandal about her seems to have made more headway in London than in Paris itself.

The next news one hears of both sisters is at Whitburn with their old friend, Mrs. Millar, where they were apparently established for a long stay, all thought of the American journey for the time being, at least, relinquished. There seems even to have been some talk of a return to their father's people in Dundee. Even Lafayette was left in complete uncertainty about their future movements.

He wrote repeatedly counting on her sympathy in the sudden serious illness of his sister-in-law, Madame de Montagu, but his letters were left unanswered till they drew forth the following pathetic appeal:

> Sunday, April 25.
> You will be sorry that you have left me without any news from you just at the moment when I am so full of anxiety as you must have learned from my earlier letters. I have only received two from you in London. You spoke to me of an old friend whom you had lately rediscovered, of some visits that you were going to receive. You promised to write to me before your departure for the North which was fixed for April 19th. I have counted on this promise, day before yesterday, yesterday, and today—and as they tell me there is no English

mail on the first days of the week, my hopes are adjourned indefinitely. I should be alarmed about your health if I had not the right to believe that one of your friends would have written me if anything serious had happened to you. My poor sister-in-law is in the fifth day of her illness which leaves us little hope that she will survive. I have passed these last days in visits to the invalid, though I have returned home several times each day on the chance of finding a letter from you. In vain.

I am leaving you now to go back to my sister-in-law where they are waiting for the doctors. I came here to look for something which I did not find, a letter from you. But I am profiting on the occasion to write you these few lines. I embrace you from far away but very tenderly.

Monday 26th.

I have time only to write one word my beloved Fanny, but the word will be one blessing the more. Your first letter from Whitburn arrived this morning, just as I was coming back from the house of my poor sister-in-law. The letter you promised me from London must have been lost on the way. [The next pages of this letter are very much occupied with his own anxieties over his sister-in-law's illness, but the conclusion is full of affection though already some suspicion of difficulties in the way of the journey to America seems to penetrate through its sentences.] I must hurry to finish this letter of thanks for yours, my beloved, my adored Fanny, the tender child of my choice.

The opinion of your maternal friend to whom I beg you to offer my most tender respects, seems to me very good. Only the cruel anxieties to which I have been subjected since your departure have prevented me from clearing up a number of things, as far as they concern me. The rest seems inexplicable to me.

Don't be afraid, my beloved Fanny. I am prouder for you than you can be for yourself. The news that you are both well gives me much pleasure. You are going to pass an entirely tranquil month of May in England with your old friends. I shall write you again very soon. I had to send this off at once so that you would not be long without receiving my affectionate messages. I embrace you both with all my heart.

But even as he wrote and dispatched this letter, Fanny was preparing her reply announcing her own abandonment of the whole

American expedition unless some way could be found to make the innocence of their relation to one another perfectly clear and unassailable to the whole world. It may be that she used all the gentleness and consideration of which she was capable in announcing this final decision to an old man whom she deeply loved and who, she knew, would be deeply disturbed by it. On the other hand one must remember her power of bitter wounding words if once she let herself go on the tide of hurt feeling and resentment against seeming injustice. And whether from the method or the reasons she used in explaining her decision or the decision itself, its effect on Lafayette was such as to throw him into a kind of fit, "which after depriving him for sometime of sense, was followed by vomiting to an alarming degree of violence." He continued unwell for two days. The first use he made of his returning strength was to seek out Fanny's particular friend, Madame Charles de Lasteyrie, for advice and consolation. She was so shocked by his changed appearance, his extreme agitation as he explained the contents of the letter, that she lost no time in writing to Fanny herself with such accounts of his condition as to send her flying back posthaste to Paris, full of grief and repentance for what she had done.

The following letter from her to her sister and Mrs. Millar, describes her at the first stages of this hurried journey.

London, Charing Cross. Tuesday morning, 8 o'clock. May 20th.

Here I am, my three beloved beings, lying in a warm comfortable little bed in a coffee house, next door to the coach office, from whence I shall set off at 6 this evening for Dover. I am wonderfully little tired although my rest at York was rather shorter than I expected owing to the order of the coaches being changed, two of those leaving at night which before left in the morning. The only mail coach was full, so I took my place in the north mail at 6 in the morning. This gave me six hours rest, however, and a much more comfortable and speedy conveyance than the coaches although somewhat dearer.

We were in London by 6 this morning, only 24 hours travelling from York. I shall now lie until 4 this afternoon when, having prepared myself for departure I shall put my letters in the post office. I shall endeavor to send a line from Calais, but do not calculate upon it as it is difficult to find a person whose head can be relied on.

Write, my dear Camilla, before you hear again from me or I shall be an age without a letter. . . . I feel sleepy, a state of mind which I have encouraged by breakfasting on a glass of ale.

3:30. I have had some sleep and am much refreshed. . . . My thoughts are always in our mother's little room, when they are not with my poor father. The nearer I approach, my anxiety increases. Truly do I feel with HIM, that in spite of all reasoning, there must be another life where we may be united in peace with those we love.

You will have heard of Byron's death of a rheumatic fever at Missolonghi where the Greek government has paid every honor to his memory. Perhaps it is as well that he has died while engaged in an honorable career before he had tarnished it by madness. But the loss of this great and unhappy genius seems to leave a blank in creation and I cannot describe the painful sensation with which I read among the advertisements pasted on every wall, "Death of Lord Byron," along with the next night's comedy, patent medicines and political tracts.

The accounts are said (for I have not yet seen the papers) to be too minute and official to admit of doubt.

Goodbye, once more my loved friends, and my own Camilla. I like to think of you together. This is my only comfort in this separation. F. W.

She was received in Paris by Lafayette in person, accompanied by the ever faithful Madame Charles de Lasteyrie, and in the General's carriage she was conducted to quarters engaged for her by Madame Charles in the Hotel Castellone. The idea was first that she should stay with the Charles de Lasteyries while she remained in Paris, but then it was decided wiser that this friend should not have the air of being too much in Fanny's own interest in case she should be needed as a link between Fanny and the other members of Lafayette's family, so that it would be better, in fact, not to be under the same roof.

"I have a room for three francs," she announces in her next letter to Whitburn, "very neat and comfortable, on the rue de Chaussée, looking out on a pretty garden. . . . My first conversation with Madame Charles was far from consolatory, nor do I at this moment see any possible step for me to take."

She was, indeed, at the parting of the ways in her future relations with her beloved old friend, and all ways alike seemed beset with insuperable obstacles. The old delightful intercourse between herself, "fille adoptive" and that revered and "paternal friend," Lafayette, had been cruelly interrupted and disfigured by malevolent slander. But the friendship on which this was founded was too precious to them both, to Lafayette even more than to Fanny, to be relinquished without a struggle. How was it to be protected? What new shape could be invented for it? Fanny's own suggestion of a formal adoption was not so fantastic as it seems today.

Pagès of Ariège, one of the few whom Lafayette had taken into his confidence on this matter, agreed with Fanny that it was possibly the best solution of the difficulty, if indeed any solution was necessary. For Pagès was at first inclined to make light of the "on dits" repeated by Fanny's friends in London.

When put on his honor by the General to state if he had ever heard such reports or anything like them in Paris he solemnly affirmed to the contrary, adding, "I am astonished, first, at its being said, but far more at its being listened to. The difference of ages, and yet more your known virtue and Miss Wright's character, all seemed to render the case simple in my eyes, besides the fact that in France such connections and adoptions into families are common, nay, of everyday occurrence."

One may add here that Lafayette himself had always been extremely free in his proposals to "adopt" this or that charming young person who had attracted his affectionate interest on his travels either for her own sake or because she was the daughter of some good friend. But such suggestions on closer analysis seem to have meant little more than an invitation for a visit of indeterminate length to La Grange, on terms of equality with the circle of grandchildren in their daily round of work and play. A formal and legal adoption such as Fanny desired and demanded in her future relation with the General, was, however, a very different matter. It was, indeed, as Pagès had very justly insisted in discussing the matter, not unheard of in French family customs. It was, in fact, legally possible, if the other members of the family offered no objection. But Pagès was a meridional, an intellectual, not particularly in touch with the habits and prejudices of a great family like that of Lafayette. Madame Charles de Lasteyrie, connected by marriage with that family, was better able than Pagès to recognize the intrinsic obstacles to such a proposition.

Virginie de Lasteyrie had been the member of Lafayette's family for whom Fanny had grown to feel a genuine affection, and whom she regarded as a personal friend. Her name and those of her children appear more frequently than any others in Fanny's earlier letters, always in terms of affection and respect.

But Virginie seems to have been the one of all Lafayette's immediate family most determined against anything like formal adoption, as her sister-in-law Madame Charles very well knew.

"Having heard my proposal," says Fanny in a letter to her sister at Whitburn, "her countenance saddened. 'Alas! you know not France or you know not that family,' she told me. 'The thing would be of no use, and as legalizing the change is impossible without the consent of the family the change itself would be impossible.' I cannot retail all her reasons. You must receive them as good and unanswerable. This conversation left my heart heavier than it found it."

Another difficulty in the way of coming to any clear understanding about the future was Lafayette's own ability to bear any new agitation on the subject.

"His countenance and complexion still retain the evidence of the force of his late seizure," says Fanny in a letter to her sister shortly after her arrival in Paris, "and in all our conversation I have constantly to watch the effect of every word, to soothe the mind and conscience, for he is ever reproaching himself either for what has been done or what not done, so that I must always represent as lighter than the reality the difficulties that surround us."

Naturally neither he nor she could discuss freely the "dispositions and characters" of his own family which so effectually blocked any public recognition of their relation along the lines she had suggested. The only other means available for legalizing their relations, marriage, had even more insurmountable obstacles. Nevertheless, there are several passages in Fanny's letters to her sister at this time, which seem to show that the subject was actually mentioned between them if only to be rejected for its obvious and inherent impossibility.

Madame Charles, it seems, had already told her of the vow he had made to his wife on her deathbed, in the presence of their children, her sisters, brothers-in-law, and many connections, never to marry again after her death. He explained later to Fanny why he had thought such a promise necessary. His wife had not exacted it from him. He had given it spontaneously as a sort of amende for the uneasiness, the suffering even, which he had occasioned her through a liaison of long standing with another woman. One continues here in Fanny's own words.

> One friendship formed in youth with a person uniting every charm which his companion might be conscious of wanting, had been often a source of uneasiness and although the advanced age of the parties might then have been sufficient to allay all apprehension, he perceived in her dying moments that her thoughts were wandering there. Wishing to answer them indirectly with that delicacy which is all his own, he bound himself by a vow, general in form, but really directed towards one person alone, the only one whom his wife had any reason to fear as her successor. This promise was given unwarranted publicity, bruited abroad even so far as to find its way into the public prints.

"When he had given this relation of it to me," Fanny continues, "he observed, 'Were I alone concerned, I know not, all things considered, whether my scruples might not give way in the contest, but when I consider the host of enemies that would rise up against them who are dearer to me than life—all the opprobrium that would be poured on them by those who might hesitate to attack me, I feel it impossible.'"

The force of such an argument was uncontrovertible even by Fanny. On the other hand nothing was said to disabuse her of her confident conviction of his need, his affectionate dependence on her for present and future happiness, in their old-established relation with one another.

One finds her saying to her sister:

> This only appears evident to me, that a separation, however much delicacy and generosity would urge his consent to it, would shorten his existence. Were he twenty years younger or had he near him one being with whom he could exchange thoughts, I should think this fear, notwithstanding my knowledge of his dependence upon me, exaggerated, but with my knowledge of his sensibility, of the deep-rootedness of his confidence in me and of the moral desert in which he would be left, I feel as certain of this fact as if I saw it passing before my eyes. Indeed we have lately had of this too full proof.
>
> Such, my loved ones is our situation. How far I and my father may be able to mend it we shall know before I next

write. In the meantime I must add that the voyage will certainly not take place before July first. My next letter will probably decide this also as the explanation will involve those arrangements. In all this the object ever uppermost, not only in my thoughts but in his also, is dear Cammy whom he loves as his own daughter. The mere idea, that he had been the indirect means of her experiencing discomfort and suffering, or of interfering with her interests, cut him to the quick. But I need not and could not repeat all he says and far deeper feels.

Sunday noon. My father has just left me. Whatever happens it will ever be sweet to reflect on the fullness of his affection and confidence. It seems to me that I never knew him until this trial . . . But I must not give way to feeling. Patience and self-possession can alone avail us. I shall not allow myself to decide on anything until I have seen Pagès. My sweet Cam, rest at least assured of my affection. I sometimes fear lest even to you I should appear to have been less occupied with your interests than my heart has ever been. Would that I could transport myself among you for one half hour or you here.

Farewell, sweet beings. Tomorrow is the post day. I shall send this early to my father that he may have it posted . . . I feel sadly deserted without you. When I opened my trunk the tears came in my eyes as I thought of the dear little hands which had packed it.

Does my mother sleep in my bed? Embrace her and the "Good Spirit."

Only one note from Lafayette himself remains from this time. Translated it reads:

I am coming to see your friend [probably Madame Charles] at the hour you have set for me, my dearest Fanny. If she does not find a double visit inconvenient, I shall see you when I leave her. If not that, we shall see each other at dinner.

How have you passed the night, my dear child? I am sending you this little note by Bastien who will at the same time bring you Black. [Fanny's dog of whom one heard last as swimming in the little fountain at La Grange.] Good day, my dear Fanny. Your father embraces you with all the tenderness of his heart.

The next one hears of Fanny and her dog is at the Pavillion Chardet, Le Havre, where the Garnetts had gone to live after they left Paris. Letter from Harriet Garnett to Camilla Wright.

Wednesday, June 2nd.

Our loved Fanny will have told you that she arrived last night, tired and I think looking thin but not looking ill. I hope that quiet and pure country air will be of service to her. . . . Pray advise her not to return to London where she can only feel pain. She has brought Black with her—her dog, and I own I like it better since she has told me it is her dog. She is so fond of it, poor dear child. It sleeps by her side and follows her everywhere. . . . She has been walking with us this evening and is very much pleased with the beauty of this place.

Fanny's own letter written on the same sheet runs as follows:

I arrived late last night, my loved Camilla and it seems to me that is all I have to tell of myself. My Father wished me to await here a packet that he will write on his return from the country at the end of the week, and indeed I am better here than in London. Harriet wishes you to join Julia in London and come here with her. You must judge, Love, whether this will be best, or for me to join you with the Trollopes at Harrow. I cannot bear to take you from our loved Mother and the Good Spirit, but I know you will be anxious to join me. Do not, however, hasten your determination but consult the dear Beings whom it is my consolation to know you are beside.

My poor father wrote to you and our Mother before leaving Paris but you may not receive them before you leave, so many have been delayed. I do not know what I have written or not written you. The agitation I have endured and what was yet worse, witnessed, has left a stupor on me which prevents my very well understanding anything.

The coming voyage, which has now lost for my paternal friend every charm, seems yet to hold out the only prospect, I say, not of happiness or peace for both are ended, but of occupation and relief. I have in part engaged, in the event of his being constrained to remain in that country if his son returns, that we should join him. Neither of the conditions may happen, and alas! how many years have the last two weeks not cut off from his existence! The tears of youth are of water but those of age are the life drops of the heart. But let me not speak of this.

Write to me, my loved Cam, what seems best to you that we should do. I do not expect that my next Paris letters can in anything change our position so that it would be possible for us to go with him. He will not at all events sail before the first of July. He would like to find us at Havre, but of what avail could this be?

If you like to join me we could spend a month here before he goes. . . . I find the Garnetts in a very pretty house, seemingly very content and living cheaper than they had thought possible at first. Dear Harriet is very kind and very glad to see me. I will write again in a day or two.

All this time Lafayette seems to have been doing what he could to bring order and amity out of a difficult situation. It was at his request apparently that Fanny had left Paris and gone to stay with the Garnetts at Le Havre while he went off to La Grange for an important interview with his assembled family. Fanny was kept several days waiting for news of the final result which would seem at first sight distinctly favorable for her own desires. See her letter of June 10th, to her old friends at Whitburn.

Today's post has brought me letters from my father, Virginie, and our dear and excellent Madame Charles. Their contents seem to open again a prospect of better accommodation and reconcilement than I had thought possible. . . . The explanations that have taken place between our father and his family have led to much contrition, withdrawal to all objections to the voyage, a warmly expressed desire that we should be with our father in America, much regret also that I should have left Paris without seeing them. I know not how far this last is true. I believe, however, that their contrition is sincere and their mortification deep. Fully convinced that they have wounded the feelings and marred the happiness of our father they are now as anxious to cement the tie as they were before to break it, and will therefore form no impediment but the contrary, to any plan we may decide on.

With one condition, however, which Fanny, perhaps rightly, considered so important that she fought desperately against it though in the end unavailingly.

Our friends and counselors in Paris also urge our making the voyage to America [the letter continues], but to humor the folly of those who are supposed to misinterpret things, suggest that we make it separately. To this I have replied in a letter which goes by return post. I believe I had better quote. I must observe that the proposal made by my father does not originate with him and that I doubt secretly whether he concurs with it.

After stating minor objections I continue thus. "There is yet another consideration which weighs with me much more. I am at Havre. I have been in France, and that in a private and somewhat singular manner. That is to say if I immediately go away again. I do not embark with you. Why? Because we aie conscious of having excited, justly or unjustly, and in these cases the world puts always the worst interpretation—the ill-nature of the public or of individuals. Therefore, as if admitting the truth, or at least the importance of such remarks, we adopt an underhand mode of doing what we desire.

"My honored father, I need not enter into details to explain my idea. You will seize it, and then I may add that not only does my character repugn from a covert way of proceeding but that I think such a way of proceeding totally inconsistent with yours, liable to cover you with reproach, and both parties, if I dared use the word, as applied to you, with ridicule. No one will believe that I and Camilla go to America at this time merely to go there. Our intimate connection is too well and universally known in both hemispheres. No, my honored friend! Might I give an opinion? It is this. If our union is to continue, it can only do so with honor to you and without prejudice to us, by your assuming openly and avowedly the air and character of a protector. You must be our father, not in a doubtful and covert way but in an open and manly one.

"I blush, my honored father, at this seeming arrogance, but it is not to you but rather to our mutual friends and to your family that I address these arguments. Forgive me, then, if I say that if you and yours approve I will call my Camilla to me, I will place her under your protection, we will assume together the place of your children, we will call you father, we will be with you as children and despising and confronting slanders, which thus met in the face will slink away, we will go and stay and return with you.

"If not this, honored father, late as it is to renounce engagements which my heart will ever acknowledge to be more sacred than any ever made on earth, we must part. Our position otherwise would be embarrassing, painful, doubtful, and even absurd."

At this point, however, she cannot resist the hint that she and her sister would be even more at the mercy of ill-natured scandalmongers if they stayed at home. As she puts it:

"I foresee also that even this cruel alternative and relinquishment of what our peace of mind requires will also seem to sanction silly gossip. It will be said that I left you because I dared not stay, that your family objected or that we had quarrelled. Reflect on all this and consult with Pagès to whom I shall explain my ideas also, and give me your answer."

You see, my beloved Cam, [so she resumes the thread of her letter to her sister] how I have ventured to dispose of you. Our London friend, good and kind as he is would doubtless censure me, but I know your generous heart better than he does. I know that in venturing to consider you as part of myself I shall best consult your wishes. Write me immediately whether you and my mother think and feel with me, I do not like to write the words as they will pain our beloved friends at Whitburn, but perhaps you should now set out for London. There you will be on the spot to join me here or for me to join you there according to what may be decided. But in the latter case how avoid seeing our good and kind friends in London? Impossible and yet how little should I have strength after all I have endured for such discussion!

She received Camilla's reply to these suggestions with its usual ready acceptance of anything and everything her sister wanted from her, before she heard again from her friends in Paris.

14th, June, Sunday.
Pavillon Chardet.
My Cam's sweet letter reached me yesterday and I acknowledge it by the return packet thinking it may still find her at Whitburn. I have not anything to communicate but so much to acknowledge that I cannot delay the post in thanking and blessing my sweet Cam and my loved mother and the "Good Spirit." Since it meets the feelings of my Cam I will

acknowledge that awaiting my sweet lamb here is far more in unison with my wishes than joining her in London. As too I have received nothing yet in answer from Paris I cannot say whether the generous wishes of my Cam may not be answered and that we may not soon be called to accompany our father. She will receive, I think, in London, something definite as she cannot avoid passing two or three days with our kind friends, the Trollopes, at Harrow. My heart does indeed yearn to see her. I shall reply by word of mouth better than letter to all the touching contents of her letter. My last contained as it were a reply.

From this one may believe that Camilla had actually forestalled her sister in her acceptance of the new role proposed for her as Fanny's companion in America, before Fanny herself was sure it would be equally acceptable to her "honored father." In the absence of further news from Paris she continues doubtfully:

So far as I can yet judge of the feelings of that ill-fated family, I see no hope that it can ever cease to be an obstacle and annoyance, except in the one unforeseen, or at least doubtful alternative of his remaining in America. I hope that letter of mine from Paris in which I detailed the circumstances and engagements between us and laid down the only measure by which I have levelled all difficulties, has been received. I cannot explain the non-arrival of the packet from my father and Pagès in answer to mine. I have expected it now for three successive days.

It would be impossible to explain by letter all the cruel doubts and difficulties which tormented my stay in Paris, and which seem now to me impossible of removal. There was but to choose between me and his family. The courage for this was wanting. Or rather there were duties and still more binding and sacred recollections of the dead, which stood, still stand between happiness and what I really conceive to be other duties not less sacred.

Never was there a case so intricate, I will not write so hopeless.

I believe the family perfectly repentant, nay, full of remorse, so far as regards their father. As regards me, I care not to imagine what their feelings may be, but none good, doubtless. They desire sincerely our going to America, but perhaps have real or pretended scruples as to our accompanying him.

Perhaps, also, they hope in case of a separate voyage to avoid an open avowal of adoption which appears to me alone consistent with dignity or comfort. Oh, it is hard to deal with little minds!

All is quiet here, and you and Julia will be welcomed by all, by none of course as your fond sister. Farewell sweet being. In thinking of you, I lose the bitterness which otherwise poisons all my feelings. To see goodness and generosity always sacrificed to petty interest, jealousy, and littleness is too cruel to witness and to feel. There must be another life, dear Mother, and I could often pray that I might come to tell you so.

This was the last word from Frances Wright before her departure to America, her last gasp of resistance to the plans and arrangements of Lafayette's friends and kindred to induce her to consent to a separate voyage. As might have been predicted considering the relative advantages of those engaged in the battle, the family carried the day. Once assured, however, of their victory, on the essentials of the situation, they seem to have made every possible effort to gild the bitter pill. The sisters were invited to Paris, to Lafayette's own apartment in the Rue d'Anjou, and treated with extreme consideration by every one connected with him.

For the account of those last days as well as of their visit of farewell at La Grange after Lafayette's departure for Le Havre, one must turn to two letters from Camilla to her young cousin James Milne.

Her first letter to her cousin is dated from La Grange, July 20th and tells of the sudden change of plan to fit what Fanny considered her obligations to her paternal friend which prevented the meeting in London already arranged between Camilla and young James.

I had hardly time to recover from the fatigue of my rapid journey from the North of England when we had to go on to Paris in consequence of a letter from General Lafayette announcing that his voyage was definitely set for the first of July and entreating us to come and meet him in the midst of his family previous to his departure.

On our arrival we found a plan which we had almost abandoned, pressed upon us with such increased earnestness both by him and his friends, that we would accompany him in his voyage to America that, though time no longer admitted of our making the voyage together, we consented to hasten our arrangements so as to follow him, if possible by the first of next month.

This we now expect to accomplish and have indeed written to our friends, the Garnetts, to secure our passage for that day in one of the regular sailing packets established on the same plan and conducted in a similar manner with those at Liverpool. Much as I dislike the thought of another voyage across the ocean to which experience has only tended to increase my aversion, I cannot but anticipate much satisfaction from witnessing the reception of this veteran of American and French liberty by a people who have never ceased to evince the most heartfelt gratitude for his services and are at the present moment vying with each other how best to testify of their love and veneration for his principles and character.

As his absence will certainly not exceed a twelvemonth, our parting from our English friends will merely be temporary and I hope you, my dear James, will not allow the Atlantic to interfere with our correspondence by addressing your letters to our friend Charles Wilkes Esq. of New York. They will be sure at all times to find us.

The rest of the correspondence with her cousin is in much the same tone. Guileless, rather commonplace letters which become not a little touching in the light of coming events. For Camilla was made for simple domestic pleasures in her own land, among her own people. She would have been perfectly satisfied to live and marry in her aunt's highly respectable vicinity at Dawlish and inherit her share of that lady's ample fortune; or to settle down as the faithful wife of one of her Scottish cousins at Glasgow; or there was a very pleasant kind of life to be lived in France with her friends the Garnetts.

But now she was to be torn up by the roots for the third time, carried off on a wild experiment of new fortunes whose outcome not even Fanny herself could predict. She did not know, as she said good-by to her old friends at Whitburn, to her cousin James, in London, to her native land, that she was never to see it or them again, that she was to return to Europe but to die.

But even if she had known the ruin of health and happiness which lay concealed under these new plans, it would not have made any difference in her devoted readiness to sacrifice everything and anything to that older sister whom she had always adored and who had always so entirely dominated and absorbed her life.

CHAPTER V

America Revisited

ON THAT pleasant day in August, 1824, as Fanny and her sister watched the fading line of the French coast from the deck of their little sailing vessel, the *London*, bound for New York, they had no other thought than that in a few months, a year at most, they would be sailing back again to take up life just as it used to be, in Paris, at La Grange, before the painful scandal which had threatened to end it.

Their voyage had been undertaken with the utmost reluctance, only after they had been convinced by Lafayette's family and intimate friends that his health and well-being would be seriously affected by any sudden break with his "adopted daughters." During those last days in Paris and at La Grange his whole family had vied with one another to remove any painful impression which might remain from their past antagonism and to re-establish the old hospitable relations with these two young Scots women as friends and intimates of the whole family connection.

It is true that all further talk of legal adoption had been dropped by both sides by common consent. Lafayette himself, however, continued to use the old familiar appelatives whenever he could, as for instance in a letter to Guglielmo Pepe written while still at sea on his voyage to America and dated off the Banks of Newfoundland.

"My dear adopted daughters have been at La Grange till the end of the month (July) but are embarking this very day, Aug. 1st, from Le Havre for New York. We expect to join them there, my son and I, on our return from Boston."

And one has only to turn to Camilla's account of their first days after landing in New York (a letter to her cousin James Milne in Glasgow preserved among Fanny's papers) to see how carefully they were included in his own plans and movements while in America,

surrounded by his affectionate consideration for their comfort and
well-being even when he himself was elsewhere.

He had arrived at Staten Island on August 14th. He had made
his first triumphant tour through New England and had been waiting in New York more than a week before the slow little *London*
finally tied up at her moorings in the East River after an exceptionally rough and disagreeable passage of forty days.

The date of her arrival, September 11th, was already overloaded
in Lafayette's calendar of engagements. A Masonic celebration of
the Knights Templar in the morning, an elaborate banquet in his
honor given him by the French citizens of New York, lasting, as such
banquets did in those days, until late in the afternoon; and a brilliant
party at the Chatham Square Theatre till after midnight. But Lafayette did not retire to his much needed rest till he had seen his
beloved Fanny.

> He could not come to us till after midnight, [says Camilla
> in her letter to her cousin.] He had been anxiously awaiting
> our arrival for some days that we might be present at the
> grand festivity to be given in his honor by the City of New
> York, and he had, through various devices, procured its delay
> and thus afforded us one of the most splendid and gratifying
> sights I have ever before witnessed.
>
> As I have no time to attempt a description, I must refer
> you to that given at length by Fanny to your father who, she
> thought, might like to have some notion of the reception of
> our valued friend by this generous people, which has indeed
> been grand and touching in the extreme.

The New York *Evening Post* in its account of the fete at Castle
Garden confirms Camilla's story of Lafayette's devices to delay it till
the arrival of his adopted daughters. It had been originally planned
for September 7th, and, in fact, its postponement till the 14th created
a good deal of confusion in the subsequent arrangements of the reception committee appointed to do him honor.

Even those persons most familiar with the present appearance of
the New York Aquarium may need to be reminded that this old
building was once a fortress, a frowning battery for the protection
of the harbor, situated on a little island jutting out into the sea and
connected with the shore by a long bridge. It was never used, however, for any warlike purpose, and in 1823, just a year before Lafay-

ette's arrival in this country it had been ceded by the Federal government to the Corporation of the City of New York, which promptly turned it into a place of amusement. Its circular wall, originally intended for cannon, furnished an ideal foundation for a circular walk, fourteen feet wide, from which the inhabitants of New York could look out over the Harbor as far as Staten Island and the Narrows, while the area within these circular walls could be made into an amphitheater capable of holding 6000 persons.

One learns from the papers, however, that there was some objection to the choice of this place for a splendid ball and reception. People were afraid that "the bleak airs from the ocean would find their way through the embrasures of the building and chill the galaxy of beauty expected at the fete and render the whole dull and monotonous. The approach also on a dark night was considered inauspicious if not dangerous. But all these possible disadvantages faded at the touch of the magic wand which directed the arrangements."

Those guests who arrived in carriages, found themselves set down with the least possible delay and disorder at the entrance of the bridge leading to the Battery Island. This had been converted for the occasion into a covered and carpeted corridor. Passage was also carefully arranged for those who came on foot. At the same time numbers of little steamboats were landing hundreds of people at the small beach of the island itself. And all these converging groups found ample room in the vast space of the interior, an immense amphitheater not less than two hundred feet in diameter and six hundred feet in circumference, with galleries rising one above the other to the extreme top of the battlement, the ascent to which was by lofty flights of steps.

"A great expanse of sail supported by a mast raised from the centre, converted the whole into a great covered ball room. Flags and festoons of all colors and descriptions entirely concealed the triple folds of the canvas forming the awning, draped in such a manner as to give a soft airy finish to the wide vault."

The *Evening Post* reporter from whom most of this description has been taken, goes on to tell about the lighting of this vast space. The whole central pillar was turned into one glittering chandelier. More than five hundred lamps and candles decorated the walls. And the guests! "Six thousand ladies and gentlemen dancing and promenading and moving in all directions to the music of two numerous orchestras in the gallery over the entrance." He even goes so far as to describe their dresses. "The gowns usually worn by the ladies were of black or white lace over satin petticoats. The hair elaborately dressed with flowers, ornamental combs and feathers. Steel ornaments, neck chains of gold and silver, with badges or medals stamped with the name of Lafayette were also much in evidence. But though 'full dress' was insisted upon for the ladies, the gentlemen were allowed a wider latitude of costume, as long as they did not come in high boots."

Lafayette himself made his entrance to the ballroom at 10 o'clock. "Immediately on the arrival of the hero and his escourt," say the newspapers, "the music changed to a national air, the gay sets dissolved as by a charm and the dancers formed a lane whose sides were composed of masses that might contain two thousand eager faces each. Through this gay multitude the old man slowly passed giving and receiving the most cordial and affectionate salutations at every step. Like some venerable and much respected head of a family who had come to spend an hour amid their innocent revels. He was like a father among his children."

From his place of honor on a sort of raised dais in the center of the hall he watched the dancing till nearly two o'clock surrounded by his official family and a group of the most distinguished persons in the assembly, chiefly his personal friends.

There is no doubt that the two sisters were included in the group of personal friends nearest to the hero on this occasion. Their faithful friend Charles Wilkes would have seen to that even if Lafayette had not himself requested it. Quoting again from Camilla's letter one finds: "Our reception by Mr. Wilkes and his family was all that was kind and affectionate. As they would not hear of our going into lodgings and we could not conveniently leave the city even for the near neighborhood of their summer quarters [in Greenwich Village] we acceded to Mrs. Colden's kind request that we should become her guests."

The marriage of Fanny Wilkes to young Cadwallader Colden, grandson of the well-known colonial governor of that name, had been one of the events of Fanny's first visit to America. The names of the couple recur frequently in Camilla's correspondence, and their house was a peculiarly convenient resting place for the sisters during those few days between their disembarkment from the *London* and the great event at Castle Garden, for the young man was one of the prime movers of the great affair, member of the committee of arrangements and special distributor of the tickets of invitation to the ball.

At two o'clock, the newspapers tell us, Lafayette himself left the ballroom to embark directly upon a steamboat which had lain alongside with steam up at the very spot where emigrant boats were later to discharge their human freight upon the new world.

In a letter to his family at La Grange, Lafayette describes this vessel, the *James Kent*, of the Northern Steamship Company as a floating hotel with ample quarters for "une très aimable societé de dames," besides the usual committee of notables who never left him.

Except for Camilla's letter to her cousin, one would never have guessed that the two sisters were included in the favored assembly. They were there, however, and from this safe vantage ground Fanny was able to see as much or as little as she wished of the festivities and civic pageants which marked his course up the river.

The trip began unpropitiously, according to newspaper reports, on a very dark night with four hours' delay because the boat stuck fast on an oyster bed in a dense fog. The General did not arrive at West Point till afternoon instead of early in the morning as was originally intended. He went at once from the landing to the parade ground to review the corps of cadets while the ladies of his party were entertained by the wives of the officers on the Post, in the spacious room adjoining the library, where they all partook of a magnificent collation.

Then came hurried stops at Newburgh, Poughkeepsie, Catskill and Hudson, where more than a thousand people had been kept waiting by the initial delays of the trip. It was quite dark when Lafayette and his party reached Albany late on the evening of the 17th.

The streets and many of the private houses of the old Dutch city were brilliantly illuminated in his honor. The whole façade of Crittenden's Hotel was covered by a magnificent transparency, designed by the artist, Henry Inman. It portrayed the landing of the hero at Staten Island with his ship the *Cadmus*, in the background. There was the usual lavish banquet, an inevitable feature of his progress through the country, the usual ball in the Senate Chamber of the old capitol, after which the weary hero was permitted to retire to rest in a bed especially imported for him from France by the proprietor of the hotel.

The very account of this interminable succession of pageants, banquets, military and civic processions becomes almost as fatiguing to the reader as to the participants, and one may be forgiven for omitting the remaining events on this trip. With one important exception however! A sudden emergence of the "Women Movement" into the plans and preparations of mere man.

The next day the whole party made a very early start and went by barge on the lately finished canal to Troy, on which occasion occurred the famous visit of the General to Mrs. Willard's Seminary for Young Ladies. The invitation to the great man was conceived and sent on the shortest notice with only a hope that it might be accepted. A beautiful arbor of evergreen trees completely encircling the school buildings sprang up over night. A floating banner adorned the entrance inscribed with the sentence: "We owe our schools to Freedom. Freedom to Lafayette." The whole school in white dresses and carrying flowers were lined up in the main hall of the seminary building, and joined in the chorus of a poem especially composed for the occasion.

At the sound of all those young voices raised in a hymn of praise the General is said to have been moved to tears. He asked at once for three copies of the poem to be presented later to his three daughters. A copy of Mrs. Willard's famous treatise on Female Education, elegantly bound, was also presented him by a child of six.

Camilla's letter to her cousin takes up the narrative again from New York. "Since our return from our excursion up the North River, for an account of which I refer you to Fanny's letter to your father, we have been spending a quiet week at Greenwich with Mr. Wilkes and his family, and I have already derived so much benefit from the care and kindness of my friends here that all the bad effects of my sea voyage have disappeared."

Lafayette also mentions this country residence of his old friend as the one place where he could find a few quiet moments for personal intercourse with his nearest and dearest. But Lafayette was already on his weary way as the honored guest of American hospitality, when Camilla was writing her letter on September 23rd.

> He intends devoting three days to the Jerseys, [she tells her cousin] where in each town through which he passes military and civic honors are prepared for his reception. We hope shortly to be present at the celebration prepared for him at Philadelphia where 30,000 militia are said to be already assembled to receive him with military honors. We

leave here tomorrow morning arriving in Philadelphia the same evening. Lodgings there have been already secured for us by Mrs. Lewis, the daughter of Mrs. Washington by her first marriage and once a celebrated toast in Virginia as the lovely Miss Custis. From Philadelphia we shall proceed to Baltimore, Washington, and so on to Yorktown where a fete is prepared for the hero of the day that is to last three days and where the Taking of Lord Cornwallis where he bore a conspicuous part, is to be acted over again . . . You will thus readily believe that for some months to come our time will be very little at our own disposal.

Camilla's letter is not the only evidence that their kind old friend was doing everything in his power to keep his "adopted daughters" by his side as far as it was possible to do so. There is a tradition that some time during his stay in Philadelphia he had his life mask taken by that strange, self-taught genius, Browere, utterly forgotten today, who also did one of Fanny at the same time at Lafayette's special request. These two masks are said to have existed for a long time in the artist's studio in an old barn near Rome, New York. She was with him so often and so conspicuously during this visit as to create a certain amount of not always pleasant comment from Philadelphia society whom she had already irritated by her ungracious manner.

"At a social gathering in that city," one is told by a respectable person who claimed to have been an eye witness on the occasion, "Miss Wright stretched herself on a sofa, spoke little, and gave herself little or no trouble about anyone, now and then breaking out into detached sentences such as this, for example. 'I believe that bears have more value than men.'"

She also came in for some unpleasantness from that small but influential group of Americans who had chosen to find her book on America too fulsome in its praise of Jeffersonian Democracy and the Revolution of 1800 which had broken their political ascendancy. The U. S. *Gazette* (Philadelphia) of that autumn has a rather sneering notice on this subject.

The courtesy due to a lady of talent should not and never will be restricted in this country but we ought not to make this gallantry a debt of gratitude for favors of which we are undeserving. . . . We protest against the expressions of grati-

tude which certain editors are making on account of this author's kindness to us in making us appear to her countrymen
better than we are. For instance, when Miss Wright learned
that in certain states proper provisions were made for general
education she made it a matter of record that the same system
obtained throughout the Union, etc., etc.

The article concludes with its own unauthorized explanation of
Fanny's presence in America at this particular time.

Miss Wright is now, we believe, travelling in the wake of
General Lafayette in order, as the papers mention, to publish
an account of his progress.

It is the first time this rather disagreeable expression, "travelling
in the wake of General Lafayette," appears in her connection, the
first but not the last, and it could not have failed to annoy her, already
sensitively alert to any hint or innuendo unflattering to her almost
morbid self-esteem.

She was no doubt entirely mistaken in believing that legal adoption would have made any difference in the world's opinion of her
unexplained and perhaps unexplainable relation to her faithful old
friend. But as long as she really thought so, her bitter resentment
against those of Lafayette's family who had opposed it, especially his
daughter, Virginie, burned higher and higher with every fancied
slight or inconvenience, and even as early as that first visit to Philadelphia she had made up her mind never again to put herself at
their mercy by any resumption of her old intimate relations at La
Grange. Her announcement of this unalterable decision, accompanied
no doubt by one of those alarming bursts of violent recrimination
from which no friendship of Fanny's was ever entirely exempt, left
the old General with a guilty sense that his own conduct during the
unfortunate family quarrel had not been entirely without reproach.
He is evidently referring to this interview in his first letter to his
beloved child after his return to Paris. After a long list of flattering
messages to her from various members of his family he concludes:

I must tell you that in the midst of effusions of this kind
from Virginie hardly an hour ago, I confided to her certain
circumstances connected with our stay in Philadelphia. But
am I certain myself not to have been entirely without blame

in your eyes? However—we must never return to those expressions of yours. I feel them still like blows from a dagger. Ah,
my adored Fanny! How could you have so misjudged me
even for a moment!

He breaks off here to resume the next day:

Forgive me, my dear friend, that I should have so brusquely
interrupted my letter. I felt myself too agitated. I wished to
tear out this page! And then that scruple which obliges me
never to hide anything from you prevents me from dissimu-
lating my feelings on this point also.

But even as one door seemed to be closing on much that she had
held as particularly precious in her past life, new doors were opening
on every side into wider fields of activity for the future. One of these,
though she little knew it at the time, was a visit to the Maclure School
of Industry on the banks of the Schuylkill some four miles above
Philadelphia. It was during Fanny's last year in Paris that she had
first come into connection with the founder of this establishment, a
Scotsman named William Maclure, born in Ayershire in 1763 of
respectable middle-class parents. He had come to the United States
at the age of eighteen, as an agent for the business house of Miller,
Hart & Company. He made frequent trips back and forth between
Europe and America, till in 1803 he was appointed commissioner to
settle the claims of American citizens for spoilations committed during the French Revolution. He was a successful business man, a man
of the world, a man of pleasure, but with all that, and even more
than that, a man peculiarly sensitive to the liberal and scientific
tendencies of his day and generation. He had devoted all his leisure
and a large part of his fortune to the study and advancement of
science and the liberal arts. He himself had made a geographical
survey of the eastern section of the United States, crossing and re-
crossing the Alleghenies many times in the process. He subsequently
made his home in Philadelphia and was one of the early members if
not the founder of the American Academy of Natural Sciences in
1812 in that city. His interest in pure science was equalled, one may
almost say, surpassed, by his passion for the general improvement of
the human race. Like so many other practical idealists of that age,
he believed that the key to health, wealth, happiness, and all the
other benefits men desire in their quest for a perfect world was a

liberal education; and he was profoundly interested in the new techniques for teaching young children that were then being developed by Pestalozzi in Berne, Switzerland. He visited the school and carried off one of its most successful teachers, Joseph Neef, to introduce its methods in a school near Philadelphia founded and financed by Maclure himself in 1812.

He spent thousands of dollars on an agricultural school in Alicante, Spain, under the protection of the short-lived liberal Spanish Constitution; while at the same time permitting his private house in Paris to be used for an educational experiment. The idea was to combine manual training and useful service by the pupils themselves with the common branches of education, under the direction of an eccentric genius named William Phiquepal D'Arusmont, who finally got him into trouble with the government by introducing a private printing press into the house as a practical way of teaching his pupils spelling.

It was during Maclure's difficulties with the Bourbon Government in consequence of this crime—for crime it was still considered in autocratic circles—that he first came in contact with Lafayette, and through Lafayette with Fanny, who thus describes her own share in the matter.

> This interesting private institution, although conducted with the greatest prudence . . . could not escape a formal domiciliary visit from the Police of the Bourbon Government. This event necessitating a hasty return of Mr. Maclure with his friend, Mr. Phiquepal D'Arusmont, to the U. S. led to their first acquaintance with Miss Wright, to whose counsel and assistance they applied to facilitate the quiet transfer of their undertaking to the U. S.

The transfer had already been effected when Fanny and Lafayette were in Philadelphia. Maclure, indeed, was still in Europe settling the affairs of his confiscated school in Alicante, and the hero of the printing press, Monsieur Phiquepal D'Arusmont, was on the high seas transporting the expensive apparatus essential for classes conducted on his "General Method," as well as some of the pupils in the school in Paris, to their new destination.

The new school itself, however, was being ably directed by Madame Marie Fretageot, a very remarkable woman whom ill-natured scandalmongers had long suspected of being Maclure's mistress. A word about her in passing for she certainly deserves it!

Her husband was colonel in the 7th Huzzars of Napoleon's army . . . later commandant of the hospice for invalid soldiers at the Bicète in Paris. She had long since ceased to live with him and no one believed that her only son, Achilles, was the child of her lawful husband. None of these things, however, seem to have made any difference with the many friends she possessed in the heterogeneous society of the First Empire. Her interest in liberal education (she had even tried her own hand at keeping a school) may have been the cause, if not the result, of her intimate relation with William Maclure. For years now she had managed his business affairs, in his various educational experiments. And perhaps the best evidence of her extraordinary capacity for unconventional adventure was her readiness to undertake the management of the girls' department of the new school near Philadelphia, without a backward look at the safe and comfortable world she was leaving behind her in her beloved Paris. Her peculiar knack of making good in the most unfamiliar circumstances is shown by her success with the respectable and circumspect society of the Quaker city, which had not hesitated to accept her as a safe and sound educator of genteel young females.

It is from her nephew, Victor Duclos, that one gets the following description of Lafayette's visit to the school.

"About five feet nine inches tall, spare built, dressed in black broadcloth. He made the boys march single file in front of him, putting his hands on their heads and bidding them to be 'good boys.'"

The next time one hears of Fanny and Lafayette together is as guests of ex-President Jefferson at Monticello. There is no doubt that Lafayette angled shamelessly for this invitation to his dear children, his two "filial friends," as he calls them in his letter to Jefferson explaining their presence in America.

> They are even now in Philadelphia [he says] on their way to Washington. She is very happy in your approbation of her book, *A Few Days in Athens,* for you and I are the two persons in the world whose esteem she values most. I wish, my dear friend, to present these two adopted daughters of mine to Mrs. Randolph and you. They being orphans from their youth, preferring American principles to British Aristocracy, having an independent though not very large fortune, have passed the last three years in most intimate connection with

my children and myself, and have readily yielded to our joint entreaties to make a second visit to the U. S.

Jefferson already knew about Fanny Wright as the author of *Altorf*. He was one of those persons to whom she had sent a copy of her play for advice and criticism. A courteous letter found in the Bixby collection shows that he actually read enough of the play to give her a flattering opinion of it. His reply to Lafayette's note from Philadelphia contains the desired invitation of the sisters to Monticello.

> Oct. 9th. You mention the return of Miss Wright to America accompanied by her sister . . . but do not say what her stay is to be, nor what her course. Should it lead her to our University . . . herself and her companion will nowhere find a welcome more hearty than with Mrs. Randolph and all the inhabitants of Monticello.

A reply from Lafayette completes the arrangements.

> Richmond. October 28th. I have communicated to my young friends your kind invitation. They are highly obliged to Mrs. Randolph and you. They ought to have been in Richmond by this time. Some steamboat arrangements have delayed them and the Ladies of their party. My way of travelling does not admit female companionship, but Miss Wright and her sister Camilla will in a few days avail themselves of the invitation which they value most in both hemispheres.

On Thursday Nov. 4th Lafayette himself arrived at Monticello for a visit of two weeks and for a part, if not all, of this time Fanny and her "Paternal Friend" were together again under the same roof in all the old easy familiarity of those days at La Grange, while he was reading and answering the six hundred letters from his family and friends in Europe which, one is told, awaited him there. And when one remembers how often in the past he had permitted his name to be used as a sort of poste restante for Fanny's errant correspondence it is not stretching the bounds of probability to believe that some small portion of this vast heap of European mail belonged to her.

Jefferson was at this time already an old man—very nearly at the end of his life—broken in health and worried by financial difficulties but still one of the most interesting and original thinkers of his day and Fanny with her passion for wise old men appeared, no doubt, at far greater advantage while listening to, and taking part in the conversation which went on at Monticello during her stay there than in the fashionable drawing rooms of Philadelphia.

She did not accompany Lafayette on his visit to ex-President Madison at Montpelier. Her introduction to that august personage and his wife was to come later. Lafayette and his "adopted daughters" were together again in Washington till his departure for the far South at the end of February, 1825.

The city was much fuller and livelier than at the time of Fanny's first visit there in the spring of 1820. The Eighteenth Congress was assembling for its last session. A bitter political struggle was about to take place among its members to decide whether John Quincy Adams or Andrew Jackson was to be the next president of the United States. But first it had much pleasanter business to attend to, and all partisan feeling having given way for the moment to the general eagerness to share in the various tributes of a grateful nation to the People's Guest.

One reads in the issue of the Washington *Gazette* of December 9th. "General Lafayette was received today by the Senate in a most distinguished manner. The Senate Chamber was crowded on the occasion. Many ladies were present, among whom we noticed the lady of General Jackson and others of the city, and the celebrated English authoress Miss Wright and her sister."

The next day was the turn of the House where Lafayette was also enthusiastically received and harangued by Fanny's old idol, the Speaker, Henry Clay. Members from the Senate, anxious to witness this great occasion, overflowed the galleries, while a crowd of ladies occupied the sofas and seats of the Chamber without the bar.

One may be quite sure, therefore, that both the sisters were present on that famous day when Congress voted a gift of $200,000 and a township of 24,000 acres of land to their honored guest as a tribute to those services during the American Revolution which they never could sufficiently repay.

Lafayette had very properly chosen this moment for a visit to Annapolis and was not in the Chamber during the discussion or while the vote was taken. In the welter of lofty sentiments exchanged by the donors and the recipient of this princely gift before it was finally accepted, one is apt to lose sight of its material results on the fortunes of a man hovering as Lafayette was at this particular moment of his life, on the verge of bankruptcy. Now he could pay the debts which had so nearly prevented his coming to America. Now he could go home and make his beloved La Grange the last word in agricultural perfection, while he continued to play the part of generous patron and protector of the hard beset liberal cause in Europe, with all the added prestige of his late glorification by the people and government of the United States.

For Fanny too, the visit to the United States had brought deliverance from a situation quite as serious and even more precarious for her than Lafayette's own, on his departure from France. Her peculiar affection for the man whom she had long believed to be the best as well as the wisest in the world, had survived the painful crisis with his family and remained intact as long as they both lived. Not so her faith in Lafayette's power to protect her from evil tongues and covert insult from his own intimate friends and kindred. All the pride and satisfaction of her early intimacy with him and them was gone forever.

It was the same with her attitude towards the liberal cause in Europe. She never lost her sympathy with peoples living under the heels of unjust and oppressive governments; but even before her break with Lafayette's family she had begun to doubt the value of the maze of secret conspiracy and futile opposition in which she had been involved for the last three years by her adoration for her "paternal friend." Now that she was away from it she could sum it up with relentless clarity, as appears in the following passage from an account of this period of her life.

> The general want of political knowledge and political experience in its accredited leaders, the frequent vanity and frivolity of individuals in responsible positions, the absurd drawing-room intrigues and fashionable conspirators, contrasted strangely and painfully though sometimes almost ludicrously with the serious character of a struggle in which human lives and those often of the young and chivalrous were the stakes of the game. And though still deeply interested in the fate of leading individuals she had ceased to anticipate success to efforts of which the object appeared to her ill-defined and those who pursued it far from agreed among themselves.

In marked contrast to the distracted state of Europe she saw America, the beloved country of her earliest enthusiasm, the one nation where "human progress was rendered safe and certain by the nature of its institutions and the condition and character of its people."

Henceforth her life and thought and dearest loyalties were to be devoted to the service of her adopted country, on lines so utterly different from anything she had thus far attempted as to divide her story into two mutually independent parts.

PART TWO

CHAPTER I

The Promise of Nashoba

IN THE last pages of her *Views of Society and Manners in America*, Fanny had devoted some time to a discussion of the evils of negro slavery in America, which she found so shocking, so entirely repugnant to the free institutions of that country and the very temper of its people that she confidently prophesied its complete disappearance at some not very distant day.

A few days spent in Virginia during her first visit to the United States had shown her only the mildest, most humane aspects of this institution, and it was not till her return to America with General Lafayette that she came face to face with one of the most hideous phases of the American slave system, a vessel just ready to set out from a Virginia seaport, where she herself was disembarking, loaded and overloaded with unfortunate blacks chained two by two and destined for the slave markets in Savannah.

From that moment the whole slave question assumed a very different aspect in her mind. It was a sin against humanity, a cancer at the heart of her dear free America which must be cut out without loss of time. She could think and talk of little else till she had worked out what she felt might be a partial cure of this great evil.

By conversations with Jefferson at Monticello, by questioning the southern planters with whom she was thrown together through her intimacy with Lafayette, and by every other means in her power, she set herself to find the real reason for the power and persistence of an institution so contrary to the principles underlying American society and government as she understood them.

From Jefferson she found out that there were approximately four million slaves in the United States. An entire economic and social system rested upon this institution, and Frances Wright was still enough of a believer in the sacred rights of private property to accept the opinion she had already received from Jefferson during their long talks on the subject at Monticello, that "any plan to remove this evil, if it was to be effectual, must consult at once the pecuniary interests and prevailing opinions of the southern planters and bend itself to the existing laws of the states."

Colonization of the whole slave population of the United States in Africa or some nearer country where their color would be no longer a handicap to their development into free people in a free country, had already been suggested by groups of men who felt their presence in the United States was a menace to the institutions of the country. Jefferson himself was on the board of the National Society working to this end.

She herself had already described at some length in her first book on America the generous action of Edward Coles of Virginia who had enfranchised all the slaves on his plantation and colonized them in the free state of Illinois where he was a little later elected to be governor. But a very short experience with the freedmen of the southern states, made her agree with Jefferson that:

> Human enfranchisement is in its beginning a slow, gradual and complex operation. It must move forward simultaneously in the soul of the internal man and in the external influences which surround him. . . . To give liberty to a slave before he understands its nature is perhaps rather to impose a penalty than to bestow a blessing. At present, when restored by some generous planter to their birthright of liberty, the sons of Africa forfeit the protection of a master without securing the guardianship of the law.

How to give the slave the education necessary for a wise use of future freedom while he still remained a slave on a southern plantation? How to supply the master with the means for carrying out some general system of colonization or immediate enfranchisement for his slaves, without utterly destroying the whole economic system on which southern society depended?

This was the problem on which Fanny had been cudgeling her brains until even she was beginning to be hopeless of success in finding the real solution, when the great English philanthropist and reformer, Robert Owen, appeared in Washington preaching his social doctrine of a new moral world.

Owen was at this time a man about fifty-three years old, small and very ugly, with a nose almost as long as that so noticeable in portraits of Lord Brougham, whom he is said to have strongly resembled.

He was already well known in the United States for the reforms he had effected in the mill village of New Lanark in the Clyde Valley, where his schools for the children employed in his factories were models of their kind. He had also been active in the passage of the various factory acts which had shortened the hours and raised the wages of the industrial workers throughout the British Isles. But it was his experiments in co-operative community living which took the strongest hold on the imagination of Americans at the time of his first visit to their country.

America had been already the scene of many such experiments, from the mere settlement in groups under a leader like Morris Birkbeck and his English immigrants in Illinois, to the religious societies of the Shakers, entirely communistic in principle and practice.

So when it became known in Washington that Owen had bought the best known and most successful of these religious communities: the whole village community of New Harmony, houses, industries, and 30,000 acres of cultivated land on the Wabash River in Indiana, from its founder, George Rapp, with the intention of establishing on the same site, one of his own co-operative communities on lines which were already well established in England, all the world flocked to hear him.

He lectured in the Chamber of the House of Representatives on February 23rd and 27th to a large and distinguished audience including secretaries, members of Congress, and the President himself.

In his first address as reported by the newspapers of the day he confined himself to an outline of his doctrine of the influence of circumstances on belief and character. In the second he gave details of his projected community with an explanation of the principle on which it was founded, his own favorite theory of co-operation. And by this, Owen meant something far more important than a mere pooling of resources for a temporary economic advantage. It was a way of life, a radical change from one social system to another: from an ignorant, selfish, competitive order where the great mass of mankind must remain, as they were at the moment, poor, oppressed, and consequently vicious and miserable, to the perfect state where all mankind would be reasonably happy and virtuous.

The chief means to this great end were to be found in small units like the one just founded at New Harmony, chiefly engaged in agriculture, carrying on factory work only as an auxiliary employment, producing all the goods required for their own subsistence, buying as little as possible from outside, selling only surplus products.

This insistence on the surplus which labor could be depended on to produce in agriculture as in manufactures, and which capital had hitherto appropriated, as the "unearned increment" of its ever-increasing resources, gave Owen his right to be called the first English Socialist.

In the Owenite co-operative village this surplus, instead of being appropriated by the employers of labor as was progressively the case in a capitalistic society, remained with those who had actually earned it. Every one must work, for on the results of collective labor the whole fortune of the community depended, but all were assured of every necessity of daily life, with ample time for recreation and education. Special attention was always given to this last, in every Owenite community, for obvious reasons.

Did not the whole Owenite theory of the co-operative village, did not the whole utilitarian philosophy from which Owen himself had drawn his first inspiration, depend on the belief in man's capacity for self-improvement to the point of actual utopian perfectibility, given the right kind of training in the right environment?

The promise of New Harmony as a new field of opportunity for enlightened and character-building education in a virgin community, far from the warping influences of existing society, raised a veritable flutter of excitement among the teachers and directors of the Maclure School of Industry already described in an earlier chapter of this work.

"I told you in my last," writes Madame Fretageot to her patron still in Paris, "that Phiquepal was going to Washington to meet Mr. Owen. He has been much delighted with that excellent man and is now convinced that you will join in his plan."

Another letter shows Madame Fretageot herself doing everything she could to bring about the new departure.

> I have seen Mr. Owen. He wishes so much to meet you when he returns to England, and I am sure, after seeing him, you will change your intention about this school. He told me that I might devote the next thirty years of my life where I am now without being able to counterbalance the evils which surround my pupils with a thousand prejudices and false opinions, which will always serve as a barrier to my best endeavors in another direction. . . . Dr. Price will be one of

the new settlers. He will arrive soon with a part of the children of New Lanark. A great many people in Philadelphia are also preparing to go to New Harmony. Troost, Say, Speakman. They all expect you to join them. I will not tell them no.

One cannot be sure that Fanny was present at Owen's lectures in the House of Representatives, but she undoubtedly had some contact with him during his stay in Washington and one cannot overestimate the effect of this new friendship on the whole aftercourse of her life.

Already they were united in a common admiration for Jeremy Bentham as the great prophet of the Utilitarian philosophy from which Owen had drawn so many of the principles underlying his whole great plan for a new moral world. And now his plan of a co-operative village seemed full of useful suggestions for the solution of her own problem. It is true that Owen himself always remained perfectly cold to negro emancipation. All his efforts for the reform of social evil and injustice were confined to the white race, to the point even that people of color were excluded from membership in his community.

But this tacit segregation of the negro as a member of an inferior race, incapable of raising himself by his own efforts from slavery to freedom, was never accepted by Fanny. On the contrary, her eager creative mind saw a peculiar applicability of the principles of an Owenite co-operative village to the unit of a southern plantation. Did not slave labor also produce its surplus? Did all of this necessarily belong to the master? Could not some part of it at least be applied towards the gradual repayment of his original purchase price plus the cost of his colonization in some country outside the United States? Was there anything to prevent the introduction of some system of education during this period of probation designed to increase the immediate usefulness of the slave to his master while at the same time preparing him for the responsibilities of freedom when it was finally obtained? Was there anything in the laws of the southern states to prevent or further such an experiment?

The same impulse which had caused her to spend hours and days in the little-frequented alcove of the Glasgow College Library, in search of facts about America at the time of her first enthusiasm for that country, drove her now to the registers of the laws actually existent in the southern states bearing directly upon the labor and government of the negro, in the collections of public records at Washington. But as she read and studied the books of written law, she grew more and more anxious to see for herself the life on a slave plantation in the deep South, to talk to some of those planters who had been so hospitable in their suggestions, to pay them a visit before she left America. She wanted to consult them on the plan which was already taking vague form in her mind, to take advantage of their experience, to get their point of view which permitted "such a monstrous anomaly in the institutions of Free America, as a system of labor which condemned a whole class of its population to social degradation, political nullity and brutal ignorance." (Her own words in a later description of this crisis of her life.)

The time soon came when, without any special effort on her part, the opportunity for just the personal investigation she so ardently longed for, fell, as it were, into her lap.

Early in February, 1825, Lafayette set out on his amazing journey through the South Atlantic and Gulf States, including Florida half cleared and still infested with hostile Indians, to New Orleans. The presence of ladies on the difficult and often dangerous expedition, was out of the question even for the intrepid temper of Fanny, but it had been already arranged between them before his departure that she and her sister should join him in New Orleans early in April by the safer, though almost equally long and adventurous journey down the Ohio and Mississippi rivers by steamboat.

One of the great disappointments of her earlier visit to America was that she had to turn back to the Atlantic seaboard from Buffalo instead of "striking south from Lake Erie to Pittsburgh to view with her own eyes the growing wonders of the Western World." She had been especially anxious to visit the settlement which a well-to-do Quaker, Morris Birkbeck, in partnership with another rich dissenter from the Church of England, Richard Flower, had founded in the southeastern corner of the free state of Illinois on a ridge of high land between the lesser and greater Wabash. It was settled for the benefit of English emigrants who were driven by the agricultural depression at the close of the Napoleonic Wars to seek new homes for themselves in the United States.

She spent some pages in her *Views of Society and Manners in America* in reply to an attack on the Birkbeck community made in an article in the *Edinburgh Review* by that cantankerous person, William Cobbett—at that moment growing turnips in Long Island—who painted the situation of the English emigrants in the darkest colors.

"I have been at pains to inform myself," she says on page 191 of her book on America, "that the worst difficulties have been surmounted and that these have always been fewer than what were frequently encountered in a new country."

She then goes on to poke a little fun at the general tendency of her countrymen to make the worst instead of the best of a new situation, holding themselves aloof, as if of a superior race from the American frontiersman, instead of letting the prejudices and predilections which they had brought from the mother country be rubbed away by free intercourse with their neighbors.

Fanny's first, rather critical attitude towards the Birkbeck experiment was changed to wholehearted respect and admiration when she heard the story of the important part this colony of freedom-loving, respectable English farmers had taken during a recent attempt to break the original compact (by which all this Northwestern territory was to remain free soil) and legalize slavery by a new state constitution. To a man the English emigrants threw in their lot with the anti-slavery party, and their vote, cast solidly against the new constitution, turned out to be a deciding factor in its defeat when the question came up for decision at the polls in 1823.

And this, their first valuable service to the free country of which they had so lately become citizens, was largely owing to the devoted leadership of George Flower, the eldest son of Birkbeck's partner Richard. Journeying up and down the state, chiefly on horseback, in his efforts to rouse the widely scattered inhabitants of that thinly populated state to the support of free institutions in Illinois, this young man had willingly incurred the bitter animosity of all those on the side of slavery, including many of the most powerful influences in the state. The threats and insults of the blackguardly element in the population culminated at last in the murder of George Flower's first son Richard, by a ruffian whom a jury of his nearest neighbors triumphantly acquitted.

George Flower had further distinguished himself by a successful effort (in direct defiance of the custom of his neighbors on this matter) to save the free negroes to whom he had rented farms from a particularly cruel fate which frequently overtook them whenever they were caught by the gang of men who made their living by kidnapping and selling free negroes down the river as runaway slaves.

At his own expense, he despatched twenty-five of his best workmen and tenants to Haiti under the protection of a man who had already made the necessary arrangements with the president of this island.

After long delays and many accidents, they all arrived safely in that country. President Boyer settled them on his own lands and Mr. Flower received a letter from him full of the best hopes for their future.

All this and more besides, Fanny must have heard retailed at length during her stay at Monticello the previous autumn, for George Flower had been a special friend and protégé of Thomas Jefferson ever since his first appearance in America in 1817 with a letter of introduction from Lafayette. He had been most favorably impressed when Flower and his father's friend and partner, Morris Birkbeck, had stopped at La Grange during a tour for agricultural information which they had been making after the close of the Napoleonic Wars.

Her early desire to visit the Birkbeck settlement in Illinois was increased a thousandfold by her eagerness to meet this compatriot of hers whom she already recognized as a kindred spirit. And now while arranging for her journey through the western country to New Orleans she was delighted to find that it could easily be made to include short excursions not only to the Flower settlement at Albion but also to the Rappite village on the Wabash which her late encounters with Robert Owen had made her even more anxious to see.

The sisters left Washington in the last week of February. Their first stop was Montpelier, where they spent a day or two with ex-President Madison and his wife Dolly, by Lafayette's express arrangement and desire. It was Fanny's fault, apparently, that the visit was so long delayed and in the end so brief. Her letter to Mrs. Madison dated Washington, February 23rd, 1825, says:

> Ten days since, my dear Madame, we were about to set out for Montpelier, when I was seized with a severe cold and sore throat which has confined me ever since to my room. I doubly regret this delay as the visit to which we had so long looked forward with impatience must now be reduced to one of a day. We shall leave here on Saturday next, to be at Grange Court House by stage on the day following, Sunday. Then, to execute in time our long journey westward so as to join our venerable friend, General Lafayette in New

Orleans, on the first day of April, we must I fear, leave you
to join the Wednesday's mail for Staunton.

One hears of her next at Pittsburgh on her way to the half-built village of Economy, soon to become the new home of the German
Rappites. The place was too far from completion to justify her attention, and Rapp was still with the body of his followers in Indiana.
The final move was not to take place till the end of May.

A drive of thirty miles through primeval forest from Mount Vernon,
port of call for steamers descending the Ohio, brought them to New
Harmony.

Her first impression of the little village which was to play so large
a part in her life for years to come, was admiration for the beautiful
orchards and vineyards, the well-planned and well-developed fruit
and vegetable gardens of the Rappite village, all the more lovely for
the contrast with the wild uncultivated regions she had just been
traversing.

Its houses, brick or frame, built along regular streets, were simply
but solidly constructed. The only buildings in the place which showed
a more ambitious design were the well-built brick house with two
lightning rods and a flight of stone steps in which George Rapp and
his family lived, and the church with its pointed roof ornamented
with a belfry and clock tower.

The community was in fact the cynosure of all travelers' eyes—and
an object of keen jealousy on the part of the settlers and backwoods-
men in the surrounding territory, who were in the process of building
up another American tradition—private initiative and individualism.
Why had its founders ever decided to move—to leave all this scene
of tangible achievement, for the uncultivated, half-built dreariness
Fanny had just witnessed in their new destination near Pittsburgh?
One ostensible cause of the change was the unhealthfulness of the
present site, but it was thought by some to be part of Rapp's policy
to keep his people on the move, lest by becoming too comfortable
and prosperous they should forget their faith and their vow of celibacy.
The Rappites were lowly peasants, believing in the purest Christian
communism. Work, prayer and the simple life were their goals on this
earth. It is interesting to note that at the height of their prosperity
in Harmony they made and sold gallons of whisky—though they did
not drink anything but water. They laboriously started a silk factory,
and wore rough woolens. All property and valuables of the individuals

were handed over to the community. All education was to be given by George Rapp and his immediate aides. Each person was to be taken care of by the community in sickness or in old age. There was to be no self-interest except that which aided the happiness and welfare of the community.

George Rapp, their leader, had been a vinedresser in his native Württemberg. He was almost six feet tall, with a slow stately walk, a fine flowing beard, keen eyes, penetrating and sympathetic. He had been a close student of the Bible and made strange interpretations of what he read in its pages: as for instance, from Genesis 26:2 he concluded, had Adam been allowed to remain in the original state of innocence he would have been able to have children without the aid of woman. Celibacy was the established order among the Rappites. We are told today that the mores of celibacy among these early religious sects made for greater labor power and productive intensity uncomplicated by the disconcerting forces of romance and the responsibilities of children.

But Fanny had too keen an appreciation of human values to be satisfied even with a paradise if it was built with robotlike labor founded on ignorance and superstition. She had not been in New Harmony many hours before she had decided that there was little difference between the intellectual and spiritual development of the German laborers and the southern negroes whose lot she was so anxious to improve. Both were slaves, the negroes under masters who bought or sold them, the others under a shrewd and practical leader who dominated them body and soul.

She and her sister spent an evening at Rapp's house where she heard some surprisingly good music, singing and playing by Rapp's daughter, Gertrude. She also met his eldest son, Becker. It was, no doubt, this latter person she meant when she speaks later of a man of singularly enlarged and philanthropic views, one of the directors of the colony from whom she obtained useful information as to its general working and government, and to whom she could free her mind as to what, in her eyes at least, were some of its most startling deficiencies.

> Well cultivated fields and gardens, and well conducted manufactures might be the result of the regular and unvarying labor of its members, broken only by psalm singing and other tedious and sometimes ludicrous ceremonies, but where

were the great and beautiful works of art, or libraries, or labo-
ratories or scientific workshops devoted to aid the progress of
invention and the sublime conquest of matter by mind?
Where were the children trained to excellence by the spur of
emulation and ever accumulating knowledge of the community to enjoy and administer its accumulating capital?

She found this man quite alive to her own point of view and
greatly desirous of seeing new moral principles and a more just mode
of administration substituted for the spiritual government of its
directors. He even promised her, so she tells us in later writing, that
if he was unsuccessful in his attempt to substitute a juster mode of
administration for the present spiritual autocracy of the directors,
in the new colony at Economy, he would leave it all, and come to join
her in the undertaking she contemplated in the southern states.

She was the more horrified therefore, somewhat later that same
year, to hear of the sudden and unexplained death of this man under
most suspicious circumstances, after a clash with his father's authority
over the property and supreme direction of the new community at
Economy. The circumstances of his death and the frightful surmises
they excited in the outside world, inspired Fanny with "additional
distrust and abhorrence of all associations not founded upon the
broadest principles of justice, and where the bond of association, the
tenure of land and capital, and the mode of direction were not made
clear to all concerned."

A brief account of this first visit to New Harmony is found in the
journal of William Owen, a younger son of Robert, who had been left
behind by his father to conclude the negotiations of the purchase.

March 19. A beautiful clear day. In the evening the Misses
Wright who were on their way to New Orleans to meet the
Marquis of Lafayette, arrived. They brought us news of my
father's proceedings in Washington. Miss Wright is a very
learned and a fine woman, and though her manners are free
and unusual in a female, yet they are pleasing and graceful,
and she improves on acquaintance.

March 20, Sunday. We walked with the ladies to the vineyards and hills, from which we had a fine view. At one o'clock
we attended a musical meeting in the church and afterwards
walked through the house and garden of Mr. Rapp. In the
evening we supped there with Mr. and Miss Gertrude Rapp.

Afterwards a good deal of music. A very fine day. River stationary.

March 21, Monday. A dull morning. A slight shower but soon clearing off and becoming a fine day. After visiting the cotton mill the Misses Wright set out on their palfreys with Mr. Flower for Albion.

A long ride across the level prairie and the dangerous passage of the Little Wabash River brought the two sisters and their escort to their destination late that same day.

Here, if one may trust the infrequent descriptions of this little settlement by contemporary witnesses, Fanny and her sister were suddenly transported into as close a likeness to an English village as was possible in a frontier settlement not yet ten years old. In the home of Richard Flower and his family, there was an almost pathetic effort to reproduce the comfort and dignity of living in the great house of a typical English community. Even the manners of the English emigrants who made up the body of the inhabitants, retained more than a shadow of the respect and deference towards their betters usually required of them in the mother country.

Under ordinary conditions Fanny herself would have been not too approving of this persistence of outmoded manners and customs on the frontier of Free America. But any inclination to make censorious judgments on the relations between Richard Flower and his English tenantry was quickly submerged by her rapture on finding herself in a world where dreams come true. For as it happened, George Flower was exactly the friend she needed to help her bring her own vague and inchoate plans for gradual negro emancipation into solid and workable shape.

His father had been for years an enthusiastic admirer and friend of Robert Owen. It was Richard Flower, in fact, who first brought the idea of the purchase of New Harmony from the Rappites to Owen's notice and carried out all the preliminaries of the sale. Both father and son were already deeply interested in the Owenite experiment about to be tried at this place. And better still, George Flower's own experience with his negro farmers had already convinced him that the negro race was quite as capable of making use of a practical education and a fair environment for its own future advantage as the whites themselves.

He saw no greater difficulties in Fanny's plan to introduce the

Owenite theories of co-operation on a slave plantation than those he himself had overcome in earlier struggles with the wilderness.

Together they plotted out the model plantation where schools, workshops, directed recreation, were to prepare the slave for his ultimate freedom, while his increased efficiency under such treatment would more than compensate the master for any loss resulting from such diversion of his labor from the main business on every southern plantation, getting in the crop in time for the market.

And as they talked, the miracle took shape: George Flower offered himself as a partner in the new undertaking. Fanny's own description of the new contract appears in a letter to her good liberal friend, Madame Charles de Lateyrie, written somewhat later that same year.

> I found Mr. Flower surrounded by a charming family, married to a woman endowed with the rarest qualities, working night and day in the cause of the negro. I talked to him of my idea, I told him of my plans, he gave me his word to devote himself body and soul to the realization of our projects. We decided that I should furnish the funds for the purchase of a plantation somewhere below the cotton line in the South, and all the first expenses thus entailed including whatever number of negro slaves should afterwards be found necessary to work it. He on the other hand would transport from Illinois all the material of the farm, domestic animals, plows, supplies, pork, salted beef, meal, etc., till the new farm can supply my needs. His wife, a charming and most intelligent person, endowed with the rarest qualities, who has devoted herself day and night in the defence of the blacks, has arranged everything exactly right. Her husband wished to sell at least part of his land in Illinois as his share of the undertaking. I did not wish this for, in case our experiment should be a failure, I thought he ought to preserve an independence for his children, and his fortune is already much diminished by ten years' effort and sacrifices.

One has had already several instances of Fanny's ability to attract and retain in her service as long as she needed them those she recognized as kindred souls. In the case of George Flower, however, one must admit that she had come upon him at a moment when he was especially vulnerable to her kind of appeal.

His second wife, the woman of whom Fanny speaks so admiringly, was a girl whom Morris Birkbeck had educated and was bringing out to Illinois to marry himself, when George Flower, also a member of the party, fell in love with her and she with him. The two young people were married at Vincennes, Indiana, and Birkbeck apparently forgave them, but all subsequent relations between him and the young man who had been like a son to him, were carried on through an intermediary, a method of intercourse which extended to the whole Flower family.

This painful element in the life of his father's community, undoubtedly increased that strange restlessness which seems to have possessed so many of those first settlers of the American frontier, and made him peculiarly susceptible to the warm appreciative flattery which Fanny knew so well how to give to those who had excited her generous respect and admiration. One may note in passing that the union of interests which resulted in this case, was as short-lived as it was sudden.

Thus all thought of a return to France with Lafayette vanished from Fanny's plan of life forever. Her fate was fixed in a new world under new conditions which were to lead her very far from the old settled way of life into which she had been born, and where she had lived for the first thirty years of her existence.

On one of her rides about the country during that very first visit to Albion she herself was witness of an atrocious example of the ugly conditions which surrounded the negro laborer even in the free state of Illinois. A vivid description of the whole circumstance is found in the same letter to Madame Charles de Lateyrie already referred to in this chapter.

> A young negro was conveyed, half by violence, half by fraud out of the state into slave territory to be sold there as a slave. I engaged two men to follow him with me. I passed two days and half a night in the pursuit of the kidnappers. I caught them at last. I actually got hold of the wretched black. He clung to my clothes. The monsters attacked us with their long knives. But some good citizens arrived and accompanied us to a magistrate who gave the wretched boy into the safe-keeping of the sheriff of the County for the night. God knows whether this man was in collusion with the kidnappers. But the next morning everyone had disappeared and the Sheriff seemed to know nothing about it. You can imagine what I suffered, especially since I must always accuse myself

for having given way to fatigue and yielded to the entreaties
of my companions to leave the task of guarding him to others.

In spite of all these accidents and incidents, however, she and her
sister reached New Orleans in time to be included in the distinguished
group of statesmen and politicians, generals and civilians who accompanied Lafayette from New Orleans to St. Louis on the steamboat,
Natchez. She seems to have lost no time in enlisting the sympathy and
interest of everyone about her in her new adventure, and to have
received a surprising amount of interest and encouragement from those
favorite sons of the South which could not all have been mere lip
service to the "adopted daughter" of General Lafayette. In fact it
would almost seem as if the leaders of the southwest country were
not so completely satisfied with the peculiar institution of slavery in
the year 1825, that they could see no advantage in some perfectly
painless method of amending it, like Fanny's model plantation.

Certainly the liberal governor of Tennessee, William Carroll, seems
to have done his little best to make her choose his own state for the
site of her new experiment. It was from this gentleman, no doubt,
that she first heard of a large tract of Indian territory in the vicinity
of Memphis, lately obtained from Congress at a nominal figure and
offering good value for prospective buyers.

There is still a tradition in that part of the country that she and
Lafayette disembarked at Memphis, and climbed those red headlands
known since early French and Indian times, as Chickasaw Bluffs.

At St. Louis, however, their paths parted. According to a local
newspaper Fanny and her sister were already at Nashville when
Lafayette and his party arrived in that city and stopped to see them,
in company with Fanny's new well-wisher, Governor Carroll. A little
later after the General's famous shipwreck on the Cumberland, a local
Louisville paper mentions another visit from Lafayette and Governor
Carroll to "the Misses Wright, the celebrated female writers who are
trailing through our country in his wake."

This same disagreeable note is struck again by Bernard of Saxe-
Weimar in his lively chronicle of the American scene, published in
1827. This gentleman arrived in Boston too late for the ceremonies of
the laying of the cornerstone of the Bunker Hill Monument at which
General Lafayette was the guest of honor, but in plenty of time to
collect and re-tell some of the gossip resulting from Fanny's presence
in Boston on the same occasion. "I was told that this lady with her

sister, unattended by a male protector, had roved through the country
in steamboats and stages, that she constantly tagged about after General Lafayette and whenever the General arrived at any place Miss
Wright was sure to follow next day. As but little notice was taken of
this lady in Boston, a literary attack was expected from her pen."

Any slights she received at this time and in this place, however,
were never mentioned by her and must soon have been forgotten
in the urgency of her own immediate interests.

She took advantage of this her last visit to the East for a number
of years, to present her plan to northern abolitionists. One of these
a certain Jeremiah Thompson, Quaker merchant and exporter of cotton goods in New York City, and friend and admirer of Robert Owen,
was so favorably impressed by her that one finds him a little later
sending three boxes full of articles most in use as stock in trade in
the plantation store, still for many years, one of the essential features
of a slave community far from the ordinary centers of distribution.
The sum spent in the purchase of these articles, $580.02, was, he told
her, his mite in aid of her good efforts and required no repayment on
her part.

And during a visit to Baltimore later in the summer she made her
first connection with Benjamin Lundy, an old friend and fellow cam-
paigner of George Flower in the late struggle against the slave interests
in Illinois. But shortly after the defeat of these last in 1823, Lundy
seems to have moved to Baltimore, transporting with him his spirited
little newspaper, *The Genius of Universal Emancipation*.

Moved more perhaps than was quite wise or prudent, by the interest and encouragement accorded to her scheme in so many different quarters, she ventured at last a trial balloon of much more
ambitious proportions than anything she had yet attempted, in a little
pamphlet printed in Baltimore in the late summer, "A Plan for the
gradual Abolition of Slavery in the United States without danger of loss
to the Citizens of the South," which was nothing more or less than a
bid for government participation on a large scale.

She proposed briefly that Congress itself should donate sections of
public lands in appropriate situations throughout the southern states;
that these should make use of this land for the establishment of experimental farms along the lines which she had already laid down
for herself on her own plantation; that the initial expenses incurred
for such experimental stations should be raised by subscription.

Here she introduced some surprising statistics, evidently furnished her by people who thought themselves authorities on slave economics.

The first cost of such an experiment was estimated at about $41,000, and it was expected that at the end of the first year, after deducting an interest charge of 6 per cent on the capital invested, there would be a net profit of close upon $10,000.

A school of industry on the Lancastrian principle was an essential feature of the experimental farm for the purpose of carrying order and co-operation from schoolroom to field. "The monitors who directed the studies of the children on the plantation would bring the same principles of order and industry to the picking of cotton as they had already established in the classrooms, with such intermissions for rest and recreation as should keep their bodies vigorous and their minds cheerful. Such a system introduced into a cotton plantation must raise the value of youthful labor nearly to mature labor."

The number of slaves required for the operation of these establishments was computed at anywhere between fifty and one hundred laborers.

The duration of service necessary to cover the initial expenses of their purchase at the current prices, as well as the rearing of infants, and possible loss by sickness or accident, was estimated at five years for an able-bodied slave on an average cotton plantation. On sugar, rice, and some cotton land it might be as low as from one to three years. In the state of Kentucky from six to ten. No figures could be obtained from Virginia, so depressed was the value of slave labor in that state.

Not the least interesting feature of this pamphlet was the suggestion that though the colonization of the freed negro in some country other than the United States was the main end and object of this form of gradual emancipation, it might later be found that colonization was not always necessary. The slaves who had bought their freedom might remain where they were on the footing of tenants, as far as the property itself was able to use them, etc., etc.

The statements contained in this pamphlet, astonishingly optimistic as they sound today, were apparently accepted by Fanny's advisors as not wildly impossible of success, under favorable circumstances. She herself was so confident in their power to appeal, that she sent copies of her plan to one and another of those august personages with whom her faithful old friend Lafayette was spending those last hur-

ried days before his departure for France, with personal letters asking
their advice and opinion.

Some of the results thus obtained are amusingly described in a long
letter from Lafayette, one of the last from him to her while he was
still in America and she already far on her way to the western country
and her own adventure.

> I have returned from my Virginia trip without finding here
> a letter from you, my dear Fanny. My table was covered
> with correspondence, American and French, partly from La
> Grange, mentioning my shipwreck and my fall, charging me
> with love for both you and Camilla. I sent, on the subject of
> your plan, before leaving here, the answer of Mr. Jefferson.
> I found him very ailing. Our mutual adieus very, very melan-
> choly, as you may believe.

> My conversations with Mr. Madison going and coming,
> have demonstrated to me that you have no better friend in
> the U. S. and make me wish that you would cultivate this
> friendship. Mr. Madison is to address his answer (to your
> letter) to Nashville, care of General Jackson. These two
> friends seem to augur well of your plans though not believing
> in so prompt a success of which the indispensable condition
> is its Southern origin and collaboration. I have shown your
> paper to Mr. Monroe, who has approved of it under the con-
> ditions just stated. He is going to sell his Albemarle Plantation
> and would like to introduce on that of Lansdowne, free white
> labor. Perhaps these circumstances might lead to something
> done with him.

> Chief Justice Marshall has, under seal of secrecy, your
> prospectus, and will shortly write me his opinion confiden-
> tially. You know he is nominal head of the Colonization So-
> ciety. They say their approbation will do more harm than
> good but I found their good will sincere and my daily con-
> versations during the Virginia trip indicate a gradual amelio-
> ration of public opinion.

> The loss of my pocket book (which has since been recov-
> ered) and therefore of your address does not prevent me
> from thinking that the two letters addressed to Mr. Rapp near
> Pittsburg will have reached you. The third has been sent to
> General Jackson.

> We dine with the President of the U. S. on Sept. 6th. when
> I enter on my 69th. year. Next morning we will go in a
> steamboat to visit the frigate Brandywine at the nearest point

where she can receive us and from there we leave for the far shores of England.

This is not yet adieu, etc., etc.

The letter of Jefferson thus briefly referred to by Lafayette appears in his published correspondence as an answer to a request received by him from Fanny that he would pronounce in some fashion on her new experiment. It is a masterpiece of Jeffersonian adroitness in avoiding any responsibility in the matter.

> At the age of 82 with one foot in the grave and the other lifted to follow it, I do not permit myself to take part in any new enterprise, not even in the great one which is the subject of your letter, and which has been through life one of my greatest anxieties. . . . I leave its accomplishment as the work of another generation. . . . Your prospectus has its aspects of promise. It may yet in its development lead to happy results. . . . You are young, dear Madame, and have powers of mind which may do much in exciting others in this arduous task . . . etc., etc.

This letter from Lafayette was directed to Fanny, care of General Jackson at the Hermitage near Nashville, Tennessee. She found it waiting for her when she and her partner, George Flower, arrived in that place to make the visit already arranged for her by Lafayette, and receive all the advice and assistance General Jackson had promised to give her in her quest after slaves and land for her great experiment.

They found at last just the site they needed for their new plantation, good and pleasant woodland, traversed by a clear and lovely stream communicating thirteen miles below with the Mississippi, at the old Indian trading post of Chickasaw Bluffs, the modern Memphis.

Already she had given it the name by which it was known for a number of years, Nashoba, the old Chickasaw name for Wolf. The whole story is related in Fanny's most attractive style in one of her long lively letters to Madame Charles de Lasteyrie.

Memphis, West Tennessee 26th. Dec.

After having passed through an immense extent of country, consulted by letter and personal interview all the most important persons in the vicinity and observed the character of the people living in the towns and villages, here I am at last, property-owner in the forests of this new territory, bought from the Indians by the United States about five years ago and still inhabited by bears, wolves and panthers. But do not be alarmed, I have traveled the length and breadth of this territory two times, doing forty miles a day on horseback, through unbroken country, spending the night in cabins open to the air on all sides, or in the woods themselves, a bear-skin for my bed, my saddle for a pillow, and I am perfectly well. My health is better—I am stronger than I have ever been in my life. I have seen bears without being attacked by them, for they don't attack—on the contrary, they run away from you. I have braved all weathers, heat and cold, and I have caught neither cold nor fever.

Before I can explain exactly where I am, you must take the map of the great Mississippi Valley and look where the 35th degree of latitude intersects the river. There you will find this little town, this dozen of log cabins baptized by the sonorous name of Memphis. Up to the moment of the pur-chase of this Chickasaw land by Congress, this modern Memphis (as wretched perhaps as Memphis, the Ancient) was nothing but a station for the fur trade of the Indians. Now, it is becoming a river port and storehouse where the new settlers, scattered through the forests, can buy their small necessities or export their cotton. But even this small trade is principally with the Indians who have withdrawn them-selves since the sale, south of the line 35°. So you see they are our nearest neighbors.

If your map is good you will also find a little river called the Wolf, which flows into the Mississippi at this place. It is on the borders of this stream and about fifteen miles from here that I have actually bought 320 acres, am in negotiation for 320 more, and shall also take possession of 600 acres which surround my plot, when they come up for sale a few months from now, at nine cents the acre, to persons already landholders in this neighborhood.

My excellent fellow-countryman, Mr. Flower, has accom-panied me in all my journeying, aided me in the choice of this land, and now having established me comfortably enough in this place, has returned to his home in Illinois to bring back my family and his own, and all the necessary farm ma-terial, domestic animals, plows, food for the cattle, salt meat, grain, etc., until the moment when our new plantation shall begin to pay.

In view of the very moderate size of my fortune, [she re-marks, with a rare flash of Scotch prudence] and since I have to run all the risks of possible loss, if one proceeds too quickly, I am limiting myself to the sum of twelve thousand dollars which, with the help of Mr. Flower will suffice to establish a good plantation worked by six men and four women whom I am buying at Nashville for from four to five hundred dol-lars each.

Behold me, quite alone, with one good negress, in a suffi-ciently comfortable little cabin, waiting for my friends from Illinois and my negroes from Nashville. In the meantime I am over-seeing the construction of houses on my land with a well which furnishes very good water. All these small mat-ters keep me very busy, for there is nothing more difficult than to make men work in these forests. But with the help of the legs of a perfect horse, gentle as a lamb and full of fire, who knows and loves me, who eats salt from my hand, and who runs like a deer, I do forty miles a day going and com-ing, with no trouble, and as soon as I become accustomed to it without fatigue.

You are afraid of the climate, and I, too, I confess am not entirely reassured on that point. However, we have taken all the precautions which depend on ourselves by settling at a distance from the navigation of the Mississippi and choos-ing second-rate soil for our plantation so as to avoid the un-healthy miasma of the swamp lands. We have also laid down for ourselves a plan of life where temperance, exercise, and a due regard for the climate, too often neglected by American settlers, with, I hope eternal peace of mind, will have their usual beneficial results. Even I am beginning to find an unac-customed joy in life.

But this chapter on the promise of Nashoba is not complete with-out some mention of a new friend of Fanny's, closely connected with this enterprise, a leading citizen of Memphis and a little later to be-come its first mayor.

His name was Marcus Winchester, son of General James Winches-ter, a soldier of the American Revolution, whose interest in Indian lands had made him one of the three original owners of the town of Memphis with other holdings throughout the whole western part of Tennessee. Young Winchester was born in Tennessee, but had received an eastern education and served under his father through the inglorious campaigns along the Canadian border during the War of 1812. When Fanny arrived in Memphis he was already established there as the town's leading lawyer. Tall, black-haired, and very handsome, with a manner which impressed everyone with its mixture of bonhomie and dignity, he seemed assured of a brilliant future in the history of his state if it had not been for one tragic limitation.

He had married a woman of mixed blood, a beautiful French quadroon, the discarded mistress of Senator Benton, who after his election to the United States Senate, had decided that he could not continue this highly irregular relation without seriously jeopardizing his future career in the Senate and before the nation. The story goes that before Benton went to Washington, he put a sum of money into the hands of Marcus Winchester to provide for her immediate needs till she could find a new protector. It was while carrying out these instructions that Winchester became so sincerely and chivalrously attached to her that he made her his legal wife, though he had to marry her in New Orleans, the state of Tennessee forbidding legal union between whites and persons of color.

Her taint of negro blood effectually excluded her from respectable white society in Memphis and throughout the state, and their children born in Tennessee were accounted as illegitimate.

It was Fanny's first introduction to a situation only too common in the southern states before the Civil War. She never grew accustomed to it, never failed to regard it as an outrage to the free institutions of America, and as long as she and her sister continued to live in western Tennessee, Mary Winchester was one of their most loved and honored women friends.

CHAPTER II

Cross Currents

THE history of Fanny's brief and tragic experiment at Nashoba was preserved for many years in a thin leather-covered book of folio size, the so-called "Journal of the Plantation." Its first entry, October, 1825, in the handwriting of George Flower, tells of his own and Fanny's arrival in Memphis "in search of land." The second, records the purchase of the first 640 acres from the agents of General Jackson. Other entries in various handwritings carry the story down to the year 1829 when Nashoba ceased to be a going concern.

The comic element so rare in this desperate adventure is furnished by a note in Fanny's handwriting early in 1826 announcing the arrival of a gentleman from South Carolina, Mr. Robert Wilson, with a large family of female slaves, a pregnant mother, Lucky, and five small children, Maria, Elvira, Isabel, Viola, and Delilah.

Mr. Wilson had seen Fanny's pamphlet published in Lundy's *Genius of Universal Emancipation.* He had read the appended notice in which she had invited the co-operation of masters "desirous of emancipating their people, but who were hesitating because of the expenses attendant on the manumission." He had come 600 miles to take her at her word by donating mother and children to her new experiment.

He appeared with his slaves early in February, before the arrival of Flower and his party from Illinois, while the affairs of the plantation were still in a state of chaos. Neighboring planters looking at the group of female slaves declared they would never earn their keep. It is more than probable that they never had earned their keep with their old master.

Fanny, however, had no hesitation in accepting this gift of very doubtful value for the hope it held of increasing sympathy and co-operation from the class she was most anxious to convince and convert to her experiment.

She entered into a formal agreement with Mr. Wilson to take charge
of the family, feed them plentifully, treat them humanely, employ
them industriously, and communicate or cause to be communicated to
them the fundamental principles of education, with a knowledge of
such useful arts as might contribute to their happiness and comfort,
at the period of their hereinafter proposed liberation and colonization. The agreement further provided that the family, at the end of
fifteen years or sooner, dependent upon the extent to which their
labor repaid the advances actually made on them, should be colonized
either in Liberia, Haiti, or Mexico. This contract was made, signed,
and witnessed by Marcus Winchester, and Mr. Wilson went away
with $446.76 in payment for expenses incurred in transporting the
family of slaves from South Carolina.

The next event recorded in the Journal of the Plantation, was the
arrival of George Flower, his wife, their three children, and Camilla
Wright on the 27th of February, 1826. Their journey to Memphis from
Illinois had been delayed by an exceptionally bad season, frozen rivers,
dangerous floods which made navigation so difficult that the travelers
were at last obliged to finish their journey in a small caravan laden
with the supplies and provisions they were bringing to Nashoba, including agricultural tools and other material required for work upon
the plantation.

Two days later, the five male, and three female slaves already purchased in Nashville, also made their appearance at Nashoba.

Then came the gruelling task of bringing the uncleared, untilled
acres into cultivation in time to produce the necessary crops for the
autumn market. The climate was against them, almost continual rain-
fall during the early spring months, followed by steaming and ener-
vating heat. Flower's children fell ill. Camilla too, suffered intensely
from the inevitable discomforts and privations of life on a half-cleared
plantation. It was finally resolved to send her back to Albion with the
three Flower children, leaving the others to carry on as best they could
at Nashoba.

May found them with fifteen acres cleared for corn, two acres of
old ground, planted with cotton, and an apple orchard of five acres
fenced. Because of the late start, however, they could hardly expect
a very good crop of either corn or cotton, for that year at least.

May also found Fanny following her sister to Albion for a long visit.
The two sisters did not return to Nashoba until the end of June. They
were not really necessary for the actual business of the plantation.

George Flower supervised the field hands. Mr. Wilson's slaves, however inadequate, were able to save their mistress most of the more
irksome duties about the cabins. And they had lately added a third
partner to their enterprise, a Scotsman named Richardson. He was well
educated (he had studied medicine at Edinburgh) and was sufficiently
familiar with bookkeeping to look after the store and keep the accounts, which included the record of hours of labor of the slaves
working to pay for their freedom.

The greater part of this long absence, in Fanny's case at least,
was spent, not with the Flower family in Illinois, but across the state
line in Indiana, where Robert Owen's new colony at New Harmony
had become the talk of the whole western country, and was, in fact,
at the height of its first success.

Owen himself had returned after eight months' absence in Europe,
in the early spring of 1826, and brought with him a group of new
colonists so distinguished in their several ways, that newspaper re-
porters of that far distant period, had jokingly dubbed them, "The
Boatload of Knowledge." The most important of these was Owen's
new partner in his co-operative experiment, Mr. William Maclure,
who had finally been persuaded to purchase the whole northern half
of the village of New Harmony as the new site of his School of Industry already described in an earlier chapter. And with Maclure had
come a veritable flock of artists, teachers, and amateurs in the useful
sciences, who had found in him a generous patron and provider when
other sources of income became inadequate for their simple needs,
among whom the most notable were Gerard Troost, the chemist;
Charles Alexandre Lesueur, the botanist and explorer; Thomas Say,
who was later to become the greatest authority on shells and insect
life in America; and William Phiquepal D'Arusmont, who had already
served his patron more zealously perhaps than wisely as head master
of his private school in Paris as well as in the later establishment on
the banks of the Schuylkill.

Last but not least there was Madame Fretageot, accompanied by
a select number of young ladies, former pupils of her boarding school
near Philadelphia, who had been committed to her charge by their
parents and guardians in some mysterious confidence that the revolutionary system of education to be established in the wilderness would
fit them better for the new moral world they saw already emerging
on the horizon, than any of the old discredited forms and formulae

still in vogue in Europe and along the eastern seaboard of the United States.

There Fanny found her when she arrived in New Harmony that summer, in complete possession of one of the large boarding houses built by the Rappites in the northern half of the village, where she had established all the necessary paraphernalia of a fashionable boarding school for young ladies, and where her pupils could continue their studies including the piano, with intervals for such useful work as milking the cows of the community. She also assumed the direction of the infant division of the School of Industry, consisting of a hundred children between two and five years old. Besides this she seems to have found time to make William Maclure exceedingly comfortable in her own quarters at No. 2, while his own private house was building.

"Queen of the North!" So she had already been called by some of the lighter spirits of the community. From the first she professed the most profound respect and admiration for Frances Wright, always, however, with certain reserves which could easily turn her into a dangerous enemy if the younger woman showed any signs of encroaching on her own unique position in the affairs of William Maclure.

Fortunately, or perhaps unfortunately for Fanny, she was much too absorbed by her own personal reactions from this first long visit to New Harmony, to make any effort to guard against a potential enemy. The busy stirring life of the community had gone to her head like new wine. She was carried off her feet with admiration for the School of Industry which Phiquepal had set up in the old Rappite church building, with some sixty to ninety boys, to whom he taught all the lower branches of education, including mathematics.

The most characteristic feature of this school, however, in which for the first and only time in his life the eccentric little French physician was given a completely free hand, was a system of education which was becoming more and more the fashion among practical educators of that time, by which the directed labor of the pupils themselves could be made to produce not only enough to supply their daily needs but also to pay all the other expenses of their education. It was Phiquepal's boast in later days that during his brief period of authority in the schools of New Harmony he had so directed his pupils' "natural energies as to have produced in six weeks nearly $900 worth of value," but he confesses that he was greatly aided in his task by the enthusiastic co-operation of three young French boys, little fellows of from eleven to twelve years old, whom he had kept with him ever since the days of his private school in Paris.

One of these boys, Amadée Dufour, was a nephew of the Count of Beauséjour, seriously compromised with Lafayette in the *Carbonari* movement of 1822. Another was a Swiss boy named Falque. And there was also Alexis, whom Phiquepal had picked up as an *enfant trouvé* in one of the public baths of Paris, on whom he expended infinite pains as an object lesson of how much could be achieved by his own system of liberal practical education on the most unpromising material.

All reports agree that he was an excellent teacher. A strict disciplinarian drilling his boys in all their studies without the help of text books. And yet he was able to prepare them for examinations in medicine and surgery before the College of Surgeons in Paris. Not all his pupils loved him, however, if one may trust the stories of Madame Fretageot's son Achilles to his own son, Achilles the younger, and related by the latter to a younger generation.

"He treated all his pupils in a very unkind way. Not so much father because he feared father's mother. But even so, I have heard father say that he thought for many years that the first thing he had to do on the arrival of manhood was to kill his old tutor."

Nor was Phiquepal any more popular with the other colonists, and not without reason. He was vain, extremely sensitive about imagined slights, a true Gascon in his love of boasting about his former achievements and rather a bore in his insistence on the all-importance of his one absorbing interest. In appearance unprepossessing, his most salient feature was a jaw quite out of proportion with the rest of his face with a large ugly mouth. But his eyes redeemed the harshness of his other features, brilliant, very dark, and scintillating with intelligence, looking out at one with something distinctly childlike, kind, and eager in their expression under the shadow of thick untidy black brows. His hair had once been as black as his eyebrows but was now turning gray at the temples. On the whole, he lacked that quality best described by the word, nobility, and in spite of his undoubted devotion to the service of his fellow men along the lines he himself had chosen, or perhaps to a certain degree because of it, he was fundamentally disloyal and ungrateful in his personal attachments, ready at a moment's notice to desert a former patron for anyone who seemed more able to help him to his life's desire. Only the fortunate chance of the partnership of interests between Maclure to whom he was already indebted in a hundred ways, and Robert Owen, had kept him true to his contract with the former as director of the schools at New Harmony.

His chief claim for Fanny's interest during these days of their early acquaintanceship was his connection with the School of Industry, those workshops, where under his personal supervision, his pupils learned their various useful trades exactly on the lines she hoped some day to introduce on her own plantation.

She was also warmly attracted to William Maclure whom she had instantly recognized as one of those wise old men in whose society she especially delighted. But for her most intimate friends and companions during this first long visit to New Harmony she naturally turned to the group gathered round Robert Owen in the boarding-house in the southern half of the village, commonly known as No. 1.

Here as nowhere else, she could feel herself in a position to judge from personal observation just how the great Owenite scheme of a co-operative village was actually working out. Even her partial eye could perceive several serious weaknesses in its general structure.

The colonists had adopted a uniform not unlike that assumed by men and women in Shaker communities, a coat reaching to the knees over pantalets for the women, and white pantaloons buttoned up over collarless jackets for the men, which even Fanny's old enemy, the Duke of Saxe-Weimar, found "to have a good appearance." Fanny herself occasionally wore this uniform which was no doubt especially becoming to her tall slender figure.

According to a constitution drawn up by a committee chosen by the settlers shortly after the return of Robert Owen to New Harmony, and approved by Owen himself, each member of the association had an equal stake in the property, and also a vote in all matters concerning the general management of its affairs. When this system of democratic control became a source of endless confusion and delay in matters which needed immediate attention, the villagers themselves had appointed Owen their general manager with something of the same power over the activities of the community that had formerly belonged to George Rapp.

But Owen had none of the practical experience, to say nothing of those special advantages which had made Rapp so phenomenally successful in his management of the earlier community. He never had under his command a group of seasoned toilers, accustomed to a hard daily round of labor, which had responded so adequately to

Rapp's autocratic lead. On the contrary the large majority of the membership in Owen's community were far better fitted to discuss the principles involved in their undertaking than to do the hard manual work necessary to put these same principles into successful practice. The whole life and interest of Owen's experiment was concentrated in the constant informal discussions which went on continually among the various members of the community. Everything else, if not entirely neglected, was left to chance and the haphazard energies of unskilled and unaccustomed workers, with the natural result that New Harmony was to continue to function as a co-operative society as long as Robert Owen continued to pay the deficit between its expenses and its income, and no longer. But like so many other experiments in co-operative living, from Brook Farm down to the last nameless adventure in the same field today, it was a glorious experience while it lasted, for everyone even temporarily connected with it.

The man who was her closest friend and sympathizer during this enchanted period, and indeed for years to come, was the eldest son of the philanthropist, usually known as Robert Dale, to distinguish him from his more famous father. This youth, for he was at this time still a youth in experience of the world if not in age, and some six years Fanny's junior, was born in Glasgow, November 9th, 1801. He had received his early education in his father's school in New Lanark and through private tutors till the age of eighteen, when he went for four years to the progressive institution of Philipp Emanuel von Fellenberg at Hofwyl, Switzerland, becoming thus a school companion of Fanny's young cousin, James Milne. "Whatever might have been then the promise of his future," says she in a letter to young Milne written about this time, "I will engage to say he has more than fulfilled it. He is a young man of decided talents and substantial requirements with every amiable quality possessed by his father and with all the judgment which his father wants."

In general appearance he seems to have been very far from handsome, undersized, with small eyes, a nose not so big as his father's but quite as irregular, and a large loose-lipped mouth. In spite of all these personal disadvantages he was evidently a being of undoubted charm, radiating intelligence—a confirmed idealist.

He had been captivated by his father's glowing account "of those plans of social reform in the new world, and the condition of things and bright promise for the future at New Harmony," and he "embarked towards the end of September, 1825 from Liverpool in the packet 'New York,' exulting as an Israelite may have exulted when Moses spoke to him of the Land of Promise."

For a time at least, he was not disappointed. "There was something especially taking," he says in his later story of this adventure, "in the absolute freedom from trammels, alike in expression of opinion, in dress, and in social converse, which I found there. The evening gatherings, too, delighted me, the weekly meetings for the discussion of our principles, in which I took part at once, the weekly concerts with an excellent leader, Josiah Warren, and a performance of music, instrumental and vocal, much beyond what I had expected in the backwoods. Last but not least, the weekly ball, where I found crowds of young people, bright and genial, if not especially cultivated, and as passionately fond of dancing as in those days I was myself."

To this easy-going genial crowd of unsophisticated, not especially cultivated young people who composed the membership of this backwoods community, Frances Wright must have appeared as an apparition from an unknown world.

The impression she made on young Owen is evident in the somewhat regretful account he gives, as a man of seventy who has outlived and repented the follies of his youth, of "this new acquaintance, who mainly shaped, for several years, the course and tenor of my life. Highly educated, thoroughly versed in the literature of the day, well-informed on all general subjects, speaking both French and Italian fluently." A woman of the world, who had traveled widely and lived for years in Europe, an intimate friend of General Lafayette, "with a personal acquaintance of many leading reformers, Hungarians, Polish, and others. A thorough republican, indeed an advocate of universal suffrage without regard to color or sex, a creed more rare at that time than it is today. Refined in her manners and her language, and yet a radical in politics, morals, and religion."

He goes on to describe her personal appearance in most flattering terms.

A tall commanding figure, somewhat slender and graceful, though the shoulders were a little bit too high, a face the outline of which in profile, though delicately chiselled, was masculine rather than feminine, like that of an Antinöus, or perhaps more nearly typifying a Mercury, the forehead broad but not high, the short chestnut hair curling naturally all over the classic head, the large blue eyes not soft but clear and earnest. Her vigorous character, rare cultivation and hopeful enthusiasm gradually gave her great influence over me, and I recollect her telling me one day when I had expressed in the New Harmony *Gazette* with more than usual fearlessness, some radical opinions which she shared, that I was one of the few persons she had ever met with whom she felt that, in her reformatory efforts she could act in unison. Thus we became intimate friends.

But he goes on to explain with much earnestness, that he never was the least in love with her. "Friends, but never throughout all the years we spent together, anything more. I felt and acted toward her at all times just as I would towards a brave, spirited elder comrade of my own sex."

It was not till much later in this comradeship that he came to see her faults:

> . . . a mind which had not been submitted to early discipline, courage untempered by prudence, philanthropy which had too little of commonsense in it to give it practical form and efficiency, an enthusiasm eager but fitful, lacking the guiding check of sound judgment. An inordinate estimate of her own mental powers, an obstinate adherence to opinions once adopted, which detracted seriously from the influence which her talents and eloquence might have exerted. With ideas on many subjects, social and religious, even more extravagant and immature than my own.

And here one needs to be reminded that the New Harmony community was, while it lasted, not only an effort to prove the effectiveness of the Owenite theory of co-operative living, but a center for radical discussion of every kind where the utmost license was permitted to the expression of all sorts of heretical opinions about customs and institutions believed by the outside world to be the very bulwarks and foundations of society. The Christian churches and the institution of marriage were the favorite subjects of attack at these informal discussions, and Fanny, perhaps to her own surprise, soon found that she had full-grown and articulate opinions on both these subjects.

During her long intercourse with Lafayette in his struggle for the enfranchisement of subject peoples, she had learned to hate the Catholic Church as the arch enemy of liberal progress in Europe, and her prompt adoption of the recognized Owenite attitude of almost fanatical intolerance of every religious influence and movement of that day was only what might have been expected. But it was not till she arrived in New Harmony and found all the young people of the community fighting like cats and dogs over the rights and wrongs of marriage, that she assumed that unconventional position towards the whole institution which was to cause incalculable trouble in her future activities for social reform.

There is nothing to show that Fanny, at the time of this visit to New Harmony, had any wish or thought of marriage for herself. She had given herself body and soul to what she felt was a great cause, and as long as she remained single she could do exactly what she liked with her money, her time and herself. But she was not the kind of woman who needs the spur of personal grievance before she feels the sting of a humiliating situation. She grew to hate and fear the very idea of marriage, not for herself only but for any woman, "whose feelings and intellect have been cultivated by education and who in consequence, is best fitted to bring forth a healthy and intellectual race."

Two other members of the New Harmony community at this time deserve special mention from the importance of their place in Fanny's story. The one, a thickset, grim little man named Robert Jennings who had started his career as a Unitarian minister and still liked to preach secular sermons in the old frame church which had been put to very different uses during the Rapp ascendancy. Tradition has it that on these occasions his favorite dress was a striped collarless jacket and striped cotton trousers. He was also on the editing staff of the New Harmony *Gazette* where his contributions showed a hardheaded vigorous intelligence and an admirable capacity for controversial writing.

He had had a constantly thwarted longing to be a successful school teacher, which made him particularly willing to listen to Fanny's ambitious plans for her own school at Nashoba. He also had a wife and family somewhere in the East and was in continual difficulties about finding money to support them in the world of competition.

The other, Richeson Whitby, was a kindhearted, unpretentious young Quaker with a good uncultivated mind and more than a touch of mild fanaticism in his wholehearted acceptance of the Owenite philosophy. His early experience as overseer in a Shaker community had not prepared him to meet two such young women as Fanny and

Camilla Wright, on anything like equal terms. He immediately conceived for them both an unbounded respect and admiration, though his natural timidity made him turn for sympathy and understanding to the younger, less brilliant sister.

The visit to New Harmony lasted till the end of June when both sisters returned to Nashoba to carry on their formidable task of raising a paying crop on those half-cleared acres of Fanny's plantation.

The summer of 1826 was remarkable throughout the whole state of Tennessee for an outbreak of dengue fever, a disease common to tropical and malarial countries and characterized by high temperature alternating with extreme debility, accompanied by agonizing pain from which it derived its more colloquial name, breakbone fever. Confident in her own power to resist infection, Fanny seems to have exposed herself with the utmost rashness, on horseback under the midday suns of July and August, sometimes even sleeping in the forest at night. She had barely escaped a sunstroke. She did not escape a fever which affected her brain and kept her prostrate for the rest of the summer and autumn.

One cannot exaggerate the discomfort as well as the actual physical suffering inevitable in an illness like hers under the existing conditions at Nashoba; the heat, the swarms of stinging insects, the lack of cooling drinks, the roughness and inadequacy of a sickroom in a hastily built log cabin, with no outlook but the half-cleared forest and those two little squares of corn and cotton fields which a bare six months' desperate labor had been able to retrieve from the wilderness! No nurse at hand but her devoted and terrified sister Camilla. No doctor but the ex-medical student and storekeeper, James Richardson.

George Flower had already blenched and fled from the impossible task of bringing order and prosperity to the plantation in existing conditions. Sometime in October of the preceding year, during one of Fanny's recurring periods of semi-convalescence he and his family left Nashoba and went back to Illinois never to return. His place as overseer and general manager of the plantation was taken by the young Shaker, Richeson Whitby, whom Fanny had learned to know during her recent visit to New Harmony; but his heart seems to have remained faithful to the desperate little group he left behind him, if one may judge from the following passage in a letter written to them soon after his departure. He longs for a cosy chat quite alone with those who thought and felt as he did.

Just to hear the sound of your voices and see the lines of
your countenances whilst you are talking to me! So one comes
to the heart of the matter and really begins to understand
those remote, those secret springs of action as they are sometimes called. That is the real pleasure. Then we feel an assurance that we have a glimmering of the truth which words
plainly printed and messages conveyed second hand, can
never give. In this age of mental reservation, the whole and
entire truth I do not expect even from the mouth of a friend
in broad daylight. But in silence, in secret and in twilight, in
soft suppressed accents it is sometimes uttered.

Anyone who could write such a letter may not be lightly dismissed
as a weakminded quitter. In actual fact George Flower remained a
faithful friend to the Nashoba experiment as long as it existed, in the
capacity of one of the ten trustees whom Fanny chose to carry on
her work in case of her own death, a possibility which several times
in the course of her long illness seemed more than likely.

This deed of trust which tied up her property for a number of
years to come, for she did everything in her power to make it a legal
instrument, was the final expression of two independent ideas which
had been struggling for existence ever since that long visit to New
Harmony the previous summer. It still recognizes Fanny's original
plan for a model plantation where slaves under a system of co-
operative labor could buy their way to freedom, "without danger or
loss to the citizens of the South." It makes special provision for the
emancipation of the slaves then in residence on the plantation as soon
as each shall have paid to the institution of Nashoba a clear capital
of $6000 with 6 per cent interest from January 1st, 1827, plus a sum
sufficient to defray the expenses of colonization. It makes special mention of the slave family of Robert Wilson whom Fanny never considered as her own property, but a trust conferred on her by their
master. It makes a special point of a school for colored children, in
which these shall receive an education in no way different from that
of white children.

But by far the greater part of the deed is taken up with arrangements for a white co-operative community superimposed upon her
original plan of negro emancipation, a glorified New Harmony with
all the virtues and none of the disadvantages of Robert Owen's co-
operative experiment; where all the hard manual labor was to be done
by the slaves, leaving the whites free to enjoy the delights of rational

intercourse between sympathetic souls, interspersed with only the kind of occupations for which they were normally fitted; a sort of Garden of Epicurus as she had once imagined it in *A Few Days in Athens*, without, however, that serene indifference to the ignorance and misery existent in the world outside, so characteristic of classic philosophy.

In fact the new Nashoba, as Fanny conceived it, was to be a place where she and those in sympathy with her could unite in a campaign of education against those forms of human evil which had their roots in ignorance, prejudice, false methods of thinking, too often encouraged and persisted in by those whose interest it was to keep whole classes of men and all women helplessly and hopelessly enslaved.

Either one of these proposed experiments alone would have been sufficient to ruin her, the first in health and fortune, the other in the good opinion of the sober middle class to which she belonged by birth and education. Both combined were to produce a crash so complete, so reverberating, in its effect upon all her subsequent relations with society, that it may almost be said to divide her life into two mutually exclusive parts.

It is possible that the whole fabric of the deed of trust, so fantastic in its plan, so diffuse in its objects, would have fallen gradually to the ground by its own weight and been safely forgotten if it had not been for a series of accidents resulting from her long and slow recovery and her absence from the plantation at a moment of particular crisis.

A letter from Camilla to Lafayette describing the serious illness of his dear adopted daughter, brought the following affectionate reply:

What news I have received from you, my dear children! I bless you a thousand times for your care to reassure me in my anxiety. Nevertheless, my heart is still overcome by a weight of anguish and terror which cannot be relieved as long as you are both so far away from me, on a plantation freshly cleared, which everyone knows is unhealthy. But though reassured of your recovery by Camilla's letter, with the touching postscript in the still feeble hand of my adored Fanny, it is an inexpressible torment to me not to see a conclusion to your philanthropic adventure, a date for our reunion which each of your letters seems to put further and further into the future . . . How glad I would be to know that you were in Washington, for instance, spreading your benevolent ideas to

those friends of yours who are always so glad to listen to you;
or anywhere, in fact, except in a position where your method
of life makes all your friends tremble for your preservation.
I am glad to know that my water coolers have finally arrived
and that my dear children are now drinking purer water,
and that they think of me at every sip they take of this simple beverage. How happy I would be to talk to them in my
writing room at La Grange where the slightest signal was
once enough to evoke their delicious presence.

The letter ends with messages from Fanny's friends, "the good Mrs.
Trollope," who had just been paying them a visit at La Grange, the
Garnetts, Madame Dupont de Nemours, the Constants, the Lasteyries.
He speaks of affairs which had been matters of common interest between him and his beloved children. Governor Coles' defeat for re-
election at the polls in November. A letter he has received from
Senator Fitzhugh of Virginia, with a new plan for the emancipation
and colonization of the slaves. An interview with the representative
of General Boyer, president of the negro republic of Haiti. His own
regret, very gently expressed, that Fanny herself, as a result, perhaps,
of being continually face to face with this stain on free American
institutions, had lost that former tolerant attitude towards the slave-
owner, so noticeable in her first book on America. This change of tone,
he confesses, "is not the least of the pains and anxieties of your paternal friend, who has received too many evidences of affection from
this class not to be deeply attached to them." He asks news about
George Flower. "You don't talk about him any more. Is he permanently
settled near you with his family, or has he gone back to Illinois? They
say that Maclure and Owen have broken their partnership."

The rumor of a break between Owen and Maclure with which
Lafayette concludes his letter was only too true. The serious quarrel
between the two partners did indeed stop just short of a lawsuit, but
nothing could save Owen's experiment from going on the rocks. The
village of New Harmony ceased to be a co-operative community in
the spring of 1827 when its founder, having expended upwards of
$200,000 in the purchase of the Harmony property, and the debts of
the community during the year of its existence, finally withdrew his
financial support of the undertaking.

From this time forth the inhabitants of the village had either to
support themselves by their own labor or leave the town. All those
who had come there in the first place to get something for nothing,

the speculators, the adventurers, the idlers and scoundrels, departed one after another for other fields. But many honest and industrious workers were glad to accept Owen's generous offers to lease them farms and houses in New Harmony at a very low rate. Their descendants are found today, among the more useful and honorable inhabitants of that little village. The Maclure-Fretageot establishment, with the School of Industry, continued to carry on, undisturbed by the changes going on about them.

Owen himself was leaving as soon as possible for England, called there by important business which required his immediate attention, and Robert Dale was preparing to accompany his father when Fanny, taking advantage of some slight improvement in her health, appeared again on the scene, full of hopes and promises for her untried experiment of a white co-operative community at Nashoba.

By her deed of trust she had placed all her lands in Tennessee in the hands of a board of ten trustees, three of whom must be resident on the plantation.

No list of her own choosing could be complete without the presence of her beloved, her honored friend, General Lafayette, and so confident was she of his sympathy and mutual understanding on any matter concerning the improvement of the human race, that she did not think it necessary to wait for his formal acceptance of this honor before she published his name among the other members of her new board.

She made a serious mistake, however, in taking the same liberty with Cadwallader Colden, ex-mayor of New York, a most conservative and venerable old gentleman, who first knew of the use she had made of his name after the events which made his published signature to such a document something of a scandal for his friends and family.

The other names on the list were Robert Owen the elder, William Maclure, George Flower, James Richardson, Richeson Whitby, Fanny herself, her sister Camilla, and last but not least the eldest son of Robert Owen, Robert Dale. This youth still in his early twenties, flattered at finding himself included in the list of important personages composing her first board of trustees, fascinated by her dominating personality, easily let himself be persuaded to cast his lot in with her. To quote his own words in later autobiographical writing:

> Assenting to these views, I accepted the trusteeship, and when in the spring of 1827, New Harmony had ceased to be

a community, I agreed to accompany Miss Wright on a visit
to Nashoba, hoping there to find more cultivated and congenial associates than those among whom for the last eighteen
months past I had been living.

Thus began that long pursuit of radical and often wildly imprac-
ticable schemes for social and political reform, which Robert Dale
Owen, in later life, was wont, rather ruefully, to call his "Earnest
Sowing of Wild Oats." It began, it would seem, not very propitiously,
if one may judge from his own narrative written many years later.

Miss Wright's health, which had been feeble at New Harmony, became so much worse ere we reached Memphis that
she had to be conveyed from that town to Nashoba in a ham-
mock swung in a covered wagon.

At Nashoba I found but three trustees, Richeson Whitby,
James Richardson, and the younger Miss Wright. We consulted daily, but even sanguine I had to admit that the outlook was unpromising. The land was all second-rate only, and
scarce a hundred acres of it cleared. Three or four squared
log houses and a few small cabins for the slaves the only
buildings. Slaves released from the fear of the lash worked
indolently under the management of Whitby, whose education in an easy-going Shaker village had not at all fitted him
for the post of plantation overseer. These were the main
facts, to which was to be added the state of Miss Wright's
health. . . . Richardson informed me that during the preceding year, intent on organizing her institution, she had rashly
exposed herself on horseback during the midday suns of July
and August, sometimes even sleeping in the forest at night.
She had barely escaped a sunstroke, and had not escaped a
brain fever which prostrated her for weeks and almost baffled
his skill and her sister's unremitting care. Fearing its return,
he earnestly recommended a sea voyage and a residence during the ensuing summer in Europe. Thereupon Whitby declared that if both sisters left Nashoba he despaired of being
able to manage the slaves. They would obey either, as their
owner and mistress, and himself only when he had their authority to back his orders.

Discouraging enough, certainly! But I was then much in
the state of mind in which more than thirty years before
Southey and Coleridge may have been when they resolved to
found amid the wilds of the Susquehanna a pantisocracy free

from worldly evils and turmoils and cares, from which individual property was to be excluded. So I adhered to my resolution. Frances Wright encouraging me to hope that in Paris
and London we might find congenial associates "for membership in the community."

The ten days of Owen's visit were duly recorded in the Journal
of the Plantation in the legible and uncompromising commercial handwriting of James Richardson, one of the three resident trustees who
were expected to carry on during Fanny's visit to Europe. The others
were Camilla Wright and Richeson Whitby. Fanny herself had already instituted weekly meetings with her slaves, a series of moral
lectures interspersed with explanations of the principles underlying
her experiment in co-operative emancipation, and intended to develop their sense of individual responsibility.

Monday evening, May 7, 1827
Did not meet the slaves yesterday evening owing to the indisposition of Frances Wright.
Met them this evening. Frances Wright endeavored to explain to them the powers with which she had invested the
trustees, her reason for investing them with this power, and
the resolutions which the trustees passed.
Dilly and Redrick were reprimanded for interchanging
abusive language, instead of laying their respective com-
plaints before us.
Willis was made to retract the threat which he had uttered
of avenging with his own hands the wrongs of Dilly.
Kitty was reprimanded for washing and receiving pay for
washing the clothes of Mr. Roe instead of carrying them to
Sukey, the washerwoman. She was also made to return the
twenty-five cents to Mr. R.

Sunday evening, May 13, 1827
Met the slaves. Frances Wright informed them of her intention to depart tomorrow on a visit to Europe for the benefit of her health.
Robert Dale Owen called their attention to the difference
between our mode of management and that to which they
had been previously accustomed, and pointed out to them
the direct and uniform bearing which our regulations had
on their happiness.

The next day Frances and Robert Dale Owen departed together for Europe. Their adventures by the way are amusingly reported in two pleasant wordy letters from Robert Dale to Camilla, the only white woman left on the plantation. "Your sister's cloak and shawl were left by mistake, on stepping on board the steam boat, at Memphis. The pillow, too, was left at Mr. John Lawrence's."

There was a tiresome delay of several days which they spent at Madame Herrie's boarding house in New Orleans waiting for a "tow-steam boat" to take the vessel on which they had engaged passage for Europe down the river.

> The weather, as you may suppose, is very hot, at least according to my Northern feelings, though the Creoles here pronounce it to be just comfortable. Mosquitoes we have, but I cannot say they plague me much. It is true they are somewhat annoying in the beautiful cool evenings when we sit out on the balconies to breathe the fresh air.
>
> Your sister, not entirely without fever for twenty-four hours, is yet stronger and better than since New Harmony.

> Since I last wrote to you [two days since] she has seen several persons of color, most of them tradespeople, introduced by Hyacinth Cimon, and apparently respectable quiet men. There is great excitement among them regarding Nashoba and they listened to the details your sister gave them with the deepest interest. Mathile has been here twice, the second time she said, "Je ne peux jamais être heureuse qu'è Nashoba," and accordingly she has spoken to her friend who has promised, she says, to take her up to Nashoba himself, next time he visits Orleans which I suppose will be next year. He is to see your sister today and she says she will express most unreservedly all our principles, that he may not take a single step in the dark. Your sister was especially pleased with Hyacinth Cimon who brought all his friends to see her.

Nothing shows so clearly how far Fanny had drifted from her first attitude towards negro emancipation than this effort of hers as described in Owen's letter to get in touch with the free black population of New Orleans.

There was a large class of free people of color in that old French city living a life apart, and yet in many ways permitted to share in the life and business of the town, within sharply recognized limitations of course. Many of these persons were of mixed blood, well-educated and intelligent, the women especially noted for their beauty, gentleness, and fidelity, qualities which made them particularly acceptable in those unlegalized unions not uncommon among young men of the best New Orleans families, before marriage.

In their old quarter round Congo Square they added to the life and gaiety of the city. But to receive someone of this class, on terms of absolute equality, as Fanny had just received Hyacinth Cimon and his friends, to invite their interest, their co-operation even, in her new liberal community, was to strike a deadly blow against the whole social system of the South, founded as it was on the principle of white supremacy. It was bound to make a host of dangerous and powerful enemies and ill-wishers among the very classes whose support Fanny herself had been most anxious to win for her new undertaking.

It may be that Fanny did not realize the strength of the forces arrayed against her when she so confidently included the abolition, not only of slavery but of the slave complex in whites and blacks alike, among the reforms projected for her new liberal community.

During her short stay in New Orleans she engaged a certain Mam'selle Lolotte, a free colored woman of mixed blood with a family of nearly white children to come to Nashoba as teacher in that infant school, always so earnestly desired but not even yet established on the plantation. The eldest daughter, Josephine, was to be entered as a probationer in the new community.

Among other matters of casual interest in Owen's letter one finds mention of a parcel containing an umbrella for Lolotte, and a bottle of lime juice for the refreshment of those left on the plantation. From that he goes on to other of Fanny's activities during this visit to New Orleans. "She has arranged to give Camilla power of attorney during her absence, written to Charles Wilkes for $2000 for Nashoba, and cleared her account with Dick, Rooker & Co. Dick has been politeness itself. His interest in the new establishment is at least as great as a man of business and the world can take in anything he does not understand, and with which, therefore, he does not sympathize."

And here follows a lively account of their departure on the sailing vessel on which they had taken their passage to France.

Thursday morning, 6 o'clock, May 30th. Off Balize.
I am sitting, my dear friends, on the deck of the *New England*, where everything is as yet in confusion, my table, a

small box of lemons which we took with us to make lemon-
ade, surrounded by sailors, passengers, and Indians, almost
deafened by the continuous rushing of steam from the pipes
of a steam boat which is alongside and about to tow us over
the bar.

We got on board last evening about 5. Your sister had, unfortunately, a slight attack of fever that very morning after
being free of it for some days. However, after being on board
a short time she found herself much better.

The Scotch woman she has engaged to go with her, will,
I think, be a great comfort to her during the voyage. She is
a cheerful, active, pleasant sort of woman with a strong High-
land accent, as if she had just left her native mountains. The
Captain is even more than usually attentive. I think we are
very fortunate in getting off in such a vessel. Much more
pleasant and convenient than going first to New York.

There are six Osage Indians among the passengers. They
are lying now on the roof of the companionway where I am
sitting. Their dark, solemn-looking faces fantastically ornamented. As we set out they commenced singing hymns to
the Great Spirit, for the success of our voyage.

At this point, Robert Dale, having no doubt a great deal of time
on his hands proceeds to moralize on the falsely placed admiration of savages, characteristic of the school of Rousseau, in the midst
of which he is interrupted by "the Captain, who comes to take the
helm close to which I had pitched my table."

They were off at last. The letter was resumed at four o'clock that
same afternoon.

Aground on the Bar [and there they remained for six days]
leading a most stagnant life. Amid swarms of mousquitoes,
which we endeavored to smoke out of our cabin last night,
without effect. Not even a breeze. The Indians lie stretched
on the roof of the companionway. The other passengers lie
in different nooks of the ship smoking cigars, coats and waist-
coats off. Your sister lies in the cabin, Mrs. Macintire sitting
beside her with a large ornamental Mexican fan which her
friend Miss Carroll presented her before she left New Orleans . . . or under an open tent which the Captain has just
erected on deck for her. If he were her brother he could not
be more kind and attentive. Besides the whiteskins, redskins
and blackskins on the vessel, we have on board two goats,

two pigs, two sheep, two alligators, without mentioning a colony of chickens, ducks, and turkeys.

This morning, June 6th. I was interrupted in this letter by the arrival of an unwelcome visitor, a great friend of yours, my dear Camilla. In plain English I had a chill and after it, as the Americans say, a smart fever. This I attribute to our residence here in the neighborhood of so many swamps and marshes.

Your sister still continues to have chills and fever more or less every other day. This will disappear when we get off now in about an hour.

This was the last word which the three resident trustees were to receive from the travelers for many months to come. But when Robert Dale mentioned this voyage in his later writings it would seem that he had been too sanguine in his hopes for a speedy recovery for his traveling companion. "I had fears for her life till we finally got out to sea," he relates. "But after that, she gradually gathered strength and when I left her in Paris with intimate friends (the Garnetts), her health was in a measure restored."

From Paris she went to La Grange to resume that pleasant petted existence which had been so abruptly interrupted by her departure to America. Now, surrounded by old friends and old associations, it was Nashoba which had become the dream, far away, and out of reach, and life in Europe the reality. Two months must pass before she could receive a word to tell her what was happening on her plantation in her absence, and two more months before those she had left in charge could receive her reply. She had every confidence in the three people she had left behind her to carry on her policy in her absence: her sister, Richeson Whitby, and a man on whom she depended more than either of the others, for his tried integrity and intelligence in past emergency, the doctor and storekeeper of the plantation, James Richardson.

Hitherto, she had been extremely fortunate in the objects of those sudden outgoing friendships, men or women whom she thought she recognized as kindred souls, and to whom she turned for special sympathy and understanding at various crucial moments of her life. Sooner or later they were bound to disappoint her. They had always brought her far more good than harm, until she met James Richardson. There was much to draw these two together by a sort of natural affinity. They were both Scots with the same passion for metaphysical argument and hairsplitting definitions so often found in members of that race. They both were in revolt against the peculiar prejudices and convictions and points of view which had dominated and warped their free and happy development when children. They both had long ago cast to the winds any belief in orthodox Christianity, though both were still willing to admit that a belief in God's existence might be "friendly to the morals and happiness of its dupes."

But there was a blackness in Richardson's pessimism, a rancor in his hatred of human shams and weaknesses and folly, a streak of cruelty and sensuality which emerged out of the depths of his nature from time to time in strange unaccountable ways. He had a capacity for doing harm even to those persons to whom he was most pledged to do good, which put him in a class by himself among Fanny's kindred spirits. Fanny herself never suspected this trait. If she had, how could she ever have left her slaves, her sister, her beloved experiment at Nashoba so entirely in his power? One need but turn to the Journal of the Plantation for the disastrous results of this misplaced confidence. For some unexplained reason the overseer, Richeson Whitby, left the plantation almost immediately after Fanny's departure, for a visit of some two months to his family in Ohio.

At the same time a new and dangerous element was introduced to the life of the community by Fanny herself, in the arrival from New Orleans of Mam'selle Lolotte, the free colored woman and her family including the young and attractive girl of marriageable age, named Josephine. The first entry in the Journal in Richardson's handwriting after Whitby's departure:

Sunday evening, May 20

Met the slaves. Camilla Wright repeated to them how the work was to proceed in Mr. Whitby's absence. She also informed them that tomorrow morning the children, Delia, Lucy, Julia, and Alfred, will be taken altogether from under the management of their parents, and will be placed until our school is organized under the management of Mam'selle Lolotte. That all communication between the parents and children shall in future be prevented except such as may take place by the permission and in the presence of the manager of the children. That Violet, one of Dilly's children, should be placed especially under the management of Josephine, the daughter of Mam'selle Lolotte.

May 24th. Two women slaves tied up and flogged by James

Richardson in the presence of Camilla and all the slaves.
Two dozen and one dozen on bare back with a cowskin.

Saturday evening, May 26, 1827

Agreed that the slaves shall not be allowed to receive
money, clothing, food, or indeed anything whatever from any
person resident at, or visiting this place whether trustee, co-
adjutor, probationer, or stranger. And that any article so received shall be returned to the giver in the presence of the
slaves and of the trustees. If the giver is absent, the article
shall be destroyed by the receiver, in the presence of the
trustees and of the slaves.

Agreed that the slaves shall not be permitted to eat elsewhere than at the public meals, excepting in such sickness
as may render confinement to their cabins necessary.

Sunday evening, May 27th.

Met the slaves, informed them of the regulations agreed to
yesterday evening. Dilly, having given utterance, a day or
two ago to some grumbling at having so many mistresses,
James Richardson stated to them that it is very true they have
many mistresses as well as many masters, and that in all
probability they will have more of both as every free person
who shall reside here, whether black, white or brown, will
be, in some sort, their master or their mistress; that this is just
the difference between a free person and a slave, and that
they can get rid of these masters and mistresses in no other
way than by working out their freedom, when they will be
transformed into masters and mistresses themselves. But that
in the meantime they will gradually find out that this multi-
plicity of superiors, so far from being a hardship, is of palpa-
ble advantage to them in preventing them from being at the
mercy of the temper of any one individual and in rendering
the concurrence of at least a majority of the resident trustees
an indispensable preliminary to the inflicting of even the
slightest possible punishment for the greatest possible offense.

30th May. Reprimanded Willis for having tried to interfere
between Lolotte and one of his children, and Dilly for having given bread and meat to one of her children sent to her
kitchen by Lolotte.

Friday, June 1st, 1827

Met the slaves at dinner time. Isabel had laid a complaint
against Redrick for coming during the night of Wednesday

to her bedroom uninvited, and endeavoring without her consent, to take liberties with her person. Our views of the sexual relation had been repeatedly given to the slaves. Camilla Wright again stated it, and informed the slaves that, as the conduct of Redrick, which he did not deny, was a gross infringement of that view, a repetition of such conduct, by him, or by any other of the men, ought in her opinion to be punished by flogging. She repeated that we consider the proper basis of the sexual intercourse to be the unconstrained and unrestrained choice of both parties, Nellie having requested a lock for the door of the room in which she and Isabel sleep, with the view of preventing the future uninvited entrance of any man. The lock was refused as being in its proposed use inconsistent with the doctrine just explained. A doctrine which we are determined to enforce, and which will give to every woman a much greater security than any lock possibly could do.

Maria tried to hang herself for jealousy of Henry which we would not support her in.

Sunday evening, June 3, 1827

Met the slaves—Willis having, a few days ago, complained to Camilla Wright of Mam'selle Lolotte's children beating his children; thinking it was allowed because hers are a little the fairest. James Richardson took this opportunity of endeavoring to explain to the slaves, our views on the subject of color. He told them that, in our estimation, all colors are equal in rank, and that whatever distinctions may be established on this place, color shall form the basis of none of them.

Sunday evening, June 10, 1827

Met the slaves—Stated to them that, as some of them have on two occasions broken the swing, by using it in a riotous manner [on a Thursday night when the two trustees had ridden into Memphis and were therefore absent from the plantation] they cannot be allowed to partake with us of any such amusement, until their habits shall become more refined than at present.

Wednesday, June 13, 1827

Willis having reported to us that Henry declined coultering [plowing] today, on the plea of pain in his knee joint, to which he is subject—we met the slaves at breakfast time, and told them that, though we did not doubt that Henry's knee gave him more or less pain, we had not sufficient confidence in his veracity to trust in his statement regarding the degree of ailment; that we would, therefore, take their votes respecting the capacity of Henry to follow the oxen today. From this vote we stated that we would exclude Willis, because he now acts as director of their work, and Maria, because she now cohabits with Henry. There were 10 votes, 5 each way. We gave our opinion as the casting vote, in support of Henry's capacity to coulter [plow]. He was therefore ordered to attend to it.

Sunday evening, June 17, 1827

Met the slaves—James Richardson informed them that, last night, Mam'selle Josephine and he began to live together, and he took this occasion of repeating to them our views on color and on the sexual relation.

If one omits the last item of this narration, one gets a not unfair example of the practical working of Fanny's grand scheme for the education of her negroes as a preparation for the responsibilities and obligations of free people. In many ways the process had a fantastic resemblance to some modern educational methods of rearing backward children, or, as in this case, of educating members of a backward race, to create in them some sense of moral responsibility and self-control by the trial and error method.

It must be admitted, however, that an experiment of this sort with its appeal to an equality of moral responsibility, an equality of ethical standards for white and black, owners and slaves, teachers and taught, undertaken on a southern plantation in the state of public feeling towards anything like negro equality, prevalent in the South of that day, needed to be handled with the utmost delicacy and discretion to have any chance of success.

A free union of two persons without marriage! Sexual relations between a white man and a colored woman, on exactly the same terms of free choice and mutual inclination which might be expected among whites! Miscegenation with all those dire consequences so widely predicted by those who believed that only the worst features of the two races are preserved by intermixture!

All these things were implied, if not openly proclaimed in the Journal of the Plantation during Richardson's term of office. To do

him justice, he was quite prepared to defend his attitude towards this
difficult situation with all the strength of his uncompromisingly logical
mind. He genuinely believed that only willful blindness or the basest
hypocrisy prevented southern society from admitting that the intermixture of the two races was going on in spite of all efforts to conceal it. He knew too much about the relations between southern slave-
owners and their female slaves to have any respect for their fine
theories about the purity of the white race.

He found nothing to be ashamed of in the record of Nashoba. On
the contrary he was ready and eager to give it the widest publicity
on the first opportunity that presented itself. He himself prepared an
article for Lundy's *Genius of Universal Emancipation*, which included
the entire record of the Nashoba Journal beginning with May 7th and
13th, the dates of Fanny's last interview with her slaves before her
departure for Europe, through June 17th, the date of his announcement of his intentions towards the young quadroon girl, Josephine.
The whole article, just as he wrote it, appeared in an August issue
of Lundy's paper, during the absence of the editor, one may remark
in passing.

The dismay and horror aroused among the subscribers to this paper
by Richardson's article may be inferred from the following letter
which appeared in the next issue under the pseudonym of "Mentor."

Philadelphia, August 8, 1827:
Mr. Lundy: No one possessed of moral or religious feelings,
can read without horror the publication in your last paper,
of the proceedings of what is termed Frances Wright's Establishment, at a place called Nashoba—a publication which
appears to have taken place by the desire of one of the trustees! . . . Are these records true? Have such principles been
adopted? Is it possible that an accomplished Englishwoman
(for such Miss C. W. is known to be) could publicly declare
to the slaves that the proper basis of sexual intercourse was
the unconstrained, and unrestrained choice of both parties?—
that a lock to a chamber door, requested by a female slave,
was refused, because it was inconsistent with the doctrine
just explained? Is it possible that one of the trustees could
shamelessly announce that he and one of the colored females
had "last night began to live together," and this flagitiousness,
announced to the community on Sunday evening, be solemnly
entered on their records? What is all this but the creation of

one great brothel, disgraceful to its institutors, and most rep-
rehensible, as a public example, in the vicinity?

MENTOR

Richardson's reply to this attack of "Mentor" did not make matters
any better.

Mr. Lundy: I have read the strictures of Mentor with your
remark that it would be both just and polite for me to reply.

You say you would fain hope that the state of things at
Nashoba is not as bad as Mentor supposes. I beg to inform
you that the state of things at Nashoba is neither better nor
worse than it is represented to be in the published records.
They are correct.

Mentor applies to us the epithet "libidinous." As applied
to me, I object not to its meaning. I possess the feeling which
it designates in common with every other complete adult animal. But the woman has never lived whom I have wronged
in its gratification. Neither am I conscious of so extravagant
a propensity to change, as Mentor seems to think must result
from an abrogation of the legal tie. Does Mentor actually
believe that when such a propensity does exist, the legal tie
ever prevents its indulgence? Mentor thinks we are instituting
a Brothel. I have seen a brothel and I never knew a place so
unlike it as Nashoba.

The letter concludes with a tirade against the Christian religion
as the chief cause of sexual immorality as a result of ridiculous taboos.
This statement could hardly have improved his standing with the religious readers of Lundy's newspaper. "For my part," he declares, "I am
an Atheist, and on the diffusion of Atheism rests my only hope of the
progress of Universal Emancipation."

Richardson apparently suffered little or nothing from his indiscre-
tion. The first, and indeed one may say the chief victim of the whole
incident was the unfortunate Camilla.

One of the persons who read Richardson's article with horror was
Mr. Charles Wilkes, president of the Bank of New York, and self-
constituted friend and protector of the sisters ever since their first
arrival in New York. This gentleman lost no time in writing a letter
to Camilla demanding rather than requesting further elucidation of
an incident which he could only hope was exaggerated.

"Nothing," says he, "but the sincere friendship I feel for you and your sister could induce me to write this letter, etc., etc."

Entirely devoted to her sister, without a grain of Fanny's saving gift of common sense, deeply grateful to Richardson who had stood by her staunchly in circumstances of peculiar difficulty, Camilla made the fatal mistake of answering this letter in a way which severed this old and useful friendship forever. She loyally defended the conduct of her friend, Mr. Richardson, "in forming a connexion in the manner described in the record which so far from exciting the reprobation of any individual here has their entire sanction and approval." She even went so far as to advance what she confidently asserted were Fanny's own views on the sexual relation, which she was only prevented by the state of her health from giving to the world before her departure for Europe.

Thus Camilla closed the door to the safe conventional world in which she was born and brought up. She ends her letter with a note of defiance most unlike the gentle being those who knew her best, had always considered her.

> So far from wishing any concealment in this matter, I request you to communicate the contents of this letter to all friends who are likely to be interested. I send by this same post a copy of your letter and my answer to the Garnetts, with the request that they will communicate them to General Lafayette and others of my European friends.

The first news of the incident came to Fanny in an outraged letter from her uncle, Professor Milne, of Glasgow, for Charles Wilkes had not waited for Camilla's permission to inform her European friends of the extraordinary state of things at Nashoba. Several days of agonizing suspense had to pass before the slow march of the southern mails brought Camilla's version of the affair.

None of the correspondence between the sisters in this crisis of their lives has been preserved, but a long letter from Fanny to Richardson furnishes an interesting light on her own reactions at the time.

> La Grange Aug. 18, 1827
> The letters of Camilla have lifted a load from my heart, restored me to quiet sleep and so decided my convalescence that Julia, now strikes me off the list of patients. But notwithstanding my restlessness is calmed for the present I am

little disposed to lengthen the term of our separation. Unless something unforeseen should arise I shall return to you the coming winter. December or January are fine months for a southern trip and if I can find a good vessel at that season, bound for Orleans, a voyage across the Atlantic in the warm latitudes will be equally favourable to my health with a journey in the Southern Alps. . . .

The curiosity which your communication to Lundy's paper has awakened respecting us is highly valuable. It may be made subservient to the progress of Truth and Higher happiness, but it increases our responsibility to the principles we have embraced and which, life granted to us, with patience, perseverance, and good temper, may widen the circle of our utility beyond the country of our residence.

Whether it was originally prepared for publication, however, or intended to be a private letter, I will say that I judge it to be very unfit for publication. . . .

It appears to me that the manner in which you have notified our opinions in the letter from which my Uncle quotes must be calculated to increase the irritation which the opinions themselves are sufficiently likely to excite. Do they not merit a statement, temperate in its language and complete in its reasoning? Do they not furnish arms which if used with temper and self-command must put their adversaries on the defensive? Do we not owe it to them and owe it to ourselves to weigh well our words in all communications with the world or is it advisable to launch our principles naked and defenceless in the midst of the enemy, leaving to that enemy itself the task of developing them?

I am not questioning, of course, our right each to his own opinions and to his own mode of expounding it. But it appears to me that each and all of us bear a double character —as an individual and as one of society associated for certain objectives. While in the circle of Nashoba, we may speak in our individual character, but it will be difficult for us hereafter to speak so in this world. Any impression thus given by us individually will be received as given by the society and does it not therefore behoove us to be cautious in provoking unnecessary hostility and misconception?

All principles are liable to misinterpretation but none so much as ours. If good taste and good feeling do not dictate their expression and guide their practice, they will fall into (at all events momentarily) contempt. I could dwell much on this subject for I feel its importance both for Nashoba and for all that Nashoba may influence. Should you not think with me, you will not, I am sure, see any other motive in these observations than that arising out of the deep interest I feel in our success and in the triumph of our principles.

I found my paternal friend (Lafayette) younger than when I parted from him in America. He touches the completion of his 70th year and shows all the freshness of manly vigor in his mind and person. This state of his health relieves somewhat the melancholy of my present visit. Little as I anticipate for myself another voyage to Europe and improbable as appears for him another to America, it is difficult to look at him and think of an approaching parting as eternal. I sometimes think, R—when I look at him that there is an aristocracy in nature herself—beyond the wit of man to surmount. Lafayette born a noble, bred in a dissolute court, sucking in with his nurses' milk the idle prejudices of his class— He came out pure from dross and preserves to this hour the artlessness of childhood and the sweetness of a gentlewoman. We have yet to prove the powers of a just education. They are great no doubt. How great we know not. But if they make the weak, strong, the crooked, strait, where, of what shall be the strong and the strait by nature, what would be a Lafayette born and bred under the new system?

Frances Wright

Reverberations of Richardson's unlucky article in the *Genius of Universal Emancipation* continued to disturb the serenity of Fanny's convalescence. A prim note from ex-President Madison asking Lafayette's opinion of these late developments at Nashoba brought a hurried reply from the latter, still the faithful champion of his beloved children, but very much put to it in his brave efforts for their defense.

The two admirable sisters have devoted their fortunes, their lives, and all their exertions to the benefit of the human and particularly of the coloured race. Miss Wright's actual system is that total colonization being next to impossibility, the object should be now to soften and finally do away with prejudices of colour, by the experiments of common education, for which a seminary should be set up at Nashoba. Her ideas on the co-operative system are congenial to those of Mr. Owen, whose ideas in the main appear to her correct and productive of social melioration. Such is the tried state of her mind and her plans which have been by several of her European friends criticised, by others admired, while all could not but agree in a sense of high respect for her person, her abilities, intentions and exalted character. She is eloquent in her cause, amiable in her admissions of every objection, more affectionate than ever in her feelings, namely towards you and Mrs. Madison, but quite determined in the pursuit of her vocation. Those particulars I am anxious to give to you both because I think your advice and your kindness may become of great service to my excellent, enthusiastic young friends not less remarkable *for the purity of their hearts than for the power of their minds.*

At the same time Fanny was receiving a letter from Mrs. Craig Millar, bewailing the effects that Richardson's article had produced in faraway Edinburgh, where that lady had lately been making a visit. "I am told he says that all religion as enforcing moral conduct or as considering moral responsibility at all requisite, is disavowed by the system of education adopted in your establishment. Will you tell me the real meaning of this as I imagine there is some mistake about it? etc."

All this unpleasant publicity might be expected to put an end to the hopes of Fanny and Robert Dale of getting valuable recruits for their new community at Nashoba from Europe.

Such, however, was not the case. One must remember that the two most startling features of their new scheme, its irreligious character and its principle of sexual equality were not nearly so offensive to liberal opinion in Europe in the late twenties of the last century, as in Fanny's dear free America.

In France large sections of Lafayette's old following among the French *Carbonari* were adopting the extreme socialistic theories of St. Simon, and had actually founded a community near Paris, far more startling in its conception of the sexual relations than anything Fanny had yet conceived.

Even her radical proposition to remove the stigma of an inferior race from the negro population of the South by "the gradual blending of the white man and the black . . . till their children became one in blood, in hue," which she was quite frank in declaring one of the important aims for her new community, was accepted with extraordinary complacency by a number of her old friends and companions in both France and England.

Her friendship with the Garnetts, mother and daughters, had remained intact apparently, in spite of everything Charles Wilkes could do to destroy it. She and Robert were quite confident that they could finally persuade the elder sister, Harriet to join them at Nashoba after the marriage of Julia to a young German-Swiss named Pertz, an event which took place during Fanny's stay in Paris.

At the same time Robert Dale was writing from London about the encouragement he had received for the new project among the radical fringe of English society, readers and contributors to Leigh Hunt's *Examiner*, admirers of Godwin and Shelley. He advised Fanny to get in touch with the young widow of the poet, living, he was told, a very retired life in Brighton. "She seldom sees strangers, so that but few people know anything about her."

The result was just the sort of letter one might have expected from someone like Fanny, pledged to the cause of moral truth and moral liberty, to the daughter of Godwin and widow of Shelley, whom she hoped to interest in her new experiment at Nashoba. She explains at some length how she had come to found it in the first place, the breakdown of her health, "under the continued fatigues of mind and body incidental to the first twelvemonth," her return to Europe as the only chance of recovery, her immediate plans for the future. "The approaching marriage of a dear friend retains me for the present in Paris and as I return to my forest home in November, I do not expect to visit London, . . . though if you share the sentiments and talents of those from whom you drew your being I feel that I could travel far to see you."

Mary's share of this correspondence is no longer in existence, but Fanny's is still to be found among the manuscript collections of the Shelley family. Living alone in deep sorrow after the death of her husband, this letter from an unknown correspondent had brought Mary Shelley a needed distraction of which she seems more than willing to take advantage. No wonder she kept Fanny's reply.

Paris, September 15th, 1827

My Friend, my dear Friend. How sweet are the sentiments with which I write that sacred word, so often prostituted, so seldom bestowed with the glow of satisfaction and delight with which I now employ it! Most surely will I go to England, most surely to Brighton, to wheresoever you may be. . . . I opened your letter with some trepidation, and perused it with more emotion than now suits my shattered nerves. I have read it again and again and acknowledge it before I sleep.

Most fully, most deeply does my heart render back the sympathy yours gives. It fills up the sad history you have sketched of blighted affection and ruined hopes. . . . I too have suffered . . . loved and mourned and felt the chill of disappointment. . . . I have sometimes feared lest too early affliction and too frequent disappointment had blunted my sensibilities when a rencontre with some one of the rare beings dropt amid the dull multitude, like oases in the desert has refreshed my better feelings and reconciled me with others and with myself. . . . But have we only discovered each other to lament that we are not united? I cannot, will not think it! When we meet and meet we must and I hope soon—how eagerly and tremblingly shall I inquire into all the circumstances likely to favour an approach in our destinies. I am now on the eve of separation from a beloved friend whom marriage is about to remove to Germany, while I run back to my forests. Our little circle (there) has mind, has heart, has right opinions, right feeling . . . but the heart craves something more ere it can say, "I am satisfied." I do want one of my sex to commune with and sometimes to lean on in all the confidence of equality of friendship.

On the 28th [September] I shall be in London, where I must pass a few days with a friend about to sail for Madeira. . . . I may leave London to visit a maternal friend in the north of England towards the 20th October. . . . Unless you should come to London, I will seek you at Brighton, or anywhere else you may name. Our intercourse begins in the confidence if not the fullness of friendship [but] however short our meetings it must have some repose in it. The feelings which draw me towards you have in them I know not what of respect, of pitying sympathy, of expectation, and of tenderness. They must steal some quiet undivided hours from the short space I have yet to pass in Europe. . . . Tell me when they shall be and where. . . . To know you is a strong desire of my heart, and all things consistent with my engagements (which I may call duties since they are connected with the work I have on hand), will I do to facilitate our meeting.

It was the beginning of one of those brief enchanted friendships with which Fanny's life was so often enriched and enlivened and from which she received in even fuller measure than she gave. There is no doubt of the impression she made on Mary Shelley who introduced her to Godwin and lost no opportunity of seeing and communing with her as often as possible during her stay in England. "She was like Minerva!" Such is the recollection of Mrs. Shelley's son Percy, then a boy of eight.

All this time Robert was writing from Scotland, letters full of references to possible recruits to their undertaking. An engineer named Skene, two young *Carbonari*, Trone and Carnot, one rather a *tête exalté*, but the other a young man, *d'un merite distingue* of good taste and sound principles. Also a young Irishman named Bell, already a member of the co-operative village of Orbiston, Scotland.

> I think we may have many with us among the oppressed Irish, but I think we must not take in inferior minds, even with a practical benefit to them, too rashly and in too great numbers. The tone of our society must be very different from any they can give.
>
> My father is determined to return to America this autumn, probably by way of New Orleans, and to take both my brothers and probably one of my sisters with him. I hope we shall be able to arrange it so that we all go together either from Havre or Liverpool. He has, I believe, already written to see what vessels sail for Orleans the beginning of November, so that I hope you and he will be able at once to arrange everything regarding our departure for the new World. We shall, I dare say, have a disagreeable enough time of it for the first week or ten days, till we get into southern latitudes, which will enable us, as optimists say, the more to enjoy the latter, quieter part of the voyage.
>
> I shall come to London as soon after my father's return as possible and I hope to pass a few days with Mrs. Trollope. What is the exact address? Strange that you have not yet heard from Nashoba. I hope your next letter will bring good accounts.

The exact address of the Trollope family at the time Owen wrote this letter, was the big comfortable house that Mr. Trollope had bought to contain his family when he finally deserted law for farming, and removed definitely from Keppel Street to Harrow, some time about 1822 or 1823. Contemporary biographers of Mrs. Trollope put this date incorrectly some five years earlier, 1817 or 1818. One finds no further reference to a visit from young Owen at this time, but Fanny certainly spent some days with her old friends in Harrow before her departure for America, and thus becomes chiefly responsible for that fantastic series of adventures which finally resulted in one of the most amusing and malicious books on the United States in the late twenties that ever was written.

Such false and inaccurate conclusions have been drawn from memorable incidents in the lives of Fanny Wright and Fanny Trollope by contemporary biography that one may be permitted to spend some moments in a brief review of the real story of the friendship between these two women which has already appeared in earlier pages of this book.

There is a family tradition that Fanny's first connection with the Trollope family came through Mr. Trollope who as an occasional reader of her publisher, Longman, and a liberal Whig, had come into touch with her during the progress of her first book, *Views of Society and Manners in America,* through the press. The friendship soon extended to the rest of the family. One remembers how many of Fanny's letters to Lafayette during her visit to London in the winter of 1822 were written from 16 Keppel Street, one of those many houses that Mrs. Trollope's remarkable quality of homemaking had turned into a lively center of overflowing hospitality.

It was she who first introduced the Trollopes to General Lafayette. Their friendship survived Fanny's years of absence in America and Mrs. Trollope had been among those invited to La Grange to welcome her on her return in 1827.

One may turn again to T. Adolphus Trollope and his book, *What I Remember,* for the impression made upon a youth of seventeen by this old friend of his mother's.

> She was in many respects a very remarkable personage. She was very handsome in a large and almost masculine style of beauty, with a most commanding presence, a superb figure, and stature fully masculine. Her features both in form and expression were really noble. There exists—still findable, I suppose, in some London fonds de magazin—a large lithographed portrait of her. She is represented standing with her hand on the neck of a gray horse (the same old gig horse that had drawn my parents and myself over so many miles of Devonshire, Somersetshire and Monmouthshire roads and crossroads) and if I remember rightly, in Turkish Trowsers.

But these particulars of her bodily form and presentment
constituted the least remarkable specialties of her individuality. . . . Her thoughts and aspirations were directed with
a persistent and indomitable enthusiasm which made the
groundwork of her character, to doing something for the improvement of the condition of the slave population in the
southern states of the great transatlantic republic. . . . She
was unquestionably a very clever woman.

No greater evidence of this cleverness, as Tom Trollope calls it, can
be found than her conversion of a woman like Mrs. Trollope, part
and parcel of the English life depicted in the pages of the novels of
her famous son, Anthony, with its love of dukes and church digni-
taries, rooted and grounded in the good old English tradition of
privilege and precedent, to her last wild scheme for an ultra radical
community, on the edge of an uncivilized wilderness.

It must be admitted, however, that in the case of Mrs. Trollope,
Fanny's powers of persuasion were brought to bear on a mind already
prepared by adversity to snatch at any suggestion, however desperate,
which seemed to promise an outlet to an already desperate situation.
Mr. Trollope had shown himself no more able to make a living by
farming than he had by the law. He was deeply in debt and growing
more so every day. The eldest son, Tom, was meagerly provided for
by a scholarship at Winchester, but both parents were at their wits'
end to know what to do with their second son, Henry, a boy of six-
teen who was already showing a tendency to that disease of the lungs
of which he was to die some few years later.

"And so," continued Tom Trollope in the book already quoted,
"when Miss Wright proposed to my mother to bring Henry, who was
then rapidly approaching manhood without having found for himself
or having had found for him, any clear prospect of earning a living,
to America, to join her in her projected establishment at Nashoba,"
both Mr. and Mrs. Trollope accepted the proposition with enthusiasm.

To such of their acquaintance, however, who were unfamiliar with
the pressing necessities of the situation, Mrs. Trollope's decision to
join Frances Wright on her homeward journey was an occasion for
unconcealed amazement.

"You will be not a little surprised," says Lafayette writing to Charles
Wilkes a little later, "to hear that Mrs. Trollope after a full explanation of the Nashoba experimental system has with the assent of her
husband (who will go next year to meet them) determined to be-

come, with her daughters and son, members of the society and to give up the habits and comforts to which I thought her peculiarly attached. Some other persons of merit, namely an engineer, have yielded to Fanny's eloquence."

In actual fact, when the time came for departure, not one of the various personages whom they had so confidently hoped to embark with them for Nashoba responded to their call, except Mrs. Trollope, with two little daughters and her second son, Henry, and a French artist of some merit named Auguste Hervieu.

Mrs. Shelley's interest in her new friend did, indeed, bring her to see Fanny off from the Tower Step of London where her vessel lay at anchor, but no further.

"Dear love," wrote the latter in a farewell letter sent ashore at Torbay, "how your figure lives in my mind's eye as I saw you borne away from me till I lost sight of your little back among the shipping."

In quite a different tone is her last hurried line to La Grange:

> On board the Edward.
> Tower Stairs, Sunday
> Morning, Nov. 3rd.
>
> I have been summoned on board with my party of recruits for Nashoba at a few hours' warning. My heart grieves at this parting from my spiritual father without another meeting. But my friend and associate Robert Dale Owen who could not accompany us because of the suddenness of our departure will see you again before he sails with a party from Liverpool on the 10th. or 12th. of January and he will say some of the things I am thus forced to leave unsaid.
>
> I have told him to present himself at your symposium in your house in Paris. You will also receive shortly a printed copy of my address to the liberal youth of France. Another copy in English you will also receive in time but I must write it now during my voyage. I am also sending a lithograph of myself by the hands of a young artist whom I have also asked to call on you.
>
> We are pushing off
>
> F. W.

CHAPTER III

Fanny Wright's Free Love Colony

THE naked reality which lay beneath Fanny's rose-colored representation of the new colony at Nashoba is told at some length in the first chapters of Mrs. Trollope's *Domestic Manners of the Americans.*

On the 4th. of November, 1827, I sailed from London, accompanied by my son and two daughters, and after a favorable though somewhat tedious voyage, arrived on Christmas Day at the mouth of the Mississippi.

So she begins her tale.

The first indication of our approach to land was the appearance of this mighty river pouring forth its waters, and mingling with the deep blue of the Mexican Gulf. I never beheld a scene so utterly desolate as this entrance of the Mississippi . . . and for several miles above its mouth, the River presents no objects more interesting than mud banks, monstrous bullrushes and now and then a huge crocodile luxuriating in the slime. As we advanced, however, we were cheered, notwithstanding the season, by the tints of southern vegetation . . . the form and hue of the trees and plants, so new to us, added to the long privation we had endured of all sights and sounds of land, made even these swampy shores seem beautiful.

The town of New Orleans has much of the appearance of a French Ville de Province. The names of the streets are French and the language about equally French and English. The market is handsome and well-supplied, all produce being conveyed by the river. The large proportion of blacks seen in the streets, the grace and beauty of the elegant Quadroons, the occasional groups of wild and savage-looking Indians, all

182

help to afford that species of amusement which proceeds from
looking at what we never saw before.

She goes on to describe with some humor her first contact with
Fanny's radical friend, Miss Carroll, the donor of the Mexican fan
already mentioned in Owen's letters from New Orleans.

The first symptom of American equality that I perceived
was my being introduced to a milliner! Not at the boarding
house, under the indistinct outline of "Miss C" nor in the
street through the veil of a fashionable toilet, but in the very
penetralia of her temple, standing behind her counter, giving
laws to ribbons and wire, and ushering caps and bonnets into
existence. She was an English woman and I was told that
she possessed great intellectual gifts and much information.
I really believe this was true. Her manner was easy and graceful with a good deal of French tournure and the gentleness
with which her fine eyes and sweet voice directed the movements of a young female slave was really touching. The way
too, in which she blended her French talk of modes with her
customers and her English talk of metaphysics with her
friends, have a pretty air of indifference in it that gave her a
superiority with both . . .
    In the shop of Miss Carroll I was introduced to a Mr.
Maclure, a venerable personage of gentlemanlike appearance,
who in the course of five minutes, propounded as many
axioms, "Ignorance is the only devil," "Man makes his own
existence" and the like. He was of the New Harmony School
or rather the New Harmony School was of him.

At the time of this first and last meeting with Mrs. Trollope, Maclure
was on his way to Mexico, having left his schools, his printing press,
the disposition of those funds on which the livelihood of teachers,
scientists and specialists of every kind who had followed him so
confidently to the extreme edge of civilization, chiefly depended—in
the hands of Madame Fretageot. Anyone accustomed to Mrs. Trollope's mischievous depreciation of every person and practice she met
during those years spent in America will not be surprised at her account of this gentleman and Madame Fretageot, the faithful watchdog
of his interests in New Harmony.

Mr. Maclure was a man of good fortune, a Scotchman I
believe, who after living a tolerably gay life . . . had deter-

mined to benefit the species and immortalize himself by founding a philosophical school at New Harmony whose principal feature was that after the first liberal outfit of the institution having been furnished by himself, the expense of keeping it up should be defrayed by the profits arising from the labors of the pupils, under the direction of a woman, a lady with whom, it is said he had had for a long time the most intimate relations who was to function as the body of the scheme of which he was to be the soul. But unfortunately the soul of the system found the climate of Indiana uncongenial and therefore took its flight to Mexico, leaving the body to perform the operation of both, in what manner it liked best, and the body, being a French body, in company with a nephew-son, stirred herself to draw wealth from the thews and sinews of the youth under her authority who being many of them lads sent from a distance by indigent parents for gratuitous education possessed no means of leaving.

Much of the venom in this digression came no doubt from an experience of her own with the Maclure School of Industry, where her son Henry is said to have been a pupil for a short time during the first summer his mother spent in Cincinnati.

Their stay in New Orleans was too brief to permit their attending any of the social meetings and elegant entertainments for which the city was noted, or to visit either the French or the English theater there. "But we were too fresh from Europe," says Mrs. Trollope, "to care much for either or indeed for any other of the town delights of the city, and on the first of January, 1828 we embarked on board the *Belvidere,* a large and handsome boat, though not the largest or the handsomest of the many which displayed themselves along the wharfs. But she was going to stop at Memphis, and she was the first that departed after we had got through the custom house and finished our sight seeing."

Then follows one of those descriptions of American manners and customs for which Mrs. Trollope's book is especially famous. She rings the changes on the handsome furniture and expensive carpets in the ladies' cabin, in absurd contrast with its dirt and discomfort, the large appetites and bad table manners of their fellow passengers, the endless political wrangles between the supporters of Adams and Jackson in the race for the presidency to be decided at the next election, the two days' delay stuck on a snag in the middle of the river; all the familiar features of her amusing parody on the American scene in the late twenties, appear in this lively narration of Mrs. Trollope's first journey on an American steamboat.

The party finally arrived at Memphis in the middle of the night with the rain falling in torrents on their landing, and the new road leading up the bluff on which the town was situated, a slough of almost bottomless mud.

At the hotel where they at last found shelter, "Miss Wright was well known," Mrs. Trollope tells us:

> As soon as her arrival was announced every one seemed on the alert to receive her, and we soon found ourselves in possession of the best rooms the place afforded. The house was new, and in what appeared to me a very comfortless condition . . . We slept soundly however, and rose in hope of soon changing our mortar-smelling quarters for Miss Wright's Nashoba. But we presently found that the rain, which had fallen during the night would make it hazardous to venture through the forests of Tennessee in any sort of carriage. We therefore had to pass the day at our queer comfortless hotel. [She describes the midday dinner.] A great bell was sounded from an upper window of the house and we proceeded to the dining room, where the table was laid for fifty persons and was already nearly full . . . The company consisted of all the shop-keepers, store-keepers as they are called throughout the United States, of the little town. The mayor, also, who was a friend of Miss Wright's, was of the party. He is a pleasing, gentlemanlike man, and seems strangely misplaced in a little town on the Mississippi. No women were present except ourselves and the hostess. The rest of the day was spent rambling round the little town which is situated at the most beautiful point of the Mississippi.

Here follows a lively description of a long street stretching in a rambling irregular manner along the cliff to a cleared space on both sides where there seemed to be good pasture for horses, cows and pigs.

> At either end of this space however the forest again rears its dark wall. The rude path that leads to the more distant log dwellings becomes wilder at every step . . . The great

height of the trees, the quantity of pendant vine branches that hang among them, and the variety of gay-plumaged birds, particularly the small green parrot, made us feel we were in a new world, and a repetition of our walk the next morning would have pleased us well. But Miss Wright was anxious to get home.

So, before the roads were fit for travel, "a clumsy sort of caravan drawn by two horses was prepared for us and we set off in high spirits for an expedition of 15 miles through the forest."

While trying to avoid one of the shaken bridges, however, they all were nearly drowned in an overflowing stream.

> We saw the front wheels disappear, and the horses began to plunge and kick most alarmingly. At length the splinter bar gave way. Miss Wright who sat composedly smiling at the scene, at last agreed with the black driver that they had best be riding out on the horses as they had got into an unhandsome fix there. With some difficulty we, in this manner reached the shore and soon found ourselves again assembled round Mrs. Anderson's fire, where the greater number of the party decided to stay till the waters had subsided. But Miss Wright was too anxious to reach home to endure this delay, and she set off again on horseback, accompanied by our man servant, who told me afterwards that they rode through places which might have daunted the boldest hunter, but that "Miss Wright took it quite easy."

Thus at the risk of life and limb, Fanny came back to Nashoba, a day and a night before the rest of her party, alone, and perhaps it was just as well that she should face the situation awaiting her on the plantation with as few witnesses as possible.

Of the three white resident trustees she had left in charge of the colony, one, James Richardson was gone, never to return. The last entry in his handwriting in the Nashoba Journal under the date December 8th, announces briefly that "having last night come to the conclusion that his previous habit will not permit of his comfortable existence on the principles essential, as he thinks, to the co-operative system of society, he proposes to leave Nashoba some weeks hence to play a part once more in the sordid world of competition."

Another entry in Camilla's handwriting three days later continues the story. "James Richardson left us for Memphis, Dec. 11th 1827."

And again without comment. "Saturday Dec. 29th. 1827, Josephine Prevot, Probationer left us for Memphis."

But there is another entry some two weeks earlier even more important in the history of Nashoba than the departure of Richardson and his Josephine.

"Dec. 15th. Richeson Whitby and Camilla Wright were married by the Justice of the Peace, H. J. Persons." This statement was followed by an elaborate apology for an act so contrary to Camilla's earlier pronouncements on this subject.

"For this apparent dereliction from one of the fundamental principles frequently advocated in these records, as in Page 14, wherein Camilla Wright stated that she considered the proper basis of the sexual relation to be the unconstrained choice of both parties; while she continues to regard the marriage tie as in the highest degree irrational and in its nature calculated to produce a variety of evils, she believes from the result of experience that by living in open violation of the civil institutions of the country, irritation and more frequently indignation will be produced in the minds of the greater portion of mankind and thus effectually indispose the public mind from listening to the reasoning which should precede the practice of opinions so novel, and repugnant to those established in the existing state of society.

This change of her views as respects the practice of these opinions she derived, in the first instance, from a perusal of Godwin's *Political Justice*. In the reflections which close this valuable production the author observes, "Every community of men as well as every individual must govern itself according to its ideas of justice. What I should desire is not by violence to change its institutions but by discussion to change its ideas."

This marriage, so obviously the result of compelling circumstances rather than any natural affinity between the rough product of a Shaker village and a gently bred, sentimental young woman accustomed from childhood to all the amenities of a settled civilization, could not be expected to result in any permanent happiness, except by a miracle of human affection and mutual consideration. And in the case of Camilla Wright and Richeson Whitby the miracle did not happen.

But even more threatening to Fanny's dreams for her new community, or for that matter even to the continuation of her first simpler plan for a co-operative negro colony under white direction was the startling change in the health of her sister and her new brother-in-law. In fact, one has only to read the Journal of the Plantation during what Fanny, in her address to the Youth of France, calls the fever season, or in other words the months of June, July, August and September and October of the preceding year, to see how often one or the other of the white residents at Nashoba, with the sole exception of Richardson, were prostrated with malaria, leaving the whole work on the plantation at the mercy of the negro slaves.

Part of the neglect and mismanagement so painfully apparent wherever one turned one's eyes about the forlorn little settlement, could be attributed to Whitby's continual ill-health. Even under the most favorable circumstances, the young Shaker showed none of the qualities necessary for the successful management of a slave plantation.

The situation was appalling but there was even worse to come, for almost immediately after Fanny's appearance at Nashoba, the whole Trollope family with the French artist, Hervieu, arrived from Memphis, and here again one's best, one's sole witness of this painful crisis in Fanny's life, is Mrs. Trollope.

> The next day, [she continued] we started again for Nashoba. The clear air and bright sun, the novel wildness of the dark forest, and our keenly awakened curiosity made the excursion delightful, and enabled us to bear without shrinking the bumps and bruises we encountered. . . . The forest became thicker and more dreary looking every mile we advanced but our ever-grinning negro declared it was a right good road and that we should soon get to Nashoba.
>
> And so we did and one glance sufficed to convince me that every idea I had formed of the place was as far as possible from the truth. Desolation was the only feeling, the only word, that presented itself; but it was not spoken, I think however, that Miss Wright was aware of the painful impression the sight of her forest home produced upon me, and I do not doubt that the conviction reached us both at the same moment that we had erred in thinking that a few months passed together at this spot could be productive of pleasure to either. But to do her justice, I believe her mind was so exclusively occupied by the object she had then in view that all things else were worthless or indifferent to her.

I never heard or read of any enthusiasm approaching hers, except in a few instances, in ages past of religious fanaticism.

It must have been some feeling equally powerful which enabled Miss W., accustomed to all the comfort and refinement of Europe, to imagine not only that she herself could exist in this wilderness, but that her European friends could enter there and not feel dismayed at the savage aspect of the scene.

A sketch drawn by Monsieur Hervieu during our visit, gives a faithful view of the cleared space and buildings which form the settlement. The clearing round it appeared to me inconsiderable and imperfect; but I was told they had grown good crops of cotton and Indian corn.

I think they had between thirty and forty slaves including children. [The record of Nashoba gives a much smaller number, not more than fifteen at the outside.] But when I was there, no schools had been established. Books and other material for the great experiment had been collected and one or two professors engaged but nothing yet was organized. Each building in the settlement consisted of two large rooms, furnished in the most simple manner; nor had they as yet collected round them any of those minor comforts which ordinary minds class among the necessities of life.

When we arrived at Nashoba they were without milk, without beverage of any kind except rain water. Wheaten bread they used very sparingly and the Indian corn bread was uneatable. They had no vegetables but rice and a few potatoes we brought with us, no meat but pork, no butter, no cheese. I shared Frances Wright's bedroom. It had no ceiling, and the floor consisted of planks laid loosely upon piles.

As for poor M. Hervieu, as soon as he arrived he asked, "Where is the school?" and was answered, "It is not yet formed." I never saw a man in such a rage. He wept with passion and grief mixed. He immediately determined to go back to Memphis and try to get some employment there.

The only white persons we found at Nashoba were my amiable friend Mrs. Whitby the sister of Miss Wright, and her husband. I found my friend Mrs. Whitby in very bad health which she confesses she attributed to the climate.

Already during her ascent of the Mississippi Mrs. Trollope had been horrified by the ravages of fever and ague so noticeable among the squalid inhabitants of the settlements where they had stopped from time to time to get wood for the steamer. "Their complexion," she tells one, "is a bluish white, that suggests the idea of dropsy, and the poor little ones wear exactly the same ghastly hue."

The mere sight of her old friend whom she remembered as a wholesome, rosy-cheeked young woman, changed now into a hollow-eyed, haggard creature who had lost every ray of youthful looks, gave new strength to the decision which she had taken the first moment she set eyes on Nashoba. Besides all the other obvious disadvantages of the situation the climate was unhealthy! "This naturally so much alarmed me for my children that I decided on leaving the place with as little delay as possible."

And under the circumstances it is quite probable that everyone else on the plantation was as anxious for her departure as she herself was to go. She had to remain for nearly two weeks before funds could be raised to pay her expenses into the world of competition to which she was so anxious to return.

These were at last furnished her from the treasury of the Nashoba community, after a meeting of all the trustees available at that time and place, Fanny, Camilla, Richeson Whitby, and, last but not least, Robert Dale Owen.

Young Owen had been even less successful than Fanny in bringing back "boatloads of knowledge" as members for their new community in Tennessee. He had sailed from Liverpool a month later than Fanny with his father Robert Owen, senior, and his two younger brothers Richard and David Dale. They arrived in New Orleans very shortly after Fanny's party. There the elder Owen stopped to give a course of lectures on the usual Owenite subjects, Co-operation, Education for Character, and the Christian churches as the chief obstacles to the advancement of human society to its desired end of perfect happiness as a result of perfect moral enlightenment.

The younger Owen, however, proceeded almost immediately to Nashoba, arriving in time for the meeting of the trustees on January 23rd, which authorized "a loan of $300 to Mrs. Trollope to assist her in removing from Nashoba to some place in the western world better suited to her future plans for herself and her children." One finds her a little later in Cincinnati. The last mention of Frances Trollope appears in the record of Nashoba.

"January 27th. Frances Trollope and family with their manservant William Abbot and Esther Rust, her maid, and Auguste Hervieu, left us for Memphis."

She had found no beauty in the scenery round Nashoba nor could she conceive that it would possess any, even in summer. But at least one pleasant memory remains from this otherwise painful and agitating experience. "The weather was dry and agreeable, and the aspect of the heavens by night surprisingly beautiful. I never saw moonlight so pure, so powerful."

The first efforts of Fanny and her co-trustees after the departure of these unwilling and unwanted guests were necessarily directed towards bringing something like order out of the chaos of mismanagement and neglect existing on the plantation.

Not without interest here is the account in Robert Dale's handwriting of exactly what the plantation of Nashoba had produced during the year 1827.

75 pounds of corn at $2	$150.00
Fodder	25.00
2,964 pounds of cotton at .02	59.28
8 dozen eggs	
68 pounds of butter	
73 chickens	

The account with the slaves, however, left them owing the trustees $159.79. A balance against them which the trustees, wishing to afford the slaves every facility in effecting their emancipation, agreed to give them, as a present.

The hand of Owen might also be perceived in the entry of the Nashoba Journal of January 29th, describing the last of those fateful meetings of the slaves called together with the design of developing in them a proper sense of their obligations and privileges under the co-operative system.

> Frances Wright stated to the slaves that in consequence of the ill health of the trustees but more especially of Richeson Whitby, and also in consequence of our perceiving that without superintendence they were extremely idle not even earning their own support, the trustees had determined to place the whole under the sole management of John M. Gilliam for the ensuing season.

Gilliam was then duly presented to the slaves and made them a polite address pledging himself to require nothing of them but what was reasonable and expressing a hope that he would find them willing and obedient, and that they would refrain from quarreling.

At the same time, Dilly, the most troublesome and intractable of all the slaves at Nashoba, because of a temper so fiercely jealous that it had occasionally threatened even the life and limb of the other negroes, was taken into temporary exile on the Davis plantation at Hurricane.

A letter from the owner apologizing for not having been present on this occasion, is surprisingly friendly when one remembers the reputation already acquired throughout the neighborhood by the mistress of Nashoba and her overseer, Richeson Whitby, who accompanied her on this occasion.

> "Hurricane" Natchez, Feb. 26
>
> I regret our absence has deprived us of the pleasure of a visit and exposed you to a very uncomfortable reception. Though aware of the little consequence you attach to such difficulties, I cannot, etc., etc.
>
> The disagreement in the family of your people at Nashoba is one under such circumstances very likely to happen. The only means to prevent it is removal. They are a race ardent in their feelings but almost without reflection as to the consequences of their actions on the lives of those about them. The girl left with us shall be kindly treated.
>
> signed J. E. Davis.

But none of these practical details was allowed to interfere with the far more important business of advertising her new experiment of Nashoba as widely as possible.

Fanny had already taken advantage of the leisure afforded her by the long journey from London to New Orleans on the *Edward* to translate and enlarge her letter to the liberal youth of France, till it became an elaborate dissertation on the principles which she proposed to put in practice in her new colony, and the general method by which this colony was to be run. Amid all the distractions and disappointments of her homecoming she found time to get this statement published in all its inordinate length in the local newspaper, the *Memphis Advocate*, under the imposing title of "Explanatory Notes respecting the Nature and Object of the Institution at Nashoba and the Principles upon which it is founded: Addressed to the Friends of Human Improvement in all Countries and of all Nations."

When one remembers that nothing she ever said or did in the varied and active course of her life, had such a disastrous effect on her good name and later reputation, it may be of interest to review its most controversial features.

The principles of Owen's co-operative village were adopted as far as possible in an establishment still dependent for its main supply of labor on the work of negro slaves. But the number of slaves on the plantation was to be strictly limited to the first purchase of the founder, excepting in cases where the planters, becoming members, might wish to place their negroes under the protection of the institution. On the other hand no slave freed by the institution could be introduced into the society as a free laborer, and since human beings raised under the benumbing influences of slavery could not be elevated to the level of a society based on the principles of liberty and voluntary co-operation, except in a few rare cases no freed slave was eligible for membership in the Nashoba community.

Fanny was prepared to admit to membership upon terms of absolute equality, respectable free negroes and their children, who would receive such education in the school of the institution as must steadily raise the intellectual and moral character of the race.

"By such means," she believed, "the amalgamation of the races shall take place in good taste and good feeling and be made, at once, the means of sealing the tranquility and perpetuating the liberty of the country, and of peopling it with a race more suited to its southern climate, than the pure European—or whether it shall proceed, as it now does, viciously and degradingly, mingling hatred and fear with ties of blood—denied, indeed but stamped by nature on the skin."

There was a word too, on the institution of marriage:

> The marriage law existing without the pale of the institution (Nashoba) is of no force within that pale. No woman can forfeit her individual rights or independent existence, and no man assert over her any rights or power whatsoever beyond what he may exercise over her free and voluntary affection. Nor on the other hand, may any woman assert claims to the society or peculiar protection of any individual of the other sex, beyond what mutual inclination dictates and sanctions; while to every individual member of either sex, is secured the protection and friendly aid of all.
>
> The tyranny usurped by the matrimonial law, over the

most sacred of the human affections, can perhaps only be equalled by that of the unjust public opinion, which so frequently stamps with infamy, or condemns to martyrdom the best grounded and most generous attachments which ever did honor to the human heart, simply because unlegalized by human ceremonies equally idle and offensive in the form and mischievous in the tendency.

Let us correct our views of right and wrong, correct our moral lessons, and so correct the practice of rising generations! Let us not teach, that virtue consists in the crucifying of the affections and appetites, but in their judicious government! Let us not attach ideas of purity to monastic chastity, impossible to man or woman without consequences frought with evil, nor ideas of vice to connexions formed under the auspices of kind feeling! Let us enquire—not if a mother be a wife, or a father a husband, but if parents can supply, to the creatures they have brought into being, all things requisite to make existence a blessing.

There is also a long paragraph explaining that "religion occupied no place in the institution." The rule of moral practice there proposed had in view simply human happiness, considering as virtuous whatever tends to promote that happiness, as vicious whatever tends to counteract it. And by the word religion Fanny meant "the belief in and homage rendered to a Being or Beings not cognizable by the senses of man." No religious doctrines were to be taught in the schools. The reason of the children was to be left to its free development and encouraged to examine all opinions and to receive or reject them according to the bearing of facts and the strength of their moral testimony.

The rest of the paper is taken up with details concerning the membership and government of the institution of Nashoba, which may be omitted without loss of interest since there is no evidence they were ever put into effect before the institution itself was swallowed up in a nightmare of disappointment and confusion.

The "Explanatory Notes" were well received by the New Harmony *Gazette*, January 30, 1828, though even this radical newspaper hinted that it might be wiser to confine the practice of the views set forth in "Notes" to a small community.

A lively description of their effect on the inhabitants of Madame Herries' boardinghouse in New Orleans is found in a handful of letters from that charming young milliner already so flatteringly mentioned in Mrs. Trollope's letters.

Mary Carroll, though she was by her own confession at heart a coward, still had the courage to continue gallantly in her role of Fanny's friend and admirer, even at the risk of ostracism by the class on which she depended for her bread and butter.

She confesses in a letter to Fanny, dated February 4th, that she kept her own copy of the "Explanatory Notes" strictly to herself, afraid to discuss it with anyone except Madame Herries and Robert Dale Owen, who was still in New Orleans when it arrived. For a time there seemed to be a veritable conspiracy of silence on the subject.

> In vain I hinted at it, [says Mary Carroll] to Mr. Dick, [Fanny's business agent in New Orleans] and to Judge Porter. [a mutual friend] They all pretended complete ignorance of the whole matter, until someone made an observation, intended for me, though not addressed to me, by the gentleman next to me at the table, that he should not be surprised if Miss Wright should, one of these mornings, find her throat cut! I quickly enquired the reason and could obtain no satisfactory reply. Madame Herries, however, resolved the enigma by informing me that Mr. Dawson, whom I know as loudly and warmly averse to your principles, had received the Memphis Advertiser and had been very industrious in circulating it all over town.
>
> Thus you see our objects are often furthered by means the least friendly. None of the New Orleans newspapers have reprinted your Notes. Mr. Dawson is doing more for you than I am for the open discussion of your principles, which once commenced cannot be put down by the affected ridicule and obloquy which narrow minds may fling upon them.

She goes on to describe some of the efforts to detach her from this dangerously unpopular cause.

"One of my friends, a sensible and amiable man, and hitherto, a very sincere admirer of yours, came to me the other day, and asked if I had seen your pamphlet. I replied, 'Long since.' 'Then I hope,' said he, 'that you have decided upon cutting all acquaintance with Miss Wright.'"

When Mary continued to assert her right to do exactly as she pleased on this point he became at last almost threatening.

"Surely you realize the necessity of having some respect for the opinion of the world."

"I live and toil in the world for my daily bread. I have nothing else to do with it, nor do I fear its displeasure while I act in consonance with its stupid mandate of conduct."

"But you forget how much you have to lose."

"I have nothing."

"You have a character to lose, which has never yet suffered in the public estimation."

This very character according to this kind friend was in danger, no less for her admiration of Frances Wright than for her tolerance of Robert Owen. One gets an amusing sidelight on this great man as a lecturer in an earlier letter of Mary to Fanny.

> His declaration of mental independence gave far more offense by the assumption to himself of the truths announced in it, which so many men have acknowledged for ages. The combination is his—and could he refrain from putting himself so much in the foreground, even his contemporaries would, I believe, freely admit all he requires. At all events he will do much good here, where almost nothing is known of the system of social co-operation. Too much can not be done to enlighten the minds of the people.

The longer Owen talked, however, the less he pleased his audiences. Note the outburst against him with which Miss Carroll's conservative advisor completes the conversation already recorded by her in her letter to Fanny.

> I tell you as a sincere friend that you cannot do exactly as you like in such matters. I tell you also that if I had a wife or sister or mother who would have returned to hear Mr. Owen after his Thursday lecture I should sever them from me and mine for ever.
>
> Thus did we part, as I thought, [says Mary] for the last time, but not so. A stiff and restrained deportment is all the result I perceive. I thought at first, and looked for a general desertion, and acted upon it, declining to go to one or two evening parties, but so far all the members of my little circle evince unusual solicitude to show their usual attention. I cannot help feeling a lively regret at this for I verily believe

that a good strong breeze of injustice and oppression w
act as a tonic upon my slovenly soul and rouse me from pas-
sivity into action, and practical honesty and usefulness, but
the sunshine of the human heart and eye act upon me as the
sun on the Lazzeroni. I lie listlessly inactive. I suffer under
my chains but I hug them like a true bond slave.

Thus you see I am still the same mixture of diffidence and
courage that you so justly pronounced me. A day of unremitting fatigue has left me both stupid and unwell. I am
tired of this mode of existence, and without anything really
to complain of I am sometimes tempted to shake it off.
Though I must confess that since I last saw you my inclination to throw off the evil of this earthly life has wonderfully
declined.

In the end, however, this mixture of diffidence and courage which
Fanny half despised, paid more dearly for her radical opinions than
Fanny herself. She gave up millinery to open a bookstore where
liberal publications could be bought and sold. She did a very bad business. Reduced at last to extreme poverty and ill health, deserted by all
her rich friends she died, probably of cholera, in 1832.

Fanny, made of sterner stuff and far more her own mistress
than poor Mary Carroll, was unaffrighted by the uproar roused against
her because of the publication, "Explanatory Notes." She continued
to urge her plan for the new Nashoba with her usual "tigerish energy,"
to quote a word often applied to her by her enemies in the newspaper
world.

One by one the more unmanageable features of her original plan
were thrown to the winds. One reads, for instance, in one of her long
letters to Mrs. Shelley after her return to Nashoba:

I hoped to have sent you, with this, the last communication
of our little knot of trustees, in which we have stated the
modification of our plan which we have found it advisable to
adopt, with reasons for the same, but we have not been able
to get it printed in Memphis so Dale is to have it thrown off
at Harmony, from whence you will receive it. The substance
of it is that we have reduced our co-operation to a simple
association, each throwing in from our private funds $100
per annum for the expenses of the table, including those of
a cook, whom we hire from the Institution, she being one of
the slaves gifted to it. Each of us builds his house or room,

the cost of which simple furniture included, does not sur-
pass $500. All other expenses regard us individually and
need not amount to $100 more, demanding, as a requisite
for admission an independent income of $200, instead of re-
ceiving labor as an equivalent.

The letter also contains some interesting reference to a mutual friend.
Could it have been Trelawney, expected home from Greece that same
summer of 1827? And did she ever hope to enlist him for her new
enterprise?

Bless your sweet kind heart, my sweet Mary! Your little
enclosure together with a little billet brought me by Dale,
which came to the address of Mr. Trollope's chambers just
as he left London, is all the news I have yet received from
our knight errant. Once among Greeks and Turks, correspondence must be pretty much out of the question, so unless
he address to you some more French compliments from
Toulon, I shall not look to hear of him for some months.
Ay, truly they are incomprehensible animals, these same soi-
disant lords of this poor planet! Like their old progenitor,
Father Adam they walk about boasting of their wisdom,
strength, and sovereignty, while they have not sense so much
as to swallow an apple without the aid of an Eve to put it
down their throats. I thank thee for thine effort to cram
caution and wisdom into the cranium of my wandering
friend. Thy good offices may afford a chance for his bringing his head on his shoulders to these forests, which otherwise would certainly be left on the shores of the Euxine, on
the top of Caucasus, or at the sources of the Nile.

Yes, dear Mary, I do find the quiet of these forests and
our ill-fenced cabins of rough logs more soothing to the
spirit, and now no less suited to the body than the warm
luxurious houses of European society. Yet that it should be
so with you or to any one less broken in by enthusiastic
devotion to human reform and mental liberty than our little
knot of associates, I cannot judge. I now almost forget the
extent of the change made in my habits even more than in
my views and feelings during the last few years. But when
I recall it, I sometimes doubt if many could imitate it without feeling the sacrifices almost equal to the gains. To me
sacrifices are nothing. I have not felt them as such and now
forget that there were any made.

Farewell, dear Mary. Recall me affectionately to the memory of your father. You will wear me in your own, I know.

Yours fondly, F. W.

A letter from Fanny written a few days later to Robert Dale's mother, still in Scotland, preserves the fiction that the community of Nashoba under this new arrangement was already a going concern.

Frances Wright to Mrs. Robert Owen, Feb. 9, 1828.

The affectionate intimacy between myself and some members of your family, my dear Madame . . . permits me as a friend of Mr. Owen, and especially as the friend, sister, and associate of your son, Robert Dale to tender my respects, etc., etc. He will himself have conveyed to you, [at the time of writing Robert Dale was still with Fanny on her plantation] his own views and feelings respecting Nashoba and its present inhabitants, etc. To worldly ambition indeed, I should be the first to confess that it offers nothing. Yet to one of your son's education and views I do believe it to offer a peculiarly fair prospect of social enjoyment and tranquil usefulness. We are now but a small circle and one not likely ever to embrace a very large one, drawn, as our companions must be, from the morally cultivated and also from those possessed of small but independent incomes.

Yet if I judge correctly of Robert's tastes and character, it is opportunity for selecting a suitable companion of the other sex. He is too amiable, too formed for the greater and purer pleasures which come through the affections not to find in that connection the chief source of his happiness or one of bitter suffering. . . . Should we receive recruits from Europe, as appears more than probable, I think they cannot fail generally to possess those tastes and manners and that tone of thinking and feeling with which his own would more or less sympathize. Nashoba is yet a young and rough settlement but if our hopes for the future are not disappointed perhaps it may hereafter offer a suitable home for other members of your family whose tastes may be in unison with those of Robert. However this may be, dear Madame, I trust you will think of him while at Nashoba as with those who love him dearly and value him highly. May I convey through you to your daughters the assurance, etc., etc.

But in this connection also her hopes were soon to be dashed. Some time about the end of February, the elder Owen stopped at the plantation on his way to New Harmony where he was urgently needed to rescue some remnant of the family fortune. Now he was departing after a few days' visit taking his eldest son with him, and Fanny was confronted with the loss of her main prop and adviser in the troubled state of her plantation.

It was just at this point in the steady disintegration of her cherished project, that one comes across one of the few semi-comic incidents which lighten the gloom surrounding the history of Nashoba.

One may remember a thickset, grim little man named Robert Jennings already described in an earlier chapter as having attracted Fanny's attention on her first visit to New Harmony. Jennings had been cast back into the world of competition when New Harmony ceased to be a co-operative community in the spring of 1827. He had finally drifted to New York where he was earning a bare subsistence on the staff of a little free-thought paper the *New York Correspondent* lately established in that city by a half-educated genius called George Houston.

In the first enthusiasm of her plan to found a successor to New Harmony at Nashoba, Fanny had written to Jennings proposing membership in her new co-operative community with a free hand in the development of the new schools for black and white children which were to be one of the essential features of her plan.

A wrong address combined with the usual delays of the mails in the United States at that time, permitted weeks and months to pass without any answer, and Fanny received Jennings' unconditioned acceptance of her offer just at the moment when the whole structure of Nashoba seemed about to crumble at her feet.

Jennings himself she would have been glad to welcome as a useful substitute for the deserter, Robert Dale. But Jennings unfortunately was a much married man. His unsuccessful efforts to support a wife and family had already roused the sympathy of the tenderhearted Camilla to whom he was still indebted for a loan of $400. But his proposal of Mrs. Jennings and his little son Bob as members of Fanny's half-born community of Nashoba was more than she could bear.

Her answer to Jennings' letter, written at the moment, and on the very spot where it was received, shows in every line the confusion of mind as well as the headlong speed with which it was composed.

Memphis, Feb. 24, 1828.

On riding into this place with Robert Dale and Robert Owen from Nashoba, Camilla and myself have received yours of the 20th. January and now remain to answer it by return post.

In reply to the letter before me, let me impress on you, my dear friend that we, the resident trustees will never cease to exert ourselves to effect such arrangements as may bring you among us.

A school is our great object, the one object to which our views increasingly point. We are equally united in opinion (setting personal feeling out of the question) that you are the only person known to us capable of forming such a school as we alone desire having.

This being premised let us look to the best means to promote our object. Certainly, my dear friend, it is not by bringing Mrs. Jennings west of the Alleghany. Her taste should be consulted in your arrangements for her.

Justice requires this no less than expediency.

So far as I can judge of your present situation with Mrs. Jennings from this distance, my counsel would be to defer the employment of Camilla's loan of $400 in your hands till we can arrange matters for your joining us here on some such footing as I mentioned in my last. And you on your side can fix Mrs. Jennings with her father or elsewhere and if you remain firm on the point of separation she may gradually become desirous of joining her father. The $400 might possibly assist you in such an arrangement. Keep them by all means, my dear friend, but do not use them hastily. Stay where you are till you can disburden yourself of your present ties. You can do nothing with your arms working on the land, nothing with a family in bringing them westward.

Land and Labor is wealth! So we all were accustomed to affirm in the old days at New Harmony. In principle we were right but with a view to actual practice in the existing generation, we were wrong. My dear Jennings, co-operation has well nigh killed us all. . . . We have all had our share of sufferings and exertion. I have had mine, dear Jennings, but they have left me only firmer in my purpose, more inflexible in principle, while they have enriched me with experience, dearly but not too dearly purchased seeing that it is invaluable. Judge what individual labor would do in your case. You cannot hold the plough, plant corn or sow cabbages. You cannot labor with your arms. If you try to put it into practice it will put you out of the world. Preserve yourself for the great, the noble task of fitting the next generation for doing what we cannot do, and unite your exertions with ours for preparing such circumstances as may in the future admit of your leaving the old world (of competition) for the more suitable life and enjoyments of the new. Launch the ship where you are. We are all navigating the same sea and our mariners are not too many. When you feel your courage slacken and your mind darken, read over this letter and think of the friends who will never cease to think of you and for you. Exert yourself for the time being in forwarding the cause of liberal principles in the east and leave it to us to open you a future home in the West. Cam asks for the remaining paper.

Then follows a little note from Camilla.

As Fanny very fully conveyed to you her views of your present situation and future prospects which are perfectly in unison with my own, I have only to add my earnest solicitation that you resign your idea of moving to the West (i.e., Nashoba) which would involve you in difficulties such as you have never yet experienced. You may believe me, and this from personal experience, that zeal in the cause will not supply the indispensable requisites of physical strength and that with persons of our habits all attempts at manual labor will end in the loss of health if not of life itself.

I trust you sufficiently understand and appreciate my friendship to believe that you could not more highly gratify my feelings than by retaining the funds you allude to, in your hands and applying them in the manner best calculated to promote your happiness. . . . While various circumstances combined to induce me to conform to the legal ceremony of marriage, my property remains at my own disposal and I have now as heretofore only to consult my own views and feelings in its appropriation. May all good be with you, my excellent and valued friend.

Camilla Whitby.

This letter, directed to Jennings, care of the editor of the *New York Correspondent*, arrived after his departure for the West and was delivered by unfriendly hands some time later to one of Fanny's bitterest enemies in the newspaper world, by whom it was twisted out of its obvious meaning into a brutal attack on her moral character.

In the meantime Jennings and his family did return to New Harmony, but they were never members of Fanny's colony at Nashoba.

One visitor from the outside world did, however, make his appearance on the plantation during those first melancholy weeks after Robert's departure. The gentleman, a certain Otto P. Braun, a friend of Sir John Bowring and through him of Fanny's old philosopher, Jeremy Bentham, seems to have walked all the fifteen miles from Memphis to Nashoba solely for the purpose of paying his respects to Fanny and making observations upon her widely advertised colony on the Wolf River.

He looked and listened to all Fanny had to say about her plans and hopes for the future, did his very best to persuade her that these were mistaken in every particular and then when he saw her still obstinately set in her original opinion, quietly and firmly walked away, all the fifteen miles to Memphis, never to return.

The letter which he sent back to Fanny after his departure, duly entered by her without comment in the Nashoba Journal, is not the least interesting of the material found therein. It begins with a fantastic account of his walk home through the forest.

Once correctly set on my course to Memphis, I let my feet take care of themselves without the least assistance from my head. I have always found such procedure the best assistance to thought. Thus wandering along the road, thinking of the other road we had just been discussing, the unknown road to happiness, reminding myself how easily one can be diverted from that road, galloping off on chimeras, nightmares, hobby horses and griffins; interrupted now and again by certain marks already noticed by me when I passed before on the way to Nashoba, signs which I took as superlative proofs that I was personally right, no matter how mentally wrong, I at last arrived not at Memphis on the Nile but Memphis on the Miss. Muddy and wet to be sure but not weary, so absorbed indeed in that old theme human happiness, so full of the question whether the world contains any ingredients with which its flavor might be sweetened, that I arrived here unaware of the time as if I had just waked from a dream. And the same string of ideas, the same dream continued to repeat themselves while I sat at the fireside before supper.

After all, I said to myself, Frances Wright is evidently well-endowed by nature. She has sense and talent and eloquence, but no chemical knowledge of the materials, or geometric skill for the construction of any fabric suitable for an establishment of human happiness.

No, Miss Wright! *Nashoba, Happiness!* They do not agree. Will Nashoba fatten your stock, load your table, or furnish you with flowers for your own and your friends' birthdays?

You pretend to me that you are never going to marry. Good Miss Wright, you are already married to a soil which I will not call poor, but which I can compare to a big, swollen, heavy, lubberly, lazy, scurvy fellow, who can be rendered tolerable to society only by physic and training. He has cost you too much already in money and health. You will have to spend $5000 more, exile yourself from your friends, take infinite trouble, and gain what in the end? Nothing but disappointment.

What spirit of immolation unites you to this place. I cannot rescue you from the grasp of Nashoba. I know it. But at least I can give you the result of my observation, and if we both live four years more, you will acknowledge how correct it is.

Come! Resolve within four hours to leave Nashoba! Take a trip, pay a visit to New Harmony. I shall wait for you, see you safe there, be your banker and steward on the road or river, and ask nothing in return.

I have no time. I must conclude. Write me within four hours, or shall I have to wait until those four years have expired.

Respectfully, Otto P. Braun.

He had to go without her. Indeed it is not likely that he expected anything else.

By the first of April, Fanny was left quite alone on the plantation. Camilla and her husband departed at last for New Harmony. The free colored woman Lolotte and her children had gone even earlier. The slaves worked quietly in their quarters under Gilliam. An occasional wanderer from the outer world continued to drift into the settlement and drift out again, their goings and comings all duly noted in the Journal of Nashoba in Fanny's handwriting.

April 30. Dr. Perkins and brother from Alabama dine here.
May 4th. Early this morning enters a quiet stranger who

gives his name as Dr. Easton and explains himself as desirous of settling in the country with a view to medical practice and boarding in the Institution. Frances Wright necessarily declined making any definite arrangements before Autumn when she would be able to consult with the other trustees on the propriety of his being accommodated here. Explained to him the nature of the Institution and the actual position of its affairs. . . . He stayed for four days. Originally from New England.

May 20. Daniel Clifton settler on the North Fork of the Wolf, called as usual from curiosity. Appeared a quiet liberal minded man for his opportunities. Promised to let him have in the fall some seed from our Irish potatoes. In return for seed of the true N. Carolina varieties. Also some seed rice.

A man from Memphis, the object of his visit I could not guess. It was probably unknown to the man himself.

May 27. A stranger from East Tenn., charged with land business from a college in that section, called and took dinner, etc., etc.

So passed the days without any special interest or significance when, almost like a messenger from another planet, arrived the following letter from Robert Dale in New Harmony.

I am here, my sweet Fanny, and find the situation much better than I expected. You know that I am a literal person, and mean what I say. There is much that must be amended but I think my father has tolerably rational views as to what ought to be done.

He is a much wiser man than he was a year ago, and I do not think he has done anything after all to involve him ultimately in serious difficulty. Most of the contracts [with dishonest land speculators on false pretenses into which the elder Owen had entered in credulous optimism before his departure for Europe] have already fallen through and are given up. Our pecuniary prospects are better than I expected. . . . Our manager, Mr. Dorsey, a quiet industrious atheist . . . who notwithstanding his avowed scepticism was lately treasurer of the Miami University and a magistrate.

Madame Fretageot is not queen of the South, but Queen of the North, i.e. the north portion of Harmony and bears her honors, I assure you with great judgment and good sense. I have seen a good deal of her and she seems to be on much better terms with everybody and to be much more popular than when I left. Her boys have established and still carry on a most respectable newspaper called the Disseminator.

There is more spirit in Harmony than when I left it. The best and most industrious citizens are doing well on the individual system, and retain much liberality of opinion and freedom from foolish ceremony, and a disposition to friendliness which even an ill-regulated community gives in a greater or less degree.

He goes on to describe the theater which has lately been set up in the body and one of the wings of the old Rappite Hall, with really superior scenery.

The first performance four weeks ago was well above mediocrity.

Mr. and Mrs. Chase are its principal supporters. They are people of the world, liberal in their opinions upon all subjects, intelligent, though not exactly first rate heads; cultivated and fond of the fine arts. Mrs. Chase is a good musician and an excellent painter. A clever little woman, take her all together! I think you would be pleased with them. But Camilla will be better able to judge when she comes on from Kentucky.

Cannot you come here with her, or at least some time this summer? You could spend a few weeks I think pleasantly and perhaps profitably.

All your friends are anxious to see you.

The Thespian Society wish much to try some of your tragedies, but I fear they can scarcely manage it unless you are here to direct them. Pray send by post half a dozen copies of Altorf. The theatre does but little real good at present though it affords much amusement but if we could set up such pieces as might be written for it, it might be made a most powerful engine to form the opinions and the taste of all the surrounding country. The Hall was crowded last night of the performance so that not a seat remained empty.

I write in haste dear Fanny. If you really wish to know the state of affairs you must come here. You will have no expense and I think that for a short time Nashoba can take care of itself, though you can judge in these matters better than I.

I shall be so glad to see sweet Camilla again. You may rest assured we will all take good care of her.

If I can find a horse likely to suit you, I think Richeson
had better buy it and Camilla can use it while she is here.
If not I dare say I can manage to hire one. Farewell dear
sister.

R. D. Owen.

One will not be surprised after reading this letter to find the
next entry in the Journal of the Plantation:

"Frances Wright leaves Nashoba to join her sister at Harmony,
leaving the property in charge of John Gilliam."

Her work was never resumed at Nashoba. The community she had
attempted, never really existed except on paper or in the imagination
of that host of ill-wishers who delighted to call it "Fanny Wright's
Free Love Colony."

But though her great experiment was by her own confession a
failure she always declared that it was a salutary, a necessary step
in her own development. As she herself expressed it in later writing:

During the 3 years and a half which she devoted to the
slave question, she learned more than during any other period
of her life. It was in the cotton field, and while watching
the extraordinary fluctuations in the cotton market, and the
fearful catastrophes in the mercantile and industrial world
consequent thereupon, that she acquired her intimate acquaintance with American institutions, the American people,
the American territory, with all those extended and varied
opportunities for observation which come from being actually involved in a practical experiment like Nashoba
whether the experiment itself is a success or a failure. And
even while granting that her own practical experiment at
Nashoba was a failure, she felt herself better equipped for
her next adventure in the field of social service than ever
before in her life.

Man species in the omnipotence of its collective humanity
is alone able to effect what I, weak existence of an hour,
thought myself equal to attempt alone.

But man species could and must be enlightened and improved by
liberal education. This was henceforth to be her chosen task as part
owner and editor of the New Harmony *Gazette*, a little weekly which
had already done gallant service in the field of radical propaganda
as the official organ of Robert Owen's great experiment in co-operative
living.

CHAPTER IV

Priestess of Beelzebub

FOR the first time in the history of the American nation, a woman, and that woman Frances Wright, had been chosen to be the main speaker at the celebration of the most important, the most august among American holidays, the anniversary of the Declaration of Independence.

The account which appeared in the issue of July 9th, 1828 of the New Harmony *Gazette* was full of fanfare.

> The morning was ushered in, in this town, by the roll of the drum, the firing of musketry and great guns, and other manifestations of joy, which usually through the United States mark the celebration. Soon after sunrise the New Harmony Light Infantry assembled on their parade ground and continued to parade our streets at intervals during the greater part of the day. At 10 o'clock A.M. Frances Wright delivered the Address which we present to our readers on our first and second pages, to a crowd of auditors in the New Harmony Hall. In the course of the morning Dr. Thompson also delivered an oration on the celebration of our National Independence, in the Labyrinth. After which a number of ladies and gentlemen partook of a barbecue under the shade of the adjoining trees. In the evening our Thespian Society gave much satisfaction to a crowded house by their performance of the *School of Reform* and *Fortune's Frolic*. Throughout the day the weather was propitious and cool for the season of the year, etc., etc.

Two years earlier, while the community was still in its heyday of popularity, Owen himself had been the principal speaker of the July celebration and pronounced his famous address on mental independence. But Fanny indulged in no such lofty flights.

Her speech on this occasion confined itself to discriminating praise of American institutions as the best possible for meeting the growing needs of a free people. How fortunate they, the American people, were in this respect she herself knew from four years' experience in a country where the only relief from governmental oppression and injustice lay in secret conspiracy or armed rebellion. Whereas the very form of the American Constitution included the power of amendment by popular consent, while almost universal manhood suffrage gave the American people ample opportunity to replace governments and leaders in whom they had lost confidence by men and laws of their own choice and making.

As it happened, she could have chosen no more fortunate time for an enthusiastic reception of such a speech than the year which saw Andrew Jackson carried to the White House by a nationwide movement of the discontented, underprivileged masses who had been left out in the cold by the conservative forces so long in control of the Federal government.

Fanny herself never had any wish to be cabined and confined by any political party, but there is no doubt that her first appearance as a public speaker owed some of its success to the rising tide of Jacksonian Democracy.

New opportunities for exercising this hitherto unused, unsuspected gift for public speaking were not long in coming. But now, instead of being borne and lifted by a favorable current, she was to find herself in bitter conflict with another nationwide movement of a very different sort and in a very different field from Jacksonian Democracy.

For some time in the past, the Christian churches had been gradually waking up to the fact that increasing numbers of the American people, especially on the western and southwestern frontiers, were growing up without religious instruction of any kind. The result had been a new sense of solidarity among professed Christians of all denominations, a willingness to forget their sectarian differences and join their scattered forces in nationwide religious associations, such as the American Tract Society, the American Bible Society, the American Society for the Education of Pious Youth for the Gospel Ministry, etc., etc. The systematic and concerted use of religious revivals as a means of exciting popular interest in the great question of individual salvation had long been one of the accepted activities of the Christian churches of America, and the summer of 1828 is especially noteworthy for the frequency and intensity of this form of religious fervor throughout the country.

At the same time there was a general movement on the part of the Christian teachers and preachers of the Atlantic seaboard to create a favorable environment for the reception of religious truth by laws restricting all forms of public amusement on Sunday, abolishing Sunday travel on post road, river, or canal, and putting an end to the Sunday mail service, etc., etc.

Those opposed to this movement retaliated by dubbing its supporters, "The Christian Party in Politics." It was not by accident that Fanny took arms against this so-called Christian Party as soon as she found herself in contact with it. Their notable service in the field of education and in various forms of relief for the poorer classes seemed to her worse than useless when combined with the supernatural side of their teaching and preaching. Their denial of man's power to perfect himself by his own reasonable efforts, their rejection of the findings of human reason for the other-worldliness of revealed religion, their promise of eternal happiness in heaven as a reward for their patient submission to all the evils and injustices of existing society, contributed to make them a formidable obstacle to the campaign initiated by Robert Owen and his followers to bring about a perfect moral world here and now.

Fanny's first appearance as a dangerous and ruthless enemy of the Christian churches in their efforts to bring back the popular mind to its old unquestioned belief in Christian dogma was in Cincinnati. This place in 1828 had already earned the name of Queen City of the West. It was built on the north bank of the Ohio River in a beautiful valley about twelve miles in circumference, arranged on natural terraces with most of its industries developed along the river front. Paper mills, foundries, and glass factories were already flourishing, and a well-organized pork-packing industry had been started in the town. Several flourishing breweries bore witness to the existence of large numbers of Germans among its inhabitants. But there was also a good proportion of Scotch, Irish, and English in its mixed population and most of the religious sects were represented in twenty-three churches, Roman Catholic, Anglicans, Presbyterians, Congregationalists, Methodists, Baptists, Moravians, Mormons, Jews, and Shakers.

The city was also an outpost for Eastern culture, in its schools and newspapers. A very active press had been in operation there for many years. There was even a good-sized theater on the south side of

Columbia Street between Main and Sycamore, which was calculated to hold some 800 people. Lane Theological Seminary, established and largely supported by Eastern capital, was a light for Orthodox Congregationalism for the whole Ohio Valley. But not till some four years later, in 1832, did it become the home of the Reverend Lyman Beecher and his even more famous daughter Harriet Beecher Stowe.

For these and many other reasons the city of Cincinnati offered special attraction to the "Christian Party in Politics" in its campaign for the evangelization of the western world. It held a series of revivalist meetings in all the little towns and villages of the Ohio Valley between the mouth of the Wabash River and Cincinnati.

Fanny herself thus describes these new activities, with the bitterness inseparable from her utter disapproval of this particular method of propaganda.

> In the summer of 1828, by a sudden combination of the clergy of the three orthodox sects, a revival with such scenes which are wont to characterise such occasions, was opened in the homes and churches of Cincinnati, a city which had stood for some time conspicuous for the enterprise and liberal spirit of her citizens.
>
> The victims of this odious experiment on human credulity and nervous weakness were invariably women. Helpless age was made a public spectacle, youth driven to raving insanity, mothers and daughters carried lifeless from the presence of the ghostly expounders of damnation, all ranks shared the contagion, while the despair of Calvin's hell itself seemed to have fallen upon every heart and discord to have taken possession of every mansion.
>
> A circumstantial account of the distress and disturbance on the public mind in the Ohio metropolis led me to visit the afflicted city; and since all were dumb, to take up the cause of insulted reason and outraged humanity, etc., etc.

On three successive Sundays in July in the Cincinnati Court House and again by special request on three successive Sundays in August in the theater on Main and Sycamore Streets, she set forth at length the theories and ideals which inspired all her later preaching in her new role of "efficient leader of the popular mind."

These three lectures, afterwards expanded to six, published in 1829 and again in 1831, may be briefly described as a glorification of true

knowledge, always pronounced by her as Know-ledge, after the fashion
of some High-Church Episcopalians of the present day; not, it is hardly
necessary to explain, the "sancta Sophia" of early medieval philosophy,
but knowledge of facts derived by sensation through experience and
thus within reach of any reasonable human being; to be sharply distinguished therefore from belief and opinion derived from sources
which may not be verified by the senses, often incorrect, always biased,
and usually directed by personal and private interests for the preservation of the very faults of human society they were originally supposed to correct.

The method she chose for the development of her subject had nothing especially new and startling about it. It was, in fact, an old story
in the Scottish school of materialistic philosophy from which she had
drawn much of her inspiration in writing *A Few Days in Athens*. The
debt she owed to Jeremy Bentham is obvious on every page of her
lectures. Many of her most telling statements may be traced to the
speeches and writings of Robert Owen.

The effect they produced was due in large measure to their extreme novelty for the kind of people who made up Fanny's audiences
at the time of their first delivery. Her insistence that man was not a
helpless victim of the mysterious caprices of a remote and exacting
divine Providence, but an independent moral agent who needed only
the judicious development of the powers already in his possession to
be completely happy, was exceedingly gratifying to the natural pride
of men who had already won such miraculous results in their struggle
with the primeval wilderness. Her emphasis on facts, the kind of facts
that can be weighed and handled and made use of by the simplest
intelligence, as the foundation of all the belief and opinion taught
by special classes of initiates and only available to the common herd
by special opportunity, was also peculiarly appealing to men who had
already begun to feel the urge towards liberty and equality even in
education.

It was not till the last lecture in the series that Fanny's general train
of reasoning brought her to a direct attack on the Christian churches
as the most formidable enemies to human progress and human happiness along the lines she had just been indicating. The whole trend
of her argument on the source of true knowledge had already relegated
the teachings of the Christian religion to the class of belief and
opinion, particularly unreliable belief and opinion, in fact, because
from its very nature it was incapable of factual proof. She went on

to show that Christian theologians themselves admitted their reliance on supernatural truths supposed to be revealed to certain favored individuals but uncomprehended and incomprehensible to the mass of humankind. She herself had no wish or intention of shackling the free human spirit in any effort it might make to find the answers to the eternal questions of human life. All she asked was that any answer which was beyond the test of factual knowledge applied by logical reasoning, should be kept strictly in the secret mind of whoever conceived it. Such dreams, such fancies, for in the last analysis they were nothing more, might be permissible to individuals but should never be allowed to cost society some twelve millions annually. [The sum total supposed to have been raised by the Christian churches in their campaign for Christian education.] They should never receive the respectful consideration, and the daily sacrifice of time and effort from credulous multitudes, etc., etc.

One need not be surprised to learn, therefore, that her most persistent and redoubtable enemies throughout her whole public career were the Christian clergy. It was from one of these that she received the nickname which stuck to her during her whole campaign for the advancement of factual knowledge and free enquiry, "Priestess of Beelzebub."

A lively account of her first lecture in Cincinnati appears in Chapter VII of Mrs. Trollope's *Domestic Manners of the Americans*:

> That a lady of fortune, family, and education, whose youth had been passed in the most refined circles of private life, should present herself to the people in this capacity would naturally excite surprise anywhere . . . but in America where women are guarded by a seven-fold shield of habitual insignificance it has caused an effect which can scarcely be described.
>
> "Miss Wright of Nashoba is going to lecture at the Court House!" sounded from street to street and from house to house. I shared the surprise but not the wonder; I knew her extraordinary gift of eloquence, her almost unequalled command of words, and the wonderful power of her rich and thrilling voice; and I doubted not that if it were her will to do it, she had the power of commanding attention and enchanting the ear of any audience before whom it was her pleasure to appear . . . I was most anxious to hear her . . . but was almost deterred from attempting it by the reports

of the immense crowd that was expected. After many consultations, and hearing that many other ladies intended going, my friend Mrs. P. and myself decided upon making the attempt, accompanied by a party of gentlemen, and found the difficulty less than we had anticipated though the building was crowded in every part.

Her lecture was upon the nature of true knowledge and it contained little that could be objected to, by any sect or party; it was intended merely as an introduction to the strange and startling theories to be contained in subsequent lectures and could alarm only by its hints that the fabric of human wisdom could rest securely on no other base than that of human knowledge.

There was, however, one passage from which common sense revolted; it was one wherein she quoted that phrase of mischievous sophistry "All men are born free and equal."

This false and futile axiom which has done and is doing and will do so much harm to this fine country, came from Jefferson. Common sense enables me to pronounce this, his favorite maxim, false.

But to return to Miss Wright.

All my expectations fell far short of the splendor, the brilliance, the overwhelming eloquence of this extraordinary orator. . . . It is impossible to imagine anything more striking than her appearance. Her tall and majestic figure, the deep and almost solemn expression of her eyes, the simple contour of her finely formed head, unadorned excepting by its own natural ringlets. Her garment of plain white muslin which hung about her in folds that recalled the drapery of a Grecian statue, all contributed to produce an effect unlike anything I had ever seen before or expect to see.

But the Roman Catholic priest in Cincinnati lost no time in taking up the cudgels against her as a dangerous atheist, warning his flock "not to listen to that woman who was teaching foolishness." An article also appeared in the Saturday evening edition of the *Cincinnati Chronicle* signed by one Oliver Oldschool, which dares to make a little fun of Fanny's "chaste diction and logical deductions from unproved data, delivered with an air of determined purpose and fortitude that seems to expect and even court persecution and martyrdom, and combined with a persuasive smile and eloquent gestures," none of which things conceal the fact that "there was nothing new in Miss

Wright's doctrines though she with the arrogance of her pride would have us all believe that the torch of truth was never lighted till she blew her breath upon it."

Fanny herself, however, was entirely satisfied with the result of her teaching in Cincinnati, which she sums up as, "A kindling of wrath among the clergy! A reaction in favor of common sense on the part of their followers! An explosion of public sentiment in favor of liberty, liberality, and reforms in education! And a complete exposure of the nothingness of the press, which at a time when the popular mind was engrossed by questions of the first magnitude, sullenly avoided their discussion, betraying alike ignorance the most gross, and servility the most shameless!"

She returned to New Harmony early in September to take up her new duties as part owner and editor-in-chief of the New Harmony *Gazette.* This little periodical had originally been established and supported by Robert Owen the Elder with the intention of making it the general reporter and expositor of his co-operative experiment for the outside world. It had continued a languishing life during those hard times which struck the village after it ceased to be a community in the Owenite sense of the word.

To put this little periodical on a paying basis, to increase its circulation, to control its future policy as the one and only publication of the West entirely removed from party and sectarian (i.e. religious) influence now became the one absorbing object of Fanny herself and her two assistant editors Robert Dale Owen and Robert Jennings.

In her own account of this period of her life she tells how she was able to make drastic reforms in the printing and publishing of the paper by turning for advice and assistance to "the talented and energetic director of the Maclure School of Industry." The withdrawal of so many of the original members of the community and their children when the co-operative plan was abandoned, followed so quickly by the departure of Maclure himself for Mexico had left this unfortunate little Frenchman in a very bad way.

Fanny herself tells us how she found him struggling with the mental depression which had overtaken him on the destruction of his high hopes for success in his "General Method," while still faithfully applying himself to the instruction of the three youths who had accompanied him from France. Touched by a disappointment which she knew from experience how to appreciate, she roused him to new life and hope by a new call to action.

Our views meeting on this ground [she says], Mr. Phiquepal D'Arusmont volunteered to acquire and communicate
to his three French pupils a thorough knowledge of the
printing business in a month's time, asking only for that
period, free access to the printing office in which the New
Harmony *Gazette*, now issued on Miss Wright's responsibility,
was set into type. She knew that the friend who made this
offer possessed at the time no more acquaintance with the
printing business than she herself, but so entire was her confidence in his ability to seize at once upon the details of any
branch of science and its appropriate art, that she made
arrangements for the whole printing establishment to be
placed in Mr. Phiquepal D'Arusmont's hands before her
departure for Cincinnati. At the close of her first lecture in
the Court House she announced that the paper would arrive
in town on the day already agreed on with its new publisher. The paper arrived on the day announced and was
universally noticed for its general appearance and correct-
ness of typography.

This noteworthy achievement of the ex-director of Maclure's School
of Industry had its unfortunate side.

Madame Fretageot never forgave Phiquepal for his desertion of his
old patron. Whenever she mentions him in her voluminous correspondence with Maclure in Mexico it is with the utmost contempt and dislike. But she was always friendly, albeit a little mischievous, in her
comments on Fanny in her new role as leader of the popular mind.
She liked all four sons of Robert Owen who seemed to be permanently
settled in the village. She was really fond of Camilla, still lingering at
New Harmony with her husband, having no clear plans for the future.
Her letters to Maclure that autumn are full of lively gossip about the
goings and comings at No. 1, still the principal boardinghouse of the
southern half of the village, under the not very efficient direction of
Robert Dale's new friend Mrs. Chase, so favorably described by him
to Fanny in his first account of his return to New Harmony.

Oct. 3

Yesterday Camilla came in and made me laugh so much
with the description of No. 1. that I want you to enjoy it also.
The little lady Chase succeeds with the three young Owens
whom she leads at her wishes. She has such a dislike for our
friend Jennings that all her efforts are put in motion to prevent

his success with his school. A new arrangement concerning Phiquepal and the boys as boarders with the family has given rise to her displeasure. She thinks herself quite disgraced by being obliged to sit down at table with such kind of people. The three young Owens are now at war on the subject with their elder brother. Camilla told me she did not know what to do and desired my advice on the subject. "Nothing else," said I, "but to desire Mrs. Chase to take her meals at her own house instead of at No. 1." "But," said she, "a violent step like that might carry her bad will to its full extent." "Do then what you think best," said I. "As I know no fear I always say and do what I think best." I told her that you had named me your agent in your absence.

From this same source one learns that Fanny had no idea of spending the winter quietly in New Harmony.

Robert Dale told me yesterday that F. W. had intention to go up the Ohio and give lectures on her way to New York and Philadelphia. She will be accompanied by Jennings who, it appears, is quite disappointed in his expectation with his school. Mr. and Mrs. Chase are not getting on together. The latter went to walk with Robert Owen. Chase ran after them with a speed that roused the suspicion of the lazy part of the population standing about. As soon as he met them ascending the hill he knocked down poor Robert who began crying saying he did not know there was any harm taking a walk with a lady that he looked upon as a sister!

Plans for this projected trip of Fanny and Jennings to the East were painfully interrupted by bad news from Nashoba. The overseer, Gilliam, had been left in complete control since Fanny's departure the preceding June, and had proved not only dishonest and untrustworthy in his management of the plantation, but, what was far worse in an experiment like Nashoba, he had also given the slaves more than a taste of the harsh treatment too often dealt out to the helpless negroes of absentee owners of plantations in the deep South.

Madame Fretageot's next letter, October 10th, gives her own mischievous version of the new catastrophes at Nashoba and their immediate effect on Fanny's grand schemes for the improvement of the human race.

You know, my dear friend what a dreadful effect this quality of imagination produces in every situation, in every undertaking. I have under my eyes a good specimen of it. Frances
Wright is obliged to go immediately to Nashoba. Whitby
has written that the whole is in a miserable situation, that
the Overseer has made use of the store in such a manner that
nothing remains, that the slaves have not produced corn for
three months for their food. She goes with her sister and
Mr. Jennings, the last a good being, but without steadiness,
in fact without head: like every one else of the No. 1 group
who do not possess altogether united that portion of good
sense so necessary in every undertaking. They never see the
advantages directly under their eyes but are always looking
forward to everything but their own interest.

I had a long conversation with them yesterday when they
came to consult me about their business. What should they
do? I told them.

"You, Frances and Camilla, go back to Nashoba and work
it yourselves for all it is worth and make it pay. Or if you
can't manage it yourself and cannot find anyone that would
manage it for you with the same interest, sell it.

"You, Robert, go to work at the *Gazette*, print it yourself
as I do the *Disseminator*. By this alone you can save $1000
a year. Sell your riding horses. You are young enough to
walk."

I told Jennings that if he wished to succeed with his school
he must remain on the job instead of going off on lecture trips.
They are already in difficulties with Phiquepal. They cannot
manage him and he means to manage them. They laughed
heartily at my advice and told me that kind of thing might
do for me but that they had higher views. "Well, my friends,"
said I, "I know you think me a booby but I shall not be
hanged for that."

Oct. 21st. Frances Wright is gone to Nashoba with Jennings as I told you in my last. Your sisters are still here with
me at No. 5. I do not know when they will get into their new
house. It is a pity they are so much against having their
cook eat with them at table because it gives an immense deal
of trouble.

Mr. Chase has turned his wife out. Robert Dale told me
that the three young ones were distracted with love for her

and think her husband very hard-hearted not to receive her back.

But Madame Fretageot's advice, that the two sisters should settle down on the plantation, and run it for a profit, however well it sounded on paper, was fantastically useless for persons so lacking in every quality necessary for the success of such an undertaking as Fanny and Camilla. They could not take any steps to sell the plantation till they had got rid of the slaves. These could not be sold without breaking what Fanny justly considered a sacred obligation to them. They could not be enfranchised without the expenditure of a great deal more money than she had at her disposal to set them up for themselves in Tennessee, even if the laws of that state permitted it. They could not again be subjected to such treatment as they had already received from Gilliam, or indeed any overseer who did not possess the same high ideals for their management as Fanny herself.

The only alternative left her in the predicament was to impress, cajole, or make it generally worth the while of her brother-in-law, Richeson Whitby, to resume the ungrateful task of overseer on the plantation at Nashoba, a position for which he had already shown himself temperamentally and physically unfit. How much this arrangement cost the two sisters in the end, is shown by a document inserted in the Journal of the Plantation under the date October 24th.

I, Camilla Wright Whitby, do bind my heirs, executors, and administrators to pay Richeson Whitby, the annual sum of $300 during his own life, the said annuity to be payable half yearly to begin Jan. 1st. 1829.

To this may be appended another paper dated October 30th.

Know all men by these presents that I, Frances Wright of Nashoba have made and appointed Richeson Whitby of said Nashoba my true and lawful attorney in fact, for the purpose of discharging the object and carrying into effect the original intentions for which said establishment at Nashoba was founded.

Signed R. S. Jennings
James Richardson
Marcus Winchester
Frances Wright.

Camilla was to remain with her husband in their old quarters on the plantation, at least till after the birth of her child sometime in January. There was nowhere else for her to go while her sister and Jennings were off on their long delayed trip to the East. The fact of her marriage seems to have made little or no change in the Camilla one has already learned to know as Fanny's devoted slave, always more absorbed in her sister's life and interests than in anything life had to offer her for herself.

Their enforced separation, until the birth of her child should permit their reunion, was almost as painful to Fanny as to the sister left behind.

Those letters sent back by Fanny at every point of her journey, dashed off in headlong haste, often before she allowed herself any rest after long exhausting days of travel, are full of remorseful tenderness and solicitude.

The first of these is from Memphis where she and Jennings were delayed several days waiting for a steamboat to take them to Louisville, their first projected stop.

We are still here, dear lamb, and employing our time busily in writing. I have not yet set head or hand to the lectures which I must have in readiness for Louisville but shall begin forthwith. We expect a boat from hour to hour to take us on, and would it were here and we off in it for I do not think the benefit accruing to this little public from our discourses will counter balance the loss of time and money to ourselves. I am losing the effect of my headache though I am still not quite as I was and shall be again in a day or two.

I pray thee, dear Love, to keep heart and mind as quiet as possible. I am convinced it is Richeson's earnest wish to assist us. The arrangements made concerning Nashoba appear to me and to all consulted, not only the best but the only possible and fair under existing circumstances. Richeson, I fear, will have trouble with the slaves, but as he has all the experience requisite and all the good feeling, there is all the chance of success that such affairs admit of.

It seems to me, as far as I understand the circumstances between you and him that our most painful feelings usually arise from misunderstandings. Take care of thyself, my Love.

I gave my lecture here last night. I think we shall do good and did so then in preventing the foundation of churches and the introduction of preachers in the place. Winchester

is going to throw the upper storey of his house into one
large room where the advocates of Truth may always find
a place to raise their voice in. He proposes also to hold it for
a dancing room and hire it for balls and other amusements
which may repay him the necessary expense.

The steamboat for Louisville still delaying to make its appearance,
she suddenly decided to embark on one going straight up the river
to St. Louis, a city not included in her original itinerary. And Fanny's
next letter to her sister comments on this visit.

My last discourse at St. Louis produced an effect beyond
any I have yet delivered, and the intelligent enthusiasm and
pure feeling which sparkled in the eyes and burned on the
cheeks of many young and old hearers in the crowd who stood
as if still listening when I had ceased, will, I think, never
leave my memory. Our agent there is a noble stirring spirit.
The "Black Swans" now form there the marrow of the population and hold their heads an inch higher than formerly.

Twenty-five subscriptions paid in before our departure,
which with the payments received at Memphis gave us exactly $100 to forward to Robert for the *Gazette*.

Her next letter from Louisville describes their journey across the
prairie states of Illinois and Indiana, by way of Vincennes on the upper
Wabash.

We arrived here night before last pretty well fagged out.
The roads and weather across the Illinois prairie were beautiful, but both veered to the other extreme in crossing Indiana.
Through the art and care of excellent drivers, however, we
escaped with our necks.

The weather cleared the evening of our arrival here after
a day of snow and storm, against which our buffalo robes
afforded a brave defense. We found our agent here, our good
friend Salmon, happy in the birth of a little daughter whom
he swears he is going to bring up to be an infidel preacher.
He and his brother liberals are making arrangements for my
meeting the population in the theatre tonight and tomorrow,
and the next morning we shall proceed to Cincinnati and
Wheeling without stopping at Lexington, Ky. fearing to lose
the water now in good order to Pittsburgh.

Cin'ti, Nov. 25th.

Jennings has just brought me your letter of Nov. 9th, my Cam, which cheers and comforts me exceedingly. To know that you are well and to imagine that you are as cheerful as is consistent with our separation, sends us both on our way rejoicing. My affectionate remembrances to Richeson. Kiss little Bob for me. I rejoice the dog was so soon comforted and that you find him more pleasure than trouble. Affectionate regards to Richardson and Winchester, my lamb! . . .

The good seed sown the previous summer in this city is not difficult to find again. I lectured twice on the Sunday we passed here and they roused to action that first evening, when a sudden meeting was called by about 50 independents who were already in the audience, for the purpose of passing a resolution to publish a circular in the Wednesday paper, calling upon all citizens favorable to the plan for establishing in that city, a popular institution [on the lines no doubt already suggested by her and finally carried out in her own Hall of Science in New York] to assemble at the place and hour appointed.

As the plan was immediately taken up by men of spirit and wealth I trust something will be carried. They are very anxious for us to settle in Cincinnati, and were we to do so I have little doubt but that we should gradually unite the great mass of the population in a wider knowledge of true moral principle and practice. We, of course, gave no pledge for our return to settle here as on the whole some city in the East may be more suitable. I am told Baltimore would be a better choice both for the climate and spirit of the people. But we shall see. . . .

I have taken up the pen again which I had to throw down in obedience to the stage's horn, at this inn on the road 20 miles east of Cumberland. We arrived here yesterday P.M. getting out of the stage after two days and two nights travelling over roads made to dislocate bones. The stage will pick us up today at one o'clock and will land us at Baltimore tomorrow night.

The winter has been mild and pleasant and it is almost warm this morning. Would that we were at the end of our peregrinations or that we knew where that end would be.

Though somewhat rested I am still too stiff and tired for writing even to our Cam. We enquired anxiously for letters at Wheeling. I fear now we shall not hear of thee nearer than New York.

Her stay in Baltimore was such a scramble of engagements for speaking and meeting all the people who wished interviews with her, that she did not find a minute for the story of her adventures there to the anxious sister she had left behind her till she was actually on board the river steamboat on her way from Baltimore to Philadelphia, where she resumes as follows:

In Baltimore, my sweet lamb, my moments were so absolutely run down by enthusiastic citizens and ardent friends that what with private talking and public speaking, neither my time and strength would admit my writing to thee of my fond and anxious thoughts, nor of our progress in the good cause. Having obtained the name of a Baltimore Liberal from William Price [an old Harmony acquaintance, settled later in Cincinnati, and one of her warmest supporters, perhaps her host, during her recent visits to that city], a Dr. Haslam, whom, by the way, he, Price, had never seen, Jennings took the precaution to write to him as well as to Lovegrove, our agent for the *Gazette* in that city. We found them both in waiting at the door of the stage office, from whence the good Doctor carried us to his house which he insisted should be our home during our stay in Baltimore.

The smaller theatre was thrown open by its owner, a warm liberal, for the lectures. I gave five lectures in successive nights to an audience whose pressure seemed to endanger the building. I can give you no conception of the stir in the public mind which my lectures have occasioned during the past week. The public reaction against their ghostly leaders seems likely to be in proportion—that is, if we should settle here but we are earnestly called for in Philadelphia and New York and must see all before we can determine.

We have arranged to give a course of lectures in the large Universalist Church in Philadelphia, and in the Chatham Street theatre in New York.

Philadelphia seems to offer the most central location, and we are told that the mechanics there are in active cooperation and want nothing, they say, but some heads to guide them. A few weeks more and we shall write something decisive. The West is out of the question, and that is all we can now see of the future.

But wherever we finally decide to fix the press I will not give up locomotion, but aid in keeping up the ball in the three cities.

We assisted at a meeting of Baltimore liberals last night, when it was proposed to take measures for the erection of a Hall of Science and a school of Industry on the plan suggested in my discourses. An ingenious mechanic who has erected many of the public buildings in the city proposes to raise a Hall, worth $20,000, for the sum of $4000, the mechanics to receive shares entitling a given number of children for gratis instruction for the work given.

A committee has been appointed of a few popular and influential citizens who are to attempt raising the necessary contributions privately, as many, it is thought, will aid the measure secretly who could not publicly.

On the last week in January they are pledged to report progress and I have pledged myself to return and assist by a repetition of the course of lectures. . . .

I write on my knee in a cabin of the steamboat which is taking me from Baltimore to Philadelphia. A cabin crowded with ladies who perhaps feel in my company as in the presence of a new importation from the South Seas, and I most certainly feel in theirs as some such unfortunate antipodian to whom the surrounding minds and manners are as uncongenial as their bonnets.

P.S. The ladies are growing tame and volunteering little civilities to the South Sea Islander!

[In Philadelphia] there was difficulty in procuring a building large enough and the pressure was so excessive that men and women fainted dead away. Notwithstanding which the attention was so highly wrought that order and silence were never interrupted. I rather think that we shall open business in the Quaker City. It is a propitious moment there. The Quakers, as you will hear, are split to pieces and the schismatics know not under what standard to rally. They were among the most eager of our hearers in Baltimore as in Philadelphia. Of course the orthodox are very loud and very angry, though they for the most part keep quiet till our backs are turned. It seems best, however, to make no decision till we have seen New York.

The mixture of apprehension and exaltation with which she entered on this last stage of adventure is described as follows in her often quoted biography:

> On a clear and fiercely cold night, the last in the year 1828, when a north-western gale detained her in the steamboat, on the contrary side of the bay from the city, she passed an hour or two on the deck, gazing on that which was to be the chief seat of her exertions, and as she foresaw, of painful and complicated sacrifice and persecution. In that city were some heart affections which dated from her first landing in the country. These, the course prescribed to her by duty was perhaps about to sever. Friends in official situations or political standing, whom considerations of propriety would oblige her in appearance to forget. Houses in which she had been a daughter, and which she must now pass with the regardless eye of a stranger. Some she knew would understand her course, and in silence appreciate her motives. Others might feel embarrassed. Among the latter her heart recalled Charles Wilkes, late president of the Bank of New York, a native of England and nephew of the John Wilkes of Opposition and Parliamentary celebrity; the same friend to whom she had dedicated her first volume on America. Imbued, as by inheritance from a fond and aristocratic mother, with other political views from herself, this difference of opinion and even feeling had never been allowed to check their intimacy or to chill their friendship. Her first care on her arrival was to address him a few lines, leaving it to him to regulate their future relations. That whatever might be his decision, on her side the remembrance of past years would always live in her heart, together with those sentiments of affection for himself and his family which she had cherished for years and which would remain unaltered for life.
>
> In a few lines couched in the same strain, he accepted, as she thought, wisely, her suggestion of dissolved or suspended intimacy. He resigned, moreover, the charge of her worldly interests and what she much regretted, those of her sister, which last had been more especially and entirely in his hands from the time of their first arrival in the U. S. This circumstance afterwards involved serious and painful losses.

Most of the daily papers gave ample space to her first appearance before the New York public, but only four need be mentioned as

especially concerned in that campaign of ruthless and derisive persecution which spared neither her person nor her sex—especially her sex
—or her reputation, past, present, or future.

The *New York Commercial Advertiser*, whose editor, William Leete
Stone, was a man only a few years older than Fanny herself, very
much like her in his unconscious self-esteem and sense of his own
importance; son of a Yale Congregationalist minister, brother-in-law
of the President of Brown College, a staunch Federalist, opposed to
the extension of manhood suffrage, equally unfriendly to any talk of
Woman's Rights. He was just the kind of man by inheritance, training and temperament, to be particularly annoyed by the appearance
of a woman of Fanny's caliber on the public stage and never lost an
opportunity to do her all the harm he could in the pages of his paper.

The *American*, whose editor, Charles King, later President of Columbia College, was in many respects the same kind of man as Stone,
although he never went to the same lengths of vilification as the editor
of the *Commercial Advertiser*.

The New York *Evening Post* had been brought into existence by
Alexander Hamilton as a Federalist newspaper at a moment of bitter
party war during the presidential campaign of 1828, had gone over to
Jacksonian Democracy, and now under its distinguished young editor,
William Cullen Bryant, was showing strong tendencies towards cham-
pioning the rights and fighting the wrongs of the common man. This
did not prevent Bryant from poking a great deal of lively nonsense at

> . . . . the new Aspasia
> From whom Religion awaits her doom
> Her quiet death, her euthanasia.

Last, but not least of Fanny's enemies in the newspaper world, was
the *Courier and Enquirer*, so called because it had resulted from a
merger between two daily newspapers of those names, both of which
had been bought by that picturesque figure in New York of the late
twenties, James Watson Webb, a very handsome, rather dissipated
young man who ran his paper by engaging the most brilliant persons
he could find to do it for him. Chief of his editorial staff when Fanny
came to town was Major Mordecai Noah (a courtesy title), of Portuguese Jewish descent, unscrupulous, witty, without genuine conviction as to the claim of one political party over the others but for the

time being a Jackson Democrat and a sachem of Tammany Hall, through which influence he had been appointed by the President to the office of Surveyor of the Port of New York in 1829, and hoped some day to be elected Mayor of the city. At one time he had conceived the idea of developing an American Zion, a refuge for the oppressed Jews of all nations, and had bought for this purpose a large tract of land at Grand Island in the Niagara River, where with imposing ceremonies he had laid the cornerstone of his future city, Ararat. The dedication ceremony was attended by civic and military authorities, and later the cornerstone was placed in a brick building erected as an Ark on Goat Island. The project never materialized, the site became little more than a real estate manipulation and the whole project was soon forgotten.

On the whole, however, Major Noah was not unpopular among his fellow journalists, though never really accepted as an equal by the distinguished editors of the *Commercial Advertiser*, the *American*, and the *Evening Post*. He was very much criticized for adopting the American spelling of I for E in the word "Enquirer," and replied with the pun, "Any man who would put out his new neighbor's eyes ought to forfeit all ease for the rest of his life."

One cannot attempt to do more than quote here and there from the flood of reportorial eloquence let loose by Fanny's first appearance in the Masonic Hall on Saturday January 3rd, 1829. Perhaps a signed article by Charles King in the *American* gives the best example of how this first lecture was treated.

When, then, I arrived in front of the uncouth Gothic edifice, Gothic in every sense except the right one, and climbed its breakneck stairway to the mysterious chamber by turns the scene of masonry and music, dancing, anti-auction protests, absurdities, preaching and profanity, I was fairly tip toe with excitement.

The whole space was occupied with well-bred, well-behaved people, Dr. Mitchell moving to and fro with uneasy step within the reserved precinct. As the appointed hour sounded from St. Paul there was a general turning of heads.

She came up the aisle, and attained the platform, accompanied by a bevy of female apostles and a single thick-set and well-constituted little Scotchman. He helped her in her little matters, received her cloak and also her cap à la Cowper, which she took off as we men do, by grasping it with a single hand.

A tall ungainly figure, of masculine proportions, dressed in broadcloth, evidently a woman's riding habit, surmounted by a ruffle fastened in front by a silken scarf, confined by a brooch. In her hand, neither white nor well-turned, her lecture. A gold watch suspended from her girdle.

An English face, proclaimed the welcome fact that she was no country woman of ours. Hair parted in the middle, ringlets on either side, complexion reddish and wind-worn. Her eye bold and fearless yet glazed and unsteady as if its energies had been wasted by midnight study or its lustre marred by indulgence and by sorrow.

She stood unmoved, broke silence in a clear strong voice, uttered coldly and with scrupulous enunciation a string of truisms.

Opinions half-way between later Scotch metaphysicians of the School of Reid and the inductive philosophy of Lawrence and the London Physiologists.

Stone, in the *Commercial Advertiser*, is on the whole complimentary.

Her enunciation is perfect and she has complete command over it. Her emphasis and pauses and the whole of her delivery are excellent, and her gestures appropriate and graceful. So far as these qualifications constitute an orator, we believe her unrivalled by any of the public speakers of any description in this city. For an hour and a half she held the attention of her audience enchained excepting that attempts made to applaud which were frequently suppressed by a majority from a wish not to interrupt her, at length succeeded, and towards the conclusion she received several distinct and thunderous rounds of applause. Nor would it be doing justice to the lady if we did not add that her language was singularly well chosen and accurate. That there was much eloquence of style added to that of manner and the keeping of the whole performance was so good that the sensation of the ludicrous, naturally suggested by its novelty was entirely suppressed.

And that Fanny herself was on the whole well-satisfied with her first reception may be seen in the following letter written to her sister a day or two after the event:

New York, January 5th.

Dearest Love

We are about to pitch our tent here. All things considered
with respect to Europe and this country, this is the most
central spot for us. The excitement produced by my opening
discourse, delivered the night before last in the Masonic Hall,
supposed to contain when well packed which it most undoubtedly was, from 1500 to 2000 people, has been very
great, though I will not say greater than elsewhere, since
the same spirit of enquiry and reformation seems to exist
throughout the land, and to require only the match to burst
into flame.

Cadwallader Colden was among the audience on Saturday which convinces me that I had not been mistaken respecting the secret liberality of his opinions. I was amused
at the fervor of Dr. Mitchell who stood during the lecture at
the foot of the platform and who running up the steps as I
closed, greeted me with all the enthusiasm he could have
bestowed upon the sea serpent itself. Good McNevin found
me this morning and seems to grow young again at the
thought of our settling here. The poor liberals are so happy
to get their breath out, and look so cheerful it does my heart
good to see them and to feel the warm shake of their hands.

I communicate on business with Charles Wilkes by letter,
a measure I trust he will adhere to, as personal intercourse
between friends thoroughly opposed in sentiment can never
produce aught save discomfort.

I board with an amiable unfortunate widow in Murray
Street whom, others shunning on account of the change in
her circumstances from wealth to poverty, we see reason for
preferring.

Jennings has taken an office conveniently situated in this
street near the corner of Broadway where he will open business which will be confined for the present to receiving
names of prospective subscribers and giving information respecting the paper. This will be of double importance here
where our present agent is dishonest.

This decision of Fanny's to make New York her permanent headquarters for her new experiment brought a wail of distress from the
unfortunate Camilla whose whole hope for the future was fixed on
the moment when the sisters should be again united.

The old scandals of Nashoba seemed to have been safely forgotten in the blaze of publicity which had attended Fanny's progress to the East in her new role of "Priestess of Beelzebub." But what could more easily revive them than the reappearance at her side of the very person most closely connected with them in the past? For there was no doubt that Camilla had been even more directly involved in the incident described by Richardson's article to the *Genius of Universal Emancipation* than Fanny herself who was known to have been absent in Europe at the time; while ill-natured gossips continued to represent that informal marriage with Richeson Whitby as no marriage at all, but a free-love covenant on the lines already laid down for Fanny Wright's Free Love Community.

Fanny, however, was not the kind of person to be disturbed by such insinuations.

> Dearest Love, I know not how to reply to all the doubts and fears expressed in your last letter. I can only state again what I have often stated in the past that I see no way at any time but to weigh all circumstances and decide upon that course which seems to present the fewest objections.
>
> I adhered to the principle of a co-operative community until I stood alone, and until I was convinced that the principle was at least one generation ahead of the human mind. It was my determination, always definitely stated, to remain in the woods for this experiment or, that failing to return into the world so far as was necessary to place myself in the reach of society more congenial in habits and manners than those the backwoods could supply, where I could be really useful. One may be as much alone in the neighborhood of a city, if not more so, than in the woods, while still having the choice of stepping forth when circumstances call upon us, without the danger of intrusion on the part of those who disagree with our opinions, with as little sacrifice of our own personal feelings as may be consistent with our new undertaking. New Harmony is out of the question, were it only from the deficiency and irregularity of communication by mail aside from all other objections which are numerous and forcible. Memphis presents difficulties of a private nature besides all the others. Men and women are just as foolish there, just as curious about what does not concern them as elsewhere, with much more opportunity for being curious than exists in a city.
>
> Keep thy dear mind at rest. Be not anxious about future

possibilities. Remember, dearest, that I am not given to shrink
from shadows or to fash my head about the nonsense of old
women either in petticoats or pantaloons. My heresies are
fully known and yet the good and wise of all classes can respect me. Why then, dearest should you think that you or
anything concerning you could interfere with my utility?
Believe it not, fear it not. Let us hold our way quietly along
the road of life and be satisfied that the many are more likely
to come round to us than to stone us to death. Everyone here
is delighted with our plans for the future. A free press is
absolutely wanted and loudly called for and there is not one
free and independent newspaper throughout the country.

In a somewhat different key one finds Madame Fretageot announcing the same event to her patron in Mexico. "Robert Dale is going
to New York to help Frances Wright found an institution on the
plan of Epicurus in Athens, as well as to continue his paper under
the title, Free Enquirer, in that city. Thus we lose them all and if I
am not mistaken, it will prove beneficial to our establishment in
removing the public attention from this place, while the spreading of
liberal principles abroad will smooth our ways."

All this time Fanny was steadily increasing her audiences in the
city of New York, till they gradually came to include a veritable following of respectable members of the female sex (to revert to the
title by which women were generally designated in those far-off
days). Even more noticeable among her audiences were certain pro-
testing elements in the population which neither churches nor political
parties had been entirely successful in assimilating.

She was equally successful in drawing a swarm of enemies against
her by her reiterated attacks on what she still chose to call "the
Christian Party in Politics."

So it happened that the tolerant, somewhat contemptuous amusement and curiosity displayed by leaders of opinion towards a new
phenomenon among the human species, a lecturing woman, which had
greeted her first performances in the city, was gradually replaced
by disapproval verging towards actual persecution, from both pulpit
and press.

An attempt was made to smoke out one of her meetings at the
Masonic Hall by placing a barrelful of combustible matter in the
doorway and setting it ablaze. "Dense clouds of smoke rolled up
through the Hall but Miss Wright's presence of mind did not desert

her and her coolness prevented a panic." A few days later in the same hall, the gas was suddenly turned off leaving some 2000 people in complete darkness.

And when the New York *Evening Post* discovered that the Park Theatre had been leased to Miss Wright for a second series of lectures, it lost its head completely and came very near inciting the very riot and bloodshed it professed to dread, in an article appearing in its pages on January 10, 1829.

Had the lessees of this theater considered what might be the actual damage to their property if these lectures were allowed to take place?

> Suppose the singular spectacle of a female, publicly and ostentatiously proclaiming doctrines of an atheistical fanaticism, and even the most abandoned lewdness, should draw a crowd from prurient curiosity, and a riot should ensue, which should end in the demolition of the interior of the building or even in the burning it down—on whom would the loss fall? Would the policy of insurance against fire which describes it as a building devoted to theatrical exhibitions of a very different description and which must attract a very different order of people, cover the loss?
>
> Is there no danger of collecting an unruly mob which nothing perhaps can restrain short of public force and bloodshed itself? We shall merely put these bare questions for the present, and let those answer them on whom the awful responsibility would devolve if any frightful consequence should happen to the city or its inhabitants. Remember the good old homely proverb, "An ounce of prevention is worth a pound of cure."

It is interesting to note here that this passionate appeal of the *Evening Post* had no effect on the lessees of the Park Theatre who continued to take Fanny's good money for the use of that building for the delivery of her lectures on the nights of January 27th, 29th, and February 3rd, 4th, 7th, and 9th, with no terrible results to the premises, or the city. In fact the desire of the management of this theater to take all possible advantage of the situation to fill their own pockets, carried them so far as to revive Fanny's play of *Altorf* which was presented on the evenings of January 22nd, and 24th, and met with a good reception from a large audience, according to the *New York Courier and Enquirer* (January 24, 1829).

Suddenly the very thing poor Camilla had so desperately dreaded came to pass. Extracts from "Explanatory Notes on the Community of Nashoba" began to appear in the *Journal of Commerce*, a business and financial sheet under the direction of those strict Presbyterians and Sabbatarians, Lewis and Arthur Tappan. All the other newspapers took them up and hastened to prove Fanny not only "a bold blasphemer aiming at the ridicule of vital religion and the pious faithful preachers of the Gospel," but a woman "impervious to the voice of virtue and case-hardened against shame, a voluptuous preacher of licentiousness"; in a word, "a female monster whom all decent people ought to avoid."

For a while she was at a disadvantage from having no newspaper of her own on the field in which she might openly reply to such venomous attacks. The New Harmony *Gazette* had begun its new series under the new name of *Free Enquirer* in October of the preceding year and had at first proposed to remain in New Harmony until April, 1829, supplying copies of the paper to the ever increasing number of its subscribers in the Eastern cities especially New York—by mail. But in the throes of her battle with the New York press, Fanny grew more and more impatient with the inevitable delays such a system entailed, till at last, in her own high-handed way, she suddenly made up her mind to print and issue a second copy of the *Free Enquirer* in New York on the same date with the New Harmony edition, and containing generally the same matter. In matters of local interest, however, it was practically a new paper, for which she and Jennings were solely responsible. This practice was carried on until both issues should be combined at the date originally chosen for removal.

Robert Dale himself had nothing to do with this sudden decision, did not like it, and did not himself come on to New York till some time after the paper had ceased to function in the West.

It was Phiquepal who hurried eastward at Fanny's first call, ready and eager to contribute all he had for the new venture. His first stay in New York was brief. He returned to New Harmony in the early winter to pack up his belongings preparatory to removing them and his three French pupils to the new establishment which Fanny was already preparing for her paper in the East.

The account of this trip of Phiquepal and his pupils down the Ohio and Mississippi rivers on a flat boat, manned only by themselves and a thoroughly inefficient and inexperienced pilot, as told by

Amadée Dufour, one of the pupils in a letter to his guardian, the Count of Beauséjour, reads like a dime novel of adventure and hairbreadth escapes from flood, shipwreck and alligators. But until his arrival, Fanny had as usual found a friend both willing and able to assume all the necessary details involved in printing as well as issuing the paper in New York. This was George Evans, an enthusiastic admirer of Thomas Paine, who constantly jeopardized his legitimate business of printer and bookseller by the production and sale of free thought literature which more cautious members of his trade refused to handle. Evans was more than ready to accept this added responsibility in connection with Fanny's new paper.

The first issue of the paper appeared on January 21, 1829, and in her first signed editorial she had her first dig at her enemies, the newspaper men.

> In the present state of the American press, it is hard to judge who are on the side of truth. Nay, were we to take the press for an organ of public sentiment, we might conceive that a mental palsy had fallen upon the nation, and that the whole people were engaged in quarrelling about trifles, libelling their public officers, insulting individuals, or sleeping away their intellects under the fumes of tobacco.
>
> But the press does not speak the voice of the nation. It does not even speak the voice of those who write for it, etc., etc.

After this preamble one is not surprised to hear that no notice was taken of this first appearance of the *Free Enquirer* by any of the New York newspapers, except the *Commercial Advertiser* which informed its readers in its issue of January 31st, that "the paper was empty, insignificant and tedious, as inaccurate as the Tour in America, as fabulous as the Days in Athens and as chimerical as the Institutions of New Harmony. Its imbecile dullness rendered it harmlessly wicked."

A contrary opinion is expressed by W. R. Waterman (in his Ph.D. thesis on Frances Wright published by the Faculty of Political Science at Columbia University, 1924):

> This interesting and ably edited little paper of which a few files still exist devoted itself to fearless and unbiased enquiry on all subjects. Although for the first two years of its life the chief topic of discussion was theology, time was found

to advocate the abolition of capital punishment, and of imprisonment for debt, social, pecuniary and political equality for women, equal civil rights for all, and the right of every man to testify in court without enquiry being made as to his religious creed. The paper also urged the adoption of a national system of education free from sectarian teachings with industrial schools where the children of the poor might be taught farming as a trade and obtain without charge, support as well as education.

Its appearance just at the moment when Houston's *New York Correspondent* was on its last legs, delighted the Liberals, to use the name by which Fanny was pleased to designate her particular circle of Free Thinkers, who were "fascinated with the charm of Style, beauty of diction and boldness of invective which they found in its pages."

It also made itself useful as a medium of exchange of views, and information concerning the general activities of those groups of young mechanics who had begun to combine for redress of the hard conditions of their daily toil. Indeed, even before the establishment of this paper in New York, it had become unpleasantly evident to some of Fanny's enemies in high places that no inconsiderable part of her audiences was drawn from exactly this class of society.

It was while she and Jennings were still alone in the field with more than enough to do to meet the requirements of a practically new issue of their paper every week in New York, and at the same time keep in touch with their old staff and old subscribers in the West, that Fanny also assumed the responsibility and advanced the money for the second of those two enterprises with which her name is most closely connected during this period of her public activities.

As she describes it in a letter to her sister.

Do not start, my love, I have turned a Church into a Hall of Science and am possessor of it. It was knocked down at auction yesterday very privately. News of it was brought to us an hour before the sale. A friend bought it in for us for three fourths of the value of the land only. Some church speculators had hoped to buy the property for a song and I suppose are sadly crestfallen at its having fallen into the hands of the Many instead of the Few.

The present building is small and old, not nearly covering

the whole lot which is in the heart of the city, the best possible situation. The Liberals are delighted.

We think we can make all the necessary repairs in about
a fortnight, and expect to open the Hall of Science after that
space of time.

The old Ebenezer Church in Broome Street near the Bowery cost
her $7000, and after some remodeling became her Hall of Science
with a seating capacity of about 1200. In the basement were located
the offices of the *Free Enquirer*. The management of the Hall of
Science, Miss Wright placed in the hands of five trustees who were
to secure competent lecturers on scientific and moral subjects and
organize a day and Sunday school which it was proposed to establish.
Late in the history of the hall the trustees provided a dispensary with
an attending physician. When not otherwise engaged the hall might
be rented for outside lecturers and this was occasionally done. The
trustees also made a little money by the sale of such works as Volney's
Ruins and other books not approved by the orthodox opinion of that
day. The ceremony of its dedication was one of the few perfect moments of her life. It took place on April 28th while she and Robert
Jennings were still the sole representatives of the staff of the *Free
Enquirer* in New York.

Free thought odes, composed by Fanny, and set to music for the
occasion, preceded and concluded her address, which she delivered
to crowded benches. The speech so clearly defines her aims and hopes
as a leader of the public mind and director of a Hall of Science that
one may be forgiven for quoting from it at some length.

The object that assembles us here this day is the same for
which through all past ages the wise have labored and the
good have suffered. This object it imports us well to understand and steadily to keep in view. If misconceived, or if lost
sight of, our efforts here will be worse than useless, they
will be mischievous.

The words engraved over the entrance of this building de-
fine *its* purpose and *our* object. Raised and consecrated to
sectarian faith, it stands devoted this day to universal knowledge—and we, in crossing its threshold, have to throw aside
the distinctions of class; the names and feelings of sect or
party; to recognize in ourselves and each other the single
character of human beings and fellow creatures, and thus to

sit down, as children of one family, in patience to inquire, in humility to learn . . .

The effects of erroneous education, and the influence of unfavorable circumstances are more or less with us all. As believers, we have learned censoriousness with our creeds of faith; as heretics or sceptics, we have learned intolerance from persecution. Judging or judged, inflicting or enduring, our bosoms have been filled with bitterness from our youth up; our hearts estranged from each other and our thoughts still bent rather on proving others wrong than on seeking the right for ourselves, and there is none among us, even the best and the wisest has not some rebellious spirit to quell, some internal censorship to execute, ere he can enter at peace with all mankind the courts of union and sit down in simplicity of heart, a pupil in the Hall of Science . . .

Our object is simply and singly the acquisition of knowledge and its diffusion among our fellow creatures . . .

Under the wise direction of men of science, honest enough to reveal what they know, and bold enough to be silent where they are ignorant, your steps cannot err, and your minds must gradually expand to the perception of all those truths most important for man to understand. But this I will say, be sure that ye mistake not between what is now esteemed earning and what *is* knowledge. Endeavor to curb that rutile curiosity which, fostered by a vicious education, is ever winging the human imagination beyond what the eye hath seen, the touch examined, and the judgment compared . . . The field of nature is before us to explore; the world of the human heart is with us to examine. In these lie for us all that is certain, all that is important.

I mean not altogether to condemn religious discussions while the world is overrun with conflicting religious superstitions; but, methinks, in our popular meetings I would condemn them here. We must bear in mind that we come together in this place as members of a family long divided and estranged by feuds and strifes; that we see in each other wanderers from every school of faith—it may be Jews, Christians, deists, materialists, with every variety of sect and class existing within the pale of each. Surely, then, prudence, if no higher virtue, demands that we set a watch upon our lips, lest haply we offend where it is our object to conciliate, and divide where we are assembled to unite.

Neither religion nor party politics have anything to do with knowledge and everything to do with quarrelling.

Let us, instead of speculating and disputing where we can discover nothing, observe and inquire where we can discover everything.

All things may we hope for man, should our efforts in this place be successful.

The greatest events have grown out of the smallest. The most important reforms have been generated by fewer individuals than now fill these walls; and effected in countries less free to thought and speech and action than this favored land. In revolutionized America one has not to contend with the bayonet, nor to encounter the scaffold and the dungeon. The battle of blood is here happily fought . . . The next great victory one has to achieve is over the tyranny of ignorance and the slavery of the mind. Noble be our weapons and spotless our cause! Let her seek them at the hand of knowledge and wield them in the spirit of peace, charity, and love to man.

As usual on such occasions she held her audience spellbound. It was also a moment of peculiar satisfaction for her, for now at last she could feel herself secure in the possession of one place of assembly from which the most powerful of her many enemies had no power to exclude her.

Neither the successes nor the rebuffs of this memorable winter could long distract her mind from the thought of her sister alone and suffering at Nashoba.

On February 10th one finds her writing:

Will your next bring me the glad tidings of your safety and our little one's entrance into this strange world? My heart longs sadly after thee, Sweetest, and my sole pleasure is in dreaming over thy arrival. You must not delay your journey by land or sea, however you make the distance. But it is in vain far away as I am, to attempt counsel. We shall have all ready for you, come when you will. A neat house in the country and our office in town.

Our paper goes on well. All things go on well and full of promise. I assure you, dearest, we have plenty to occupy these good heads. Jennings is busy from morning till night in the office without ten minutes to spare for writing which will fall on me till Robert comes.

I have stood the winter well without inconvenience from cold. Latterly I have flagged a little from over work.

Last night we dropped into the Park Theatre (now stamped for Infidel!) to see the Hypocrite (an English version of Tartuffe). The house was crammed. Formerly the piece had been attempted with all the pith of it subtracted and even then was repressed. Last night more than the text was given. A favorite actor extemporized a sermon at the end of his character of itinerant preacher, sending the whole audience to the Devil for being in that hell upon earth, a theatre, adding that they need not think to creep in through his agency as he would hold up the skirts of his coat that they might not catch at them. He was encored and gave a second sermon in finale. The poor orthodox priests are at their wits' ends!

We live as quietly, though more busily here than at New Harmony. When we move into the country we shall be really more uninterrupted than either there or at Memphis, quite as much as at Nashoba.

My own sweet lamb, my head would get through its duties better were my heart lighter on thy score! Only keep thy mind as easy as may be and join me soon and do pray take the advice and guidance of Robert who will certainly come this way as soon as he is released from the business of editing the paper in Harmony which I trust is by this time, although I fear he will not leave Harmony earlier than the middle of March.

Yours fondly, My Life F. W.

Camilla's child, a little boy, was born the third week in January at the house of Marcus Winchester in Memphis, though owing to long delays of the mail Fanny received no news of it till a month later, February 21st, on which date one finds her writing:

My own dear—my heart is too full to throw its feelings into words. How sadly I feel the wide distance between us and then how I rejoice over thy safety and that of thy newborn lamb. I tremble to think of thy sufferings and the danger we have all escaped. When shall I hold thee and the babe to my heart? I cannot write. Your letter has shaken my nerves, darling. Come to me as soon as possible.

If you cannot come under Robert's charge one of us will
come and fetch you at the time you may name. But do not,
I pray, throw it late in the season. If you must be detained
beyond March when Robert would bring you up the river
leaving all luggage to be brought by Phiquepal, who with
his boys will take the southern route.

And about the same time that she entered into her bargain for
the church in Broome Street she also seems to have reached the limit
of her endurance as boarder with the indigent widow in Murray
Street where she had made her home on her first arrival in New
York. As one reads in a letter from Jennings to Camilla after the
birth of her baby:

We are very busy removing from our boarding house to a
small neat house of our own. Large enough to accommodate
F. and her servant with a spare room for a friend. (William
Owen and I sleep at the office.) I am going to buy some tubs
and buckets, and since we received your letter announcing
the arrival of your baby, I intend to bespeak a tub that will
hold a hogshead to bathe the *little* no, not the *little* stranger,
but the little monster on his arrival.

Around our *own* fireplace last Saturday evening we talked
and laughed and were happy while reading of our Camilla
and her darling. Fanny and a very severe winter seem to
agree very well.

But this "small neat house" mentioned in Jennings' letter was only
a temporary resting place in Fanny's plans for the future of her life
in New York. She was already making arrangements for purchasing
an old rambling farmhouse on the East River, the property of Richard
Riker, about a mile above the present Queensborough Bridge, and
five or six miles distant from the center of the town.

This house she thought contained, "all that we shall want for the
summer, convenience, comfort, retirement, and beauty of situation.
A garden, 10 acres of land, stable, cow house, poultry-yard, good
water. If we can obtain it under $400 which I have little doubt of, it
will be ours for a year, with permission of a lease afterwards."

It will be necessary, [she goes on to tell her sister] to make
all our arrangements now or we shall lose the season for

planting our garden. A good servant of all work, with a couple
of cows and our own poultry and garden and we shall live
for little.

Possibly we shall also move our press into the country,
and the house will hold our whole establishment, but we
can't decide on that till the arrival of Phiquepal and Robert.
Unfortunately the expenses of the two establishments must
begin as soon as I take the house, for we must have a servant
at once to work in the garden, and I cannot leave town until
you all come.

It was a long time before Camilla gathered the health and
strength necessary for the long journey from Memphis to New York,
with a young baby, "a dear monster," as Fanny put it in one of her
tenderest letters, "whom you talk of carrying in your arms while you
ought to be carried yourself."

> My health comes back slowly, [Camilla writes to her sister
> on the 13th March] and yet not more than I might reason-
> ably expect considering what I have passed through. I owe
> more than I can ever repay to our good Lolotte [Richard-
> son's mother-in-law]. Indeed without her care and attention
> neither I nor my child would be in existence. My son in the
> meantime is growing so fat and heavy that I can hardly carry
> him across the room. Dearest Fanny, when shall I have the
> unspeakable pleasure of shewing you my fair son who al-
> ready smiles on me with his blue eyes and distinguishes me
> from all the others as the being on whom he most depends
> for care and nourishment. His resemblance to you is noticed
> by many. James Richardson most especially says he never saw
> anything so striking. But this resemblance is effaced with me
> by another far more striking which moreover increases daily
> with the enlargement of his face and features. And Whitby
> agrees with me that another tale is told there which will be
> more forcibly depicted in later years. How often I anticipate
> our meeting, my boy in your arms and your first gaze on his
> sweet face where so many see *your* image reflected!

There was never any question of her husband's going with her.
Whitby was bound by his promise to both the sisters to remain on the
plantation till Fanny had completed her arrangements for removing
her slaves to Haiti. The uncertainty of their future, the dread of exile

among strangers in a foreign land, had created a sense of tension among those poor ignorant negroes which made the task of the unhappy overseer more difficult than ever during those last days.

"Only by the medium of fear alone," his wife describes its afterwards, "is quiet preserved on the plantation but Whitby remains undaunted and he will carry his plan or perish in the attempt."

He seems, however, to have tried desperately to get rid of the chief disturbing element on the plantation, Dilly, the wife of Willis, who had returned from the Davis plantation near Natchez, as difficult and dangerous as ever.

At one time it seemed possible that Camilla should take her and her child to New Orleans on their way to New York by sea. But the plan fell through when Camilla confessed herself quite unable to undertake the care of Dilly and her child.

"For aught I know," she told her husband, "they may be altogether rejected as stage passengers, while I am persuaded that nothing short of violence could induce Dilly to trust herself and her child in New Orleans under the guidance of any other person than you or myself. The very sight of Dilly affected my nerves so severely that I entreated Whitby to take her back to Nashoba as speedily as possible. This was effected yesterday to my no small relief, for her mere presence here occasioned me real pain."

It was finally decided that Camilla should go to New York by the river route to Pittsburgh where Fanny promised, as it turned out in vain, to send someone to meet her or even go herself if she could possibly spare the time. Neither Camilla nor her husband had any illusions that they would ever be reunited in the place where they had spent their short married life together. Neither he nor she seem to have questioned the inevitability of their separation. Their future relations were friendly, not without a sort of melancholy affection very evident in the letters which continued to pass between them, but they never saw each other again.

Camilla's last days on the plantation were spent packing up all the movable property both sisters had collected during the four years they had made their home there. Everything was to be boxed and sent to the steamboat landing at Memphis to await the arrival of Phiquepal and his boys who would pick it up, load it on their flat boat and take it the rest of the way by sea.

Not so easy a task, this last, as it would be today, if one may trust Camilla's letter.

Though quite ignorant of the time of Phiquepal's passing here I shall endeavor to have all in readiness. The boxes for the two fountains [the gift of General Lafayette] and the two baths, are nearly made, but I have as yet discovered no person competent to pack them so as to ensure their safety. As to straw or any material for fitting in the sides of the fountain, it seems to be unattainable here.

I have at the suggestion of Whitby decided to avail myself of Mr. Winchester's escourt as far as Cincinnati where his business will call him sometime between the 15th and 20th of April. This time will suit me perfectly as I hope by then I shall have completely regained my health.

From Cincinnati I shall take passage for Pittsburg or Wheeling from whence it will be no way difficult, however fatiguing, to perform the land journey without you or your coadjutors employing their valuable time in meeting me at either place.

One note on her long journey across the country with her baby, is sufficiently characteristic of the habits and customs of high officials even under the democratic Jackson administration, which had come into power the preceding March, to be inserted here, a passage in her letter to her husband announcing her arrival at Pittsburgh, May 28th.

By an unfortunate combination of circumstances, as Mr. Owen would say, I find myself in this smokey town awaiting the departure of a stage for Philadelphia. I had to give up my seats at Wheeling to the present postmaster general Mr. Barry, who has standing orders that whenever his family should arrive by steamboat they should be sent on by stage to the exclusion of other passengers, so I arrived here only last night. The trip to Philadelphia allowing rest and sleep by the way takes four days.

Some time early in June, therefore, Camilla was at last in peace on Fanny's farm on the East River with her baby; re-annexed body and soul by her sister's absorbing and dominant personality. Robert Dale arrived from New Harmony a little later.

There we lived, [he says in the autobiographic article, "An Earnest Sowing of Wild Oats," which appeared in the

Atlantic Monthly of June, 1872] and there our paper was handsomely printed by three lads who had been trained in the New Harmony printing office. They boarded with us and we payed them a dollar a week each. We lived in the most frugal manner giving up tea and coffee and using little animal food, and being supplied with milk from a couple of cows and vegetables from our garden. We kept two horses and a light city carriage, had two female servants and a stout boy who attended to the stable and the garden. I was my own proof reader, rode on horseback to and from the city (ten miles) daily. I was occupied fully twelve hours a day and having a vigorous constitution my health was unimpaired.

There was also good salt water bathing in the unpolluted tidal river which ran just at their door, a special delight to poor Camilla after her four years exile in the malaria-haunted forests of western Tennessee. Everybody worked hard and gave a good account of himself in his own particular way. Jennings kept the accounts and subscription lists besides writing constantly for the paper and giving lectures on education at the Hall of Science, with what relief to the thwarted soul of the continually unsuccessful schoolmaster, one can well imagine! He was not the only lecturer at the Hall of Science. One hears of a series of discourses on physiology by a Dr. Charles Knowlton and other lectures on the natural sciences, geology, anatomy, chemistry, geometry, history. There was also a weekly Sunday school in the morning for small children where reading, writing, and arithmetic were taught.

On the whole, this summer of 1829 may be counted as one of the most soul-satisfying periods in Fanny's lifelong struggle for noble fame. It is a pity it was so brief.

CHAPTER V

The Fanny Wright Party in Politics

SHORTLY after her return to the North, Camilla described in a letter her experiences during a trip she made in her sister's company on one of the latter's visits to Philadelphia.

> I had the satisfaction of hearing Fanny deliver her address there on July 4th to a crowded audience who assembled in one of the largest theatres of the city and though she, on this occasion announced many sentiments little in unison with the popular feelings of the day, her animadversions and even re-proofs were received with enthusiastic applause such as made the solid walls of the building shake to their foundations. Many Quaker broad brims and Quaker bonnets were mingled with the crowd and by far the larger portion of those who called on her during her stay in the city of Philadelphia were of that sect.

The lecture was one of a new series, "On Existing Evils and their Remedy," which Fanny had written for the *Free Enquirer* in the series issued from March 18 to April 22. The poverty and suffering of large numbers of the population, which she had seen during the dis-tressing winter of 1828 and 1829 had changed the tone of this lecture, from the rather academic handling of existing evils typical of her earlier lectures.

It happened that her return to the East after an absence of several years fell in one of those periods of hard times so lamentably fre-quent in the history of our country. Fanny was startled as well as deeply distressed by the shocking, disquieting alterations which had taken place in the cities of the Atlantic seaboard where on her first visit to America she had been so delighted to find no slums, no poverty, no ostentatious contrasts between the rich and the poor.

Broadway had, indeed, become a much grander and handsomer thoroughfare than when she had first seen it in 1818 and 1819. Jewelry stores, bookstores, fashionable tailors, hatters and drygoods stores dotted its three-mile length from the Battery to Union Square. Fine residences built of the new fashionable brownstone which was gradually replacing the homely red brick face of old New York, gave every evidence of the increased wealth and personal pride of the ruling classes. But in the alleys and side streets along the water front, and in the neighborhood of the historically famous Five Points there was a teeming population, crowded together in unsanitary tenements and always on the edge of starvation. Over and beyond these chronic centers of distress, "the check which our commerce has lately experienced," one reads in a New York newspaper of the day, "has produced greater embarrassment and distress among all classes of our citizens than has been known here for a long period. Hundreds of our laborious citizens who in this great and populous mercantile metropolis, followed occupations in some way connected with commerce, have found themselves without employment or means of support. For the want of employment is followed by the want of money as a natural consequence."

A soup house was established at Mercer and Houston Streets for the free distribution of soup to the poor unemployed, the first of many such undertakings supported by private charity. "It makes the heart bleed," says Lewis Tappan, owner of the *New York Journal of Commerce,* on January 11, 1829, "to look at the hundreds of shivering, hungry applicants for charity who have thronged the old Alms House in the Park this forenoon pleading their cause in the most woeful and supplicating terms. . . . There is unquestionably more intense suffering at this moment than there has been for many previous years if ever."

Committees were appointed from the leading men of the most seriously affected communities to look into the general situation of wage earners during the depression. Fanny's old publisher, Mathew Carey, served on the most important of these in Philadelphia, and found the most deplorable conditions everywhere, especially among the wretched women employed as seamstresses. Even the wisest and best of these public-spirited men could suggest no way out but private charity. The churches contributed generally to the relief funds while at the same time preaching submission to the will of God.

The truth was that American society, founded originally on the principles of liberty and equality, had already begun to produce conditions which for an increasing number of its members provided neither one nor the other.

As a result of the Napoleonic Wars, including our own little affair of 1812, which temporarily closed the seas to American commerce, the industrial development of the United States had proceeded fast and furiously, with its inevitable consequences for all concerned. The industrial workers in the new mills were generally ill-paid, overworked, badly housed, and frequently discriminated against by laws passed under the influence of property-owning employers, for their own protection and in their own interest.

Carey's committee discovered that the wages of expert spinners were not more than one dollar and twenty-five cents a week. From this, fifty or sixty-two and a half cents must be deducted each week for room rent, and twenty-five cents for fuel, and the half dollar that remained must needs stretch to include meat, drink, and clothing. The committee urged the establishment of a society for bettering conditions of the poor and a drive for relief funds.

The growing discontent among mechanics and unemployed was brought to a head by the hard winters of 1827 and 1828. One reads of strikes and riots among the stevedores and riggers on the New York water front, strikes among the textile workers in Marstown, Pennsylvania, and workers on the Pennsylvania canal, who became so indebted to local storekeepers during the months of unemployment that they struck for twenty cents a day increase to bring their daily wage up to one dollar. Riots occurred on the new Baltimore and Ohio Railroad, and the workers tore up the tracks with their bare hands from sheer desperation. Meanwhile the mechanics and unemployed of Philadelphia formed a city organization of wage earners—the Mechanics' Union of Trade Associations.

In the preamble to its constitution a vigorous protest was made against economic exploitation and social inequality. The association was convinced that many of the evils which beset the laborer could be attributed to an "injudicious use or criminal abuse of the elective franchise." It decided to enter politics in Philadelphia with a program advocating the elimination of all property qualifications for voters, intensive political education, and attacking certain grievances. Chief of these was imprisonment for debt. Some 75,000 people, it was estimated, were imprisoned annually in the United States for debt. Most of the workers, unable to pay their creditors, languished in the town jail, with not even a chance to earn the amount of their debt. The rapid growth of monopolies granted to private corporations by state legislatures also fostered concentration of wealth and power to a degree that alarmed the workers who were taking democracy with its ideal of equal opportunity most seriously. The Mechanics' Association hoped to crush monopolies, however, by appropriate legislation. The first labor paper ever published in the United States, the *Mechanics' Free Press*, appeared in Philadelphia during the summer of 1828, urging the election of men in sympathy with the new movement to the state legislature.

Fanny's appeal to her audience of Philadelphia mechanics was well received by them. She declared, "I speak to mechanics who are uniting for the discovery of their rights. I speak to a public whose benevolence has been long harrowed by increasing pauperism, and whose social order and social happiness are threatened by increasing vice."

Fanny always insisted that her "Lectures on Existing Evils" were not addressed to any one particular sect or class or political party but to all mankind. But there is no denying that there was much in her lectures distinctly provocative to these discontented elements in the population, and one need not be surprised to find an increasing number of discontented workmen present. They listened patiently to her long and careful dissertations on factual knowledge for the sake of that part of her speech which dwelt on the right of workers to a fair share of the results of their labor and which attacked all special privilege as contrary to the principles on which the American nation was founded.

She soon came to have personal friends among this element in her audience. Such, for instance, was the first printer of her paper before the arrival of Phiquepal and his boys, the free thinker, George Evans, and many like him who had been drawn to her in the first place by her insistence that the Christian churches presented the most formidable obstacle to her campaign for free thought, free institutions and free enquiry.

An increasing interest in the deistical and sceptical doctrines of the French Revolution is a noteworthy phenomenon of the whole Jacksonian era. On the 29th of January, 1825, a few friends of Thomas Paine in New York City celebrated his birthday by a public dinner. In January 1827 the ceremony was repeated and so greatly had the number of friends of Tom Paine increased in the meantime that they were able to organize a permanent group of Free Enquirers, a free debating society and a free press association for the purpose of putting on sale philosophical works of deistical tendencies at prices so low as to bring them within reach of the smallest incomes.

The year 1827 also marks the birth of the free thought newspaper, the *New York Correspondent*, already mentioned in connection with Fanny's friend, Robert Jennings.

Fanny was therefore by no means alone nor even the first in the field when she flung down her challenge to the Christian churches in that first series of lectures delivered in the Masonic Hall, and one must take with a grain of salt her confident assertion that when she arrived in the city on that bitterly cold night, the last of the year 1828, the number of atheists in the population could be counted on the fingers of one hand, while when she left it some eighteen months later, that number had increased to as many thousands.

One cannot deny that the followers of Tom Paine in the city of New York were enormously heartened by her sudden appearance on the scene. One need only repeat the list of toasts presented on the anniversary of his birthday to prove her influence.

> Equality. May an equal share of education be bestowed upon our daughters as on our sons to make them the most competent as they assuredly are the most influential instructors of Youth.
> Miss Frances Wright. Song: "The Banks of Dee."
> The Hall of Science.
> Robert Owen.
> Voluntary Toast from the assemblage: The *Free Enquirer*.

She and Robert Owen the Elder seem to have shared the honors of the occasion.

A little later that same winter one finds her again flouting conservative public opinion by a visit to Paterson, New Jersey, to give an address to the Jackson Democrats of that place. Paterson was the site of the first silk mill in this country. Hard times had closed the mill, and Fanny's audience was largely drawn from the class most seriously affected by the situation.

Her lecture was received with enthusiasm. The mail conductor who was a good Jackson Democrat and a good Liberal furnished the four gray horses for the carriage which took her back to New York. These were the horses which had had the honor of transporting General

Jackson. Fanny offered to compensate him for his generosity. He refused, declaring that he would never have used them for any money, nor for anyone but Fanny herself.

Fanny's appeal in all these lectures was for the establishment of a free school system which would house, feed, and educate all children regardless of class and background. She called upon her audiences to bestir themselves and to prepare themselves to use the vote and the ballot box as a means of accomplishing their program. The hostility of the press and the clergy increased with her power to attract the discontented mechanics. One could readily understand how such evidence of good understanding between Fanny Wright, "Priestess of Beelzebub" and "Angel of Infidelity," and the restless mechanics would annoy the conservative property-holding classes of the Atlantic seaboard. Certainly the barrage of attacks which was hurled upon her gave her a far more prominent place as a leader of the workingmen's movement than she actually deserved.

The workingmen's political and economic movement of this period was decidedly an American product. The unconscionably long hours, the lack of universal education, and the low wages were of long standing; and the workingmen did not need Fanny to tell them that without leisure time for effective participation in the social and political life of their country, or proper education to fit them for the duties of citizenship, the control of government and society, even in democratic America, must fall into the hands of the rich, while the working classes remained an ignorant, discontented, easily exploited mob.

The last restrictions of the right of free citizens to the ballot had been pretty well swept away in time for them to vote for Andrew Jackson before Fanny came exhorting the restless mechanics to unite with the industrious classes and all honest men for a gradual but radical reform to be achieved by electing their own kind of men to the state legislatures.

By the summer of 1829, the mechanics in New York, Philadelphia and Boston were already developing a strong political movement, to the deep dismay of the conservatives and the consternation of the politicians.

Just three days before Fanny's dedication of her Hall of Science, on April 27th, a large and enthusiastic number of young mechanics and others met in the Military Long Room of the tenth ward, one of the poorer wards of New York City, and passed a series of resolutions surprisingly radical for the time, as a challenge to the unfair practices of their employers.

The latter, hard hit by the depression, had frantically attempted to minimize their losses by lengthening the working day. The meeting of the mechanics was called, however, to consider the propriety of remonstrating the further extension to the working day. The resolutions adopted strikingly reflected the ideas which Fanny had been enunciating.

> Resolved, That ten hours, well and faithfully employed, is as much as any employer ought to receive or require for a day's work, and that it is as much as any artizan, mechanic, or laborer ought to give.
>
> Resolved, That all men hold their property by the consent of the great mass of the community and by no other title. That a great portion of the latter have no property at all. That in society they have given up what, in a state of nature, they would have an equal right to with others, and that in lieu thereof, they have a right to an equal participation with others through the means of their labor, of the enjoyment of a comfortable subsistence.
>
> Therefore, Resolved, That if those in whose power it is to give employment, withhold such employment, or will only give it in such a manner as to exact excessive toil, and at a price which does not give a just return, such persons contravene the first law of society, and subject themselves to the displeasure of a just community.
>
> Resolved, That we offer the foregoing as reasons to our fellow-citizens for remonstrating against increasing the time long since established in this city and elsewhere, as being sufficient to perform a day's work, and that we trust it will meet their approbation.
>
> Resolved, That we will work for no employer who attempts to violate the rule already by long practice established and found to be consistent with the best interests of both employer and employed.

A week later another meeting was called by the same leaders and in the same spirit. About five or six thousand workers were present, and passed resolutions to blacklist all employers who continued to exact longer than ten hours a day from their workmen, and all workmen who continued to submit to this injustice. The meeting then proceeded to appoint a standing committee of fifty to keep in touch with the situation during the approaching summer and draw up a political program before the November elections for the labor interests in New York State, in co-operation with Thomas Skidmore.

This man, a machinist by trade and a devoted admirer of Thomas Paine, had just published a book on the Rights of Man to Property, in which his chief thesis was that the unequal distribution of property was the cause of all "the evils of society." His hand is clearly visible in the attack on the private ownership of property which appears among the resolutions passed unanimously by the first meeting called by the committee of fifty.

Fanny Wright was still too rooted and grounded in the money-making, property-holding middle class to which she belonged by birth and education to have any natural sympathy with the extreme doctrines of Thomas Skidmore, and even Robert Dale, at this most radical moment of his existence, was not radical enough to believe in the abolition of private ownership of the soil. But the whole staff of the *Free Enquirer* was sympathetic enough to the general aims and objects of the new party to justify the opinion of conservative society that the paper's aims were, in fact, identical with even the extreme pronouncements of radical philosophers like Thomas Skidmore.

When it came to the question of a more democratic education for the citizens of the American Republic, the whole staff of the *Free Enquirer* with Fanny at their head outstripped the workmen in the radical extent and quality of their demands. They were, in fact, the first to insist that the children of the nation were in some respects wards of the state, which should be responsible for their education from earliest infancy to manhood and womanhood, for their health, and for their training in some useful trade or occupation on which they could later depend for support—very much the lines state education is following today.

The plan which was proposed to meet these requirements was the joint production of the Free Enquirers and showed all the marks of this group of ardent reformers, most of them late-comers upon the American scene and therefore less fit to understand the fundamental quality of the workingman's movement than those who had actually developed within the situation which produced it. Though in later years young Robert Dale was to serve three terms in the lower house of the Indiana Legislature and one term in Congress at Washington, when he came to join his fellow workers on the staff of the *Free Enquirer* in New York in the summer of 1829, he was not even an American citizen.

Fanny herself, in spite of her theoretical knowledge of the history and institutions of the United States, and her peculiar skill in analyzing the origins of existing evils, was never sufficiently aware of the character of the American worker to realize that he could not accept the remedies which she proposed. She had heartily shared old Robert Owen's prejudice against religious instruction. She was influenced by young Robert Dale's experience in the Fellenberg School at Hofwyl, Switzerland, where boys of every class of society were subjected to the same treatment and training. She was also impressed by Phiquepal's general method of instruction, by which pupils learned useful trades (an essential branch of the new system of democratic education for rich and poor alike). Students could be made to produce enough value to cut down the expenses of the proposed plan which otherwise might have to be supported by state funds.

The Free Enquirers further declared in their plan to the workmen's movement of New York City that in order to obtain the best results from the proposed plan of universal education the children of the nation from the age of two and through childhood and early youth must be segregated in boarding schools. By no other way could they be removed from the pernicious influences of society as it actually existed. Only by such drastic means could a generation fit to carry on in the true spirit of the American Republic be brought into existence.

The states were to be laid off into townships or hundreds. The legislatures would then organize, at suitable distances and in convenient and healthful locations, establishments for the permanent reception of children between certain ages. Parents might visit these at suitable times but in no way would they be allowed to interfere with the form of instruction carried on in them.

> In these nurseries of a free nation, [says Fanny in one of her many lectures on this subject] no inequality must be allowed to enter. Fed at a common board, clothed in a common garb, uniting neatness with simplicity and convenience; raised in the exercise of common duties in the acquirement of the same knowledge and practice of the same industry, varied only according to individual tastes and capabilities in the exercise of the same virtues, in the enjoyment of the same pleasures, in

the study of the same nature; in pursuit of the same object—
their own and each other's happiness—say, wouldn't such a
race, when arrived at manhood and womanhood work out
the reform of society, and perfect the free institutions of
America? etc., etc.,

How keenly the lack of free non-sectarian education was felt by
the more intelligent among the workmen themselves is shown by
the surprising response they gave to proposals of so radical a nature,
so full of startling innovations, and interfering with the right of
every American to do what he pleased with his life.

During the whole summer of 1829 the Free Enquirers worked
desperately at their formidable task of educating public opinion to a
sympathetic understanding of their new plan.

One of the ways proposed for getting the subject discussed favorably was the establishment of separate units all over the country, somewhat on the plan already adopted by the *Carbonari* in Europe,
without its conspirational secrecy, however.

In one of Fanny's lectures given in New York, Philadelphia and
Boston, she describes this at some length.

I would suggest the establishment of local groups through
which the attention of the American nation may rapidly be
awakened, the spirit of popular union fostered, useful enquiry
set afloat, the plots of orthodoxy and priestcraft defeated,
pledges interchanged for supporting at the elections men
pledged to the defense of upright measures, and first and
chief to the carrying the one great measure, a system of
equal universal republican education. All these units to be
connected at some central point, by standing committees
who may thus impart greater energy and unity to the whole
plan.

The first of these scattered centers of propaganda, later dubbed
by enemies of the movement, Fanny Wright Societies, was formed
in New York City in the autumn of this same year, under the name
of an "Association for the Protection of Industry and for the Pro-
motion of National Education." Its creed, as drawn up by Robert
Dale and published in the columns of the *Free Enquirer* on September 23rd, 1829, runs as follows:

I believe in a National System of Equal, Republican, Protective Practical Education, the sole regenerator of a profligate age and the only redeemer of our suffering country from the equal curses of chilling poverty and corrupting riches, of gnawing want and destroying debauchery, of blind ignorance and unprincipled intrigue.

The Parent Association was to be supported by contributions, chiefly from the sums derived from a small entrance charge to Fanny's lectures. Twenty-three dollars and fifty-five dollars were collected at two lectures which she delivered in Providence, Rhode Island, the last week in September.

And the ghost of the first Nashoba rose from its grave and took new life in a memorial drawn up by this same Parent Association of New York for presentation before the New York State Legislature, urging the adoption of a state guardianship system of education and asking that $100,000 be appropriated for the establishment of a model school somewhere near the center of the state.

But even in the midst of her intense preoccupation with this new project for the good of the human race, Fanny could still find time for an interesting pronouncement on the subject which had once been of paramount importance in her thought and life—negro slavery.

A lecture delivered at Wilmington, Delaware, in one of her many tours through the country that summer, is especially noteworthy because she formally declared her complete lack of sympathy with the abolitionist movement, which was just beginning to take new life under the leadership of William Lloyd Garrison.

Garrison had pronounced the first of his innumerable public addresses against slavery at the Park Street Church in Boston on the very same day (July 4th, 1829, that Fanny was lecturing her audience in Philadelphia on "Existing Evils and Their Remedy." Later that same summer he was in Baltimore helping Lundy edit his weekly journal, *The Genius of Universal Emancipation*. Although Garrison was far from being the first American abolitionist, as has been frequently asserted, he was one of the earliest to demand immediate and complete emancipation of slaves by the national government.

Delaware was a slave state. Fanny's earlier efforts to correct the evils of slavery were common knowledge among the cities of the northern seaboard, thanks to the unfriendly publicity given her "Explanatory Notes" on the nature and object of Nashoba by her enemies of the New York press.

But Delaware was also a Quaker state, and the Quaker ladies who turned out in numbers for her meeting, drawn as usual by her uncompromising attitude on Woman's Rights, were also earnest abolitionists.

Thus she was sure to offend two diametrically opposed elements in her audience, by beginning her lecture with the announcement that she "had but little sympathy with professed abolitionists among whom she usually found much zeal, with little knowledge, and not infrequently more party violence than enlarged philanthropy. Hatred of the planter seemed oftentimes to be a stronger feeling than interest in the slave," and continuing it by a fearless justification of her experiments at Nashoba. She still believed that the best solution of the problems introduced into Free America by the introduction of negro slavery, was her own plan of gradual emancipation by the co-operative principle which permitted the slaves to buy their own freedom while at the same time being prepared for their new state. This was to be accomplished by a liberal education on a southern plantation. She believed that a slow intelligent amalgamation of the two races now forced to live side by side in the unnatural relation of master and slave would produce a new blend, better fitted to endure the climate and hard conditions of agriculture in the southern states while at the same time fulfilling the duties of free American citizens.

Her own failure to bring this plan to any degree of success had convinced her, not that her theories were wrong, but that the public mind was not yet ready for any fundamental reform of an evil which had become the very warp and woof of the economic, political, and social system of the South. American negro slavery was in fact but one form of the same complex of evils which pervaded the whole frame of human society. And as in common with all human errors it has its source in ignorance, so must one common panacea supply the complete remedy. The spread and increase of true knowledge alone could enable man to distinguish that the true interests of each pointed to the equal liberties, equal duties, and enjoyment of all.

In spite of the provocative nature of this and several other of the lectures she delivered to audiences which must have included a number of people who did not agree with her, or in centers where a majority of the population must have been actively unfriendly to her campaign, only occasionally does one find any mention of attempts to break up her meetings. The worst instance of the kind was in Philadelphia, where crowds assembled round the door of the Walnut Street Theatre, which she had engaged for one of her Sunday evening lectures, to find it closed by virtue of a last minute appeal from the stockholders. She met with no interference when she drove in a carriage to the place of meeting, and spoke to the crowd, urging her hearers to take steps to build a hall of their own, where they could listen to whom they liked without waiting for the approval of the "clergy or the aristocracy."

And she had no difficulty in hiring the Arch Street Theatre for another meeting and filling it to the doors for two of her lectures on "Existing Evils and the Need of a National Republican Education."

One hears of her also in Boston where the public halls were refused her and she had to be satisfied with the Federal Theatre. There was also a request on the part of some important Boston business firms that Boston newspaper editors should take no notice of her during her visit, that in fact she should be boycotted by a policy of silence. But there was too much curiosity already aroused about her in the public mind to make this possible. Long notices of her lectures appeared in most of the papers, including such bits of human interest as the following description of the way she wore her hair:

> Short, close curled in her neck and around her forehead. This arrangement has something of singularity about it, yet it forms a pleasing contrast with the perched up head-dresses of our young ladies, who in their four wrought India combs, pile up about their brows a tower of tortoiseshell and tresses newly purchased from the frizeurs which converts those of dwarfish figures into giantesses, and the tall ones into something very like a Chinese pagoda looming aloft in the air.

Fanny's overweening confidence in herself as the one person who had found the way, the only true way out of darkness and error into perfect light and truth, laid her open to some justifiable criticism from people who might otherwise have been her friends.

Note the following passage from a letter to William Maclure in Mexico, from G. W. Erving, a wise old gentleman who had been the friend and well-wisher of Maclure during most of his adventures in the field of liberal education in France, in Spain and the United States.

One word of Miss Wright. She appears to be a woman of a very extraordinary genius or talent, though somewhat masculine in her mind as well as in her person. What she says has been said a thousand times and is to be found in an hundred volumes. It has hitherto done neither good nor harm to the readers nor will it to her hearers now. People go to hear her as a curiosity, that is all. She is not one of those commanding spirits who now and then appear and form a new religious sect. She has nothing of the prophetess in her. It is not by her preaching that the progress of the priests can be arrested. She is bold enough but too little prepared. She has the language of philosophy taken from the books but she has not the true philosophic spirit, and she is without eloquence or tact. She is too monotonous. Her dominant motive, personal vanity, is too apparent. So she will pass away as so many more worthy have done before. We have Paine's Age of Reason, but the worms are eating it. It produces no good, though so admirably calculated for effect and when Adams says "It is worse than useless," all the world applauds.

Poor incorrigible race! I tell you again and again, time is the only reformer, man does nothing. So all the Owens and Wrights in the creation are mere passing bustlers on the scene.

Even if Fanny had heard his unflattering judgment of her and her cause, she would not have believed him. She still believed that she could do a great deal to make the world a better place to live in, by her plan for a liberal non-sectarian universal education of the youth of the land. But just at the high tide of her effort to that end, she was suddenly called to fulfill her unpaid obligation to her first experiment in the reform of existing evils. She had solemnly promised her brother-in-law when she left him at his ungrateful task as overseer at Nashoba, to wind up her affairs there at the earliest opportunity by removing her slaves to some region outside the bounds of the United States, preferably the new negro republic of Haiti.

In her own words:

As I purchased my people for their benefit, I must renounce the trust in the manner most consistent with their feelings and with justice. I have now made arrangements for embarking with them this autumn for Haiti, having already given a public pledge that I would not set them free in the United States.

Thus she explained her departure from New York in her last address in the Hall of Science before she set out on her long wearisome journey across the western country to New Orleans on October 17th.

She promised her audience, however, that she would continue the work of rousing the public mind to the necessity of a national system of free education by lectures and personal propaganda as long as she remained in the United States, and she was comforted by the thought that the cause would be in good hands during her absence from New York.

So, as it happened, it was after her departure, though not, perhaps, without her knowledge and approval that the Free Enquirers made their plunge into the perilous sea of party politics.

It is difficult to say how much Robert Dale Owen and his fellow editor of the *Free Enquirer*, Robert Jennings, had to do with the calling of the great meeting of October 19th when the workingman's movement emerged from its first tentative beginnings and became a political party. Owen and another Free Enquirer were present at the meeting in the capacity of secretaries of the proceedings, and they had enough influence in its counsels to get some form of communal education accepted in its platform. The rest of the report and resolution presented to the workers for adoption were largely the work of the radical, Thomas Skidmore, and were deeply imbued with his particular theories on the rights of private property. Thus the resolutions presented at this meeting were indeed radical in character.

It was resolved, for instance, that private ownership of the soil was eminently barbarous and unjust; that the hereditary transmission of wealth was the prime source of evil; that chartered banking and auction monopolies represented a rapacious and cruel plunder of the people; that the exemption of the churches and clergy from taxation was direct robbery of the public. "Just experience," it was declared, "teaches that we have nothing to hope from the aristocrats of society and that our only course to pursue is to send men of our own description, if we can, to the Legislature at Albany, etc."

The Free Enquirers did their best to detach their cause from the most extreme of Skidmore's proposals. An article appeared in their newspaper as soon as possible after the meeting explaining that "inequality is often of the mind as well as of property and that the only security for the enjoyment of equal rights is, not agrarian laws or any laws whatever but equal, national, republican education."

Fanny too responded in the same vein, when the news of the meeting reached her at Auburn, New York.

> Only a generation brought up equal in knowledge and similar in habits, tastes and occupations can be trusted to produce equality in rights and enjoyments. Let us train that generation to be what they ought to be and let us leave them to decide, to judge for themselves how their property shall be inherited and divided. What now would cost heartburnings, wranglings and complainings may then perhaps be passed by acclamation. Nay! may necessarily result from the altered feeling of the community, as present injustices and inequalities result from the present feeling about them.
>
> The human mind cannot be forced, it must be convinced. Let reform move faster than its conviction, its calm, its well-reasoned, its well-digested conviction, reform will halt, reform will stumble. It will have against it all the timid, all the shorter sighted, all the slower heads which are many, and not always the least sound, all the suspicious. If it move precipitately even in the right direction, it will have for it all the rash and the headstrong and soon all the ambitious and the dishonest, etc. etc.

But the conservative opinion of the general public refused to be deluded by what it looked upon as mere splitting of hairs. The city press to a man accused the Free Enquirers of organizing and guiding the new party, the "Fanny Wright Party," as it was quickly dubbed by the *Evening Post,* since no other name could properly designate the crew of which Robert Dale Owen and Robert Jennings were leaders.

And Colonel Stone of the *Commercial Advertiser* wastes a great deal of malicious pity on the "poor deluded followers of a crazy atheistical woman," who have allowed themselves to be enticed, against their sober judgment "into the new political party which has lately emerged from the slime of this community, and which is more beastly and terrible than the Egyptian Typhoon."

But Mordecai Noah of the *Courier and Enquirer* takes a livelier tone.

> At a numerous and highly respectable meeting of the friends of Wright Reason, held at the sign of "the World

turned upside down," in the Five Points, last evening, Mr. Ichabod Ragamuffin was called to the Bench and Messrs. Rag, Tag and Bobtail appointed secretaries. The meeting being properly disorganized, the following preamble and resolution was passed unanimously.

Whereas all men are born free and equal and bring nothing with them into the world, it stands to reason they ought to remain so, and take nothing with them out of it. It is therefore contrary to Wright Reason and the laws of nature for talent, industry, economy, enterprise and honesty to raise one man above another, in reputation or property.

Resolved unanimously that the social state as it exists at present is contrary to Wright Reason, and a great evil.

That it is against the laws of nature and the principles of Wright Reason that because one man chooses to work and another to do nothing the former should get rich and the latter remain poor.

That it is bad enough for a man to have the exclusive enjoyment of his labor during his life; but that he should be permitted to leave them to his own children instead of ours, is a crying sin against law and Wright Reason, etc., etc.

All this abuse and ridicule, however, did not prevent the workingmen from meeting again to draw up a party ticket of bona fide workingmen, men of their own sort as they expressed it, for the coming election.

A panel of eleven men was selected to run for Assembly. Though none of the candidates were very well known to the mechanics, enthusiasm for the great principles of the Workingmen's Party ran high. The opposition parties, to be sure, were not slow to twist and color the program. The great increase in the number of voters since the repeal of the property restrictions to suffrage, made it necessary to extend the period required for casting the city vote from one to three days—November 2, 3, and 4, 1829. During this time the whole city was given over to shocking disorder. Crowds of repeaters hurried to the polls in the interests of one party or another. Violent attempts were made to prevent opposition votes from being cast. The ballots themselves were written and presumed to be secret. The new labor paper, *The Workingman's Advocate*, which first appeared on October 31, urged in its editorial and exhorted the members of the Workingmen's Party as follows:

Your fathers of the Revolution secured to you a form of government which guarantees to you almost universally the elective franchise . . . If you possess the rights of freemen, you have exercised them as the privileges of a slave . . . Awake then from your slumbers and assault not the memories of the heroes of '76 by exhibiting to the world that what they risked their lives, their fortunes, and their sacred honor to obtain, you did not think worth preserving.

On the evening of the first day of the election the New York press began to recognize with something like hysteria that the workmen's movement was carrying the city. Tammany Hall called the workmen's ticket an Adams ticket; the Federalists called it a Tammany Hall ticket. All opposition parties dubbed it a Fanny Wright ticket.

All this time Fanny herself was moving farther and farther away from this battle of interests and parties so closely intertwined with her name. One may still read of her progress up the Hudson to Albany, Utica, Syracuse, Auburn, Rochester, speaking every night and often in the daytime, preaching to every one she met in stage and packet boat, everywhere entreated by letters and expresses to visit towns and villages not included in her proposed route, yet still finding a moment here and there to exchange blow for blow with her antagonists the gentlemen of the New York press, in copious contributions to the *Free Enquirer*.

She was at Buffalo when she received the last details of the New York election and the last word of her enemies, the editors of the New York dailies, in their usual campaign of vilification directed chiefly against herself.

As it happened she had more than enough time to answer these last as they deserved. For she was marooned a whole week in Buffalo by one of those storms of mingled wind, rain and snow, which still descend from time to time on the western part of New York State with paralyzing effects on all communications from the outside world. She spent the time scribbling her writings on the backs of letters. She pretended it was a translation from a Hebrew manuscript which had been unearthed in the ruins of Mordecai Noah's famous city of refuge for the oppressed Jews at Grand Island in the Niagara River.

But under its Biblical name, *The New Book of Chronicles*, it is really nothing more nor less than a lively description of her own encounters with the conservative forces of New York since her arrival there in

1827. All her enemies of pulpit, press, and respectable society generally, are held up for derision in Biblical language, which permitted her even more freedom in expressing her opinion of them than she could have in her lectures or editorials.

She describes New York as it had expanded, since her visit there, into "a rich and populous city, lying on the shore of a large and fruitful continent."

> The industry thereof was great and the streets thereof were spacious and many until they stretched themselves far along the river of the north and the river of the east and across from one to the other.
>
> But the people had become greedy for gold wherewith to make fine their houses and showy their apparel. Their hearts were set on the vanities gold could buy. They did bow down before the rich merchants and money-makers and money-lenders and took no heed as to who ruled them nor in what manner they were ruled. And the labor of the poor counted for nothing . . . and the people were bowed down beneath their burden and sore vexed.

She describes the secret combination which she always believed existed between the rich merchants and money-makers and money-lenders and the Christian churches to keep the toiling masses in their place so that they might continue to give "of the fruits of their industry even ten fold and a hundred fold."

> And lo! there dwelt in the land, soothsayers and prophets and dreamers who worshipped an idol exceeding fearful to behold. Three heads had the idol, painted of many colors acording to the fancy of the soothsayers. And round the idol was smoke and fire which the soothsayers had cared to feed.
>
> And the rich merchants and the money-makers and the moneylenders called unto the soothsayers saying: "Come now and help us. We will give ye a tithe of our possessions and we will build temples for your idol and we will show respect for you" etc., etc.

The other side of the bargain was, of course, that the soothsayers should blind the eyes of the people by teaching them that their misery was by decree of the idol, and that according as they did the will of the idol in the life which was, "even so should it be done unto them in a life which was to come."

It was by the advice of the soothsayers, according to Fanny's *Book of Chronicles*, that the last step of this combination against the rights and liberties of the working classes was taken in the complete subjugation of the public press, which she describes as a great engine "that multiplied the words of the dead and the words of the living, originally intended for the people's good but had been turned to the people's hurt by creatures of a base spirit, cunning perverters of words who wrote after the fashion the soothsayers showed them for money."

She describes herself as a woman from a distant isle who knew the city and the great continent on which the city stood, and the people who dwelt therein, their laws and their customs and their usage and the vexations with which they were vexed. For behold the woman had journeyed much through the land and tarried in many of its cities and villages. And she also knew the tribe of rich merchants and money-makers and moneylenders, for she herself was born of that same tribe in her own country. "Yet so it was that she loved them not because she knew them."

She describes her own coming to the city at the moment when the people were growing impatient of their burdens, and even the rich merchants and the money-makers and moneylenders had begun to feel a little restless under the exceeding pride of the soothsayers and the voraciousness of their idol.

Then did the woman raise her voice in the midst of the city and smote the pride of the soothsayers and measured the maw of their idol and showed how it devoured of the fruit of the people and took the money of the merchants until all together were confined in the coffers of the Christian Churches.

Then raged the soothsayers with a great rage and straightway sought the creatures of base spirit who held the great engines that were for the people's good but which they had turned to the people's hurt.

"Are you not ours?" cried the soothsayers to the editors of the New York press. "Have we not bought you? Fulfil your tasks and work the engine against the woman and heap on her of the filth whereof ye have such a store and lo! if the filth that ye have be not filthy enough to poison her in the eyes of the people, we will supply you."

She goes on to tell, at too great length to be repeated, of her own newspaper, the *Free Enquirer*, planted by her for the good of the people "against the idol and against all those who lived by the idol"; of the Hall of Science that displaced the idol from one of his hundred temples that stood in the center of the city; and of her own efforts to show the people how "because the fruits of their labor were absorbed by the money-makers and by the churches, the poor were without bread, the children without protection, the widow without comfort and the people without knowledge." And finally most deadly crime of all, to show them how the power was in their hands, and how it befitted them to use it for their own vantage and their own honor.

> Till it came to pass that the people in the great city gathered in the public places and took counsel together saying: "Are we not many? Are we not the strength of the land? Is not the pride of our cities the work of our hands? And the fruits of the earth, what are they but the earnest of our toil? How is it that we suffer . . . when the earth groans beneath the fruits of our labor, and the markets are glutted with the various productions of our skill?
>
> "How comest it that our rulers are chosen from our oppressors? Are they not chosen by the breath of our own mouths?" Then looked they one upon another and they said: "Lo! our ignorance hath done this."
>
> Then pledged they one to another their troth to choose their rulers from amongst themselves at the hour appointed for the choice of rulers, and sealed the vow in their inner hearts. And when the hour came they gave in the lots of their choice and behold 6000 lots fell the first day to the men of their choice.

Here for the first and only time during her career as a public lecturer and writer did Fanny attack personally a man who among all the crew of her enemies in the New York press had done the least to deserve it.

Major Noah of the *Morning Courier and Enquirer* had, in fact, been almost friendly with certain members of the staff of the *Free Enquirer*. "He hit us from time to time," says Robert Dale Owen describing this period of his life, "but always good naturedly. He was a man of infinite humor and I used to enjoy his jokes even when made at my expense."

It was Major Noah, however, who drew upon himself the most scathing shafts of Fanny's ridicule in the fourth chapter of her *New Book of Chronicles*.

> Now there was in the city among the creatures of a base spirit, [she begins] a man who called himself the high priest of the Jews. He who founded the great city of Ararat whose ruins are on the shores of the great island among the waters of the mighty cataract.
>
> The man was of the tribe of Israel and worshipped the Israelite idol (which was not the idol of the soothsayers) yet was he said to be of the sect of the Sadducees, not laying much store by any idol and treating all prophecies of other worlds as fables.
>
> And behold the Israelite worked his engine and put forth a great scroll and his praise was always to the strong and his eye to money. Yet his heart did love a joke and except for the money which was with the idol he would have laughed merrily at its three heads and at its maw, huge as that of the fish that swallowed Jonah.
>
> But in the day when the woman from the distant isle came to the city and took up testimony against the idol of the soothsayers and measured its maw and exposed its emptiness he worked his engine as one distracted. At one moment he was on the side of the woman and the people against the idol, at another he was on the side of the idol and the soothsayers against the people and the woman.
>
> And lo! while the Israelite was divided between his hatred of the idol and his love of money which was with the idol, there was a place given him at the receipt of customs, surveyor of the Port of N. Y. which brought to him eight thousand shekels of silver and more also.
>
> At the same time he increased the size of his newspaper so that it brought him 4000 shekels over and above the receipts from the place in the great port.
>
> And there was a wigwam in the city and a tribe of savages therein. Whence these came, none knew or cared to enquire, so busy were the people with the worship of the idol, but they had taken the city in possession, selling its places and its rich offices to the highest bidder, and at the head of the savages in their wigwam was an Israelite and his engine.

And so it was that when the day came for the choice of rulers and 6000 lots were thrown to the men who appeared on the side of the people's vow, great was the stir in the wigwam, as great as in the temples of the soothsayers. The Israelite swore by the idol of his fathers and all the savages in the wigwam swore by the idols of their fathers and a clamor as of a war whoop arose in the city.

Then cried the Israelite with an exceeding bitter cry for he thought of his seat in the customs, "Verily this regards us all. Money-makers, and moneylenders, and gamblers on change! Look to your coffers! Look to your crafts! Look to your houses! Look to your lands! Rebellion! Sedition! Treason! The people have broken loose! The workers are looking abroad, and we shall all soon have to work for our living!"

And he made a compact with the soothsayers and their party among the moneylenders and money-makers, for though they were not agreed on all matters they were all thoroughly agreed in one purpose, namely "To eat the fat of the land that is produced by the sweat of the people, and to fill the high seats of honor which are seats of easy profit, and to protect the bills of the money-makers from challenge by the men of toil." Therefore, said he, "You who count upon the idol and upon its power among the people will cry Heresy and Atheism! But I who care little for any idol with three heads or with one, will cry, "Robbery and Murder! Fire and bloodshed and rapine are abroad. Lo! they that have nothing are about to seize all, and they who have all are about to lose everything. The people have drunk wine and are distracted. They have hearkened to the woman whose purpose is that every man shall pick his neighbor's pocket, and every woman seize her neighbor's husband, and that the earth shall be chaos as before the days of Adam and that men and women shall live in chaos no wiser than the first pair before they eat the apple."

But while these parties raged in the city the people themselves learned a thing or two about their rulers and the makers of their laws, and began to ask themselves, "Is it such as these, roaring like bulls of Bashan, telling lies and imagining absurdities about us which our forefathers would have despised? Is it such as these who have been chosen to make the laws under the great charter?"

We will make our own idols, fashioned each to each man's fancy and keep them in our own closets, and shut the door upon it, and worship them as we like in secret. As for the money-makers and their craft, we will put them aside entirely. And as for this Israelite and for his wigwam, lo, they are too foolish to be regarded.

Every man to his post. While the people have slept, the strongholds of the nation have been seized by robbers, and the great charter of their equal privileges has been infringed by traitors.

Every man to his post, and let him prepare his mind and his heart to win for himself what he hath felt the want of himself, equal knowledge, equal protection, equal maintenance, equal privileges, equal enjoyments. Then in the generations whose youth shall be reared in wisdom, all crafts that are useless shall disappear from the land, industry shall be held in honor, crime and misery and oppression and violence shall be no more remembered by men.

And now this is the history of the first wakening of the people in the great city and all they did, and all that was imagined against them. And lo, the farther doings of the people shall they not be written when they have performed them.

The *New Book of Chronicles* appeared in four issues of the *Free Enquirer* through late January and February, but by that time Fanny was out of the country.

She had cut across the state of New York from Buffalo to Pittsburgh, already a smoky center of the manufacturing interests of Pennsylvania.

My visit here [she writes the Free Enquirer on Dec. 4th] was much needed and will I think be productive of much good. This city has been the very donjon keep of priestcraft, the very New Jerusalem upon earth of sanctified, mystical fanaticism for the honor of God which translated, you will understand to mean "for the benefit of the clergy." This indeed is the chosen throne of Levi, from whence they declared the Christian religion to be part of the law of Penn., where honest citizens a few years since were arrested for holding a free debating society, where Sabbath laws yet reign in all their glory, and where the very packet boats hush their steam at the wharve during the solemn hours of church service.

And yet so it is that the wicked woman whose plain matter

of fact creed had made even a Jew editor of the New York Courier and Enquirer turn Christian, has been attended by a crowd of all varieties of auditors for three successive evenings. The great body of the crowd is by this time satisfied that the female monster is after all a very harmless personage, showing neither horns on her head nor hoofs on her feet, but breathing forth some sound counsels from her lips.

I hear there is some low growling of Presbyterian thunder, and that the Masonic and anti-Masonic partizans are beginning to ask what effect the new excitement is to have upon their tickets. Alas! Alas! When will the rule of priests be at an end and the people universally see through the nonsense with which knaves and fools alternately bamboozle their understanding?

A great part of the population here is low Irish, a race of being which the corrupt government of England has been molding for centuries to its shame.

She arrived in New Orleans the very end of the year 1829, nearly at the end of her physical strength, but with enough of her indomitable courage and energy to write the following letter to William Maclure in Mexico.

New Orleans Jan. 3rd. 1829

I have been long without news of you, my respected friend and you without news of me, excepting so far as public report may have carried to your ears and to your eyes through the newspapers travestied accounts of the popular movements in which I have been through the past year an agent. I send you herewith with young Bennet who will deliver them to you in Mexico City, copies of my lectures, files of the Free Enquirer and the first 6 numbers of "The Workingman's Advocate" conducted by the former printer of the Free Enquirer and assisted by R. Dale and others. We found our paper insufficient to supply all the business matter of the cause in New York. The two papers together will show you the spirit which is abroad.

I have no hours of leisure, my every moment being now employed in the public service. Otherwise I would attempt an account of the important reform made in N. Y. and Philadelphia and the measures taken to secure their progress at the last election. But as I and my fellow reformers are too hard worked to describe them in letters, I can only say, "Come and see." Visit Phila. and New York as soon as you can. They are the headquarters of our reformers, albeit the whole country is awakening . . . It has taken me three months to reach this place from N. Y., being stopped everywhere by popular curiosity to learn what is doing elsewhere. I was stopped in stage and packet boat, met by letters and expresses inviting me to visit towns and villages on the route, so that to have met fully the popular wishes would have taken me as many years as it did months to arrive here. I have now work chalked out for the whole of this winter and following summer and I wish, when revolving it in my mind that I could be in 20 places at the same time. My discourse on Existing Evils has united the people of the northern cities on the great measure of republican education as there explained; to this their hearts and votes are now pledged. This is the question which in one day polled 5600 votes in New York and which would have carried the whole city ticket had it been properly chosen or had time permitted its revision. But the whole was the work of a few days.

I close in haste wishing you all health and a safe and speedy return to these states. This country is at length started and merits the attention of a mind like yours . . .

CHAPTER VI

Haiti and After

IT HAD been a painful effort for Fanny to wrench herself free from her absorbing campaign for the new plan of state and national education and take back on her shoulders the old intolerable burden of her plantation and slaves.

For a while she had hoped to find someone willing and able to assume the difficult task of winding up her affairs and transporting her negroes to Haiti. But in this she was doomed to disappointment. Her good friend Marcus Winchester was, indeed, more than ready to help in all the preliminaries of the undertaking, but neither he nor Whitby could be prevailed on to accompany the slaves to Haiti.

There was for a while a faint chance that James Richardson and his wife and mother-in-law, Lolotte and her children, who were finding their trace of colored blood a more and more insuperable obstacle to any sort of honorable existence in free America, might consent to act as escort to the expedition in return for a free passage to the Black Republic.

But Richardson himself soon put an end to that hope in a letter peculiarly characteristic of that curious mixture of faults and virtues which made his friends continue to love him, however much he failed them in any real emergency.

He was full of a new plan for making his living in New Orleans as teacher of free colored youth, at six and one-fourth cents a lesson of three hours, supporting himself and his family meanwhile on $1000 which he had lately received from Scotland.

He refused his approval of her system of State Guardianship Education, or any education, as a cure for human depravity.

> I am not in love with your motto, "just opinions." It involves, as I think, the same species of mistake as does the

religious identification of creed with conduct. Knowledge, even omniscient knowledge, seems to me no more to involve rectitude than a belief in gods or witches involves good will to men. I do not deny the tendency of knowledge to lessen crime but still think that crime is sometimes different from ignorance, for to my feeling all crime has been perpetuated, not by the comparatively ignorant but by the comparatively knowing. It is the blindfold attempt of the injured to redress and avenge the wrongs committed on them by their comparatively intelligent oppressors. By enlightening the Many therefore, you will doubtless emancipate them from the tyranny of the Few. But when all are enlightened what shall prevent the Many from tyrannizing over the Few?

A few really benevolent beings exist now, a few have always existed but they are not necessarily particularly intelligent. I know a benevolent spirit joined to a very high grade of intellect; it is the spirit of my friend F. W. I know a benevolent spirit joined to a very low grade of intellect. It is the spirit of my wife, Josephine Richardson. She is now on her passage to New Orleans where I shall follow her in January.

The letter ends with a request for books to be bought for him by Fanny in Cincinnati and sent ashore when her steamer touched at Memphis. Thus he put himself out of the question.

It was only at the last moment when all her other friends had failed her that she turned in her extremity to William Phiquepal, and Phiquepal, as usual when called on by her for special service, did not fail her. He had deserted his first patron, William Maclure, to help her print the New Harmony *Gazette* when she first assumed its direction with Robert Dale Owen. He had followed her to New York long before her other partner was ready to make the transfer. He and his French boys were largely responsible for the excellent printing and proofreading of the *Free Enquirer* as long as she had anything to do with it.

But the farm on the East River, which the other members of the establishment found such a delightful retreat from the storms and struggles of daily life, had already begun to bore the little Frenchman, and the opportunity of accompanying Fanny to Haiti came to him like a godsend.

He had already spent years in the French West Indies and would be interested to revisit them. He knew the language. He could flatter himself that he was a far more appropriate companion to his patron than men like Robert Dale Owen, or Jennings or even Winchester, in a country so strange, so savage, so lately emerged from the worst conditions of slavery and civil war as was the Black Republic under its ruler Jean Pierre Boyer.

This man, a mulatto educated in France though Haitian by origin, had combined with the pure black Christophe to overthrow that monster of cruelty and vice, Dessalines, and then with another mulatto, Alexandre Pétion, to overthrow Christophe they established a republic of sorts of which he became president and sole ruler when Pétion died in 1818. He later managed to extend his rule over the whole island of Santo Domingo, Spanish as well as French. In 1825 he obtained from Louis XVIII the recognition of Haitian independence by saddling his government with a debt of 150,000 francs to the mother country.

He is described as a "little intelligent-looking man with keen black eyes which he whirls about with extraordinary rapidity." His manners were a good imitation of the best French models, but his taste in dress was fantastic. At a public review of his troops, for instance, he is said to have worn a blue frock coat very richly embroidered in gold, Hessian boots made so that the foot, the ankle and upper part were of different colors and bordered with gold tassels, with a belt of velvet and gold suspended across his shoulder, holding an enormous sword. He also carried a gold-headed cane as tall as himself.

During his presidency, however, he did much to set the finances and the administration of the island in order, and to encourage the arts and sciences. He was especially anxious to improve the character of the backward Haitian inhabitants by the introduction of a more active, industrious and generally efficient type of negroes from abroad, and for that reason he was particularly open to suggestions from the colonization societies in the United States that Haiti become a haven for those American slaves whom their masters wished to free and at the same time remove from their own country.

The arrival of George Flower's shipload of free negroes in 1823 had been such a boon to the island in this respect, that Boyer immediately authorized the Secretary of State of the Republic to open a fund in the United States by the sale of 50,000 pounds of Haitian coffee, "to facilitate the emigration of . . . individuals of the African race who should be disposed to come to Haiti."

Such a record could not fail to excite the interest and sympathy of a man so deeply hopeful for the future of the negro race as General Lafayette, and Fanny herself had shared the General's enthusiasm for "Boyer's noble effort to set up a free self-governing republic in a land of lately enfranchised slaves."

At the height of their old affectionate relation, it would have been the most natural thing in the world for Fanny to turn for sympathy and assistance to her friend Lafayette as soon as the prospect of her own visit to Haiti with a cargo of newly enfranchised slaves appeared on the horizon.

Ever since her adoption of her new role as educator of the public mind, however, letters between her and her paternal friend had ceased, and she had to break a long silence when she wrote to ask for the letter of personal introduction to the president of the Black Republic, which she believed would open all doors to her during her stay in Haiti. It came. When had he ever failed his dear child in her wildest experiment for the benefit of the human race? And on this point at least, he was completely in agreement with her plan to settle her colony of slaves in the "free country of Haiti" as soon as it was practically possible.

For the first time in his long correspondence with his dear adopted daughter, however, he adds a note as nearly critical of her late adventures as leader of the popular mind, as was possible for his kindly tolerant nature.

See the following passage from the letter addressed to Robert Dale with the request to forward the enclosed letter of introduction to Boyer in case Fanny had already left New York.

You have very properly concluded that my love for her cannot be impaired. I believe that her lofty philanthropy, her sincerity and the purity of her heart are equal to the brilliancy and power of her mind. Nevertheless I can not but regret her disregard for public opinion to a degree that necessitated her withdrawal from any connection with those friends I had hoped to attach to her interests, and even though I do not expect you to agree with me, I still venture to express my profound dislike for her exhibition of herself as a female lecturer in a whirlwind of anti-religious propaganda, etc., etc.

Before Fanny had obtained Lafayette's letter of introduction, she had already received a reply from her own appeal to Boyer—a long, cordial letter, not from the president himself, indeed, but from one of the distinguished members of his cabinet, General Inginiac.

General Inginiac was a man of color descended from one of the first French families in the island, owners of a large plantation called La Concorde in the Parish of the Croix des Bouquets in the jurisdiction of Port-au-Prince, who had fled before they could be massacred by their revolting slaves, and received indemnification for their losses in 1832.

The name, however, was not unworthily borne by General Inginiac, whom everyone visiting the island at this time speaks of as unusually intelligent and obliging.

General Inginiac assured Fanny that her people would find on their arrival the full and complete liberty which she desired to procure for them. As agriculturalists they would be placed on farms, the proprietors of which, known for their wisdom and justice, would bestow on them every care which their situation rendered necessary; and they would receive half the product of their labor.

I pray you, madame, [the letter concludes] to believe the lively interest with which you have inspired the chief of our state not only by your proceedings themselves but by the motives which prompted them and be persuaded of the pleasure which I shall have in continuing a correspondence so dear to the Haitian nation and so precious to the heart of him who is with the highest consideration
Your very humble and obedient servant
Secretary General of his Excellency, Inginiac.

It had been already arranged between the two sisters that Camilla and her little boy should not rejoin her husband at Nashoba, but remain quietly at the farm on the East River till Fanny's return from Haiti.

The sudden death of this child in the late summer did not alter these plans, though it made the separation of the two sisters all the more painful.

The loss of her baby was the last blow to all Camilla's hopes of personal happiness and reduced her to a state of patient despair from which she never recovered. On September 6th of that same autumn one finds her writing to her husband.

For myself, dear Richeson, I am weary of existence and
while reason tells me the folly of indulging in regrets as vain
as they are useless, the source of my sorrow is still the same.
My lovely babe is torn from my bosom, my soul's best treasure is departed and there is now nought on earth that can
yield me satisfaction. My days pass in bewildering and wither-
ing recollections of past comfort and fondly cherished hopes
now for ever blighted. It is true I can yet look on the satisfaction of others and rejoice in their utility but as I can no
longer participate in the one or contribute to the other, my
life is as useless as it is miserable. The extent of my misfortune is known only to myself while the depth of my affliction is beyond the reach of sympathy or of alleviation.

Ah! Could you have seen him a few days before his seizure,
his large blue eyes beaming with sweetness and intelligence,
his rosy and dimpled cheeks and sweet endearing smile, as
he held out his arms for me to take him, you would not marvel
at his mother's anguish, as she recalls the lovely image that
so lately filled her heart with hope and gladness now the
abode of sorrow such as death alone can vanquish or efface.

The rest of the letter is taken up with details as to the removal
of the slaves from the plantation in time to arrive in New Orleans
not later than the first of January on which date they were expected
to embark for Haiti. It ends with a word of encouragement to her
anxious husband that nothing further was expected of him after that
point by his dominant sister-in-law. "Fanny will not fail to be in
readiness to relieve you of your charge. Phiquepal, having been
obliged to abandon his intended visit to France, will accompany her
from thence to Haiti."

Whitby and the slaves arrived in due time from Nashoba. As
might have been expected from his inefficient management of the
plantation, there was also a long bill of expenses for the last year's
operations, for never in the course of its history did Nashoba produce
anything but a deficit for its owners.

Fanny may be excused, therefore, for listening to her friend Marcus
Winchester, and his friend, a certain James Breadlove, already in
trade with the West Indies, when they advised her to turn an honest
penny in an affair which might better have remained from first to
last an act of pure benevolence. They assured her that by loading
the vessel already chartered by her for the transport of her slaves, with

a cargo of lard and pork, she could make enough profit out of her return cargo of Haitian coffee to pay the expenses of the trip.

Further details of this engagement are found in a farewell letter from Fanny to Robert Dale as follows:

New Orleans Jan. 6th. 1830

I have done my best to comply with the wishes of my friends, and I might add, with my own wishes not to absent myself much longer from these states and from our own city, but as I have told you and as I have told the public, my first duty is towards the helpless beings who look to my countenance and lean upon my protection. I need not enter into details for which I have no leisure but must content myself with simply stating that I shall myself convoy the people to Port-au-Prince, perceiving no other arrangement capable of affording at once equal satisfaction to them and equal facilities for the voyage.

After seeing many vessels and weighing many plans and proposals I have finally with the assistance of our excellent friend [unnamed] chartered a fine little brig of 163 tons [the *John Quincy Adams*] to make the voyage out and home, and as soon as she is freighted, which will be some time next week we shall put to sea.

My little colony, which is now thirty in number, (13 adults and 18 children) arrived some days since and will go on board from the steamboat where they have continued since their arrival, during the course of the day.

I grieve to think that you have received such exaggerated impressions respecting the hazards and inconveniences of the passage. I own I should now close my eyes with regret upon a world which Free Enquiry is quickening with a new spirit and that consequently, I should feel as averse needlessly to risk my life at this moment as my warmest friends could desire. Say this for me to those who are kindly anxious on my account, and should you or they still dream of shipwreck and pirates, just call to mind that we may break our necks in going down stairs or be blown up in the bursting of a steamboat boiler, and that really I do not see before me more chances for the former accidents in my run to Port-au-Prince, than from the latter on the Mississippi River.

With the greater part of the trip I am familiar, and I find my own calculations respecting the term of time likely to be consumed in it confirmed by those made here with better

knowledge. From twenty to thirty days may be considered
the average passage out and from ten to twenty home. I shall
return to this port both to avoid the dangers of our more
northern coast in the months of February and March and also
that I may be enabled to visit some towns on the Mississippi
and Ohio which I was obliged to neglect on my way hither.

In these close calculations for a speedy return to the work which
lay nearest to her heart, she had not made sufficient allowance for
the difficulties and delays connected with any commercial relations
with the West Indies, and none at all for the bribery and corruption
inseparable from this trade, even in the case of respectable merchants
who hoped to make a reasonable profit out of its inevitable risks and
losses.

The adventure in the cargo of the *John Quincy Adams* seems to
have been no exception to this rule, with all the risks and losses
connected with it to be borne by the one person who was least able
to afford them, Fanny herself.

James Breadlove, Marcus Winchester, and Frances Wright were
the three partners in the cargo. A paper found in the box of manuscript inherited by Fanny's daughter furnishes interesting evidence
as to how the affair turned out for all involved.

Adventure to Hayti in account with James Breadlove.

Investment in pork etc. and lard...............	$6165
Return duties on coffee &	550
Expenses (Drayage, weighing, storage)........	150
Insurance from Hayti to New Orleans..........	100
Commission for selling. 2 1/3% on $12300......	307
Freight paid	15.15
Interest 6 mos. at 10%.......................	31.95
Guarantee	275.50

as compared with $14,044.45

By 11,000 barrels of coffee at 11 cents a pound	$12,100.00
9 tons of logwood...........................	200.00
Cash from Miss Wright for transportation of slaves	450.00
Loss Frances Wright	431.48
Loss J. W. B.	431.48
Loss M. B. Winchester.......................	431.48

$14,044.45

Thus it would seem that far from getting any profit from the adventure Fanny had to pay for the transportation of her slaves and also shoulder a third of the loss on the cargo. This was the least part of the troubles and losses she had to bear. Her people had been enfranchised before they left Tennessee, but until she got them safely off to Haiti, they might at any moment be arrested and imprisoned on the pretext that they were really slaves escaping from their master. Furthermore her own partner in the adventure, Breadlove, seems to have taken advantage of the situation by insisting that the best way to hurry their departure was a cash payment of $2000, Fanny's third of the invoice on the cargo, instead of allowing her the usual credit till the business was concluded.

It thus happened that she started on her journey so short of ready money that except for the generosity of President Boyer she would have been in serious straits to meet the necessary expenses connected with the actual placing of her people whon they all arrived in Haiti.

Phiquepal, who had taken advantage of the occasion to pay a visit to his friends at New Harmony, arrived at New Orleans in time to sail with the party on the *John Quincy Adams* but not in time to be of any help to Fanny in the difficulties and anxieties of her departure.

The little vessel made the harbor of Port-au-Prince, the capital seaport of Haiti, after an uneventful journey of thirty days. This part could be approached by sailing along one or the other of the two long sides of the gulf on which it is situated, which look on the map like the two jaws of a great alligator, with the island of Gonave lying half way between them. The passengers must have been struck at once by the total absence of visible cultivation on both island and surrounding coast. No sign of human habitation, nothing but the wild impenetrable wilderness of tropical vegetation. The harbor also strangely without signs of life. Not even a solitary fishing boat broke the almost sinister monotony of its approaches. The town itself lay in a glare of light reflected from the naked white surface of the rocks of its immediate neighborhood. A few buildings in a state of absolute ruin and a miserable wooden pier marked the landing place. The nearest approach to European civilization was to be found in the few neat looking cottages scattered over the hills close to the city, the residences chiefly of foreign merchants. The city itself, its streets torn and left unmended after the ravages of the torrential rains from which the whole island suffered during the rainy season, was composed of small wooden houses never more than a story in height, except for the president's palace, a large building with a handsome flight of steps leading into good reception rooms. Here General Boyer lived in some state, but the town itself was so unhealthy that the more important members of the community preferred to reside on their plantations on higher ground outside the city.

One of the most important of these, "La Coupe," seven or eight miles east of the city, was the country seat of a French gentleman with a colored mistress and family, brother of the distinguished naturalist, Victor Jacquemont, the friend and correspondent of Lafayette. "Roche Blanche," "Mon Repos," and "Letor" were the names of other plantations in the vicinity of Port-au-Prince, where life was carried on with that freedom from the ordinary restraints of European civilization which was to be expected in a people hardly a generation removed from slavery.

But Fanny, by choice and reputation "the female friend and advocate of the African race in America" seems to have had no difficulty in accommodating herself to her new role as favored guest of the president of the Black Republic in Haiti, accepting all its startling contrasts and personal inconvenience with her usual self-confidence and assurance.

Thanks to Lafayette's letter of introduction, the welcome she received was a cordial one. The negroes, supplied with tools and a month's provisions, were placed on property belonging to President Boyer and located in one of the finest sections of the island. Cabins, gardens, and water were provided for them. Having given evidence of good conduct and responsibility, and shown a desire to become proprietors, they were to receive a grant of government land in fee simple. Fanny herself, as the adopted daughter of General Lafayette—whose name was still one to conjure with among the inhabitants of the island—lived again in his reflected light, in familiar intercourse with the men and influences that made the laws and directed the policies of the republic.

By one of the strange contrasts so common on this island, there were several bookshops in Port-au-Prince, of a more respectable appearance than could be found either in Barbadoes or Antigua, and two printing presses. The most important of these was owned by a pure black named Courtois, bookseller, editor and publisher of a lively little newspaper, the "Feuille de Commerce," noted for its sharp editorials advocating the supremacy of the blacks in contradistinction to those of mixed race such as the president and most of his council of state.

Soon after Fanny's arrival on the island there appeared in the columns of this newspaper a long flowery poem from the pen of one J. B. Romaine, lauding her to the skies for her *"belle action philanthropique"* and offering *"les plages que ses pieds ont touchées pour un refuge contre la persecution, un asile contre l'injustice."*

An acknowledgment of Romaine's letter, in Fanny's very best French, appeared a little later in the columns of the newspaper. *"La bienveillance de cette nation interessante me touche jusqu'à l'attendrissement,* etc., etc."

Indeed, if her sole business on the island had been that "beautiful philanthropic action" which they all united in commending, she would have finished her business and sailed back home in a week or ten days at the most instead of remaining the month or more which passed before she was ready to depart.

Here again it was that unfortunate cargo of merchandise with which the *John Quincy Adams* was loaded, which kept her day after day, week after week, while the return cargo was being collected from outlying plantations, loaded and finally cleared for its return passage to New Orleans. The Haitians were proverbially unbusinesslike and procrastinating in such matters. But Phiquepal's knowledge of the language, habits and customs of the people made up for his natural ignorance and inexperience in affairs of this kind, while his zeal in Fanny's service made him willing to assume the entire responsibility of the return trip of the brig and the disposal of its cargo in New Orleans, thus leaving her free to sail directly from Port-au-Prince to Philadelphia not very much later than the date she had originally set for herself.

They parted with mutual regret, for their common experiences in Haiti had created bonds between them that could not be lightly broken. He was too old to have fallen romantically in love with her, but there is no doubt that he had come to regard her as a rare and wonderful being, worthy of a man's deepest devotion, while she had grown to depend on him for those thousand personal services which she always managed to extract from everybody who ever came into daily intercourse with her, while at the same time becoming more and more interested in the man himself, most eager to help him in all his plans for the future. If the great scheme for a free national education ever passed the legislature of the different states, she would certainly use her influence to get him appointed to one of the regional schools which were expected to rise up throughout the country.

In the meantime, however, she encouraged him to return to France as soon as he had concluded the business of the *John Quincy Adams*, and sent him off with the following letter of introduction to Lafayette, to be presented to the General as soon as possible after his arrival in Paris.

Port-au-Prince March 15th 1830

You will receive this, dear friend, from the hand of a valued friend, already frequently announced to you, but whose departure for France has been as often deferred from his kind respect to my interests. Monsieur Phiquepal who has been my escourt hither will return with the vessel and cargo which I have upon my hands, to New Orleans whence he will close the very troublesome commercial affair in which circumstances have engaged me and embark immediately for Havre. I take my passage hence to Philadelphia in a vessel which is to sail in a few days. My visit here has been one of great interest, and my reception in the highest degree gratifying and satisfactory.

Not only from the president but from all the members of his government and from the citizens generally, I have received every flattering attention.

I expected to view this country with interest but I own it inspires me with yet deeper interest than I had anticipated. The singular beauty of this island, its delicious climate and the mild and kindly disposition of its inhabitants would alone expand the feeling of a stranger, independent of its past history and of the great principles involved in its present and future destinies.

In this country there is one evil evident to every eye and it strikes me as being the only one, the total absence of industry. To create this, none of the means employed in other climates and on other soils would suffice. The wants of the people which are few, are more than satisfied by nature herself, who pours forth her riches on every hand. Here, therefore, necessity will never teach industry, education alone can do it, an education which should embrace agriculture and all the useful arts and raise up a new generation capable of developing the resources of the country and of adding a moral bulwark against its enemies to the physical one which nature has supplied in its mountains and rugged defiles.

The philanthropist need not desire a better moral soil than that supplied by the natural temperament of this people. Gentle, humane, grateful, and hospitable, even the white stranger calls forth their ready sympathy and some decided demonstrations of enmity or insulting contempt from him would be necessary to recall past wrongs to the mind of the kindly Haytian.

Monsieur Phiquepal will give you more interesting details than I can supply in writing. He will tell you too, how often your name is here mentioned with affection and respect. I must, however, myself recount a little circumstance, not only illustrative of these sentiments towards the patriot of the two worlds, but also of that tact and ready sensibility which lead this people to divine so frequently the secret feelings of others, and to address them in the most touching language.

At a dinner at the house of General Inginiac, after a toast to myself too flattering (though delicately worded) to repeat, the private secretary of the President introduced the following. After observing that it would be difficult to add more to the sentiments already expressed by the company and echoed by the nation to the female friend and advocate of the African race, he continued: "I believe we shall reach her heart in pronouncing the name of the just and good, the venerable and the venerated patriot, *qui lui a voue toute sa tendresse le General Lafayette, l'ami des hommes et l'homme des peuples.*"

I need not say that the tears started to my eyes, dear father. I have frequently experienced the same emotion during my conversation with the President. He regrets extremely that you did not visit Hayti at the time of your visit to America. I thought I distinguished even that he had been pained at it. I gave good explanatory reasons, not omitting the one I found you had advanced yourself, viz. the death of a near relative. I mention this because you may perhaps find occasion in your letters to re-iterate your regrets on the subject.

Nothing can be more pleasing than his manner of speaking of you and much of his attentions to myself it pleases me to think springs from your recommendations. I could wish you, my honored father, to write to him, as soon as possible.

I must trust to Monsieur Phiquepal all the American, as well as all the Haytian news. If some foolish travellers, lovers of ghost stories and inventors of the marvellous should have inspired any fears respecting the projected reforms in the U. S. and the nature and tendency of the influence I exert over the popular mind in that country, fastness of human liberty, his relation will I think restore your confidence. By returning from hence directly home I shall leave unfulfilled many engagements in the western states but I am anxious to embrace my Camilla and also to know the progress of things in the leading cities of the North Atlantic border. Dear Father when the measures now fomenting in the popular mind shall be adopted by the legislatures of some leading states, would that health and other circumstances might permit you to revisit America. Your blessing could then set the seal to that revolution you aided in youth with your blood. Certain it is, the revolution will only be completed when a national education shall be adopted and surely in such an assertion there is nothing to alarm the patriot or the philosopher.

May all good be with you, my excellent friend. May all the wishes of your heart be fulfilled in your family, in France and in the cause of liberty throughout the world.

Your Filial Friend, F. W.

Anyone reading this letter might have been hypnotized into forgetting the bloodstained past of Boyer and many of the other members of his government; the atrocious cruelty of those "gentle, humane, grateful, and hospitable people" in their successful efforts to exterminate the whole white population of the island, the thin veneer of French civilization hardly concealing depths of savagery, strange voodoo rites and superstitions practiced side by side with the formal religious observances of the Catholic Church, indubitable facts for anyone who chose to recognize them. On the other hand, it is just as noteworthy that a white woman like Fanny, completely submerged in a black and mixed population, was perfectly safe, entirely free from the slightest insult or misunderstanding through her whole visit to this island, during the last week of which, after Phiquepal's departure to New Orleans, she was alone.

One wonders, however, exactly where and how she was lodged. A passage in one of her letters to Phiquepal after his departure, seems to show that they were not together during his stay in Haiti although a note found among her papers shows that they were often invited together on expeditions to the neighboring country houses.

"March 16th, 1830. Invitation to Pickpal to spend next Thursday with General Inginiac in the country where the General hopes that Madame Frances Wright will also favor him with her presence."

On this occasion, however, she went alone for Phiquepal was already on board the *J. Q. Adams* waiting for the vessel to clear out of the harbor on its return voyage to New Orleans.

> The little sloop which was to have taken this [thus she begins her first letter to him] cleared out by help of oars just after your vessel had raised anchor and a few hours later passed you in the bay, as we observed from the garden of General Inginiac! I know not if you understand the position of the General's farm, or with the help of the glass I think you might have distinguished us, so near and so slowly did you take your course along the shore. With a good glass, which we had not, we thought we might have distinguished you.
>
> I found myself throughout the day in the midst of a cheerful party but I had no longer anyone to observe with me the beauties of the scene or the peculiarities of the company and had often to make an effort to rouse myself from a revery.
>
> The appearance of a French corvette in the harbor gave rise to much interesting conversation on the subject of the French treaty just concluded with the Bourbon government, for the vessel is supposed to convey the envoy charged with definitive answers to the latest Haitian demands.

[The demand of the huge indemnity of 150,000,000 francs to make good the losses of the original owners of plantations at the time of the slave revolts which exterminated or expelled the French population of the island, was so unpopular with a large portion of the Haitians that the president at first refused to ratify it.]

> Inginiac defended the French treaty, including the clauses in it allowing France especial privileges in the payment of duties. Simonize was the only one who hazarded criticism. The rest were silent. Alas! How confused are human heads, black, white, or colored!
>
> *Sunday.* I was interrupted on Friday by a summons from the carriage which was to take me to General Serbones. I found a party of twenty, comprising some new faces and more acquaintances. The sugar farm is more profitable than

General Inginiac's but even the best, how far from what they might be!

With this generation, however, I do not see at what end a reformer could begin. I find Inginiac has some vague project of a school of young agriculturists and thinks to push it forward through the club of Freemasons. It will probably never come to the experiment, and if it should, could only bring disappointment. . . . No natives, I am persuaded, would ever start the enterprise unless with a view to individual profit and the attempt of foreigners would need the powerful protection of the President as I think they would be suspected by the natives of views similar to their own.

Yesterday I was oppressed with lassitude and passed the day reading on the sofa, feeling my solitude and often speculating respecting the progress of the J. Q. Adams. Towards evening I roused myself to pay a parting visit to Madame Granville [the wife of the Haiti envoy sent by Boyer to the U. S. in 1823 to facilitate colonization of American slaves to Haiti]. For I expect, or hope at least to embark on Monday. I did not find Granville when I called but left your compliments and mine for him with his lady.

In returning I paid a visit to your old hostess and took a bath. The premises looked to my fancy very forlorn, about as much so as I feel myself, and today I find that the "Enterprise" will not sail before Wednesday morning. This will make out the week from the time of your departure. Truly I feel the hours very long.

Monday morning. I breakfasted yesterday and passed the greater part of the day with Jacquemont and his two female friends, and this morning before dawn I rode with him to his farm and distillery in the plain. He is active and enterprising and seems in a fair way of making a successful and very profitable establishment.

Our friend Windsor (one of the business acquaintances they had made in the process of buying their new cargo) has been ill for three days past. He is better today and I hope to see him well before I leave. The greater part of the coffee is on board. Some little remains to be brought which will be done today. I hope to enclose in this a detailed note of the duties duly signed.

One rather wonders about this second consignment of coffee which Fanny brought with her to Philadelphia. Was it part of the original venture of the *John Quincy Adams* collected too late to go with the rest of the cargo to New Orleans, or was it the form in which the President's present of doubloons took its final shape?

> The hours now hang heavy on my hands. You know how disagreeable it is to be always on the eve of departure and always delayed. I shall be anxious to hear how you get through the business in Orleans.

The last letter written just before her departure on March 25th is in French (translated).

> I wrote you two days ago, dear friend, by a boat which has not sailed yet, so I am sending this last word on board to tell you of my departure. I shall be on board two hours from now, just one week after you left me. And even as it is I am leaving without all my coffee. But that is not my fault, neither is it the fault of Mr. Windsor.
>
> We were told that the custom house was so overburdened with business that the "Enterprise" could not possibly get off before Friday so we thought we had plenty of time to finish everything. But this morning we are suddenly informed that the brig has settled her cargo and is due to sail this evening. At the same time the demand for coffee has been so great that there is none to be found in the town today. An especially good lot is expected tomorrow, however, which will be loaded on another boat for Philadelphia, leaving three days later. About 150 sacks I think. I am taking 422 sacks with me now and leaving full powers with Mr. Windsor, in case of trouble with the other party in the transaction, from whom it may be difficult to get what he owes us from one pretext or another. I am leaving all the necessary papers and receipts with Mr. Windsor. He has been ill these last days but is again on his feet. Here is his compte de charge. Cartage 21.50 Bags 259.50. I have coffee to the amount of 4012 Haitian dollars. *Je pars. On m'entoure. Je n'ai pas un instant!*

Her announcement of her return to New York appears in the *Free Enquirer* of May 1st as follows:

> I greet once more our readers from this city after an absence of 6 months. Having seen my colored colony advantageously

and happily settled under the immediate protection of the Haitian President I sailed from Port-au-Prince on the 25th of March and landed in Philadelphia on Thursday last. The fatigue of a rough and tedious passage during which I suffered much from the sudden change of climate in passing from the genial airs of the tropics into the cold northeastern gales which lately swept the whole extent of our coast, and some private business which demands immediate attention, prevent me from adding more at present to this short notice of my return and the satisfactory completion of the business which took me to the West Indies.

I purpose to deliver an address in the Hall of Science on the evening of tomorrow week next, May the Ninth.

Very interesting changes had taken place in the popular mind since her departure to Haiti the previous autumn. The workingman's movement was still formidable to the classes whose special privilege and personal possessions it seemed to threaten, but in spite of its brave appearance, it was already falling a prey to those temptations which have so often interfered with the development of a strong labor party in the United States.

Its unexpected and surprising successes at the election of the previous autumn had drawn into its ranks a number of persons, who, in Robert Dale's and Fanny's opinion at least, had no genuine interest in the cause of the workingmen or sympathy with their real aims and grievances, but had joined the movement from personal ambition, or even as secret emissaries from Tammany Hall, engaged for the express purpose of bringing back the workingmen to their old party.

The first act of these "political workmen" (to give them the contemptuous name bestowed on them by the Free Enquirers) was to read Thomas Skidmore and his Agrarians out of the party.

At a meeting of the party held the previous December, the extreme radicals, under Thomas Skidmore (whose program of confiscation of landed property had so alarmed the conservative classes of the city at the previous election) were denied a hearing by the more moderate elements among the workingmen, who had no objection to private property provided they could be assured of a fair share of it as a reward for their labor and a safeguard for their old age.

Skidmore and his followers, apparently few in number, promptly withdrew from the meeting, to organize a small but vociferous party of their own, which took the name of "The Poor Man's Party," and set up a small weekly newspaper called "The Friend of Equal Rights."

But soon afterwards it was the turn of the Free Enquirers to suffer similar treatment at the hands of the same moderate element which was gradually getting control of the main body of the workingman's movement.

The demand for a free and equal education, and that of the best, for all the children of the community, rich and poor, the leisure classes as well as the toilers, under conditions that would make it possible for poor as well as rich to take advantage of it, had already been responsible for a large and enthusiastic following among the more intelligent of the young mechanics. These workers could easily understand the argument that without such equality of opportunity in education, no government could remain a democracy in fact as well as in word.

But the novel and startling features of the state guardianship plan on which the Free Enquirers depended for the regeneration of society must sooner or later have caused a falling off even among this class of followers. These features were the segregation of the whole child population between the ages of two and twelve in boarding schools where the parents themselves were admitted only as visitors; the suggestion that the expenses of these institutions, where the children of the land were to be clothed and fed as well as educated at public charge, should be met by a poll tax on the head of every parent, whether his children were sent to the schools or not; and the further suggestion that a tax should be laid on all incomes to produce the revenue necessary to meet the very large cost of such establishments, if the poll tax proved insufficient.

A steadily increasing opposition to the whole plan, which the "political workmen" were quick to take advantage of, had already begun to show itself in the rank and file of the party.

Several of these had long been active among the members of the Committee of Seven originally entrusted with the task of drawing up the final report on education which was to be submitted to the General Committee which determined the final policy and direction of the workingmen's movement.

The Free Enquirers confidently believed that they had a majority in favor of the State Guardianship Plan in the Committee of Seven. They felt equally sure of a majority on the General Committee. Time was to show, however, that on both these points they were bitterly mistaken.

When the report of the Committee of Seven finally appeared early in May, a few days after Fanny's return from Haiti, it was found to contain nothing of a constructive nature, contenting itself with a statement of general principles which could offend no one. "A base example of time-serving mediation, with no better end in view than more votes for the party at the next election," to quote Fanny's slashing editorial in the next number of the *Free Enquirer.*

This was not the worst. Appended to the report was a series of resolutions denouncing the whole plan of the Free Enquirers "as unwise in its details, impolitic in its operations, based upon the doctrines of infidelity," with more than a hint that it concealed "the hidden purpose of a few misguided men to indoctrinate the whole child population of the nation with the virus of infidelity, to subvert the present order of things, to create disturbance in the bosom of our families and sever the strong ties of affection that keep families together. 'Can a Mother forget her child?' We hope no system of education will ever be introduced into this country which will compel an affirmative answer."

The Free Enquirers, however, did not take this rebuff lying down. They believed their plan of State Guardianship still had the main body of the party behind it. They really had strength enough on the General Committee to issue a call for a great public meeting of the workingmen to be held in the North American Hotel on the evening of May 26th to reconsider the whole question.

The "anti-guardianship men," as the opposition was called, instantly raised the cry which had been so successful against Skidmore and his Agrarians. On the evening before the meeting they went about busily distributing the following handbill:

Liberty! Principle!! Mechanics and other workingmen, to your posts! Another base attempt is being made to palm upon us
Infidelity and Agrarianism!
You, then, who love your country, your children, and the cause of Liberty and Principle. You who wish to preserve the civil institutions of your country free from the baneful levelling system of a fanatical set of Foreigners, attend; rally round the standard of Liberty, at the North American Hotel,

Wednesday evening May 26th at 7 o'clock and put down forever these infuriated individuals who wish to ruin the Working Men's cause.

The meeting as reported in Major Noah's *Courier and Enquirer*
was "probably without exception one of the wildest, most singular
scenes short of personal violence and bloodshed that the city had ever
witnessed."

Not only the room hired for the occasion, but the lobby and stairs
of the hotel and even those parts of the Bowery and Bayard Street
neighboring on the place of meeting, were filled with the crowd collected by the appeals of both factions in the party, fighting for entrance. Once they were inside the hall, they clamored for recognition
from Ebenezer Ford, sole representative of the Workingman's Party
in the New York Assembly, who had shown his sympathy with the
Free Enquirers by consenting to take the chair on this memorable
occasion. Robert Dale and his fellow workers had not been wrong in
believing that they still had a large number of the party behind them
in their campaign for State Guardianship and Support.

They remained in control of the situation in spite of strenuous efforts
on the part of the "anti-guardianship men" to adjourn before the
passage of resolutions condemning the action of the General Committee on the evening of the 21st, or failing this to break up the meeting
by uproar and interruptions. Several such objectors were removed
from the hall with violence. A motion of censure for all who had any
share in the attack on the Free Enquirers was carried by a large
majority with cheers.

For the moment the "anti-guardianship men" were defeated, though
the final outcome of the meeting was a serious schism in the ranks
of the party itself. This was quickly taken advantage of by the politicians within and without the party in their efforts to weaken the
workingman's movement in every way. The Free Enquirers believed
that all the trouble came from the "political workmen" who had
joined the party after its first successes. Fanny attributed it directly
to the machinations of the chief sachem of the Tammany wigwam,
her old enemy Mordecai Noah, whom she pilloried in one of her
editorials in the *Free Enquirer* as "a vacillating, cowardly unprincipled
advocate of regular nominations in his Courier and Enquirer."

Noah responded in kind with a flippant notice supposedly facetious.
"There is a scandalous report about town that Miss Epicene Wright

has abstracted or rather Agrarianized a pair of Mr. Jennings' inexpressibles and means to appear in them at her next lecture which report says is to be delivered at the sign of 'All Things in Common.'"

And very shortly afterwards a long article appeared in the same newspaper under the title "Fanny Wright, unveiled by her own Pen," making rather shabby use of the private letter, already quoted in an earlier chapter, which she wrote to Jennings while he was still on the staff of the *New York Correspondent*, in which she dissuaded him from coming to Nashoba on the new venture of school teaching, unless he could leave his wife behind him with her father.

The whole text of the letter with a running comment by its editors drawing the most offensive conclusions from its most innocent statements, holding her up to public ridicule as a destroyer of the family relation was afterwards issued as a pamphlet and received such wide circulation that a copy of it finally reached the Library of the British Museum.

Its immediate purpose which was to show improper relations between her and her fellow editor on the *Free Enquirer* rather missed fire, however. Jennings had already left the staff of the newspaper and removed to Boston at the call of one of the local societies of Free Enquirers which had sprung up in the wake of Fanny's campaign for the State Guardianship Plan the preceding summer. With their backing, Jennings hoped to establish a practical and scientific school which would give him the long-looked-for opportunity "of more essentially benefiting that cause to which he had hitherto devoted his time and energies along lines better fitted to his peculiar abilities than his work on the Free Enquirer." His place was filled for the moment by Robert Dale's proofreader, a young man named Baxter.

But Fanny's enemies of the New York press had already found a new point of attack, which for the first time in the long series of insult and ridicule at her expense, drew blood.

On May 28th, four weeks after her return to New York and two days after the victory of the Free Enquirers over their opponents within the Workingman's Party, a long detailed article appeared in the pages of Colonel Stone's *Commercial Advertiser* declaring that the whole expedition to Haiti was nothing but a money-making venture. It stated that:

Twenty-seven out of her thirty alleged slaves were free persons of color whom she had accepted as passengers on the *J. Q. Adams* for payment received before she left New Orleans.

That she had received a rebate of the duties paid on the cargo which she took with her to Haiti as a special favor from the Haitian government.

That she had accepted lavish presents from President Boyer.

That the return cargo of Haitian coffee was much larger than it should have been under the circumstances, etc., etc.

Her letter of reply met and dismissed each one of these accusations with proof.

To all who may have any curiosity to ascertain whether the now emancipated colonists were purchased by me or not, I state that the original bills of sale paid by me when I bought them are in my possession and may be seen at the office of the Free Enquirer. Also the account of the duties regularly paid into the Haitan treasury.

I did receive [not in doubloons, but in what I believe will prove equal to the amount, or somewhat over the amount specified, namely 100 doubloons] a gift from the President, which gift would have sufficed to cover the immediate expenses of colonization, had I not encountered from other parties, not Haytian, nor connected with that nation, a disposition to profit by my ignorance of commercial affairs, as well as my peculiar and anxious situation in the port of a slave state, charged with the responsibility of emancipated people of color, whose motions are ever watched with peculiar jealousy.

Notwithstanding my unwillingness to allude publicly to a transaction involving sacrifices and exertions on my part, which consumed four years of my life and which have reduced me from comparative affluence to a moderate competency, I should before this, have publicly supplied the details of the President's generosity, had he not, with a delicacy which at all times distinguishes his character, requested that they might rest between him and myself alone.

In thus departing from the promise he drew from me, the necessity of the case will plead my excuse to him, while it supplies to myself an opportunity which I could not otherwise have sought, of rendering a testimony thus public to the

unostentatious generosity and gentlemanly deportment of the
Chief of the Haytian nation.

This statement, or perhaps even more the threat of a libel suit,
brought an ungracious apology from Colonel Stone in the June 2nd
issue of the Commercial Advertiser. The campaign of insult and
ridicule went on unabated, however, in the other New York journals.
The old scandals about Nashoba were revived by more extracts from
her "Explanatory Notes" in the columns of Major Noah's *Courier and
Enquirer*. The old jokes and jibes about the Fanny Wright Party in
Politics assumed new importance as they began to strike home among
that portion of the workingmen who had grown tired of hearing
themselves called infidels and atheists, deluded followers of a crazy
virago, etc., etc.

Fanny's power to draw large and sympathetic audiences wherever
she appeared on the lecture stage was unaffected. Her editorials in
the *Free Enquirer* were as trenchant and apposite to the occasion as
ever. But now for the first time she began to wonder whether her
presence in New York in the thick of the struggle for the State Guardianship measure was not doing more harm than good to the cause
she had so deeply at heart.

Private reasons also may have contributed to her sudden decision
to withdraw from the field of battle, at least for the rest of the summer.
On June 8th she announced her coming departure for Europe at a
crowded meeting at the old Bowery Theatre in the following words:

> And now, my fellow citizens! after two years of public ex-
> ertion in a work I have believed righteous, I feel warned for
> a season to retire. The people are now awake to their own
> interests. And the same boldness which, while they slum-
> bered, I was encouraged to assume, would now appear to
> me as presumptuous, as it has, perhaps, at all times appeared
> to others. But this is not all.
>
> The unwarrantable use of my name by the abettors of old
> abuses during and since the period of the late elections
> would alone determine me to remove this poor pretext for
> party cries and appeals to old prejudices . . . So long as I
> alone was concerned, the noise of priests and politicians was
> alike indifferent to me, but I wish not my name to be made
> a scarecrow to the timid, or a stumbling block to the inno-
> cently prejudiced, at a season when all should unite round

the altar of their country, with its name only in their mouths and its love only in their hearts.

For these motives, which I trust my fellow citizens will appreciate I shall take the present season for attention to some more private interests of my own and shortly leave this city and this country for a few months, not to return until after the decision of the autumnal elections.

In her farewell address at the Hall of Science a few days later, she resigned all share in its management to a board of trustees to be elected by the subscribers themselves.

Her passionate faith in the ultimate perfectibility of mankind shows itself in every paragraph of this address, but her last words were a warning to her young friends in and out of the Workingman's Party.

> I have already stated why I regard you as destined to supply the best props to the reformed political edifice of your country . . . But it is not rashly or presumptuously that you should reach forth your hand to steady that sacred structure. No unrighteous ambition, no petty vanity, no thirst of worldly gain, or worldly influence should lead you to lift your eyes to the State's Service . . .
>
> Youth is accounted hasty and is so, for it is inexperienced. Yet do I believe it far more capable of self correction and self government than maturer age. To the young, then, do I look for the most zeal in the cause of reform, and most tenderness of its honor.
>
> With such reliance on the good sense and good temper of the frequenters of this Hall I leave them for a season.

The Hall of Science remained for some time the one tangible sign of her campaign for a juster and more liberal public opinion in the great cities of the eastern seaboard. Bought with her own money, supported largely by the receipts from her lectures, its classes in geology, chemistry, physics, and other like subjects, its forums of free debate furnished a much needed center for free enquiry among the more intelligent young mechanics of the Workingman's Party to whom all other institutions of higher learning were hopelessly closed.

However mistaken she was in her plans for the elimination of error, prejudice, and false ways of thinking, no one can deny her generous and single-minded devotion to the highest causes. This did not prevent her from being regarded by those who considered themselves the flower of American civilization of that day, such men, for instance, as Charles King, the future president of Columbia University, Colonel Stone, the editor and proprietor of the *Commercial Advertiser*, the two Tappans, honorably remembered today for their service in the cause of anti-slavery, as fair game for such absurdities as appeared in the pages of the *Evening Post* describing her farewell meeting at the Bowery Theatre.

One of these attacks took the form of a poem, too long to be given here except in brief extracts. It is supposed to be addressed to her young friends in the Workingman's Party who, because of the short workmen's coats commonly worn by young mechanics at their daily work, are here called the "Jacket Boys."

> Oh, Fanny Wright, sweet Fanny Wright
> We ne'er shall hear her more.
> She's gone to take another freight
> To Haiti's happy shore.
>
> She used to speak so parrot-like
> With gestures small and staid.
> So pretty in her vehemence.
> Alas! Departed Maid!
>
> She beat Jemina Wilkinson
> Joana Southcote quite
> E'en Mother Lee was nothing to
> Our little Fanny Wright.
>
> For she had gold within her purse
> And brass upon her face.
> And talent indescribable
> To give old thoughts new grace.
>
> And if you want to raise the wind
> Or breed a moral storm
> You must have one bold lady-man
> To prate about reform.
>
> Fare well ye young mechanics
> Ye lusty men and true

All—one and all—both great and small
My heart is warm for you.

Thus cried she on that Tuesday night
When in her whitest gloves
Her grey eyes at the Bowery
Looked on her hundred loves.

Her Owen was forgotten
And Baxter looked an ass;
Though one hung up her Leghorn
The other filled her glass!

Those dignified Philosophers,
Those Platos of the West
Were nothing to the Jacket Boys
Who fired her virgin breast.

Ye are the bone and sinew
The marrow of this land
And yet ye are but blockheads
Who cannot understand.

So I have come to teach you
What Spence has taught before,
That—if mankind were all made rich
They would be poor no more.

Tom Skidmore he came out too soon
And now we tread him down
Because we find his monstrous plans
But horrify the town.

Thus spake this gentle maiden
Not more than six feet high
How beautiful her curly wig
How restless clear her eye!

She had a very little book
She seemed to look upon;
But buxom boys with peachy cheeks
Much more her notice won.

But now she's gone alack alas!
Och hone and ullaloo!
She's ta'en old Spence for Boyer
And we have nothing new. etc. etc.

Gone, but not either disconsolate or defeated, if one may trust her last words before her departure which contained a threat to her enemies and a promise to her friends that just as soon as the private business which was taking her to Europe was concluded, she was coming back to take up the cudgels for a free republican system of education just where she had left off and never give up the fight till she had brought it to a triumphant conclusion.

CHAPTER VII

Wifehood and Motherhood

THE news of Fanny's departure from New York was announced by her fellow editor of the *Free Enquirer* in the issue of July 10th:

> Frances Wright left this city for Europe on the 1st. Instant, on a visit of some months. She has left with me a variety of articles for the Free Enquirer which I shall give our readers in course. She will continue from Europe to supply matter as usual, and will probably find more leisure to do so than she found while here in the bustle of lecturing and of other public business.
> The reasons which have induced her to select the present period of political excitement as the best opportunity for attending to some more private interests of her own, are given at the conclusion of her Farewell Address. I think them good. It is ever undesirable that the name of any individual should be associated too intimately with the cause of popular reform, etc., etc.

A wise and good conclusion. One wonders, however, whether Fanny would have been so easily convinced of its applicability in her particular case, if it had not been for those "more private interests" hinted at in her brother editor's announcement.

The condition of her beloved sister, Camilla, had filled her with dismay on her return from Haiti. There was still the hope that a complete change from scenes and persons already closely connected with the loss of her little son might rouse her from her settled melancholy.

Fanny herself was to confess a little later, however, that anyone who hoped to find relief for strained nerves, and distraction for an over-charged mind, on the continent of Europe in the summer of 1830 was doomed to disappointment.

The sisters landed in England shortly after the reactionary ministers of the Bourbon king, Charles X, had published their famous ordinances which precipitated the Revolution of 1830. For a time it almost seemed as if Lafayette's dream of a French Republic was coming true with Lafayette himself in his old position as commander-in-chief of the National Guard.

But then too soon from her vantage ground across the Channel Fanny could perceive the old familiar forces of reaction slipping gradually into the foreground. Louis Philippe was acclaimed King of the French by the crowds assembled round the Hotel de Ville, while Lafayette had allowed himself to be used, all unwittingly, as a tool for the re-establishment of irresponsible power on the throne of France, in the place of the liberal constitutional government expected by the men who had shed their blood on the barricades.

It was at this crucial moment that Fanny elected to dip her own small oar into the sea of counterrevolution. The following is the last page of a letter to her honored and beloved friend, General Lafayette, announcing her own and her sister's arrival in France.

> I say not how I long to reach you and yet perhaps it is as well that I should not be seen at your side just at this crisis, the more so as I feel it must soon be decided.
>
> I have done what I could to make myself forgotten at this moment in America, and the public motives which decided me to this have made me less regret that private ones should have led me just now into retirement. I could wish, however, that these had been unconnected with the health and spirits of our dear Camilla. These are, as I have assured you, reviving and will authorize me, I trust, ere long to embrace you.
>
> Adieu, fondly and reverently F. W.

And Lafayette's reply.

> I have read and read again your excellent letter, my beloved Fanny, and what has most struck me along the high thoughts and tender sentiments that it contains, is the news that my dear daughters have returned to live in France, and that we are about to renew those ties whose interruption has been so painful to me. "There will never be any more ocean between us!" I have taken these words as a sort of refrain till

I clasp you both again in my arms. I am amazed that I have let so long a time go by without having actually answered your letter though I have dwelt upon its contents since I received it almost without ceasing. But only when you are here beside me can you imagine the wild confusion in which I live, the endless stream of interruptions which surround me.

My position and duties as head of the chief military force in France on whom depends the defense of the land, and especially of this capital city, are the least part of what actually depends on me. Deputations from all the departments, and fractions of departments, succeed each other continually, wishing to be assured by me as to the real intentions of the new government. While all the patriots of Europe are pouring in upon me, disappointed that the government is going no further towards helping their cause, than a very firm system of non-intervention which would, at least, prevent the neighboring powers from interfering between an absolute monarch and his subjects who have risen in revolt to make themselves independent and free.

I preserve my individual independence, moderated of course by my actual connection with the ruling powers in France at this moment, and my position is sufficiently recognized for me to receive confidences and offer services, though I must confess, as you yourself can see from the newspapers, the Chambre and the Council of State do not proceed so courageously and quickly in this respect as my own inclinations, so well known to you, would wish. That takes time and then, my dear Fanny, I have to confess it to you. Side by side with the admirable disinterestedness and generosity of my dear population of the barricades, there are other populations better dressed but more greedy for place and perquisites than can possibly be imagined, who are asking for more than enough to pay all the debts I myself contracted, both in the war of the American Revolution, the Revolution of '89, during my captivity in Austria, besides a dozen conspiracies during the Restoration, to say nothing of the great week of July.

Everyone who has anything important to say, including strangers of liberal views who wish to be informed as to the general situation, come to see me with the result that I sleep just enough to keep from falling ill—eat just enough to sustain life; and days pass without a moment's time to write a letter with my own hand.

But everything in me must be devoted to this great affair of my old age, which so strangely completes the vocation of my whole life. God grant that we carry it safely to the end, in spite of the efforts of hidden interests, personal ambition of all sorts, including that of vain-glory. And the priests, especially those representing foreign powers who are prostituting every means they have to disorganize the situation!

But we shall be talking about all this face to face, my dear friend. I cannot say your letter surprised me, so accustomed am I to the way you see and feel and think about all these things, but I can tell you that I have made its political comments a special subject of meditation. On this point, my Fanny, have not our hearts always spoken in unison? Fortunately, we are soon to be reunited.

You will not find our friends, the Garnetts, in Paris. They have gone to live in Switzerland. They had left, I believe, before I received the news of your return.

And then comes a very tender charming message on the subject of Fanny's old lover, the faithless Eugene.

We have had here among all the projectors of future revolutions a man who was once your friend. I cannot express to you with what interest I regarded him, fixedly, all the time he was talking to me about the affairs of his country. I did not risk the slightest mention of you. An indifferent reply on his part would have irritated me too much. Any other sort of response would have affected me too deeply. And yet I was really anxious to ask him a certain question if I had only had the courage. He leaves tomorrow for England. Perhaps when I see him again before parting I may bring myself to say a few words. Forgive me if I revive old painful memories but I had to tell you that I have seen him.

Farewell, dear Fanny, dear Camilla. Write to me again. Be sure and tell me when I am going to see you. Je vous embrasse, etc.

This friendly flattering letter, so entirely in the old tone of affectionate confidence which had distinguished all their early relations with one another furnished Fanny with just the excuse she needed for a long elaborate exposition of her own reasoned conclusions and prophetic opinions on the actual political situation in France as she saw it, especially as it concerned the honor and reputation of her old friend, in the form of a long letter sent him at his headquarters in the Hotel de Ville.

An amazing production! Amazing as an expression of her supreme confidence in her own power to advise, exhort, and even condemn a man so enormously her superior in every way as General Lafayette. Amazing also in its absolute trust in Lafayette's comprehension of and sympathy with the motives and principles which had inspired her in its composition!

There are a few words at the beginning still in the spirit of the humble admiring disciple writing to a man whom she believed to be the wisest as well as the best in the world. As the letter proceeds one is struck with its increasing confidence in her own power to see and feel aspects of the situation still concealed from him.

I needed not the expressions before me in your last to satisfy me of the sympathy existing in our views and feelings at this crisis so long, so anxiously expected by us both. They quickened my hopes and strengthen my confidence that the temporary difficulties which impede the progress of human liberty will be speedily mastered.

It seems to me possible, however, that as a quiet looker on, interested in watching the course of events and yet removed from their immediate personal influence, accustomed to study the popular mind, and now enabled to study it unnoticed, and unsuspected, I may distinguish some tendencies which the very elevation of your position might have caused you to overlook.

From this point she went on with the utmost frankness to enlighten her old friend as to the dangers actually surrounding him, dangers which false friends and secret ill-wishers were taking great pains to conceal from him. She especially pointed out the grinding poverty and unappeased restlessness of the under-paid, over-taxed working classes of the country who had hoped for some amelioration of their condition by the new government and had so far received nothing, not even promises. She reminded him of the deep-rooted antagonism of the other nations of Europe, especially England, toward anything like a smooth progress of reform in France. She told him of the dark designs upon Lafayette himself as the only popular leader trusted at home and for that reason feared abroad; the constant secret efforts

of men of high position in foreign governments to destroy his "dangerous popularity by pinning on him every error, every weakness of the
new government," and thus involving him every day more and more
in the popular disrespect into which this was falling.

She told him that he was surrounded by spies, English spies, especially, whose business it was to circulate rumors involving his honor
and good faith toward the men of the barricades whom he still professed to represent.

In her own words:

> Caution, extreme caution is necessary, even in your rela-
> tions with your most trusted friends. If the boast secretly
> whispered in the circles of British diplomacy have any truth
> in it, the enemy may have channels of information through
> the most honest of your own household. Those whom you
> confide in with reason, may, in all simplicity of heart confide
> in others less trustworthy. This troubles me little however,
> as long as you remain in control of the National Guard. My
> fears as well as my hopes are fixed on no other object. Keep
> this bound to yourself and all is safe. Be sure of this. There
> are no means left unemployed to loosen it from your hold,
> etc., etc.

But she believed there was still hope. Not any longer for a republic.

> That is a name, dear indeed to you as to us, but still only
> a name. If the essential foundations underlying it can be
> obtained without the name, I say with you, Let the name go!
> And what are the necessary foundations for any good gov-
> ernment. Honesty and courage and economy. Such is what
> France expects. Such is what the time requires. Such will
> silence the opposition of the hour and put to shame the dis-
> honesty of which the new ministry is suspected. It will make
> room for the quiet progress of reform by curtailing the ex-
> penditure of place money [the old name for graft] simplify
> place service and substitute honest public servants for preyers
> upon the public spoil.
> Go to Louis Philippe in person. Tell him what is required
> of him. Can a citizen king refuse the counsel of him to whose
> disinterested and perhaps too scrupulous delicacy he owes

his crown? Should he do it, it is my impression that evil threatens him more than it threatens France.

The evil particularly threatening to which she returns again and again in this letter and in an analysis even more clearly written in an article for the *Free Enquirer* about the same time, was nothing more or less than a class war. In her own words:

> The working classes of the world have begun to reason, and in France especially it is no longer the well dressed populations but the toiling millions who are destined finally to effect "le salut public." It is no longer nation pitched against nation for the sport of kings, nor sect persecuting sect for the glory of God, nor army butchering army to transfer from a James to a George or from a Charles X to a Louis Philippe, the privilege of making laws, coining money and creating peers and dividing the good things of the land among his followers. It is now everywhere the oppressed millions who are making common cause against their oppressors. It is the ridden peoples of the earth who are struggling to throw from their backs the "booted and spurred" riders whose legitimate title to starve as well as work them to death, will no longer pass current. It is labor rising up against idleness, industry against money, justice against law and privilege, etc., etc.

She had to wait nearly twenty years to see this opinion confirmed by the flight of Louis Philippe before the Red Revolution of 1848. But not two months after Lafayette had received her warning letter, a motion to deprive him of his supreme command of the National Guard was put and carried at a session of the Chamber from which he was absent.

Deeply wounded, he lost no time in sending in his resignation to what was left of his command on December 26th, 1830. His public career was ended. Henceforth he was to remain only a figurehead in a world of sinister tendencies which he no longer understood, and over which he had no control. What he had described to Fanny in his letter of October 13th so touchingly as "the great affair of his old age which was so strangely to complete the vocation of his whole life" had somehow missed fire!

But this inglorious anti-climax to a life devoted to the most lofty ideals of public service was not the only setback Fanny was to suffer in her own dearest hopes for the future, in the closing weeks of the eventful year of 1830.

Almost immediately after the retirement of Lafayette from public service came letters from her brother editor of the *Free Enquirer* announcing the serious losses sustained by the Workingman's Party of New York at the November elections. Wrecked by internal dissensions, ultraradical leadership and the machinations of designing politicians, its members had been able to cast a bare 2000 votes instead of the 6000 which had so alarmed the conservative elements of the city on its first appearance at the polls the year before. The plans of the Free Enquirers to present their State Guardianship bill at the next session of the New York legislature went down with the defeat of the radical party at the polls.

Fanny, in her first characteristic reaction to bad news, wrote to announce her return to New York in the early spring to renew the battle, but long before that date her life was inexorably settled on other lines.

The voyage, the change of scene, the renewal of old associations had brought some temporary improvement in her sister's condition, but the time soon came when she could no longer close her eyes to the unhappy truth. Camilla was dying.

The end came on February 8th, 1831 at seven in the evening. The Acte de décès required by the city laws of that time, was destroyed with the old Hôtel de Ville owned by the Commune in 1871. But the blackened fragments of all these records were reconstructed as far as possible and reconstituted legal documents by the law of 1873. So one may still read the brief details of the original statement thus preserved.

"Camilla Wright, aged thirty years, wife of Richeson Whitby, proprietaire, born at Dundee, Scotland, died at Paris No. 2, Rue Montaigne."

Her death meant far more to Fanny than the loss of a deeply loved sister. It was a staggering blow which divided her whole life into two parts, before and after. For the first time in her life she saw herself desperately, dangerously alone with all the generous objects and aims which had once filled her mind and heart to overflowing, broken in pieces around her.

It was during this time of painful disillusionment that Phiquepal D'Arusmont was finally successful in assuming that position of paramount importance in her life which he had long desired. One can only guess at his movements after he disposed of the cargo of coffee in New Orleans. How soon he joined the sisters in Europe one has no means of knowing. But a memorandum on Fanny's copy of that long letter of advice and warning to Lafayette, already quoted, states that he was the messenger chosen by her for the delivery of this highly compromising document to the General in person.

He was living in the same street, No. 10, while they were at No. 2 Rue Montaigne during the last days of Camilla's illness. He was one of the two witnesses to the Acte de décès—the wine merchant, Charles Vidal Copin, No. 20 Rue Montaigne being the other—and in the complicated business required by the French law on the death of a stranger in that country. Fanny could hardly have done without him. For with all her masculine initiative in the general management of her affairs she was always strangely dependent on some one, any one, who could act as a buffer between her and those troublesome details of daily living which she was temperamentally unfitted to handle for herself. One is a little surprised, however, to see how completely successful this ugly, virile little Frenchman, vain, irritable, hard to live with, as even his best friends were obliged to confess, was in entrenching himself in her affections during those days of physical and mental prostration which followed her sister's death.

They were agreed in their dislike for the institution of marriage as the direct negation of a woman's natural rights to her own individuality. They made no effort to legalize their relation to one another till they were confronted with the startling discovery that she, a woman of thirty-five and he a man of fifty-two, were to become the parents of a child of their own. Then, indeed, they seem to have lost no time in taking the necessary steps for a formal marriage as soon as it was legally possible. No marriage could be legally performed in France, no matter what the age of the participants, without first obtaining the consent of their parents, if living. It was more than thirty years since Phiquepal, a young man of nineteen, had left his birthplace in the south of France for Paris and the new world. For the greater part of that time he had dropped all connection with his family. He had no difficulty now in finding out that his father was dead, but that his mother and an unmarried sister, Caroline, and a married younger brother, Hipolite, were still alive, the latter a Judge in the Cour Royale, Rue Suderie at Agen, Lot-et-Garonne. His family seemed both ready and willing to welcome back the wanderer to their midst, and even to bring the old mother to Paris if her presence was necessary to legalize his approaching marriage.

Before this could take place, however, Phiquepal or Fanny, and in Fanny's state of health it would necessarily be Phiquepal, must return to America to arrange her affairs there preparatory to the gradual transference of all her interests to France. It was Phiquepal's wish apparently, that their future home should be in his native country. At one time, Fanny tells us later, there was even some idea that they should buy and settle down on a family estate in Lot-et-Garonne near Agen.

There was also a great deal of troublesome business to be transacted in connection with Camilla's will, drawn up and signed in those last days in New York before the sisters sailed for Europe.

By the laws affecting a married woman's property in those days, Camilla had no legal right to make a will or leave her fortune to any one except her husband. But in 1827 Richeson Whitby had signed away his claim to everything in his wife's possession "at that time or in time to come," in return for an annuity of $300, and Camilla's will begins by acknowledging the obligation of this annuity by her heirs to the end of her husband's life.

It may be of interest here to insert a letter from Fanny to her brother-in-law on this subject.

> June 29th. 1831. Among the arrangements which I, as heir at law to Camilla now deceased, feel most desirous to know duly met is that to yourself. I should wish it to be secured not only during my absence from the U. S. but under all circumstances which the fluctuations in the commercial and moneyed affairs of the world may render possible. The following occurs to me as an arrangement at once advantageous to you and agreeable to me. In lieu of the annuity of $300 I propose to cede to you for life the plantation of Nashoba as well as the house and lot lately acquired by Camilla in Memphis. This would place in your charge and to your profit a property interesting to me for many recollections, associated in the memory of both of us with our lost Camilla, etc., etc.

Whitby, however, does not seem to have been tempted by the alternative thus suggested by his sister-in-law, and the annuity remained a continual drain on Fanny's resources to the end of her life.

There was another charge and behest in Camilla's will which could not have been altogether pleasant reading to her sister.

> I do bequeath to Robert Dale Owen of the City of New York an annuity of three hundred dollars payable half yearly, and in the event of the death of Frances Wright, my sole heir and executrix, I leave all my property to R. D. O. charging him with payment of an annuity of three hundred dollars a year payable from my death and the death of my sister, to William Phiquepal now of New York City.

Why did Camilla thus single out this particular young man for such generous consideration after her death? Had Robert Dale been more kind than wise to his gentle and unhappy "sister" during those melancholy months at the farm on the East River while Fanny was away in Haiti? Was there another reason hidden away under those so confidently advanced by Fanny to explain the sisters' sudden flight to Europe?

There is no doubt that Robert Dale had been sincerely attached to both the sisters. He had confidently expected their return in the early part of April 1831 when he suddenly received the news that both were lost to him, one by death and the other quite as completely by her new relation with Phiquepal D'Arusmont, a man whom he had always disliked and even a little despised.

It was not that he had ever been in love with Fanny. That relation he himself ruled out by repeated denials. But there are other forms of jealousy besides that induced by passionate love, which produce almost as painful results.

For nearly six years he had been, not only her intimate friend and companion, but her business manager, the chosen dispenser of her open-handed generosity to the causes they both were so ready to support and encourage. And now he was to see another man invested with all these rights and privileges he had enjoyed so long.

One need not be surprised, therefore, when he gravely announced in a later account of his relations with these two sisters that the two great misfortunes of Fanny's life were the death of her sister and her marriage with Phiquepal D'Arusmont.

Camilla, he confessed was on the whole inferior to Frances in mind and firmness of character, "but, unassuming, amiable and temperate in her views, she exercised a most salutary influence and in her death

Miss Wright lost her good angel." In her husband, on the other hand, she found a man gifted indeed with a certain attractive enthusiasm but an unwise, hasty, fanciful counselor and ultimately a suspicious and headstrong master. "His influence was of injurious effect alike on her character and on her happiness."

It speaks well for the mutual tolerance and tact of these two men thoroughly ill-disposed to one another from the beginning, that when Phiquepal appeared in New York in the spring after Camilla's death with full powers from Fanny to act for her as executrix of her sister's will and take whatever other steps were necessary to reduce her always chaotic affairs into some kind of order, they managed to carry through the business which brought them together without an open break.

For a while at least Robert Dale refused to accept the annuity left him by Camilla's will. He also made no difficulties about Phiquepal's withdrawal of the not inconsiderable sum of $10,000 from Fanny's depleted capital for transportation abroad. They both agreed as to the advisability of selling the Hall of Science as soon as they could get a satisfactory price for it. This was effected the following November when a congregation of Methodists purchased the building and at once began to use it for their Sunday services. As the Methodists had no use for the assembly room for the other days of the week, they offered no objection to the Free Enquirers carrying on their secular activities for which the hall was originally intended.

Thus came to an end the only one of Fanny's ventures in the cause of human improvement which had achieved an immediate and tangible success. It had attracted a following by its evening lectures on the higher sciences, on history, popular education and political economy; its weekly debates where free enquiry was permitted and encouraged even when it seemed to threaten the very foundations of conservative society; its circulating library of liberal, secular literature; and by the public dispensary offering medical attention.

The other venture, the *Free Enquirer*, almost equally dear to Fanny's heart, continued to appear with her name on the front page as one of its editors and proprietors till 1834. Phiquepal's connection with the paper, however, was definitely closed when he carried off the three young French boys who had served in the printing office ever since their arrival in New York with their erratic tutor in 1828. It was, indeed, high time to return them to their parents and guardians in Europe.

Another interesting record of this visit of Phiquepal to America just before his marriage is found in naturalization papers, taken out for no very understandable reason, since at that time he evidently intended to spend the rest of his life in France. He may have thought by that means he might strengthen his position as Fanny's representative in the management of her various holdings in real estate in New York, in Cincinnati, and Nashoba.

The paper dated May 10, 1831, reads as follows:

> William Phiquepal D'Arusmont, a native of France, exhibited a petition praying to be admitted to become a citizen of the United States, and having on his solemn oath declared that he had resided in the United States upwards of twenty-eight years within the state of Pennsylvania preceding his application; that he was residing under the jurisdiction of the United States between April 14th, 1802, and 18th June, 1812. He renounces all other allegiances, etc., etc.

All this time Fanny was living quietly in Paris under the care of Dr. Francis Magendie, an old friend of Phiquepal's and also one of the leading physicians of his day, creator of a school of experimental physiology, professor in the College de France. A warm appreciative friendship had already sprung up between Fanny and her new doctor which lasted as long as he lived.

She also took the occasion of Phiquepal's absence in America to establish cordial relations with his family in the south of France. How well she succeeded may be shown in the following letter from her prospective brother-in-law, judge in the Cour Royale at Agen.

To Mademoiselle Frances Wright chez Dr. François Magendie
30 Rue de Seine, Paris. June 6th, 1831.
The portrait you paint of my brother, influenced as it may be, a little too much by your feeling for him, is nevertheless just what I would like to believe about him. In fact, I rediscover him all together in the few words you have used to describe him. He loves good for the mere pleasure he finds in doing it, without a thought of praise. His labors in the field of thought have no other object than what is useful for the human race, quite regardless of any honor or profit for himself. He has the most humble opinion of his own attainments and this, as you tell me, because he has already found out how simple is the real truth underlying all science, how

easily it can be taught to the simplest intelligence. Everything else is mere charlatanism, tending to perpetuate ignorance. In this he little resembles our science and scientists, in France today. Characters such as you describe are very rare and not much appreciated when found. How fortunate then is my brother, Mademoiselle, that favorable circumstances and a fitting occasion have enabled you to discover the real worth of his nature and judge him as he deserves! The sentiments that you are good enough to tell me you have for him, and those he has for you, are your best recommendations for my esteem and affection.

It is true that from now henceforth you two are to have all things in common, but with so many good qualities to choose from in him, I beg you not to share his habit of leaving us in ignorance of everything he is doing and thinking as soon as he goes away.

When you have settled where you are going to live in Paris, I hope that you will send us your address. I am giving Mamman an opportunity of adding a few lines to this letter, but before I cede my pen, I wish to assure you, etc., etc., signed Hipolite D'Arusmont.

A little more than a month later one finds in the registry office of the Tenth Arrondissement of the City of Paris the record of their marriage.

Friday, 22nd July, 1831, at 11.00 o'clock in the morning, at the Mayor's office, Guillaume Jervis Casimir Phiquepal D'Arusmont, physician, aged 52, born in the commune of Monsant, Department of Lot-et-Garonne, on March 7th, 1779, residing in Paris No. 30 Rue de Seine, eldest son of Guillaume Phiquepal D'Arusmont, deceased, and of Frances Lacombe, his wife, living at Agen, who consents to the present marriage according to Act in Agen, July 1st, and Act of decease of father, May 25, 1814.

To Frances Wright residing No. 30 Rue de Seine, after publication made in this office Sunday, June 26th and 3rd July.

Witnesses: Pierre Jean Turpin, landlord, aged 56, living Rue de la Vielle Estrapade No. 3.
M. Leon Rostan, physician, Rue des Beaux Arts No. 10.

General Lafayette, Member of the Chambre des
Deputés, aged 73, living Rue d'Anjou St. Honoré
No. 6.
François Magendie, physician, living No. 30 Rue
de Seine.

The first-named witnesses were supposed to vouch for the husband,
the last two for the wife. All, however, with the sole exception of
General Lafayette had been friends and companions of Phiquepal
during the years (1814-1819) when he was studying medicine in
Paris. No effort was made by Fanny to secure her property for herself
beyond the provisions of the law of France for persons marrying without express contract. This was an omission which Fanny in later
years had good reason to regret.

Their first home in Paris was in the Rue Fréjus near the Luxembourg
Gardens. The boy Alexis whom Phiquepal had brought back with him
from New York was also included in their modest ménage.

One gets an unforgettable glimpse of the first months of their married life from Phiquepal's former friend and partner in the Maclure
schools, Madame Fretageot, in her perennial correspondence with her
patron in Mexico. At last this faithful friend and watchdog of her
master's interests at New Harmony had permitted herself an overdue
vacation in her own country among her own people.

She sailed from Philadelphia and while waiting the departure of
the packet boat on which she had taken passage to France, she paid a
visit to Mrs. Sistaire, mother of her favorite pupil Lucy, now the wife
of Thomas Say the naturalist. Her old resentment against Phiquepal
as the man who had deserted her in her utmost need, received new
occasion through what she heard that gentleman had been saying
about her on his last visit to America.

A letter from her to her patron before she left America, pours out
her injured feelings in the following words:

"Mrs. Sistaire told me that P. had done everything in New York to
injure my reputation. He is a miserable being! I don't know where
he is now neither will I enquire."

She was soon to find out without inquiring.

She arrived in Paris at eight o'clock on Monday morning, December
25th, and on that very first day, Christmas morning, she went to call
on General Lafayette.

He was unwell and I did not see him. But as I was turning away [she tells Maclure] it came into my mind to enquire of his secretary, the address of Frances Wright. He gave it to me thus, No. 8, Rue Fréjus, at the house of a Madame Debison, or de Busson. I went to No. 8 and having enquired from the concièrge if Madame de Busson lived there, and being answered that she did, I went on to ask for Miss Wright. The woman opened great big eyes in token of astonishment and did not answer. Well, I walked upstairs to the fourth story in the dark and ready at every step to break my neck, and there I saw a light on the right side. I knocked at the half-opened door. A young lad, after my enquiry about Madame de Busson, took a key on a table by which he was standing and coming out in the entry, he went to the left side, opened a door and I followed him. In a kind of antechamber, as well as a dining room, I met a man who was standing there without light as there was none in the room but the one brought by the lad. I would have passed him without noticing him at all had the lad not stopped before him with an appearance of great embarrassment. Think of my surprise! But you will never guess who it was till I tell you his name—Phiquepal! And the boy, Alexis! When I thought both in New York! You may imagine how we greeted one another. "Monsieur Phiquepal!" "Madam!" both at once, "but," said I, "I had not come to see you. Where is Miss Wright?"

No answer. In my astonishment I was looking around me and saw a door at the other end of that room. I went there in search of one of the ladies of the house. One was there indeed, looking at me speechless. It was Frances, with a little girl of about six months old that she was undressing to put to bed. The baby was nearly to fall if I had not put my hands in the way. That movement gave an impulse which returned in part the speech to Frances. She asked me who gave me her address. I did not answer that question but said, "I thought you would see me with some pleasure."

"I receive no visits," was her answer.

"Then I suppose you write much?"

"I do not. I am totally occupied with my family."

I did not ask who that might be because I perceived she was much disturbed. I asked if she visited the General Lafayette. She said she had discontinued all visits since several months. I observed to her that it was believed in America that she was occupied writing the biography of the General.

"Oh!" was her answer, and then she proceeded to put the child to bed in the same room. While she was thus occupied, I looked and saw a furnished bed, some chairs, and a stove with a top of marble as is the fashion in France. The whole together has not the appearance of comfort. When the child had been lulled to rest by rocking she returned to me without a sound.

"Will you not come and see me?" I asked.

"No," said she, "I never go anywhere."

"May I come to see you?" She did not answer.

"Frances, I am sorry for having disturbed you. It was not my intention."

In the meantime the child began to cry and I observed that she appeared not well. She said it was caused by her cutting four teeth at once and that she was growing so fast that it debilitated her frame—that she had been fatter but had grown thin of late. I rose to take leave. She did not move and as the door of her room fell shut, I remained in perfect darkness in that front room where I had already met Phiquepal and the boy. I groped my way not without blunders, knocking against chairs and table, but she did not come to my help. However, at last, I found the door, but was unsuccessful in opening it for several minutes, cursing the impulse which had brought me there.

Even when I at last managed to open the door into the ante-room where I had first met Alexis with the light, all was in darkness and I had more difficulties in going down than in coming up.

Glad I was to find myself in the carriage and well out of such a scrape.

Now what do you think of that! As I remember one of Phiquepal's first names sounds something like the one by which she is now called. He lives there, because his dress when I met him is what a man wears when he is at home, and the little room where I met Alexis appears to be a kitchen. Now what the devil does this mean? Is she his wife?

Her burning curiosity on the subject was satisfied at last. In the midst of a long account to Maclure of the flattering attention showered on her by her various distinguished friends during this visit to France, she broke off suddenly:

About that man! A celebrated doctor here and neighbor of Madame Daubigny in the country being also her family doctor, a Monsieur Férus, came to dine with us the other day and as the conversation turned on education, he spoke of Phiquepal as a man well acquainted in these matters and also of his intimacy with you. Mdm. Daubigny, having many times heard your name from me, said, "But Mdm. Fretageot knows Mr. Maclure very well." This attracted the doctor's attention.

"You knew also M. Phiquepal, Madame?" he asked me.

"It is true," said I. But I declined speaking further on that subject until after the doctor's departure . . . However the curiosity of the family was roused. They wanted to know what was behind my reserve so after a good deal of reflection I told them what Phiquepal really was and showed them one of your letters confirming my opinion by yours. But among the other things M. Férus told us before he left was that P. had really married Miss Wright and that she was known everywhere as his wife. Now if that is true, poor Frances! I really pity her with all my heart. Is it possible she would have ended in such a manner? Better if she had drowned herself!

Madame Fretageot's power to influence public opinion to the disadvantage of Fanny and her husband, by ironic pity for the one, and slanderous attacks on the character and reputation of the other, was not of long duration.

On December 30th, 1832, just a year after her arrival in France she sailed, not to the United States, but to Mexico, to take her old friend Maclure by surprise by joining him in Mexico City. There is a letter from her to Maclure dated February 17th, 1833, from Vera Cruz, announcing her arrival after a trip of forty-eight days with continual bad weather. The next thing one hears of her is in a letter from Maclure to a friend in New York announcing her sudden death in the following August.

"You have suffered a greater loss than ever you did before," writes this sympathizing friend in reply. "A cheerful companion, an attentive nurse, kind friend and disinterested manager all in one person. And although your habit of making yourself comfortable alone will come to your aid in this new affliction, still the sudden privation of renewed comforts will be sufficiently hard to bear." She could have had no better obituary.

Nor was she alone in her ironic surprise over Fanny's sudden desertion of her public career for the commonplace duties of wife and mother. Note here the comment of Maclure's old Boston friend G. W. Erving whose uncomplimentary opinion of Fanny as a social reformer has already been quoted in an earlier chapter. In a letter to Maclure in Mexico he remarks casually:

> Apropos of marriage I hear that Phiquepal has married Miss Wright. Happy pair!
> And apropos of Phiquepal, I hear that his old enemy Madame Fretageot has gone from your Harmony to Paris on leave of absence. I prophesy she will never return to you. She would have been a far better wife for Phiquepal than Frances Wright, supposing marriages are made in heaven!

One word here in passing on the change of name which had so confused Madame Fretageot on that famous visit to the Rue Fréjus. Fanny herself, as soon as she became aware of its existence "after ten years' friendship," says her daughter in later years, instantly requested her husband to adopt his second name of D'Arusmont. He who had already in his own quiet way discovered how unpronounceable, not to say ridiculous was the name he had chosen to be known by as better fitting a plain sympathizer with the equalitarian principles of the French Revolution, "willingly acquiesced."

Fanny's first real sorrow in her new role of wife and mother came with the death of that delicate little child whom Madame Fretageot had discovered in her arms on the unforgettable visit to the Rue Fréjus. Phiquepal's personal situation was also a source of concealed anxiety to her during those first years of marriage.

To do him justice he was only too ready to work along his own particular lines if given a fitting opportunity. It was not his fault, but the misfortune of his erratic and unconciliatory temperament, that even the most promising of these experiments of his, became a more or less costly failure.

He had been anxious to obtain the appointment of director of a model agricultural school which, during the reign of Charles X, had been under the control of the Jesuits, but when through the influence of his wife, this appointment was actually given him by General Lafayette, he could not keep it. Shortly after his marriage, a serious malady of his eyes, which was finally to reduce him to almost total blindness, still further interfered with his power to earn a living.

The condition of the world at large also continued deeply disquieting. The year 1832 was noted for a terrible epidemic of Asiatic
cholera whose ravages extended over the whole western world including America, and were nowhere worse than in Paris. One of the
earliest victims of the disease had been Casimir Perier, who alone of
Louis Philippe's first prime ministers had been able to bridle the revolutionary forces to which that monarch owed his throne. His death
was followed by a renewal of street fighting in Paris when the National Guard fought side by side with the regular army and was able
to restore order throughout the city only after wholesale massacre of
the ill-armed men of the barricades near the famous cloisters of St.
Méry.

It was into a world so convulsed with public and private tragedy
that Fanny's second little daughter came to fill the place left vacant
by the death of that first child.

Frances Sylva D'Arusmont was born in Paris, April 14th, 1832, in
a small house in the village of Passy No. 10, Rue des Vignes, where
Phiquepal and Fanny had gone to escape the heat of the summer; a
seven months' baby, "the smallest my father in six years' hospital practice had ever seen, a perfect miniature of my mother," so the child
herself retells what she heard over and over in later years from
Phiquepal. "I awoke his fatherhood in such incomprehensible, over-
powering way that he said on seeing me, 'I devote myself to this little
thing for ever,' and then, giving me my first plunge into cold water, 'I
baptize thee in the name of the Father, the Son, and the Holy Ghost.'

"Father told me this in the early '40's. From one who would not
have allowed a priest to touch me, this seems a great inconsistency,
but I was too much moved to question him at the time, and I knew
him incapable of doing such a thing in jest. It was a bona fide impulse in him."

This beloved little child became more and more of a factor in the
life of both Phiquepal and his wife, to the exclusion of outside interests. Absorbed and distracted by her own domestic affairs Fanny
made no effort to respond to Lafayette's suggestion that she should
take up her pen to defend her beloved Free America from the jeers
and jibes which had appeared about its customs and manners in Mrs.
Trollope's famous book on that subject.

A word from Fanny as to the real story of the motives and plans
behind Mrs. Trollope's journey to America might easily have changed
to malice and bitterness the adulation her book received from ill-

wishers to the American experiment. No such article ever appeared from her pen.

One brief flash of her former energy appears during a visit from Robert Dale Owen, full of new life, new plans and in the new role of a happy bridegroom.

On his way home from New Harmony the previous autumn, where he had been called on business connected with the family holdings of real estate in Posey County, Indiana, he had met and fallen in love with a young woman named Mary Jane Robinson. Owen himself described her to his friends and acquaintances as in no way remarkable for either good looks or mental capacity. She had, however, a greater gift of winning the hearts of all about her than any young person he had ever known. Her conquest of his own heart, he confessed, followed very shortly after their first meeting in Petersburg, Virginia. She consented to return with him to New York unaccompanied by any older person and they were married there on April 12th, 1832, a mutual agreement in writing taking the place of the usual religious ceremony. On May 19th, he sailed with his wife to Europe, never to return to his work as editor-in-chief of the *Free Enquirer*. The paper languished under the uninspired directorship of Amos Gilbert, a little longer, and then expired.

He appeared in Paris in August full of a new plan of life. In the first enthusiasm of his reunion with Fanny, he nearly persuaded her and her husband and child to join in it.

In a letter to Amos Gilbert he says:

> I found our friend Frances, in as good health as, after a recent and severe attack of remittent fever, I had expected to find her. Her husband and child also in indifferently good health.
>
> She must not, at least for some time to come, venture upon the mental exertion to which as editor she formerly exposed herself. Her constitution, at first shattered by an almost fatal attack of fever, superinduced by her exertions during the first settlement and arrangement of the Nashoba colony, then further enfeebled by too continued mental efforts during her editorial career, has felt deeply and painfully the shock of her only sister's death; and for some time longer it demands repose.
>
> I have learnt with pleasure, then, on more accounts than one, since my arrival here, that she and M. D'Arusmont in-

tend to remove next year to New Harmony. Considerations connected with the management of the small independence I possess there, which, while occupied with public objects I was constrained to neglect, demand my presence. Both our families, therefore purpose making the banks of the Wabash our place of residence; and I shall proceed in a week or two by way of N. Y. to Indiana, in order to superintend the erection, in the immediate neighborhood of the town, of a small country residence, to receive our united party. Mary remains, meanwhile, with Frances.

Needless to say this fantastic plan never materialized. In the first place, Robert had to give up his idea of an immediate return to America in order to spend the winter in London, where his father had recalled him to take the management of a new paper lately founded by this indefatigable old man in the interests of Co-operation, *The Crisis or the Change from Error and Misery to Truth and Happiness.*

He still counted on sailing in the spring before the rest of the party, and he still proposed to leave his wife behind him in Paris till that later date. Perhaps he really believed that the help she could render Fanny as *femme de ménage* and general factotum in the household would amply compensate for her board and lodging and even some instruction in French.

For a time at least, the arrangement seemed to work, if one may judge from Fanny's first letter to Robert after his departure.

Sept.

Dearest Robert:

The days have seemed very long to us since your departure: house is still and silent even in spite of the monkey (little Sylva) who gains in strength and spirits. I and Phiquepal have both been ailing until yesterday. Mary, I rejoice to think, is recovering her general health— Would that she had not to lament your absence and to suffer under a separation so calculated to depress the life within her. But she, sweet gentle creature, bears up under her affliction with that good sense which I think distinguishes all her thoughts and actions. I am satisfied, dear Robert, that you found in her what will soften the rough road of life . . . Phiquepal and I will come with Mary this spring when we can judge better than we

have been able to here, touching Harmony. Let our affairs
there be forgotten, therefore, until we join you!

But a note from Mary to her husband enclosed in the same letter
is full of grave doubts whether, when the moment actually came
for departure, Fanny would consent to go herself or let Phiquepal
go without her. She was really afraid of the effects of the climate
not only for herself but for little Sylva. And, as the days went on,
the relations between these two women, so delicately placed towards one another in the first place, so unlike in every way, grew
more and more strained. Mary's letters to her husband became more
and more complaining. Try as she might, do what she would, she
told him, it was impossible to satisfy two such nervous and irritable
persons as Phiquepal and Fanny. "All I wonder is that you who are acquainted with them both did not foresee how it would end." Robert
himself finally had to admit that Frances and Phiquepal with all
their excellent and admirable qualities, were "figgetty."

One does not know exactly how long this unsatisfactory visit of
Mary to the D'Arusmonts lasted. She herself seems to have been
half right and half wrong in insisting that neither of the D'Arusmonts
had any real intention of returning to America. In the end Fanny
and her child remained in Paris but Phiquepal sailed with Robert,
Mary, and Robert's sister Jane the following spring. Phiquepal also
took with him his adopted son, Alexis, and left him in Cincinnati to
learn the brewing business with Fanny's old friend and admirer Dr.
Price. But a very short stay with the young Owens in New Harmony
was long enough to convince Phiquepal that any plan to unite their
two families in one common center was doomed to failure.

He rejoined his wife in Paris in the beginning of December. The
next few years of their married life were spent in a little apartment
in the "Quartier des Écoles," No. 3, Rue de la Vielle Estrapade. Their
nearest neighbors were the famous botanist Pierre Turpin and his
childless old wife. This typical bourgeois environment was soon to become a sort of second home for Sylva, now rapidly growing into a
delightful, precocious little being.

Even Fanny's restless spirit found for a time an unaccustomed
calm in the thought that "her noble child" might some day attain
to those heights of fame hitherto denied her mother.

In Sylva's own words written many years later, "My childhood
was one of the healthiest and happiest possible. I grew up in the

united care of my parents, so proud of each other, and they of me, that I invented a sort of ceremony which consisted of pressing my cheeks between both my dear ones, with a kiss, given and taken by all three together, *tous les trois,* the words themselves thus spoken serving as a sort of magic spell against all outsiders."

She speaks also of a portrait painted of her mother at this time by the Swedish artist, Gorlitz. "He desired my father to draw my mother out on some congenial topics, and never looked again after he had seized her expression. To my mind it is the very personification of her bewitching words, 'God bless thy innocent face!'—the only religious training I ever received from her. It was a great success and reproduced a number of times in good lithographs which have long survived the delicate pastel."

Another household which had almost as important a place in Sylva's happy childhood was that of the de Boinvilles in Clichy. Madame de Boinville was an Englishwoman, the widow of a French emigré whom she had met and married during his exile in England. She was in close touch with the circle around Godwin, a help and comfort to the poet Shelley during those melancholy days before his final separation from his first wife. Shelley always thought and spoke of her under the name of Maiume, the mysterious spinner of Southey's poem, "Thalaba the Destroyer," whose face was bright as a damsel's face, and yet her hair was gray.

Fanny's first introduction to this delightful being was during that brief intense friendship of hers with Mrs. Shelley in the summer of 1827. At that time neither Madame de Boinville nor Fanny were especially attracted to one another. The intimate relation which held them together for a number of years began with the removal of the whole de Boinville family to Paris about the same time that Fanny herself, still desperately lonely after the death of her only sister, was most in need of a sympathizing female friend. Phiquepal too was petted and admired by the whole de Boinville household which contained, besides the head of the family—Fanny's particular friend—a married son, Alfred, and his wife Pauline, their child, the little Pauline, about the same age as little Sylva, and a married daughter, Mrs. Turner.

Another member of the tiny circle of friends who had gathered round Fanny and Phiquepal during those early years of their married life was the great positivist philosopher, Auguste Comte, and his wife. Comte, a much younger man than Phiquepal, had been one of the under teachers at Maclure's School in Paris and had been even a little tempted to follow its fortunes to America.

At the time of his greatest intimacy with Fanny, Comte was still very largely under the influence of that particular brand of French socialism known as Saint-Simonism. The main objects of this new doctrine were much the same as those laid down by Owen in his *New Moral World*. Both urged an entire reorganization of human society in the interests of the working classes so that all members of it might be happy and free, each working according to his capacity and each receiving according to his need. Both insisted on the complete emancipation of woman from male domination, with the recognition of her entire equality with man in all important matters. But there was an element of extravagance and mysticism among the Saint-Simonians which Owenism entirely lacked and which left Fanny herself cold.

On the other hand their belief in human history as the elucidator of the great fundamental truths underlying human conduct, later to become an important factor in the positivism of Auguste Comte their almost religious belief in Humanity—written with a large H—to take the place of the Christian idea of God, had a deep and lasting effect on all her later thinking and writing.

Nothing of this was apparent, however, on her first reappearance as public lecturer in the early summer of 1833. Notice of the coming event appeared in an issue of Robert Owen's newspaper the *Crisis*, which gave as her subject those four lectures on factual knowledge originally delivered in the State House in Cincinnati some five years before.

The description of the meeting as it appeared in Owen's paper has the old familiar ring.

"On Tuesday evening last, Madame D'Arusmont, late Frances Wright, delivered a lecture to a large and respectable audience in Freemason Hall, Great Queen Street."

The notice goes on to emphasize the beauty and simplicity of her language, the ease and dignity of her manner, with a hint that the subject itself was more theoretical than practical.

Another lecture was announced for Thursday June 26th. Her power to hold large audiences had not been affected by its disuse during the last years, but the fact that she was no longer a free spirit was made sufficiently plain by her husband's daily letters, full of intimate details of his life with his little daughter in her absence, interspersed with earnest requests for her speedy return.

> June 1st. Sylva insists that I write to you. She has dictated this letter: "*Chère Maman, revenez voir et embrasser Papa. Sylva voudrait bien aussi te voir et t'embrasser.*" We have often told each other that she was a remarkable child, but she is more so perhaps than you think. She perfectly understood your preparations for departure. I hope, dear friend, that you are now in London and that you are not too tired after the journey.
>
> Sylva and I get on beautifully together and are very well. I haven't taken a new *femme de ménage*. I manage perfectly without one and I believe I shall continue to do so.

Here he digressed for a moment to tell her that Madame Tracy Lafayette had responded very kindly to Fanny's request for the return of her portrait and any letters of hers that might be found among Lafayette's papers. This was the only mention one finds in her correspondence of what must have been a painful blow, the death of her faithful old friend, in Paris, May 30th of that same year.

> Tuesday, June 3rd. Monsieur and Madame Comte who returned a week ago came to see you and were not a little surprised to learn that you were in London . . . Sylva is very well. She keeps me very busy taking care of her, but fortunately for me she likes to be with our next door neighbors, the school teachers, so that I can confide her to their care for part of the day.
>
> It is very warm. The thermometre rose lately to 85 degrees. I am most impatient to know how you are placed, if you are in the city or the country, and whether you have decided what you are going to do there? You had better follow carefully all that is going on in the United States Senate, President Jackson's protest against their measures. As for me, I am persuaded that it is all part of a gigantic plot, just like the one which followed the Three Days Fighting here.
>
> I beg you, if you speak at all in public, not to allow yourself to be deflected from the plan which you laid out for yourself before you left.

> Thursday, June 5th. at eight o'clock in the evening. It

rained yesterday, but not hard. Today we have the most beautiful weather possible. Sylva has written you a great many letters. She is growing sweeter and sweeter every day. We went together to return Mrs. Turner's shawl and when we did not find her at home we stopped at the Palais Royal. She was much delighted with the fountain. "But see, Papa, isn't it funny water? Water which looks like a bunch of flowers. No, not flowers, great feathers which fall back into the water." In fact, her remarks on everything she saw constantly surprised me. However, by four o'clock she announced to me that she was very hungry and as we had eaten very frugally before we went out, I thought that a dinner Chez Hurbain would not be amiss. I happened to have a ticket of our old subscription in my pocket, so in we went and had quite a little spree. Sylva was delighted and made a little comedy for everyone around us.

But you, dear friend, what are you doing? I hope all the exercise which you must be taking has been good for your health. Have you found comfortable lodgings? Are you surrounded by interesting people? I hoped to find a letter from you on my return answering all these questions, but I am not yet really disturbed by your silence. I shall wait patiently till tomorrow, or even day after tomorrow. But after that I sha'n't be able to keep from worrying.

Sylva wants to go to school. It might be worth while to try the experiment. I put her to bed this evening with the promise that she should go next day.

Saturday, June 7th. It is nine days today, dear friend, since your departure and still not a word. I confess that I am growing very much disturbed about you. Are you ill? I can't tell you all the evil possibilities which are passing through my head about you. I have not sent this scribble, begun a week ago, because I did not know exactly how to address it, and have been waiting for a letter from you.

Then comes more about Sylva, the extraordinary precocity she showed on her first day at school.

"Can you imagine, Papa," she told me. "There is a little girl there who doesn't want to learn. Isn't that funny? Isn't it strange?" And not content with hearing the fable of *Le Renard et le Corbeau* at school, she made me repeat it to her afterwards more than fifty times till she knew it nearly all

by heart. I should be surprised at her readiness to apply herself if I did not remember that she was your daughter. She
is more like a little woman than a little child. I never have to
punish her. All I have to do is to explain the necessity of
what I want from her and she submits immediately. It is
impossible to spoil her. Everything would be perfect here
if I could only hear from you. We sha'n't try to get another
femme de ménage till your return. I keep the house cleaner
than it has been for a long time and I have bought a new
table for the salon which I hope you will find pretty.

Sunday, half past ten in the morning.
I wish I dared to be angry with you but I am too afraid
that there is really some serious cause for your silence beyond
mere negligence. Whatever it is, dear friend, do not leave
me any longer in this painful uncertainty. If you are ill you
can surely find some means of letting me know. But I am not
even sure that you are in London. However, unless I hear
from you before Sunday week, I shall come myself and look
for you.

And this was what in the end he had to do. One sees by their pass-
port that the two returned together from England to France on
July 3rd, 1834.
But the old passion for a life of active service, once awakened, was
not so easily put to sleep again. When Phiquepal was confronted
with the disagreeable necessity of another journey to America, in
search of further sums of money accruing from Fanny's investments
in that country, she was no longer content to let him go alone.
She sailed with her husband on November 3rd, 1835, leaving Sylva
behind her with the Turpins. It was the first and only time in her life
that the child was separated from both her parents at once. At the
moment of departure, they expected to be absent only a few months,
a year at most. In actual fact it was nearly four years before Fanny
returned to France, four momentous years, full to overflowing with
feverish activities as lecturer, writer, and editor of a radical newspaper which she had relinquished—as she thought forever—on her marriage to Phiquepal and the birth of her child.

CHAPTER VIII

Sowing the Wind

ON THEIR return to America in 1835, Phiquepal and Fanny took the southern route, so familiar to them both from past voyages to and fro, disembarking in New Orleans and then proceeding directly up the river to their final destination, Cincinnati. The fact that Phiquepal's adopted son, Alexis D'Arusmont, was already established in that city, had no doubt something to do with this. Alexis had grown by this time to be a worthy young man in every particular, a credit to Phiquepal's "General Method of Education" and devoted to both his adopted parents.

But an even more important reason for this visit to Cincinnati was the transaction of some very necessary business in connection with Fanny's investments in America. These were mortgages on real estate scattered widely throughout the United States from New York to Memphis, Tennessee, but chiefly in Cincinnati.

A little black notebook in her husband's handwriting, found among her papers at her death, shows some $9000 invested in this way in that city between the years 1827-1837. A number of these mortgages became due in the early months of 1836, involving new loans at the most advantageous terms.

As soon as this business was concluded, however, there was nothing to keep Fanny and her husband in America. Nothing except the fact that Cincinnati was the place where she herself had begun her career as a public lecturer just eight years before. It was a city full of dangerously disquieting memories to a woman barely forty, still in the plenitude of her powers of mind and body, with unplumbed, unsatisfied depths in her nature still clamoring for expression.

Eight years ago the American people had been preparing to elect a new President, startlingly unlike any of his predecessors in that great office. Andrew Jackson came into power as the champion of the forgotten man, who at that moment in the history of the United States happened to be the man of the frontier states, whose possibilities as a member of the American Union had been largely neglected hitherto by the upper classes of the eastern seaboard. And now, after eight years of service during which President Jackson had shattered many of the precedents and shocked most of the prejudices of the conservative property-holders of the country, who had grown to believe themselves its predestined leaders, the American people were preparing to elect his successor. The fact that he still remained the idol of the democratic masses of the country through his whole term of service, had not prevented the rise of a strong opposition party which was only waiting for the next election to put a candidate of its own in his place, and undo as fast as it could some of those reforms which he considered the chief triumph of his administration.

As it happened, the new Whig party was composed of just those elements in the community that Fanny most feared and hated as enemies of the essential principles which she believed to be the foundations of the American Union. It was the old combination of rich merchants, money-makers and moneylenders in league with the soothsayers who worshipped the idol with three heads "to deprive the toiling millions of the just rewards of their labor," which she had excoriated in her *New Book of Chronicles* at the time of her memorable campaign for a National Republican System of Education.

The slavery question, too, had assumed new importance under the leadership of William Lloyd Garrison. There was no longer any idea of co-operation for its reform among the southern planters. It was war to the knife, a fight for the extermination of the whole evil, root and branch, by Federal intervention.

This new call for immediate action had roused violent opposition throughout the country, but it had also galvanized the whole movement for the reform of negro slavery into sacrificial efforts to spread this doctrine through the South as well as in the North, regardless of consequences. In the summer before Fanny's return to America had occurred that famous meeting of the Female Anti-slavery Association so vividly described by Harriet Martineau, when Garrison was dragged through the streets of Boston by an angry mob with a halter round his neck. Disgraceful scenes had occurred during the spring of her return to Cincinnati. The anti-slavery newspaper owned by James Birney, *The Philanthropist*, which was similar to Fanny's own *Free Enquirer* in its willingness to publish both sides of the question, was raided, its press and type and material defaced or destroyed, and Birney himself had narrowly escaped tar and feathers.

From the very first, as one may remember, Fanny had conceived a strong prejudice against the abolition movement, partly no doubt, whether consciously or not, from her personal bias against the Christian churches which furnished such a large number of its early membership. It may also be that, even if she had agreed with their general procedure and policy, which she did not, there existed a temperamental disinclination to play second fiddle in a field where she had already made the supreme sacrifices of fortune, health, and personal reputation.

With all her passion for the service of humanity along unorthodox and often startling ways, she always returned sooner or later to the safe moorings of her deep-rooted belief that all progress must wait on the slow process of education and free enquiry. At this time, in the face of the new abolitionist doctrine of immediacy, she again insisted that the enfranchisement of the negro could be achieved only by the enfranchisement of his master, also in the chains of prejudice, ignorance, and unwillingness to see where the best interests of both really lay. The salvation of master and slave must be left to time and the inevitable spread of liberal opinion.

Here was another matter on which she felt she had something really valuable to say.

She resumed her role of public lecturer and reformer on the platform of the Court House at Cincinnati on Sunday, May 15th, 1836, with a great map of the United States hanging on the wall behind her and a copy of the Declaration of Independence in her hand. The newspapers of the city tell us that she held a large audience enthralled for an hour and a 'nalf while she discussed the nature and object of America's political institutions from the Jeffersonian, anti-Hamilton point of view. Her success continued through the remaining Sundays in May when she addressed her audiences on the various burning issues of the day.

Her lecture on slavery was practically identical with the one already delivered by her in Wilmington, Delaware, the autumn before her departure to Haiti.

But in her speech on Chartered Monopolies, she boldly entered the field of party politics with a violent attack on the Bank of the United States, whose destruction she had always considered one of the triumphs of Jackson's administration, and which it was the avowed intention of the new Whig party to re-establish in all its former pride and privilege if they were successful in electing their candidate for President, William Henry Harrison.

Her future biographer, the Quaker Amos Gilbert, describes this new political development as a sort of insanity, unworthy of the woman whose lofty exposition of true knowledge and free enquiry had set her in a place by herself far above the partisan struggles of the multitude.

He was wrong, however, if he believed that Fanny was actuated by anything but the purest idealism in her campaign against the Whig candidate for President. Her fear and hatred of banks and bankers was a thing of long standing, dating back to those three years of her experiment at Nashoba. The people of the back country in which her plantation was situated, including all her most trusted friends and advisers, had an instinctive fear of borrowed money. To them a debt was a terrible necessity born of poverty and to be repaid as soon as possible. Loans and credits were painfully necessary in a community where there was very little ready cash, but the general attitude of the frontiersman to the chartered monopoly which made its money by its management of just these matters, was one of the deepest dislike and distrust.

It is hard to tell just how far Fanny was influenced by this local prejudice, but she certainly believed that one of the chief functions of the banking system was to make the rich richer and the poor poorer, and thus intensify those class distinctions which to her mind, at least, were gradually reducing the Declaration of Independence to a dead letter.

In France too, she had seen, or thought she had seen, all the hope of a great nation for a freer, more generous form of government, put to nought by secret pressure from the powerful money interests of the country in combination with the Bank of England. From her exile in Paris she had followed with the deepest sympathy the various phases of Jackson's war against the Bank of the United States, and rejoiced in the veto which reversed the decision of Congress to grant this institution a new charter. In her opinion the new Whig party was the lineal descendant of all the most anti-American elements in the nation from the time of the Great Federalist, Alexander Hamilton, till the present crisis. The election of the Whig candidate to the presidency would be a great disaster for the future of Free America, a disaster which it was her duty and pleasure to resist by every means in her power.

Once set forth on this new road, nothing could prevent her from following it to the end. In throwing down her challenge to bankers in general and the Whig party in particular in the heated atmosphere of the presidential campaign of 1836, she showed even more courage and self-confidence than was necessary in her first encounters with the conservative forces of American society. For the temper of the nation was vastly changed, and not for the better, since the time when she was able to travel from one end of the country to the other preaching her startling doctrines of rational education and free enquiry to peaceful audiences, with the minimum of interference and interruption from those elements in the community who found her teaching shocking and subversive. A new intensity of partisan conviction was abroad in the nation, with its inevitable accompaniment of an increased unwillingness to listen to or even permit the expression of contrary opinions. Many of the early meetings of the Whigs had been broken up by open violence and now the Whigs were adopting the same tactics towards any efforts to discuss the financial situation on the part of those opposed to the United States Bank.

As long as she remained in Cincinnati, where she had many personal friends and well-wishers, including the editors of the principal newspapers in that city, she was listened to with respect and toleration even by those who entirely disagreed with her. When a little later in the summer she turned her step to Philadelphia, one finds quite a different series of events.

She was refused admittance to any public hall suitable for the delivery of her lectures. When by a fortunate accident she at last got hold of a spacious building formerly occupied by a wire factory at the Falls of the Schuylkill, her meeting was disturbed by "boys urged on by men in genteel garb, among whom was observed some of the police who did not prevent the throwing of stones," in which disturbance some of the thousand people assembled to hear her were slightly injured.

From Philadelphia she went on to New York and Boston, everywhere drawing large and attentive audiences, till at last, with the election of Martin Van Buren to the presidency, she could really flatter herself that she had contributed to his success to an appreciable extent. In the city and state of New York, however, the Whigs had made alarming encroachments on the normally democratic preserves because of a split in the Democratic party ranks. It was a recrudescence of Fanny's old party in politics now calling themselves the

"Equal Rights Party" and dubbed by their enemies the "Locofocos" from the use they made of matches of that name when the light went out at one of their meetings. Fanny was so deeply convinced now that the fate of the country depended on the defeat of the Whig party that she was strangely impatient of this diversion of Democratic strength from the regular party nominations, with a possible advantage to the Whig candidates in both state and city.

In fact the victory of the Jacksonian Democrats at the polls in 1836 was not nearly so safe and sweeping as its leaders wished and expected. The Whigs had made alarming inroads on the great cities of the East. They had already nominated William Harrison as their next presidential candidate, and were settling down to the four years' campaign which was to result in the victory of their party in 1840.

Having once put her hand to the plow Fanny would not turn back. One finds her settled in Philadelphia for the winter of 1836-37, hard at work over a new newspaper, the *Manual of American Principles*, a successor to those better-known ventures of hers in the newspaper world, the New Harmony *Gazette* and the *Free Enquirer* which had already won such notable success for her. Only two numbers of this magazine still exist in the Yale Library. Unlike its predecessors, the *Manual of American Principles* seems to have been financed, edited, and written almost entirely by Fanny herself. Where were the friends and fellow workers, that gallant band of Free Enquirers who lived together so happily and had helped to make those earlier publications so remarkably successful? Jennings! Robert Dale! All mention of the first disappears from the *Free Enquirer* after the dissolution of their partnership in 1830. Fanny and Robert Dale were already hopelessly alienated by their quarrel over that fertile source of broken friendships—differences about money.

Her letter to James Richardson, asking his aid and encouragement in her new undertaking, received the usual charming and evasive reply which Richardson was accustomed to give in such emergencies. He described his new position as tutor, at $500 a year with board, in the family of a rich planter named McGoven living on the outskirts of Memphis.

> Thus I have obtained, [says he] the highest object of my ambition an office for which I consider myself eminently fit, and the only one for which I consider myself fit at all. It enables me too, to fill the measure of justice to my most

amiable wife and two promising children, by their emigration to Haiti, where their foot will be on their native heath
and their name no longer nigger. I shall follow them whenever the separation shall become intolerable, by which time
they will have built a nest and I shall have a few feathers
to soften it when I go.

I have received the little picture of you and live in the
hope that we shall sometime and somewhere meet again and
again enjoy the glorious laugh of a common sympathy.

Affectionately,
your friend Jas. R.

There one may leave him once and for all. He never appears again
in Fanny's story.

Her final appearance in the field of party politics was in New York
during the campaign for the election of a new Congress in the mid-
term of Van Buren's administration. She never had permitted herself
to be identified with any political party. For that matter no party,
except perhaps the Abolitionists, would have openly accepted aid
from her.

The Democrats, however, while holding aloof from her officially,
were quite ready to help her when they could do so, to their own
advantage. It was through the good services of a Tammany alderman, for instance, that she was able to engage the Masonic Hall for
a series of lectures to be delivered the four Sundays before the
election.

Fanny herself solemnly declared, however, that she was innocent
of any special intention to annoy, in her choice of the Hall for the
delivery of her lectures. As she herself explains it:

> Most unsuspectingly and altogether undesignedly I have
> come to station myself in the hornet's nest of the great
> Whig Headquarters, mistaking it for an altogether neutral
> and peaceable, if not friendly region. I had applied for the
> Hall without any reference to its being the Whig Headquar-
> ters and simply in the natural course of things. It was in this
> hall that I first addressed the public of New York in 1828. . . .
> I came here because it was the only hall I had ever hired in
> the city. Had I known at the time of any other procurable
> building at once as large and as conveniently placed and also
> better aired and better seated and better constructed, I should
> most certainly have preferred it. All who may ever have had

occasion to exert their voice within these walls for any length of time, will know that it is not done without difficulty, nor without pain, and will feel with me that some other and more suitable place of meeting for the purpose of public instruction is much wanted.

A mischievous joke had appeared in one of the Democratic newspapers: that the Whigs were making a bid for favor with the radical fringe of society by inviting Fanny to speak in the Masonic Hall at that time. This was too much for the Whig party and the Whig press. Fanny, who had been left surprisingly alone since her return to the New York lecture stage, was now to be given a taste of mob violence and editorial blackguardism which put her former experiences of that sort quite in the shade.

Her old enemy, the *Courier and Enquirer,* was now a Whig newspaper, under the personal management of one of the founders and baptizers of the new party, James Watson Webb. Fanny's own particular enemy, Major Noah, had also turned Whig and was editing a paper of his own in that interest, the *Evening Star.*

An article in the New York *Daily Express*, also a Whig newspaper, began the campaign against her in the old familiar tone.

> The great she-Loco-Foco continues her political harangues on Sunday night, of which the Public had the second of the series last evening. The audience was large and about thirty women disgraced themselves by appearing on the stage. Well-clad enough and well-looking enough! To do our She-Benton justice, however, she showed herself quite equal to her Humbug prototype. Were the Loco-Foco's of the City to take her to their ward meeting, etc., etc.

In the heated atmosphere of an especially bitter electoral contest it was a very easy step from fierce abusive words to fierce abusive deeds.

> On Sunday October 6th, [says the New York *Gazette* in its issue a few days later] serious disturbances occurred among the audience which nearly filled the Masonic Hall with a mixed multitude of friends and foes assembled to hear Fanny Wright, the high priestess of infidelity, lecture on her anti-religious doctrines as she understands them.
>
> It was soon apparent, however, that more opposers and

reprobaters of her doctrines than friends and supporters were present. She was soon assailed with hisses and after she had lectured for nearly an hour, a fight sprang up and then another and another until six sturdy fellows were pounding and bruising each other most magnificently.

With the help of the police and a Tammany alderman who appeared as her friend on this occasion, these disturbers of the meeting were finally arrested and one of them sent to the watch house but soon after discharged. But the disturbance still continued. Discordant noises and hisses were uttered from various parts of the hall, with cries of "Put her out! Put the old bitch out!" "Down with her!" etc., accompanied with sundry expressions too indecent to mention.

She was seen at last, [says her old friend Amos Gilbert in the brief biography already mentioned] descending from the second story of the hall with thousands of grim faces peering upon her, giving savage indications of murderous intent, so soon as their masters should give the word "go." But her calm intrepidity awed them and she was permitted to pass through the formidable crowd to the carriage unscathed. When she was ensconced out of sight in the vehicle, where her tranquil firmness was invisible to them, they several times lifted and leaned the carriage trying themselves whether they had the audacious courage to overthrow it. Prudent resolute men walked slowly before the coach horses, repeating "steady! steady!" The noble animals, as if proud of their office, moved gracefully on, as if cognizant of the contemptible bipeds around them. Meanwhile Frances sat gently fanning herself and in easy conversation with her friends.

But indignation against the disgraceful exhibition of mob violence upon respectable "females" some of whom had not even attended the meeting in question had already begun to spread among the law-abiding portion of the community, and Fanny was able a week later, Sunday Oct. 28th, to appear on the same platform in the same hall with perfect impunity, to complete her engagement with the public in the last lecture of the series, "What is the Matter?"

She could and did answer her own question in her own way as to the rights of man and the independence of the new world to which Federalism had given the lie, and which British fraud had thought to encompass and break. "It is the bowels of Federalism that are racked with anguish and her own mother on the banks of the Thames whose empire feels the throes of dissolution.

"Rejoice then rejoice in thy deliverance, young eagle! Full fledged art thou this day. Thou art ready and willing to achieve thy last victory. Henceforth and forever thou art thy own. Soar then aloft on the strong pinions which Freedom gave thee. Scatter to the four winds of heaven the foul and foreign harpies who battened on the blood of thy children. One bold defiance, perchance one fierce encounter and the Leopard of England shall spring back to his jungle all the tiger monarchs of the earth shall crouch in their littleness before thee, and all her peoples shall rise up and bless thee in the name of Freedom."

The Tory Federal Whigs, as she called them, were trying to set the public on a wrong scent by reviving all the old scandals connected with the name of Fanny Wright. But, "Say they should succeed in tearing me to pieces," she concludes with all her old fiery temper, "or stoning me to death, as they have at different times attempted, what then? Admitting that my life and labor have somewhat advantaged the cause of the people and the interest of humanity at large, even if they were now both stopped on the instant and forever, that would not prevent the passing of the Independent Treasury Bill, and the passing of that bill knocks Federal Tory Whiggery on the head and gives it its quietus forever, etc.

"Fellow citizens I have answered the question. It is the Independent Treasury Bill which is the matter. It is the safe snatching of America's young eagle from the greedy clutch of the English leopard. It is the fast sealing of that golden charter . . ."

The Democrats did indeed retain control of the next Congress by a small majority and therefore they did manage to pass the bill on which Fanny had expended so much fervid oratory before their fall from power in 1840. But the Whigs were triumphant in the city and state of New York, and signs were not wanting all over the country that the wave of Jacksonian Democracy which had carried all before it in 1828 was already beginning to recede and give place to a confusion of petty political ambitions and compromise measures which could have little appeal to a person of Fanny's general tendencies of thought and noble desire for the spread of true opinion as the only corrective for the human misery still existing all around her. She had by no means relinquished her old self-appointed task of efficient leader of the popular mind, assumed so gallantly some ten years before. Her new field of activity, however, was much wider and more speculative than anything she had attempted in those early days, even in those first six lectures on the value of scientific and factual knowledge. It was, in fact, nothing more nor less than the presentation of the history of human civilization: its beginning in India, Egypt, Greece and Rome and its later phases in medieval and modern Europe; the history of the origins of the evils which especially plague and disfigure our modern society—the subjection of women, the degradation of human labor—with special attention to the sinister influence of England upon the fresh life of free America through the introduction of her banking and funding system.

She had evidently taken infinite pains in the preparation of these lectures, which had apparently been on her mind for a long time. They show an enormous amount of general information, the result of wide and voracious reading during all those years spent in seclusion in Paris. They are, also, peculiarly interesting as they show the rise of a new star in the constellation of great innovators which one after another had exerted such extraordinary influence over her mind and heart and even the direction of her life: Epicurus, Byron, Jeremy Bentham, Lafayette, Robert Owen the elder, and now Auguste Comte. There was much in the philosophy of this great positivist thinker in line with her own natural tendencies and beliefs. Comte was also a Utopian, who believed that the final perfectability of the human species could be effected by moral development rather than by violent changes in the present order.

But Comte also believed that the highest instincts of mankind could be developed by religion and religion only, the religion of humanity exalted on the throne already occupied by the supreme being of Christian theology, and exercising a power so superior to ourselves as to command the complete submission of our whole life.

One need not be surprised, therefore, to find Fanny beginning her new series of lectures with a careful correction of the error which had crept into her earlier writings, namely the confounding of religion with theology.

> Theology from the Greek words theos, God or gods, unseen beings and unknown causes, and logos, word, talk or, if we like to employ yet more familiar and expressive terms, prattle or chatter! Talk or prattle about unseen beings or un-

known causes, Religion from the Latin *religo* to tie over again, to bind fast, a binding together, a bond of union.

The religion of priests was the binding principle behind the civilizations of Asia and Egypt. The religion of Kings held all Europe together down to the present time. And now in this new world of America we see the binding force of the Religion of the people, bright prototype of that final religion of Humanity which is to bind together all the nations of the earth under the apotheosis of the American principle of Justice, sole divinity whose reign once established is to extend peace, love, and universal prosperity over the whole surface of our globe, etc., etc.

These last lectures were never published but they still exist, beautifully written out in longhand and conveniently bound in neat little booklets that their author might the more readily handle them on the platform. One finds in them all her most salient characteristics of sincerity, nobility and earnest desire to serve the cause of Human Improvement to the limit of her powers. In her effort to reach the stars she lost her exceptional capacity of attracting and holding the average American audience. A rather melancholy impression of one of these later meetings is found in an article by the notable feminist writer and lecturer, Elizabeth Oakes Smith, giving an account of the only time she saw and heard Fanny Wright.

It was a cold winter's night when I prevailed upon my honored husband to go with me to hear the famous woman. There might have been fifty persons or more present who presently began to shuffle and call for the speaker. It was all so much more gross and noisy than anything I had ever encountered where a woman was concerned that I grew quite distressed. At length the door in the rear of the desk opened and a neat foot was placed upon the platform. She was a full-sized woman, with well-developed muscle and handsomely shaped, dressed in black silk with plain linen collar and cuffs. Her head was large but not handsome, her forehead comparatively low but broad indicating force and executive ability. Her gestures were all good, and her smile sweet with a touch of feminine sadness. Eyes well set, under broad brows. She was pale but not sallow and there was an earnestness and wholesomeness about Frances Wright that made their way to the mind and heart. She was at intervals ap-

plauded but did not seem to care for it. Her self poise was
very fine.

Whatever might be the seeming indifference to the applause of her
scanty audiences, Fanny was both surprised and chagrined by the
lack of response to this, her latest and most seriously considered effort to instruct the public mind in the things nearest to their best
interests. She continued the series, however, in the face of continued
disappointment, till at last some time in April, with a burst of ill-
temper very unusual with her, she brought them to an abrupt close
with the following announcement:

> I have conducted thus far most conscientiously, though not
> with the detail I should have given it under other circum-
> stances, the important enquiry to which at the opening of
> this winter I invited the attention of a steady and select audi-
> ence imagining I was doing so to meet the wishes of a large
> portion of the more staid and enquiring friends of American
> Independence, human liberty and happiness, among the peo-
> ple of this city. Since it seems however, that mere curiosity is
> the only motive which drew them in the first place, it is cer-
> tainly more than time for me to desist not only from the pres-
> ent but from all other labors in the public service.
> I made not a few personal sacrifices in order to pass this
> winter in this city and it may possibly not be in my power
> to pass another here for some time. This is then probably
> the last time I shall address a New York audience.

Some six weeks later one reads of her departure from that city for
another prolonged stay in France.

It has seemed best for the sake of clarity to keep to the main thread
of Fanny's public activities during these last strenuous years even
though this involves the exclusion of all the more personal and intimate side of her life during the same period. But one would carry
away a very incomplete idea of the essential Fanny during this period
of her development, if one were not able to fill in certain details about
the other side, the intimate, personal side, full of passionate affection,
and deep-rooted loyalties, which may sometimes have been overlaid
but never extinguished by the demands and interests of her public
career. She never ceased, for instance, to mourn the death of her much
loved sister, Camilla. Her sense of bitter loss when her first little child

died in infancy was never entirely assuaged even by her beloved little Sylva. Rather touching proof of this is found in some verses written by her on that long sea journey chiefly over tropical waters which took her away from her little girl to America in 1835.

A Dream at Sea. Jan. 2nd. 1836.

I saw the golden and the dark haired child;
Shadowy and pale the one, as soft moonlight.
The other as Aurora dazzling bright.
And side by side they stood and on each other smiled.

And near them sat a being in whose air
Was all a woman's love and woman's grace.
Ah! Why has sorrow faded that sweet face,
And dimmed the eyes' soft light and silvered the pure hair?

And to her feet the children come to lay
Their heads upon her knee; their cheeks have met,
The rings of gold have mingled with the jet,
The lily with the rose, night with her sister day.

Before the angel group I gazing stood . . .
"Sylva, my child!" she turned her sunlit eyes,
Opened her arms . . . Ah me! The vision flies.
Around me is the midnight vault and ocean's boundless flood.

Even clearer proof of her profound affection for both her husband and the one child still left her, is found in a handful of family letters covering all the period between 1836 and 1839.

The first of these is in Phiquepal's handwriting dated from Cincinnati early in June, 1836.

Papa to his dear child. My dear Sylva, our dear little treasure. We have just received a letter from Maman Boinville who tells us that you are big, fat, fresh and well, that you are growing like the wind. All this good news makes us very happy, but what puts the last touch to our content is to learn that you are always gentle, good, and kind, ready to do everything that can please Papa and Maman Turpin.

They are so good to you, dear child, that you can't do too much to repay them for the trouble they take to make you happy. Every day we think of you. Every day papa and

maman look at your picture and imagine ourselves holding
you in our arms and giving that threefold kiss. Do you remember it? What we used to call *"Tous les trois."*

Give our best love to Maman Boinville, Maman Pauline
[the wife of Madame de Boinville's son Alfred] and Maman
Turpin.

Fanny's letter (the 7th of a series of which only this one remains)
is dated from Philadelphia, July 3rd, 1836.

Maman to her dear little girl.

Thy poor mother has been very very anxious about thee,
my treasure. On our arrival in Cincinnati in February, Papa
and I found the first letter from Maman Turpin, but for the
last four months we have lived without any news from our
little Sylva. At last a letter from Maman Pauline dated March
11th came to relieve us a little from our anxiety. But we have
not yet received any answer to our first letter written while
we were in New Orleans.

Dear Child. The letter of Maman Pauline was written at
the time of your bad toothache, and told us how you had
suffered for three days, before the naughty tooth could be
extracted but that now you were again quite well and gay
and happy, and came frequently to play with little Pauline
in the Rue Clichy. Dear Child we imagine ourselves beside
you in all your little occupations, your plays, your walks,
your visits to the Rue Clichy, your visits to the country. At
this moment you are probably settled at Les Gres for the
summer. Madame Turpin has recovered her health, Monsieur
Turpin has lost his rheumatism.

But I must not write any more now. Papa is just setting
off for New York where he will write again to you and Monsieur Turpin and enclose this little word from thy tender
mother.

Then comes a letter from "Locust Grove on the borders of the
Susquehanna, August 10th."

My dear child. We have at last received thy little letter
and how many times we have read it and how many times
we have kissed it!

Dear Sylva, I shall keep it always to the end of my life.

[And indeed it was carefully preserved in the box of papers inherited by that same daughter at her mother's death. Seven lines written in a big neat childish script.] The first that thy little hand has ever traced. Immediately after thy letter arrived, my friend, in one from Monsieur Turpin, Papa left me to return to Cin'ti, while I am staying on here during the weeks of his absence which may prolong themselves to two or three months. I know my child, that in no part of the world could you be better off than where you are, surrounded by care and love, and far removed from stupidity, bad examples, and bad influences. I know all that perfectly well, my dear child, but nevertheless very often when I am wandering beside this river, in these woods, among these meadows and mountains, the most beautiful in the world, tears pour down my cheeks when I picture to myself, my little Sylva playing in the midst of this lovely nature and then have to remind myself "How far away she is from here!"

I am surrounded by kind friends in a charming family who all talk to me of you and would love to see you, to embrace you, to play with you, take you on walks among the mountains and on the lovely banks of this river, three times bigger than the Seine at Paris and as clear as the water in the fountains but all broken by rocks and waterfalls and rapids and sown with little islands, so that there are no great steamboats here as at Cin'ti, though the river is quite as large and beautiful as the Ohio.

But to meet these difficulties of navigation the inhabitants of this country have built a canal beside the river on which one can travel very agreeably in pretty boats.

Good bye, my darling. Papa is going to bring me back thy portrait which I left in Cin'ti for fear I would hurt it in the journey at a time of pouring rain, which was the case when we set out for Philadelphia.

The letter ends with tender messages to every member of Sylva's circle and promises to write again as soon as possible.

The next letter in the series is from Phiquepal in Paris, where he was sent apparently by Fanny, as soon as it became quite evident to her that her life and work for the present was in America, to bring Sylva back to join her mother in Philadelphia.

The letter is addressed to Fanny at the office of the *Manual*, 103 North 3rd Street, Philadelphia.

December 27th.

Chere Amie— Your absence alone prevents me from being perfectly happy. I have the inexpressible pleasure of pressing your dear child to my heart every day and seeing her return my caresses a hundred fold. Our first encounter turned exactly as I would have wished. I found her alone and stood there quietly beside her for nearly ten minutes. At first she did not recognize me but as I stood there motionless before her, to let her get the full impression of my person she looked at me earnestly with a certain surprise and then flung herself into my arms with the cry, "It is Papa. It is Papa! But where is Maman?" We passed the rest of the day joyfully together with reciprocal caresses, but when I had to leave her at night although I promised to come and get her early next morning to take her to Mrs. Boinville in the Rue Clichy where we were to pass the day, her tears flowed in abundance, in spite of all the efforts she made to hide them from me.

Yes, my dear friend, you have always perfectly understood our little angel. Sensibility, intelligence, beauty! She possesses them all and everything else that can charm. Besides which as she grows older, every day she resembles you more and more, to a degree which makes me hope that she will one day take up the task to which you and I have devoted our existence, the service of our fellow men.

But thou, dearest friend! Where are you at this moment? What are you doing? Don't work so hard as to injure your health. The fear of that always makes me anxious. Madame Boinville and her daughter, in fact everyone who loves you, all have the same fear. Heaven grant that on my return I may find we have been mistaken. As for me, all our friends say that I look better than I have for 15 years and I feel so in spite of the fact that Paris ever since my arrival has been in the grip of glacial cold and snow and the walking has been so bad that I have hardly seen anyone and so have very little to tell you. I would only suggest that you write a long and very friendly letter to Turpin. I know how busy you are but if you can spare the time I know it will have a good effect and do away with any idea that he has been a little neglected.

All the interesting family of the Boinvilles are well. Comte has been having some trouble with the Institute about a course of lectures on the general history of science which he hoped he would be permitted to deliver there, but I believe affairs have turned out better than his enemies expected, for a position has fallen vacant in the Ecole Politechnique which no one in Paris is as fit to fill as he. Even so, the Institute whose business it is to present such subjects, has refused to include him in their list of candidates. Comte wrote them a letter making no secret of his independence of mind which will probably close for him the post in the Ecole Politechnique, but in the meantime the Minister of War, General Bernard has appointed him interim professor. The students are so enchanted with the opportunity of hearing him that they have quite deserted the nominal appointee and otherwise express their satisfaction almost too frankly for safety.

I don't know whether you have read in the newspapers that Magendie has been made President of the Institute. He fills his new position with *beaucoup d' aplomb.*

Sylva has learned to read very well and I see now that she could easily have written the letters she sent you, though, why! I don't exactly see, Madame Turpin usually dictates them. Her next to you shall be written without help in my sight so that you can know exactly what she is capable of by herself.

Another letter a month later speaks of the ravages of la grippe in Paris that winter.

I hope this cursed epidemic, which has not been so bad here as in London and Berlin, has not reached America. We have all had it. Turpin has been confined to his room for the last month, and our dear child has also been attacked though only lightly. But now we are all in full convalescence, and I am starting in a few days with Sylva on a visit to my family in the South. My brother writes me that the hope of seeing her soon has put them all in a holiday mood. But I wish this were not necessary. I am longing to have the child entirely to myself so as to have a real opportunity for forming a just opinion of the development of her mind after our long separation. I have not as yet found any serious faults in her education but . . .

The old teaching instinct in Phiquepal had already set him planning on the old lines.

As soon as I get back to the U. S. we must try to find some half dozen little girls two or three years older than she, gentle, good, and intelligent, whose education I could undertake at the same time as hers. I know this would be rather a heavy burden upon me, but I think that three or four years would completely suffice for my task and I am sure it is the best thing we could possibly do for Sylva.

Needless to say, that with so many like plans in his old age, this scheme never materialized.

I shall try to get passage from le Havre directly to Philadelphia in view of the heavy articles that I am bringing back with me. Among others something called a Divan because it is at the same time an elastic bed of the kind you said you wanted, and a sofa. My room as you remember is so small that I prefer to sleep on a divan—instead of filling it up with a bed. *Je t'aime, je t'embrasse.*

Further details of the visit to France are found in a letter from Madame de Boinville, the intimate friend of both Fanny and Phiquepal with whom he made his chief home while in Paris.

Rue de Clichy, Friday May 20th

While waiting the arrival of your true half to take his soup with us I write a few lines to you, beloved friend. Many a sweet line have I received from you which have gone straight to my heart and filled my eyes with tears, etc., etc. Shall we ever meet again? I hope so. I almost feel that we shall—moment and place I do not now see, but methinks we are not to be parted forever.

'Tis a sad parting of Sylva from her loving protectors. Madame speaks her sorrow loudly and Monsieur Turpin feels it not less. This is a trial to your sensitive half and I shall be glad for his sake when the parting is over . . . Sylva spent the whole of yesterday here and I took her home to Madame Turpin in the evening who began to weep and lament bitterly. She must miss the dear child painfully for a long long time. The life her presence bestowed, once extinguished, I know not how they will endure their silent empty rooms.

[The letter is interrupted here by the arrival of Phiquepal]

. . . Very late! We had most given him up. And tired! Sadly tired he was, having been wet thro' more than once in the morning. We compelled him to put on dry slippers and socks. We then blew up the fire, drew the little dinner table close to it and cheered and refreshed him to the best of our power by heartfelt friendly chat in which he was lively and interesting as he always is, in spite of fatigue.

But for three days he was so ill from a return of grippe with all its miseries, harassing cough and fever that I felt actually alarmed about him and would have had him sacrifice everything to the care and repose which his state so imperiously demanded. My imagination was painfully struck and went off at full gallop into calamities which I could not bear to trace distinctly to myself, but his impatience to be with you was such that it would have been impolite to detain him, though I did keep him two days longer than he intended.

When this is delivered to you, you will have both your treasures safe and be able to bear the account of the stormy week which preceded their departure. All things going wrong, no room on board either of the Packets! The financial struggle in New York extending itself as it does to other countries has occasioned a commotion amongst the numerous Americans here and all are returning to their country at the same time. But, at the last moment Monsieur D'Arusmont has taken passage with an American merchantman bound for Philadelphia.

It was the same Captain French with whom Phiquepal and his wife had made the trip to New Orleans two years before. For a short time one finds all the Trio as Madame de Boinville likes to call them, together again in Cincinnati. It was the place above all where Phiquepal was to feel himself at home during the rest of their stay in America. Fanny too was obliged to spend the rest of the winter and the following spring of 1838 in Cincinnati, in slow recovery from a serious breakdown in her health brought about by too hard work as editor and chief contributor of her new periodical, the *Manual of American Principles*, already mentioned earlier in this chapter.

It was during this period of enforced leisure that one finds another letter from Phiquepal to his wife, written from Philadelphia, where he had been despatched to pick up the loose ends Fanny had left behind her in that city as well as in New York unavoidably because of her serious illness the preceding summer.

For some reason best known to himself, he had taken Sylva with him.

1838

Chère Amie

Here we are both comfortably settled in your old quarters in Philadelphia *chez* Mrs. McClosky.

Sylva is enchanted with her journey . . . Our two days by coach in the Alleghenies were not too fatiguing. I took great pains to protect our treasure from the cold one must be prepared for in these regions at this season of the year. In any case the little scamp always manages to find people ready to oblige her. Some of our fellow passengers were going to Washington. She instantly insisted on joining their party, and I couldn't refuse her, so we spent 24 hours in that city. Our representative from Ohio, Mr. Duncan was staying in the same hotel and offered to present Sylva to the president. I am enclosing her own account of the interview.

At Philadelphia Mrs. McClosky insisted on giving us the big room you and I occupied together last summer but as it does not contain a stove, the air was glacial when we arrived, I am having one put in as soon as possible. I beg you to take the utmost care of your health. Tell Mrs. McIntyre that I count on her especially in that matter. Remember me to Dr. Price and all his family and say something friendly from me to Alexis. Address your letters Care of Mrs. McClosky, 132 South Second Street.

Sylva's letter is rather a remarkable production for a little girl not yet six years old.

Dear Maman—I am very well. I have seen Mr. Van Buren, the president of the U. S. I have seen the Capitol and think it very pretty. I have been to the Senate and heard Mr. Buchanan make a speech. He talks so distinctly and I heard what he said so well that for a moment I thought he was speaking in French . . .

Dear and good Maman. I love you with all my heart. I hope that on my return I shall find you very well. Good Bye, Sylva.

Another glimpse of father and daughter on this visit to the East is found in the *Life* of Dr. Charles Follen, German liberal refugee,

first professor of German literature at Harvard, Abolitionist and Unitarian preacher of some note. He and Phiquepal had been fellow passengers on the *Cadmus* when the latter was on his way to join Madame
Fretageot in the New School of Industry in Philadelphia after the
failure of the school in Paris.

Dr. Follen was at that time much impressed with his philanthropy
and with his admirable views upon the subject of education, as with
his signal success in the actual management of some boys under his
care.

When Monsieur D' Arusmont came to New York, hearing that Dr.
Follen was in the city he passed a long evening with him, striving
to engage his interest and aid in a plan he had much at heart for
establishing a community upon the principle of exact justice. Here
each one should have an equal opportunity for efficient action of
the kind best fitted to his nature, and should receive an adequate
compensation for his labor; and here the surplus wealth should be
employed for the mutual benefit of all, so that the best education
and the highest civilization should be secured for each and all. Such
a project could not fail to interest a mind like Dr. Follen's. But he
thought such a state of things must be the result of religious training,
which had no place in Monsieur D' Arusmont's plans. "For," said the
latter, "wherever religion has had any power there has been persecution and cruelty."

D' Arusmont believed in the immortality of the race. Follen believed
in the immortality of each and every individual. Monsieur D' Arusmont
tried to convince Dr. Follen that they did not disagree except in words,
and after the discussion, writes Follen, "the benevolent old man left us
in a depressed state of mind, very different from the eager enthusiasm
with which he had commenced the conversation. He had with him a
most beautiful little girl of about eight years of age!"

But this plan of a community established upon the principles of
exact justice which Dr. Follen mentions in his account of their interview never really emerged from the mind of its creator. Though
Fanny still persisted in thinking and saying that her husband was like
herself, "an active fellow laborer in the good cause of human reform,"
her assertions to this end were becoming daily farther from the truth.
Though not yet sixty, Phiquepal was beginning to be in very truth, an
old man. He had long ago given up his old ambition to be a great
teacher of liberal youth by his own special method of education. He
had easily relinquished his vague plan of gathering a small class of

little girls for the same end, mentioned in one of his letters from Paris. He was quite content with one small pupil, his little daughter. And, as an inevitable result of the long and frequently recurring absences of his wife during all the later time of their stay in America, he was becoming more and more satisfied with a plan of life in which she, Fanny, had an increasingly small share.

He became absorbed in what he fondly hoped was to be his *magnum opus*, an elaborate exposition of his general method of education, profusely illustrated with charts and models. He had found exactly the man he wanted to help him make these last, an intelligent young carpenter named Joel Brown, with whom his adopted son Alexis had struck up a friendship as fellow member of a workingman's club established in Cincinnati. Brown himself describes this club in an unpublished biography of Frances Wright at which he was to try his hand after her death.

> Every Wednesday night the club held debates, every Sunday, a lecture by some one of the members. As is generally the case, working men are poor. They wanted a library. A committee was appointed to solicit books to be loaned to the institution, for the use of its members, also newspapers . . . The Committee called on Frances Wright and Phiquepal D'Arusmont who were both very much pleased with the objects of the society and both loaned quite a number of books, and F. W. gave some European newspapers and periodicals while Phiquepal loaned a fine telescope worth $60.
>
> I did considerable work for Mr. D'Arusmont at this time in the construction of some wooden blocks intended for teaching arithmetic and geometry by a plan on which he had been at work for 20 years. He designed it for the use of schools . . . He thought every principle of mathematics ought to be demonstrated. Hence he had what he called blocks to demonstrate every angle, or circle in geometry, or fractions in arithmetic. Even philosophy, astronomy or chemistry could be taught by demonstration, tho' books too were useful. He thought that every school room should be provided with suitable apparatus for demonstration at the expense of the state.
>
> "Are you acquainted with Frances Wright?" he asked me one day.
>
> I told him I was not personally acquainted with her.

"Then I will introduce you," he said, and gave me the introduction in the most approved French style, for Mr. D'Arusmont was one of the most polite men I ever saw, a perfect gentleman, if politeness makes a gentleman.

I was so embarrassed I did not know what to say. She saw my embarrassment but she was so well acquainted with all classes of humanity she soon put me at my ease. F. W. received me with all the simplicity possible, said she was glad to meet me, asked in what part of the city I lived, if I was a native of Ohio. I told her I was born in Connecticut.

"Ah!" says she, "Then you are of English descent. Perhaps we are distant relatives. I told her my ancestors emigrated to this country in the Mayflower, and landed on Plymouth Rock in 1620.

"Yes," she said, "your fathers fled from England to avoid persecution but were more relentless persecutors than those they left behind. They banished Quakers, bored their tongues with hot irons, cut off their ears, hung witches, banished Baptists. There was no end to their persecution, all in the cause of religion, etc., etc."

Fanny's sojourns in Cincinnati at this time were few and far between. Before the end of the summer of 1838 she was again in the East preparing for her lecture campaign for a Democratic Congress, which was to reach its climax in the tumultuous meeting at the Masonic Hall already described earlier in this chapter. She took up permanent quarters in Canal Street, New York, with every intention of spending the winter in that city unless she went to Washington to watch the process of her favorite bill for an Independent Treasury through the new Congress.

But Phiquepal evidently had no intention of joining her in either of these places as long as he could possibly avoid it. He contented himself with long, affectionate letters full of tender anxiety about her health, her general well-being in her new lodgings which he suspected of being anything but comfortable, her business affairs both in Cincinnati and Nashoba, and added detailed accounts of their little daughter, who in her father's eyes at least, was growing up to be a fascinating and remarkably precocious child.

Taking a passage here and there from these letters at random one finds him telling his wife that the trunk he was sending after her full of warm clothes and books and unbound pages from the *Manual of American Principles,* had been despatched at the beginning of November.

I am sorry I did not wrap it in a piece of carpet which you could have used for the floor of your room. I am sorry that your landlord looks like a walking spectre, sorry for him and also sorry for you. It is not pleasant to have a walking spectre for a landlord.

And again.

I have just come home from voting for Dr. Duncan [Representative for Congress from Ohio], I am sure he will be elected. He invited Sylva to come and pay them a visit at their home in the country. But I refused, of course. This dear child is in perfect health and growing to resemble you more and more every day. She would read from morning till night if I permitted it. She has already a large library nearly 60 volumes and uses them with a facility which amazes me. She can find any passage she wants in any one of them. . . . She herself has lately begun to ask me questions on the two subjects which you have most at heart, anatomy or physiology, and mathematics, and at such times, I assure you, she learns more in a quarter of an hour than from many lessons when she is not in the mood for it. She has the best possible memory for anything that interests her and none at all for everything else.

I follow all your suggestions for her health to the letter. Her two glasses of milk in the morning and again at night are always cold. She never takes tea or coffee, or soup if it is too hot, etc., etc. And though we spend three fourths of our time alone together in our room I doubt if there is any child in the world more perfectly happy than she is. All that we lack is the opportunity to give our dear Maman a good hug. We have on my table your portrait by Gorbitz, which is for us both, a source of delightful emotions. Every evening and every night and many times a day we kiss each other before it in your honor, and you seem to smile upon us. It is really very charming, that picture!

I am afraid I shall have to put off my visit to Memphis till next spring. In the mean time I see from a letter just received from Winchester that Whitby has found a good farmer for Nashoba and wants our consent for this new arrangement.

He had better have it for this year as I shan't be there myself to do anything about it. No purchasers as yet for Camilla's house.

Then comes an interesting reference to the almost complete disappearance of hard money throughout the country before the resumption of specie payment by the local banks after the panic of 1837.

Even the Whigs are turning against the banks in these days. I remain on my guard against another catastrophe like that of 1837. There never was such a demand for hard cash as just now in Cin'ti. The Cin'ti banks are issuing no notes at all. All the bank notes now in circulation come from somewhere else. Keep all the money you have and I would advise you too, to draw out all your money and keep it with you after having converted it into gold eagles. I don't know how people are going to manage here this winter. One already lacks coal, salt, sugar and many other necessities of life. For the present, however, Sylva and I are perfectly comfortable and have everything we want except the power of clasping dear maman in our arms.

He was deeply sympathetic over her failure to draw her usual audiences for her last course of lectures.

What difficulties one always experiences, chère amie, whenever one tries to do good. No one ought to know that better than you do. But how can one help it? The more advanced one becomes in one's ideas as compared with the ideas of one's time, the more fear there is of being misunderstood. I love the United States because I believe that the cause of humanity will finally triumph in this country before anywhere else, but I also believe that at the present moment there is no country in the world where the truth is so little understood either by those who sympathize with its advancement or those who seek to retard it. Some day they will render you justice but till that time comes there is no one to aid you because no one really understands you. They are all carried along by force of circumstances without having the least idea where this is taking them, etc., etc.

There are no more of these letters after December, 1838. The next news one has of Phiquepal and his little daughter is their arrival in

New York some time before the date of Fanny's departure for Europe on June 16th, 1839. Then, by a perfectly amicable arrangement between husband and wife, as far as one knows anything about it, Fanny and Sylva sailed alone, leaving Phiquepal to go back to Cincinnati to finish his book and prepare generally to rejoin his family in Europe.

The anguish this separation inflicted on his child is reflected in the tender letter he wrote her after her departure addressed to "Mlle. Sylva D' Arusmont a sa pension ou chez sa maman. Impasse Gramont No. 3 Paris."

My dear little Sylva, thy letter of the 10th April pleased me very much. I see that my little treasure is making progress in her spelling and writing which convinces me that she is making the same progress in her other studies. But what I care for even more is that my dear Sylva should be always good, gentle and obedient to the wishes of her maman who has no other desire than to contribute to the happiness of our dear child. Thank the owner of the house where you and Maman are living for having given you a little garden. If you take great care of it you will always find a source of real joy in it, besides an opportunity for doing useful work. I embrace with all my heart my dear little Sylva. You notice I say "my *little* Sylva," although I hear that you are already growing very big. But this makes no difference to me for I must always look back to certain occasions in the life of my little girl which make me think of her in that way. As for instance the last time I saw her, before she went to France, when she said to me in such a touching manner, "*Et toi donc, aussi, Papa, et toi donc aussi tu m'abandonnes.*" Maman can explain to you, I think, what a mistake you were making then.

Good bye, my dear child. Kiss Maman very tenderly for me till I can press you both against my heart and renew those delights *tous les trois* from which I have been so long deprived. Papa.

The last in the series of these family letters is one from Fanny, full of affection and sympathy with her husband in what she knew to be for him a great and irreparable loss, the death of an old and very dear friend. This was Pierre Turpin, a naturalist of real distinction, member of the French Academy of Sciences since 1833, and also closely connected with Phiquepal's own life as a young man in the West Indies, and in Paris one of the four witnesses to his marriage. His modest apartment in the Rue de la Vielle Estrapade had been a second home for Phiquepal and Fanny during their life in Paris, intimately associated with the tender comradeship between father, mother, and child which little Sylva liked to call *"tous les trois."*

Fanny's letter dated from Paris, May 7th, 1840 begins as follows:

I told you in my letter of last December, my bien aimé, how anxious we all were over the health of our friend Turpin. Well, as it turned out he passed the winter better than I had expected, and by taking the greatest care of himself, even escaped the dangers of a singularly treacherous spring. So we really had all begun to think that he might be spared to us for another year at least. Just two weeks ago on Good Friday, while Sylva was with me for her Easter vacation, we dined together, Sylva and I, with him and his wife, both in the happiest spirits in their reunion with our child.

It seems that two weeks later he went into the country with his wife to over see some renovations which they had arranged to have done the maisonette that you know so well. He worked in the garden till drenched with perspiration and then went to rest in a little arbor, even colder and damper than the house itself. He was seized with an attack of pain, passed three days at Les Gues, badly lodged, with no other care than what his wife could give him, and you know how inefficient she is in such emergencies. Then she took him to Paris in a covered cart, the best they could find in the little town near by.

He died the 1st of May at one o'clock in the morning, having suffered very little, supported to the last by a slight fever. He had been talking about his flowers, and the country in Spring and his future plans till the morning of his death.

You can conceive the state of poor Madame Turpin, knowing her deafness, her extreme unreasonableness, her suspicious character. I only heard the sad news that evening. Sylva was out with little Pauline de Boinville and her nurse to see the fireworks at the fête in the Bois, from the house of a lady living in the Champs Élysées. I had to wait for her return and knowing Madame would be surrounded by friends, I did not get to see her in a quarter so far removed from mine till the next morning. I spent the whole day with that unhappy woman, as she wandered from one room to another of their apartment, from the body of our poor friend whose face still preserved the gentle smile habitual with him while he was alive, into the salle à manger, into the little room next to Turpin's study, returning always to the fatal room where he was lying, at which point she began it all over again until at last towards evening, at the end of her strength the poor woman fell exhausted on our old sofa in the little parlor and permitted us to move her into the apartment above, whose kind owner, has received her for the present. There she is still and there I go to see her every day. "*See*" is well the word, for the only communication one can have with a being so entirely deaf and entirely self-centred as Madame Turpin, is by the eyes.

Our poor friend cannot be buried till Tuesday five days from now, because in this country so given over to legal forms, one can't get "an acte de décès" without an acte de mariage, and an acte de décès is absolutely necessary before one can put a corpse under ground. The poor widow couldn't understand or hear enough to give the necessary information.

Our dear child is still ignorant of the loss we have suffered. I thought it best to conceal it from her at least till after our friend's funeral, and even until the poor widow has come back a little to herself. I would be glad, if it were possible, to save Sylva entirely from her first real sorrow. . . . Not the very first, it is true, for she still suffers from our separation from Papa in New York, last year. But it will certainly be the first sorrow of exactly this kind. She was deeply attached to Turpin and he loved her tenderly in return.

The wind has changed, the rain is falling. I am waiting for a word from you. In the meantime I have enough money to last me till the end of the year. All these misfortunes make me apprenhensive. Ah! If I only could follow the impulse of my heart, it would not be this letter that the steamer carries off to-morrow but thy friend and thy daughter. May we soon meet again, cher ami, and after that no more separations! I give you my word. From henceforth my life shall be devoted to you and our child.

In this confident hope for the future she was, as so often in the past, bitterly mistaken. Between the date of this letter and her death in 1852, she crossed and recrossed the ocean seven times, and Phiquepal nine times, but never together; and only for the briefest interval in the years still remaining to them were husband, wife and child united in any semblance of unity and friendship.

CHAPTER IX

Reaping the Whirlwind

IN THE early autumn of 1841 Phiquepal returned to France, broken in health and nearly helpless from a return of that malady of the eyes which had once before attacked him, shortly after his marriage. He was also in need of the funds necessary for the completion of his book on education, which only his wife could supply. To add to his list of misfortunes he was immediately called upon to prepare his defense in a lawsuit between himself and his former pupil Amadée Dufour, involving sums claimed by him for expenses and service during those six years that Amadée spent with him as his pupil, in Paris and in the United States.

Phiquepal himself had brought the first suit on refusal of the boy's uncle and guardian to pay the sum required of him. After a lapse of years the Count de Beauséjour was bringing a countersuit claiming indemnity against the boy's master for "serious faults in his education."

All Fanny's early affection for her husband, combined with the generous indignation she always felt at any act of injustice and oppression of the weak by the strong brought her to his side. She undertook the long ocean voyage back to Cincinnati alone. She withdrew her adopted son, Alexis, from his work in William Price's brewery and sent him to take care of his father during her absence. She managed to collect the sums necessary for an expensive legal action and was back again in France in time to render substantial help in the preparation of her husband's case against the Count de Beauséjour. One must suspect, indeed, that she made herself almost too prominent in this connection. Otherwise it is difficult to explain the personal animosity against both Phiquepal and his wife so noticeable in the whole conduct of the case.

It came up for final decision before the Cour Royale in Paris, March

30th, 1842, and is cited at length in the *Gazette des Tribunaux* under that date.

First, came the claim of payment for the expenses of education by a master against his former pupil. Second, the claim of the pupil against his master for an indemnity on account of serious faults in that education. Third, details on the system of utilitarian education as set forth by Robert Owen and further developed by Phiquepal.

Monsieur Sudre, lawyer for Amadée Dufour, describes his client as an orphan, ward of his uncle, Monsieur de Beauséjour, member of the Chambre des Députés, and summarized their side of the case. His client recognizing the disadvantages of a university education under the reactionary policies of the Bourbon Restoration, confided his nephew to Phiquepal, whom he believed to be a well-educated and well-born person already very successful in the education of young boys. This man promised to prepare Dufour for any one of the liberal professions, the bar, medicine or engineering. For the two years they remained in Paris everything went well. But in 1823, Monsieur Phiquepal, disturbed by the constant interference of the University of Paris, proposed to take his pupils to Philadelphia where they could continue the education which he had already begun, and at the same time learn English. Nine months later, under the influence of Robert Owen, rival of Saint-Simon and Fourier in his system of education, he removed his school to New Harmony, Indiana.

The humanities, the sciences, the French language were all abandoned for manual labor of the roughest and hardest description, the blacksmith's forge, bricklaying, making of clothes, preparing and cooking their daily food which was largely supplied by their own exertions on the farm and in hunting, and finally at a printing press where they took the place of workmen who had left disgusted by the communist doctrines of the newspaper published in the place. In this occupation they were kept hard at work from five in the morning till ten at night.

Then came a voyage of 1200 leagues down the Mississippi on a flat boat sailed by the four boys aided by one inexperienced sailor, to New York where they continued to print the *Free Enquirer* without instruction or pay or support except the coarsest food and clothing prepared by themselves.

All this time the families of the boys could get no news of them. Finally a single letter appeared from Amadée Dufour to his uncle which was submitted as evidence of the kind of education he had been getting.

He could write English passably. He expected to improve his French when the opportunity presented itself for printing articles for the newspaper in that language. He was quite confident of being able to provide himself with all the necessities of life with his own hands, in any emergency. He could make his shoes, his hats, his bread, his soap, his candles, manage a garden and a farm, build his house, his boat, and swim like a fish if he happened to fall into the water.

But when Phiquepal finally returned him to his uncle declaring his education finished, it was soon too evident that he had forgotten his French, was entirely ignorant of science or letters or any of the requisites for entrance into a liberal profession. After three years spent in the effort to correct all these faults of education in a school of commerce he finally got a place as a clerk at 1000 francs a year.

The distinguished French lawyer, M. Mairie, had been engaged by Fanny for the defense, and proceeded to show that Phiquepal belonged to an honorable family. His father had been president of the Parliament of Bordeaux and his brother was now counselor of state in the Cour Royale of his department. He himself was highly educated, having studied law in his native town, and medicine in Paris. He had adopted a new system of education which was very highly thought of by all sorts of important people, including the Duke de Plaisance and Baron Cuvier.

But at this point Monsieur Mairie was interrupted, silenced, and seated by the presiding judge before he could finish reading these testimonials which, in Fanny's opinion at least, would have satisfactorily proved his client's disinterested, enlightened and valuable work in the cause of juvenile education.

In citing various instances of Phiquepal's indifference to the welfare of his pupils while they were still under his authority, M. Sudre asserted that the main reason for his desertion of them for several years was in order to wander through the world with a lady named Miss Wright, a rich Englishwoman who had founded an Owenite community of black slaves, and whom he afterwards married!

At this point [says Fanny in her own story of the case] not in consequence of any argument or evidence which ap-

peared in the official account, Monsieur Sudre proceeded to
deliver a violent tirade against the public career of the wife
of the defandant, in the United States which, astounding as
it was to those who heard it, was not even alluded to in the
published record.

Let not the public accuse those who shrink from rendering it disinterested service! [she continues] At the present
time there is no prudence that can ward off vengeance from
those who bear the reputation of serving humanity for herself, M. and Madame D'Arusmont, thus outraged in a case
which presented in itself no one political feature, were residing in all but absolute seclusion from a world with which
in its present state they have no sympathy. They have never
either of them had any direct or indirect relation with the
reigning government of France nor indeed with any government of any country.

She always remained convinced that the attack upon a person as
entirely foreign to the case as herself, was the sole cause of the partial
denial of justice in the sentence of the Bench in as much as both
Phiquepal's and the Count's claims for indemnities were denied.

She was also convinced that an entirely false impression of her had
been given the whole French nation by M. Sudre's unwarranted and
insulting attack on her in his speech for his client. The following
letter, written evidently for publication and found among her papers
after her death, is a painstaking effort to explain her real position.

The idea of a woman leading an active life in political
matters must necessarily appear a strange thing in France.
For that reason Madame D'Arusmont has never made any
attempt to occupy herself with such things as long as she lived
in France. She perfectly understands that each country ought
to follow its own natural inclination on such points. But if
in Europe the principles of political liberty work under re-
straint, in America quite the opposite is the case. There each
individual has not only a right but a duty to express his
opinions on public matters, and this duty a woman can sometimes fulfill better than a man, because of the natural respect
and confidence she inspires in the other sex.

In this country it would be impossible for a woman to
make a rendez-vous with the public, in the Hôtel de Ville, a
church, or theatre, or any other place large enough to let in

all who choose to come to discuss the gravest political and social subjects, to examine and criticise both laws and customs as well as any other matter which occurs to them, with all the freedom and frankness that happens to belong to their talent or to satisfy their desire.

But in America, a country where there is no populace but a population composed of free equals where all force is moral not physical the presence and word of a woman armed with nothing but the truth is as powerful as that of a man, and Madame D'Arusmont may very easily owe a considerable part of that influence upon the public minds which even her enemies concede to her, from the very fact of her sex.

But anyone who believes that she ever used that influence with an anarchistic intent, is mistaken. Anyone at all familiar with the adopted country of Madame Phiquepal D'Arusmont would understand not only the falsity but the absurdity of such a statement.

The surest way of losing all influence in the United States is to foment disorder or to attack in any way the institutions and laws of that country. In her defense of truth and her defiance of evil, Madame Phiquepal has often been the object of base and lying attack. But this is the fate of every friend of truth. And the Americans accustomed to the unbridled license of the public press are well accustomed to distinguish the true from the false in their daily newspapers, etc., etc.

In spite of all she could do or say in self-justification, the sense of maladjustment with her surroundings, combined with a very clear knowledge as to just how disagreeable continued police surveillance could be for people as unorthodox in their political opinions as herself and her husband, brought her to a sudden decision, in which Phiquepal apparently entirely agreed, to return to America and resume her residence in Cincinnati, where Alexis had already preceded them.

Again one finds her undertaking a long ocean voyage alone. Phiquepal was still too handicapped by his late illness to be of any help to her in the new plan, to put in order and prepare for occupation the old house of Josiah Warren in Cincinnati, which she had bought some years before, and which was now standing empty.

Now one can turn again to the unpublished narrative of the carpenter Joel Brown, where one finds the following detailed account of his relations with her in this matter.

"The house we live in," she told me, "is a clay house. The walls are built of clay and straw. I think it dangerous, for when it rains and the wind blows hard, it washes the clay, and after every rain the walls get thinner. Did you know Josiah Warren? He was the architect of this house."

I told her that I had read his "Equitable Commerce" but that was all I knew of the man.

"I want this building torn down," she told me, "the rubbish removed, a brick building erected (here she gave me the exact number of dimensions of the rooms), the lot fenced in, and a cistern of 200 barrels. I desire you to tell me what it will all cost, make your estimate and bring it around to me. I must know what it will cost beforehand because I am ignorant of building."

I made the estimate, told her I would do her work, find all the materials, for $2000.

Her answer was, "I want it all done by the day. I think I will get a better job." So it was arranged that way. I did the work by the day, bought all the materials, hired the masons, plasterers and painters and she paid all the bills punctually as they came due. She was very exact in her dealings as the whole D'Arusmont family was.

After the building was partly enclosed I moved my bench into it. In those days carpentering work was all done by hand, and at the same time F. W. also moved in a few things, a charcoal furnace, a sleeping cot, two or three chairs, a table and a writing desk. Her food consisted of a boiled potato or two, a boiled egg, a piece of boiled beef, crackers, tea or coffee. She was a plain liver. My wife says she was the most ignorant housekeeper she ever saw. She could not sweep a room and do it correctly, could not pack a trunk properly when about to start on a journey. She regretted this very much. "How much better it would have been for me," she often said, "if I had been taught general housework when I was a child instead of the aristocratical nonsense I learned while with my guardian."

At first I did not like the idea of her moving into the building before it was finished, thinking that she hoped that way to get more work out of me and my brother, for my brother was working with me, but I soon found out my mistake. She did not seem to have any desire to hurry us, in fact it was the other way. She actually hindered us by talking to us, advancing her theories for the advancement of working

men. We carried our own dinners with us, but she insisted
we should eat our dinners at her table. In this way I learned
a great deal about her private thoughts on different subjects,
never yet published.

Her manner of getting up an address was new to me. She
would write a few minutes, then get up and walk whispering
to herself, repeating what she had written. She learned all of
her lectures by heart and delivered them extempore. I have
often met her in the street talking to herself in whispers.
She never rode in a carriage or on horseback. If she embarked
on a steamboat to go up or down the river she always walked
to the landing. I have known her to walk three miles to see
friends, whispering to herself, looking neither to the right
nor to the left. She was never idle, always reading, writing,
or repeating what she had read. She had a wonderful memory.

"That is because I take an interest in what I read if it is
worth reading," she told me. "You would have just as good
a memory as I have, if you took the same pains I do repeating
to yourself what you have seen, heard, or read." She was the
most entertaining controversialist I ever saw. Her language
was as smooth as oil and as entertaining as it was smooth.
Every word left her tongue finished. No corrections after it
was uttered. She could entertain you by the hour on ancient,
or modern history, on the sciences, geology, chemistry, astronomy or natural history. She was a walking encyclopedia,
an orator, inferior to none and superior to any I ever heard.

Joel Brown then goes on to describe the family life of *"tous les
trois"* now at last reunited in the renovated house of Josiah Warren.

If they weren't happy together they were the most deceitful
hypocrites I ever saw. All later stories to the contrary were
invented by their enemies in the religious world to smirch
their character and destroy their influence as educators.

Joel Brown was not the most discriminating judge on such matters.
The habit of living together, like all other human skills, must be
kept in practice by constant use, and is seriously injured or even
destroyed if interrupted too often and for too long a period.
And even Joel Brown had to admit that this period of married
happiness which he had just been describing, lasted a very short time.

In the fall of 1843 [says he] M. D'Arusmont left Cin'ti
for France taking Sylva with him to finish up her education.
Another object he had in view was to get his manuscript
printed for the use of schools which he had been at work on
for twenty years. He told me he could get his School books
printed for half the price in Paris that he could in Cin'ti. I
know Frances Wright was anxious Sylva should accompany
her Father. If for any reason she had lost confidence in her
husband why did she trust the education of Sylva to him
3000 miles from her home in Cin'ti?

Now, for the first time in her life, it was the others who went away
and Fanny who was left behind. One can only guess what she did
with her new solitude. The political scene in the last years of Tyler's
administration did not interest her. There is no record that she made
any effort to return to the lecture stage at this time. The Woman
Suffrage Movement had been born some three years before at the
World's Anti-slavery Convention in London, June 12, 1840, but Fanny,
in spite of her ardent stand for Women's Rights during her active work
on the lecture stage, never had anything to do with the movement as
such, nor with any of its leaders except Lucretia Mott. And she
had dropped all intercourse with this faithful friend and supporter
when she withdrew from activity in the East, after the failure of the
State Guardianship Plan.

If one may trust Joel Brown's random quotations from what one
might call her table talk at this time, she had a great deal to say
about various concrete examples of the growth of capitalism in the
United States, the financing of the railroads, the exploitation of the
limitless resources of a great continent by the few at the expense of
the many. She had already begun to enlarge and arrange those old
lectures of hers on the History of Mankind which had failed so
signally with her New York audiences in 1839, for the book, which
she published four years later, under the name of *England the Civilizer*.

Then all at once, in the early winter of 1844, everything was changed
by a most unexpected piece of news, a letter from the British Em-
bassy at Washington containing the formal announcement that she
had just fallen heir to the remainder of the family estate in Dundee
through the death of her last remaining cousin, Margaret Wright.

The whole large family of her father's uncle, James Wright, with
whom he had spent his youth and young manhood after the early
death of both his own parents, had been wiped out one after the other,

till now in the fourth generation from the great man of the family, the first Alexander, town councillor of Dundee in 1724, Fanny was left sole descendant of the name, and heir general to the family holdings in Forfarshire, Scotland.

She had never had much to do with her father's family since the death of both parents had removed her from their care to that of her mother's sister in the south of England. For years now she had almost forgotten their existence. None of her father's cousins seem to have married. They lived carefully and cannily and inherited one from the other without ever troubling to make a will, till all their most cherished possessions had fallen into the hands of a woman they knew so slightly that the notice of her heirship spells her name Francesca D'Arusmont. The Dundee inheritance consisted chiefly of real estate scattered through the town and suburbs of old Dundee in separate parcels, amounting in all to some twenty acres drawing rent and other returns of money which increased her income by nearly a third.

The part of it that impressed her most deeply when she came to take possession of it was the house where the merchant descendants of the first Alexander had lived for more than a hundred years, the old family dwelling in the very center of that huddle of grim gray stone walls, many feet thick, threaded by sunless wynds and gloomy closes, long known as "The Vault," now almost entirely pulled down and rebuilt more in accordance with the modern requirements of comfortable living.

It was a house filled to overflowing with the possessions of a family who never threw anything away even after it had outlived its usefulness; with closets which had not been opened for years, full of mouldering dresses in the fashion of a former generation, and heaps of family linen with the names of Alexander and James Wright interwoven along their borders. Here was a notebook which had belonged to Fanny's own father. With what a thrill she recognized "the singular coincidence between a father and daughter separated by death when the first had not reached the age of 29 and when the latter was raised in an opposite quarter of the island and removed from all acquaintance with her Scotch relatives!"

"The spirit of law and the tenor of the conduct of government in order to be well-adapted to the mutable and ever-varying state of human affairs, ought constantly to change according to existing circumstances and the progress of the age!" Indeed this was part of the main thesis of her very first lecture at the Fourth of July celebration at New Harmony in 1828.

Here also was the record of young James Wright's share in the publication of Thomas Paine's *Rights of Man* to make it available for the working classes, etc., etc.

This unexpected revival of memories and associations stretching back to the very roots of her long distant past was indescribably moving to a woman like Fanny, who had been cut off so long from every connection with her youth and childhood.

Many of the friends and relatives who had been closest to her during her own life in Scotland were dead, as for instance both her uncle and aunt Milne, Mrs. Craig Millar and her sister, "the good Spirit," otherwise Miss Margaret Cullem. Her cousin David Milne consented, albeit rather unwillingly, to serve as one of the four trustees for her Dundee property. Another of these trustees was William Watson, brother of Fanny's first suitor, James. The Watsons were also Campbells through their mother, a sister of Fanny's grandfather, General Duncan Campbell, and from them she learned that Miss Frances Campbell was still alive, still living in her own house on the outskirts of Dawlish; but any suggestions on William's part that she should renew her intercourse with her mother's only sister and her own nearest living relative, were without result as far as Fanny was concerned.

All this time Phiquepal seems to have held himself strangely aloof from his wife's good fortune, as if he had been vaguely disturbed, even made a little jealous by it. A serious illness of Sylva's had sent Fanny hurrying to Paris before she finished her business in Dundee. Husband and wife were united then, perhaps for the last time, in nursing their child back to health. But when Sylva was at last well enough to be left behind or even to accompany her parents to Dundee, Phiquepal still refused to leave Paris and let Fanny go back alone to complete her business with her lawyers. He was both annoyed and hurt, however, when with his wife's consent or even by her suggestion, her Scots lawyers took steps to tie up the whole Dundee inheritance in a trust which excluded her husband from any share in its management or power to dispose of it, if he should chance to survive her.

On this second visit to Dundee she had an amusing interview with a lively young reporter of the *Northern Star*, a North British newspaper of some importance at that time.

As the reader may be curious to know [says he] how I arrived at the information herein contained, I may briefly state that as soon as I knew of Madame D'Arusmont's arrival in Dundee for the settlement of important business connected with the property she had inherited from a cousin of her father, the last of her name, feeling anxious to see a woman whose eloquence has gone so far to effect a revolution in the mind of America, I embraced the earliest opportunity of soliciting an interview. I was received with the greatest kindness.

Madame D'Arusmont is among the tallest of women, being about 5 ft 10 inches high. She walks erect and is remarkably handsome. Her brow is broad and phrenologically speaking, magnificent. Her eyes are large, her face masculine, but well-formed, etc., etc.

In the course of our conversation I mentioned to her that certainly little was known of her life as I had seen it stated in the *Edinburgh Review* that she belonged to Glasgow . . . Before her departure from Dundee, she revised with her own hand the proof sheets of the biography here presented.

This is the article so often quoted in earlier chapters.

The narrative ends on the eve of her settlement in New York as editor of the *Free Enquirer*. The autobiography was not brought up to date because she had to take the steamer sailing from Liverpool to New York on August 17th of that same summer.

Her own explanation of this sudden return to America at this important crisis of her life was the necessity of effecting a similar business arrangement with her American holdings as that already entered upon with her Dundee property.

There is no evidence to prove that she was influenced in this by any lack of confidence in her husband, and a number of reasons why he should have been rather relieved than not by proceedings which, while securing him a share of his wife's fortune as long as he lived, relieved him of all responsibilities for its management—which the condition of his health would have made more and more onerous.

On her way back to Cincinnati, she made a stop in Haiti to see for herself how her enfranchised slaves were prospering in their new condition, and went away all the more convinced that her original plan of education followed by colonization was the best, in fact the only solution of the slave problem in America.

She also made a long visit to Nashoba and drew up a new deed of trust for her Tennessee property, on the same lines already proposed for her Dundee holdings. Arrived in Cincinnati she lost no time in making an elaborate will leaving everything to Sylva on the death of her parents, but also containing certain conditions which Phiquepal found particularly disquieting when he received a duplicate copy with the request that he would execute, sign and return it to his wife as soon as possible for safekeeping in the Cincinnati Life and Trust. Only by such means could a married woman make a legal disposition of her own property under the restrictions of the English and American law at that time. By this will Phiquepal was assured of an adequate income for life whether or not he should survive his wife, but new evidence of a revival of some of those expensive schemes for the benefit of the negro race, from which Fanny's marriage with him had effectively weaned her, appeared in a codicil providing for the disposal of a considerable sum of money to form a school for manual training in Shelby County, Tennessee, after her death.

At the time he could find no reason to refuse this request. The duplicate will was duly executed and returned to Cincinnati. A letter from Alexis D'Arusmont to his little sister that same winter also shows entirely friendly relations between husband and wife.

Dear Sylva.

I ought to make papa and you a great many apologies for not writing sooner, but when Maman is on this side and particularly in Cin'ti I deem it altogether unnecessary to write, as she gives you in her letters all the information I should be able to. I am in the brewery business on my own account, in connection with a young man of the name of Harris. I have been at it for 15 months and business is improving rapidly.

I sometimes do not get out of the brewery more than once a week that is on Sunday, when I generally go and dine or take tea with Maman, where I am at present writing these few lines, having dined with her. She returned from Memphis only three days ago. The weather has been intensely cold and it was with a great deal of trouble owing to the great quantity of ice in the river that she reached here. She seemed improved in health by the journey.

He goes on to speak of a young colored girl, daughter of the overseer at Nashoba, whom Fanny had apparently adopted as her maid.

She had rather a lonely time of it, being left alone in the house while Maman went to Memphis.

I shall not enter into business. I shall leave Maman to attend to that, as she is more capable of doing so than I am. Hoping these few lines will convince you that I have not quite forgotten you, I shall conclude by assuring you that my friendship for Papa and Sylva is as strong as ever it was and will continue I hope through life.

Alexis D.

She expected to return to Europe early in the spring of 1846 and had already written to her husband and daughter to meet her in England. By this arrangement she would be saved a long journey back and forth from France before they should all proceed together to Dundee for the final arrangements with her trustees, since Phiquepal's signature as well as hers was required for the disposal of her property as a married woman.

A letter from her to her cousin and trustee, William Watson, tells how gravely she was disappointed in this plan.

May 6th.

Having sailed for London Apr. 4th, I landed Apr. 27th at Portsmouth, [Already one sees the difference the introduction of steam had made in these voyages across the Atlantic] leaving my baggage with my maid to go round by the Thames while I took the railroad to London where I expected to find my family. In their stead a letter from Sylva communicating her indisposition and her father's request that I would proceed to Paris. I went at once and on my arrival here a week since I found Sylva languishing from the effects of another sudden growth, her whole growth having been made in rapid sudden shoots. She is already better.

Thus I could not, as by letter, see you in Liverpool in April to examine my affairs previous to taking action about Scotland. You have already received my letter of Sept. 1845 requesting you to receive and hold in your keeping the trust deed of the Dundee estate desiring that no action might be taken under that deed in my absence.

Send me a line to Paris. Warmest wishes from our little circle.

But now for the first time Phiquepal began to develop obstructive tactics in the settlement of his wife's new inheritance.

A wrangle occurred about the final terms of the deed of trust, a bitter scene between husband and wife when the former accused the latter of lack of consideration for his own and his daughter's rights, and insisted that the deed should be altered on several points before he consented to give his signature. When the three came to settle down all together in Phiquepal's apartment in Paris, they soon found out that the old affectionate, mutually admiring relation between husband and wife which had made life possible and pleasant during those occasional intervals of common existence in the past, was gone beyond all power of resumption.

Even their thoughts and opinions on great human questions were no longer in harmony. Her abounding energy of mind was already occupying itself with portents of the coming revolution of 1848 and she was planning a complete readjustment of human society which seemed to him only so many threats against his own safe and comfortable old age. She saw him at last as he was, a selfish, ineffective, troublesome old man, whose early loyalties to the high cause of human service had gradually been replaced by a timid attachment to personal interests, while his former devotion to her, on which she had so long depended for a thousand useful services, had been entirely replaced by a doting absorption in their only daughter.

Sylva was at this time a delicate girl of fifteen, who had passionately loved and admired both parents, until the painful difference which set one against the other in bitter enmity. Spoiled and petted from infancy, charming, intellectually precocious, but without mental discipline of any sort, she was incapable of preserving an even balance of affection and consideration for both her parents in time of crisis and it was inevitable that between a doting old father who asked nothing more from her than to have her near him, responding to his caresses, and a mother still in the prime of life, formidably active, absorbing and dominating the lives and interests of everyone about her to the exclusion of any individual life of one's own, there was, there could be, only one choice.

For the last five years, moreover, she had spent far more time with her father than with her mother. She had learned to think of him as the best and wisest of men as well as the tenderest of fathers. And in the mutual recriminations to which she was constantly witness in those last unhappy days in Paris it was only too easy to see her mother always in the wrong, her father always in the right.

Long ago in friendly discussion of the essential principles under-

lying human intercourse, husband and wife had agreed that as soon
as two people found each other completely incompatible it was better
for them to part. Now, however, when Phiquepal found himself confronted with exactly that situation he was peculiarly embarrassed by
one complication of the issue which neither of them had thought of
before. So far in their married life it had never greatly mattered to
either of them that the money they lived on came from Fanny. Now
all at once it began to matter very much. Suppose she agreed to
their separation! Could he trust her in her present frame of mind to
go on furnishing the means for his support, or if she let Sylva go
from her, which was very doubtful, trust her to support both himself
and his daughter in a life in which she no longer had any part?

Phiquepal had always been a man of very simple inexpensive tastes,
but he was also a man who had shown himself over and over as
peculiarly incapable of earning his living in the world of competition.
He was nearing seventy, infirm beyond his age, nearly blind, having
lived all his married life on Fanny's bounty. He was suddenly faced
with the possibility of having to relinquish not only the physical comforts to which he had gradually become accustomed but, what was
far worse, the companionship of his beloved child.

One must not blame him too much for the means he took to remove
himself from this painful predicament, but one will not cease to blame
him for the strange ruthlessness which characterized so much of his
later dealings with his wife.

By the law affecting a married woman's property in both England
and America, unless it was already secured by legal settlement before
marriage, everything Fanny possessed in the world, already belonged
legally to her husband. Hitherto it had been Phiquepal's pride and
boast that he had never taken any advantage of this law. Every penny
of his wife's fortune as well as her maiden name and her complete
independence of action, was hers in the same degree after his marriage
with her as before it.

In April, 1847, after months of almost intolerable provocation from
his wife's disturbing presence in their confined apartment in Paris,
Phiquepal suddenly made up his mind to a new course of action
which must put an end to the insufferable situation forever. He
abruptly announced his intention of returning to America taking their
child with him and leaving Fanny to do what she pleased and live
where she liked without them.

From New York he went directly to Cincinnati where he proceeded to take all necessary steps for asserting his marital rights over his wife's property in that city. According to his own later explanation of his conduct in this matter, he never meant to keep all Fanny's property for himself and his child, or even in his own hands. His first idea had been to divide it fairly between himself and her, so that each should be financially independent of the other for the rest of their lives.

But after long and careful consultations with his adopted son, Alexis, when as he himself confesses, he saw the large amounts which she had previously squandered on various visionary schemes, he became satisfied that if she was clothed with power to dispose of the principal as she wished, it would be wasted and she become destitute. For that reason he secured the portion already allotted to her, by a new deed of trust in which he and Alexis D'Arusmont as co-trustee should have power to collect and reinvest all interest as it became due, and to pay a yearly annuity to his wife at such times and in such measure as they should find wisest and best for all concerned.

Alexis D'Arusmont was by this time no longer an immature boy but a man of thirty or more, entirely American in thought and speech, though yet retaining many of the characteristics of the meridional Frenchman. All the traditions which preserve his memory in his adopted country speak of him in the highest terms as a citizen and later as a husband and father.

He had always been devoted to his adopted father, to whom he owed everything he was and had in the world. He was already half in love with his fascinating little foster sister. On the other hand he had never received anything but kindness from Fanny, whose ready generosity in a time of crisis had enabled him to set himself up in his own business as a brewer.

But when it came to a choice between Fanny and Phiquepal in his future relations with his adopted father and mother, he could have had little or no hesitation in throwing in his lot with the latter.

Very shortly after the return of Phiquepal and Sylva to Cincinnati, one finds him replying to Fanny's urgent request to be kept informed as to what was going on in her absence, that "he had been with his father and sister continually during their stay in the city, had concluded to espouse their cause and declined all further correspondence with her."

Indeed, so completely was Phiquepal in his legal rights in what he was doing with his wife's property that even Fanny's own lawyer, a Mr. Morris, saw nothing better to do than help her husband draw up the articles of the new trust and himself send it to her with a letter urging her to sign it as promptly as possible so that there would be the least possible interval before she began to receive the income therein assured to her.

She received this notice some time in the early summer of 1847 while she was in England working feverishly on her new book, *England the Civilizer*.

More than once in the past one finds her so absorbed in some compelling dream of her own creation, as to be for a time at least, completely oblivious of personal suffering, disappointment, discomforts of every sort and kind. Now again it seems possible, even probable, that the best explanation of her strange indifference to her own personal misfortunes through nearly a year after she had been left deserted in Paris, may be found along the same lines.

The longer she worked on this book the more exclamatory, fragmentary, and full of strange symbolism did it become, till it was nearly incomprehensible to the average reader. Its excitement reflected that fervid summer on the eve of the Red Revolution of 1848, when Fanny's old friends the toilers of the world, the oppressed millions who had been so long and so cruelly used by "their booted and spurred riders," seemed for a moment at least to be coming into their own.

In her own words, Liberty, Equality and Altruism: science, industry and woman, the last finally emancipated from the subjection in which she had been held so long by the dominant male, were now at last coming to the rescue of a ruined world. England the Civilizer, France the Simplifier, and the United States the Federator, all played different but essential roles in the great denouement.

Remnants of Utilitarian philosophy and sharp practical criticism of existing evils quite in her old tone of refreshing common sense are found side by side with pages that might have been taken from the apocalyptic extravagances of a second adventist. Indeed this book of hers was essentially apocalyptic in its form and tendencies, though instead of the Second Coming of Christ when all things shall be made new, there is the perfect state in which the various populations of the globe had come to live together in a great federated, yet unified society, where those selfish interests Fanny had fought all her life had been superseded by justice, liberty and righteousness, where every man worked to the limit of his capacity, and every man received to the limit of his individual need, under an administration formed from the people themselves.

Even the most perfect society must have leaders and these, by a sudden and strange reaction on Fanny's part, were to be chosen from the aristocratic class of the "Haves" in the old society, purified by the essential power of collective humanity so that they were at last fit to serve as wise and efficient administrators for the needs of the many. But side by side with these in Fanny's new state there were to be a few rare individuals, naturally belonging to the dominant class who had voluntarily stripped themselves of all their possessions and taken their place with the toilers. And one of these devoted souls she proposed to be herself. On the last page of *England the Civilizer* she announces that at the first dawn of the social revolution she would relinquish all her personal possessions to the general cause.

Already in preparation for that event she had long since ceased to own anything herself. All that was once her property stood in the name of her family.

By the beginning of December her book was in the hands of the printers and she herself at leisure to answer her lawyer's announcement of the formation of the new deed of trust with her husband and Alexis acting as co-trustees.

On December 3rd, 1847 came the following letter from her in London.

Dear Sir

I have been detained at the seashore by illness during which time my letters were not forwarded to me. I write now, dear sir, in the American consul's office, tired, weak and standing in a dark room.

I think I should have a right to half my property, but no doubt all has been settled with a view to the best possible security. I can say no more at the moment. Within is the power of attorney I have just executed for the raising of $5000 pledged in Mr. D'Arusmont's name and mine. I did not feel authorized to execute it before, ignorant as I was of all the proceedings taken or intended. I wrote Alexis in June telling him of my ill health and requesting another remittance but have received nothing so far. Do not neglect to see that the money is forwarded immediately as I am at this moment all but without funds.

You say Mr. D'Arusmont and Sylva left Cin'ti in September. Where are they? I pray you to give me news of my dear daughter's safety. I will write again soon but I beseech

you to have a draft forwarded to me care of Isaac Ironside,
Bank Building, Sheffield, Yorkshire, Great Britain.

For one reason or another this letter did not satisfy either Alexis
or Phiquepal. Alexis enclosed it in one to his sister in Paris, Sylva
having already assumed the office of amanuensis-in-chief to her half-
blind father which she continued to fill faithfully till his death. Referring to the request it contained for money, he remarks that he
had not sent any and was not going to send any money for two reasons.

> The first is that I can't, having already invested all the
> funds on hand. And secondly I see nothing to satisfy me
> that all necessary documents will be signed by her, as ex-
> pressly stated in the deed of trust made by Papa and me
> before she can be entitled to her portion of the trust fund.
> I send you the copy of her letter so that you and Papa may
> fully understand what she says for herself and if he thinks
> that upon what she writes he can advance her what funds
> she wants for her necessary wants, he can do so out of the
> funds he has on hand and I can forward him the amount at
> his request.

And Phiquepal's reply, dated February 5th, 1848 from Paris, shows
how little Fanny had to expect in her future dependence on her husband.

> Thank you for sending us so promptly Madame D'Arus-
> mont's reply to Mr. Morris. You have done exactly right in
> refusing to satisfy her demands. We have already sent her
> some three days ago £100 by an intermediary without writ-
> ing ourselves, or making any mention of the Trust deed,
> though Mr. Morris has already told us that we could with-
> hold all funds till she sent a clear statement of her intentions
> towards it. We have asked him to set a definite time for this
> and tell her that if she does not reply within these limits she
> will receive no more funds. One suspects her good faith. At
> one moment she says that the trust pleases her thoroughly,
> and at the next she evades all its conditions. I have also
> asked Mr. Morris to tell the president of the bank in Cin'ti
> of our intention to go on living here for the next four years

during which time it will not be necessary to make any change in our investments in Cin'ti.

For the rest, dear friend, since in my moments of leisure, I very much like to pass our business affairs in review, I beg you to send me every detail of the receipts and expenditures of the property as they are entered in your account book.

A very few days later the fall of Louis Philippe was followed by a furious insurrection among the working classes in Paris. For three days—June 24th, 25th, and 26th—the eastern industrial quarter of Paris was given over to the most terrible scenes of bloodshed and struggle which resulted at last in the almost complete annihilation of the radical workers by the army under Cavaignac.

Sylva and Phiquepal had weathered these storms without personal danger or any inconvenience except that resulting from the prostration of financial credit which accompanied the establishment of the short-lived Red republic in France, with the consequent interruption of their American income.

One finds, for instance, Alexis writing Sylva as early in the year as April 18th.

"I am sorry to see by Papa's last letter, the embarrassing situation in which your financial arrangements may be plunged by the great change in the French government. I can't send any assistance for every commercial house in Havre has suspended payment." He urges them both to come home. There is also a brief mention of Frances, in reply to Phiquepal's reference to his wife's new book, both father and son being very much annoyed by her personal statement as to the condition of her own fortune. "What connection she makes between private affairs and subjects treated in a work intended for the public, is a thing I do not at all understand!"

It would seem that Phiquepal did actually make a flying visit to Cincinnati to settle the difficulties of the money exchange with Europe, but he went alone and returned as soon as possible to his daughter, left behind in Paris.

He had hardly settled down to his peaceful pleasant life in the Rue Clichy in Paris, however, when he received a most disquieting piece of news in a letter from Alexis to Sylva, July 26th, 1848.

The very day after I sent a letter to Papa in New York before he sailed, [says he] Madame D'Arusmont arrived here.

I was a little surprised at the manner in which she wished to meet me, just as if nothing had happened to create any coldness between her and me. The first thing was, "How are you, my dear boy!" drawing me to her to embrace me. This last compliment I declined receiving, and merely gave her my hand and asked her how she was.

I was astonished to see her look so well. I never recollect seeing her look better. I had imagined from the tenor of her letter that she would have looked care-worn and much emaciated but to my great astonishment she looked as blooming as a young girl of 18, a very convincing proof to me that all she pretends to have suffered is all affectation and for effect.

She is stopping at a boarding house not far from my place of business. She frequently calls there and I have called once on her at her particular request when she did everything in her power to prejudice me against Papa and also to work upon my feelings. But I believe I know you and Papa too well to shake my faith in the love and friendship that we all feel for one another. Madame D'Arusmont betrays her wish to estrange us by talking too much.

She has had a great many interviews with Mr. Morris, and now that she finds things are arranged so that she can't change them, appears to be satisfied. She talks of going to Memphis in a short time as though she intended to make Nashoba her future residence and at the same time improve that property. She also speaks of some work that she is engaged on which requires a great deal of her time. I don't know how she will be able to manage both, but that is her business not mine. She has said to me once or twice that she had predicted all the events that have taken place in France and takes credit to herself for having averted the same catastrophe in England. It may be, but I doubt it. I had almost forgotten to say that Barbara came with her and will accompany her tomorrow or next day to Memphis.

Another letter speaks of Fanny's continued residence on the old site of her wildest dreams and bitterest failures.

She has been making purchases of farming implements and household articles, salt provisions for the use of her people until such time as they should be able to raise their own supplies. She has also turned off the family of Barbara's father, as she says they were too lazy and now has taken on a white overseer with several negroes whom she hires to work the place under her own control, etc., etc.

She has found a bad advisor in her new lawyer at Memphis and I hear that some of her friends there are persuading her to have the deed of trust set aside by a suit in the court of Chancery here. But I am happy to say that the manner in which Mr. Morris met that proposition soon made her see the absurdity of such a course.

It would have been better for the peace of mind of all concerned if Fanny could have remained in the mood of lofty detachment from personal possessions in which she wrote the last words of *England the Civilizer*, but perhaps that would have been asking too much from a being as proud, as passionate, as peculiarly sensitive to real or fancied grievances as she.

Very soon after her return to Cincinnati she allowed herself to be persuaded by a number of her friends in Cincinnati who thought she had been badly used to bring suit against the two D'Arusmonts, father and son, for the restitution of her property in Cincinnati and Nashoba, which she claimed had been illegally taken out of her control by a deed of trust to which she had consented against her will and without clear understanding of what she was doing.

Before she could obtain the legal status necessary for the prosecution of any suit against her husband, she must obtain a divorce. Only by such means was a married woman restored to the rights of femme sole which she had forfeited under the law affecting the status of a married woman in both England and America.

A petition of divorce in the courts of Shelby County where she had already established residence during her long visits to Memphis, was thus inextricably involved in the Ohio suit before chancery, and the two actions, though tried in different courts and even in different states, depended on the same evidence and were practically part of the same legal process by which Fanny was trying to regain possession of her property.

On July 1st, 1850, accordingly, one finds Alexis writing in some agitation to announce the wife's last *démarche* to her husband and child in Paris.

"She has been encouraged in this by Dr. Price, meddlesome old nuisance." Thus does Alexis describe his first employer in the brewing business in which he was now, through Fanny's generosity, established for himself. "I find her principal council is an old intimate friend of Dr. Price and offers to share the expenses with them in case the process goes against them."

One need not follow the details of these two suits further than is absolutely necessary. The sight of two people who have lived together in peace and mutual confidence for a number of years, pouring out abuse and recriminations against one another in their desire to prove one another in the wrong, is especially disagreeable when the two people involved had so much that was really fine and good about them as Fanny and Phiquepal.

In justice to the latter, however, one must quote some passages from the very long letter he wrote his wife as soon as he received the notice of her petition for divorce, begging her to desist from this intention.

> I must own, my dear friend, that I suffered most cruelly while reading the long document which you have drawn up against me . . . you whose great qualities I have so deeply loved, you the noblest of women in my eyes, whom I had the happiness of rendering mother of a daughter worthy of her, I hoped, in every respect.
>
> When we were united to each other, it was after a long and intimate friendship. We felt a deep and mutual esteem, and from the depths of our hearts came those vows by which we bound ourselves to support and assist each other in pursuing that ideal towards which our steps were equally directed, although by different routes—you by outward life, written or spoken, I, more humbly and certainly more modestly in education of children. These vows, I believe, Frances, I have most loyally kept. Your desire to keep them loyally, I feel sure, was equal to my own. Whence then, proceeds this discord between us? I believe I know my friend, and will tell you frankly, leaving the appreciation of my words to your own conscience.
>
> Your life was essentially an external life. You loved virtue deeply, but you loved also, and perhaps even more, grandeur and glory; and in your estimation, unknown, I am sure, to your innermost soul, your husband and child ranked only as mere appendages to your personal existence. You could not even conceive their individuality, as distinct from your own; you imagined you possessed that which we mutually agreed no human being possesses over others, the right of stopping

their personal development and forcing them to live your life without examining whether that existence coincided with their wishes or their ideal. . . . You could not conceive that my daughter and myself should be anything but satellites revolving in your orbit, and I must also sorrowfully add, my friend, that since an epoch closely corresponding with your Scotch inheritance, your simple and austere disposition seemed suddenly to expand into desires of luxury, and at the same time your character and political opinions underwent a complete transformation. Frances Wright, the champion of democracy became the warm defender of aristocracy! This is attested by your last publication, "England, the Civilizer," which offers a most striking contrast to your earlier writings.

Constant discussions owing to the utter change in your sentiments and character made our life together impossible.

He then went on at some length and with some show of reason to explain his plan for the division of her fortune.

We had never asked ourselves, I fully believe, to which party belonged the wealth we enjoyed, nor what was its origin. It belonged to us, the community, and not only did we enjoy it together but its distribution was free to both according as the opportunity presented itself. Having both reached that age when there is no further chance of increasing family, we considered our fortune as the property of our only child, and spending our income freely, we mutually wished to insure to her the fee simple as her right. All the deeds you are now seeking to destroy were made in view of those two objects—to insure to you and myself a perfectly mutual independence, and the enjoyment of all our property after our death to our daughter. More than half our income is settled already on yourself, while I and our child whose education has cost and still costs me considerable sums, content ourselves with the other moiety. The delay you have recently met with in the payment of your income only became known to me through reading your suit, etc., etc. Whence arises, then, your claim that I have drawn anything from you violently and fraudulently? Your former love for me was undoubtedly excited by the belief that you thoroughly understood my character, but to commit what you have charged me with I must have lost my senses, and thanks to the life I have led I am still in possession of all my faculties, etc., etc.

Phiquepal lost this gentle and reasonable tone as the proceedings for divorce developed.

He was apparently absent when the case came up in Raleigh, the capital of Shelby County, Tennessee, in October. But the speech of his lawyer urging that Fanny's petition be rejected is ingeniously insulting.

> He believes you are about 55 years of age, being 16 years younger than himself: that you are frequently afflicted with ill-health, although still active and enterprising in your habits and persevering and unrelenting in your persecutions of himself and Sylva. He also admits that the bodily infirmities which have their origin in the brain fever you had in 1827 and the severe relapse you experienced in 1845 in consequence of too much application in composing your lectures, and great disappointment in not delivering them in America, may have been greatly aggravated by the mental sufferings endured by you. But these mental sufferings have not been produced by any improper act done or omitted by him, but by your restless and aspiring disposition and implacable hostility to him. Said hostility having been excited by his opposition to your plans respecting your daughter and the various measures, shifts, and devices resorted to by you subsequently in order to bring Sylva under your power through the aid of your property. And he states that he believes that your almost constant application to your political works when in England (1847-1848) especially the severe disappointment you experienced in the little sensation produced in England by your lectures and your book, must have been to you a great cause of mental suffering and he verily believes that you have been so engrossingly occupied with your political and social schemes and have so engrossingly brooded over your imaginary wrongs that the intellect itself has become diseased and deranged and upon this supposition alone can he account for the numerous misstatements and perversions contained in your bill.

His plea was rejected by the court, however, and Fanny obtained her divorce.

The scene now shifts to the Ohio Court of Chancery in Cincinnati, where Fanny was represented by a lawyer of good local reputation and both Phiquepal and Sylva as well as Alexis were present at the trial.

The following brief statements are found in the *Daily Commercial* of Cincinnati, August 5th, 1851. "The D'Arusmont Case. Judge Walker began his argument yesterday."

"August 12, Judge Walker pronounced in favor of the complainant on the whole bill, besides granting her alimony, as an allowance during the suit and before the final verdict."

But this court decision turned out in the end to be only an empty triumph for Frances Wright. She had hoped and believed that when she won her suit she would also recover possession of her daughter, but in this she was bitterly disappointed.

A meeting between mother and daughter was finally arranged by Fanny's lawyer, Mr. Gholsen.

> I thought it my duty to accept, [says Sylva in her diary] without any great hope of success. Mr. Gholsen proposed his own house but my mother insisted on another and herself fixed the hour between three and four. I went early accompanied by Papa. He left me at the door urging me to be prudent. I waited. She came in and for a moment on first seeing each other everything else was forgotten. Then a word, a look and I could see that it was all as bad as ever. Our talk lasted five hours and left me perfectly hopeless of any good coming from further intercourse. She wanted to be alone with me on my way home and appeared very much irritated when our host insisted on accompanying us. The next day she came to the hotel to bring me some fruit that I had left behind and wrote me a charming letter, but since then I am told that she is more furious with us than ever.

Phiquepal had in the meantime appealed the judgment handed down against him in Cincinnati and was preparing another suit in Memphis in connection with the Nashoba property.

"It will wear us out," cries Sylva to her diary. "It will kill my father and waste all those precious years when we might still be living together." But the end came much sooner than she had feared.

In the beginning of January, 1852, Fanny fell on the ice in her own front yard and broke her hip. She was carried from her own house to that of a good old friend of both husband and wife since their first residence in Cincinnati, a Frenchman named Dennis, where every arrangement was made for her comfort, but she remained in great pain and quite helpless while the broken limb was kept extended by weights so as to prevent it from contracting while it healed.

"It is not my hip which makes me suffer," she is reported as saying over and over during those last weeks of illness. "Not my hip but my head, my head!"

This torture lasted for nearly a year till the middle of December, 1852, when after weeks of delirium brought on by extreme suffering she died in full possession of her senses at the age of fifty-seven.

Sylva and her father were no longer in Cincinnati when the end came. Some six weeks after Fanny's serious accident Phiquepal was also knocked down by a horse and buggy driven by a Dr. Chamberlain in a hurry to visit a patient. Though no bones were broken the shock of the fall was so serious for an old man already nearly blind and growing deaf, that a change of scene had been prescribed for him.

He was still in New York with Sylva when the news of his wife's death was telegraphed him by Alexis.

One finds the note of it in Sylva's diary. "It arrived on Dec. 14 at half past four in the afternoon. I sent this reply: 'Wait. I start tomorrow. Sylva.'"

And four days later, the following Saturday, she was writing in Cincinnati.

> Today I have fulfilled a melancholy duty, which brought with it, its own reward. I have been to the funeral of my poor mother and I have learned that her last hours were calm, that her last words were for me, her last blessing, her last kiss. And out of all this trial comes this much consolation, that all her old love for me had returned while she was dying. Everyone who surrounded her treated her with the greatest tenderness.
>
> I saw her again for the last time in her coffin, looking once again as I always remember her, the beautiful and lovely mother whose likeness was perpetuated by the Gorbitz portrait.

On the last morning of her life, December 13th, she made her will, "being of sound mind and memory but very ill and not long to live," leaving everything she possessed to her only daughter, Frances Sylva D'Arusmont, "who has been alienated from me but to whom with said property I give my blessing and forgiveness for the sorrows she has caused her mother, etc., etc."

Announcement of her death appeared in the *Cincinnati Gazette*:

> On Monday the 13th inst. in this city, Frances Wright
> D'Arusmont in the 57th. year of her age. Her friends are
> invited to attend her funeral from her late residence on 7th.
> Street west of John, on Wed. the 14th inst. at half past one.
> Interment postponed to the 18th. at 2 o'clock. Her friends are
> invited to attend.

Very little notice was taken of her death except by some radical
papers, *The Reasoner and Secular Gazette*, Great Britain, and the
Boston Investigator where one finds a notice of two lectures given at
the Sunday Institute in Philadelphia by one Thomas Curtis to commemorate her life and death.

Her husband did not long survive her. He died in Paris on March
22nd, 1855, "with as clear a mind and as warm a heart as possible,"
says his daughter, "while just completing his 76th year."

His tomb is in the Montparnasse Cemetery in Paris, marked by
an elaborate monument with a long inscription. Fanny's grave in the
Spring Grove Cemetery in Cincinnati is marked in the same elaborate
way, both monuments being raised by their daughter with the filial
desire of preserving the memory of both parents to a forgetful world.

Of the two, one must admit that Frances is in less danger of being
forgotten than Phiquepal. For in spite of the sorry trick fate played
on her at the end by bringing her to final defeat over a petty personal
struggle with her nearest and dearest for such poor things as money
and power, after a life wholly dedicated to the noblest ends, she
yet remains a person whose permanent achievements in the field
of social service far outweigh the many obvious and disastrous
failures of some of her most cherished intentions. Her failure as a
wife and mother and even as a faithful friend cannot be overlooked.
Her overweening confidence in her own genius, her thirst for public
recognition, her inability to see life at all unless she was in some
fashion in the center of it, must be included in any just estimate of
her character. But with all her faults, and perhaps even because of
some of them she still remains a woman who will not let herself be
forgotten until she is properly remembered by the country to which
she gave her first love, which drew forth her one successful book,
Views of Society and Manners in America.

For she was not content to stop at mere empty love and praise of her adopted country. Her youth, her health, her fortune, and her own good name, were recklessly sacrificed in one attempt after the other to make and keep the land of Free America worthy of its high heritage. However barren of tangible success her work may seem today, at least in its first intentions, her efforts to stir up and quicken the somewhat stagnant currents of the popular mind in the early nineteenth century have had incalculable results and still continue to work and bear good fruit in all sorts of unexpected nooks and corners of this great country, where old local tradition of the origin of some work of social service still points back to the long-dead friendship of some forward-looking woman of an older generation with Frances Wright.

This book is a belated attempt to pay some measure of the debt we owe her.

THE END

ACKNOWLEDGMENTS

THE authors are particularly indebted to the Pennsylvania Historical Society for the use of the letter from Lafayette to Madison, August 28, 1826, and the letter from Lafayette to Robert Dale Owen, October 28, 1829, vols. 40-41; to the Philadelphia Historical Society, Gratz collection, for the Mathew Carey manuscript; to Walter P. Gardner and Stuart Jackson for the Lafayette letters in their private collections; to Grace Zaring Stone for the letters of Mary Robinson Owen to Robert Dale Owen; to Nora Fretageot, librarian of New Harmony Library, New Harmony, Indiana; to André Girodie, director of the Museum of Franco-American Co-operation, Blerancourt, France, and to the Rev. William Guthrie, formerly of St. Mark's-in-the-Bouwerie, New York City, for the courtesy of extending the use of the collection of family papers, including letters, diaries, unpublished poems, lectures, etc., of Frances Wright D'Arusmont, his grandmother.

BIBLIOGRAPHY

BOOKS, PERIODICALS, AND MANUSCRIPTS

Abdy's *Journal of a Residence and Tour in the United States of North America*. April, 1833–October, 1834.

Bentham, Jeremy. Works–11 vols. Edited by John Bowring, Edinburgh: 1843.
    Mss. Portfolio No. 10, folder No. 9–Letters from Frances Wright to Bentham, March 7-9, 1823.

Berrian, Hobart. *Origin and Rise of the Workingmen's Party*.

Brown, Paul. *Twelve Months in New Harmony*, 1827.

Carey, Mathew. Mss. Select Scraps. Vols. No. 10, No. 13, No. 28.

Chinard, Gilbert. *The Letters of Lafayette and Jefferson*. Introduction and notes by Gilbert Chinard. Baltimore: Johns Hopkins Press, 1929.

D'Arusmont, Frances Wright. *Altorf, a tragedy*. Philadelphia: 1819.

—— *Views of Society and Manners in America—in a Series of Letters from that Country to a Friend in England, During the Years 1818, 1819, 1820*. By an Englishwoman. London: 1821.

D'Arusmont, Frances Wright. *A Few Days in Athens*—Being the Translation of a Greek Manuscript discovered in Herculaneum. London: 1822.

—— Course of Popular Lectures. New York: 1829.

—— Introductory Address—delivered by Frances Wright at the opening of the Hall of Science, New York, on Sunday, April 26, 1829. New York: 1829.

—— Address—containing a Review of the Times, as first delivered in the Hall of Science, New York, May 9, 1830. New York: 1830.

—— An Address to the Industrious Classes—A Sketch of a System of National Education, New York: 1830.

—— Fables. New York: 1830.

—— Parting Address, as delivered in the Bowery Theater to the People of New York in June, 1830. New York: 1830.

—— "What is the Matter?" New York: 1838.

—— Tracts on Republican Government and National Education addressed to the Inhabitants of the United States of America. New York: 1832.

(Robert Dale Owen wrote the tract on Republican Government and Miss Wright that on National Education.)

—— *Biography, Notes, and Political Letters of Frances Wright D'Arusmont* (From the Dundee, Scotland, *Northern Star*.) Printed in Boston, by J. P. Mendun, 1849.

—— *England the Civilizer—Her History developed in its Principles*, London: 1848.

—— Articles from New Harmony *Gazette*, a weekly magazine published in New Harmony, Indiana, 1825. In 1828 it became The New Harmony and Nashoba *Gazette*.

—— Articles from *Free Enquirer*, a weekly magazine published in New York, 1828-1832.

—— *Manual of American Principles*, 1837. Vol. I, 1-7 issues (to be found in Yale University, New Haven, Conn.).

—— Most of the lectures delivered by Frances Wright and much of her poetry are reprinted in the *Free Enquirer* and New Harmony *Gazette*.

Davis, James. *History of Memphis*.

Edwards, Martha. "Religious Forces in the United States, 1815-1830." *Mississippi Valley—Historical Review*.

Erving, G. W. Correspondence to William Maclure—New Harmony Library.

"Etudes sur l'Histoire d'Haiti," tome 10—pp. 174-175.

Evans, George. *History of the Workingmen's Party*.

Faris, John T. *Romance of Forgotten Towns*.

Flower, George. *History of English Settlement in the Illinois*.

Follen, Mary. *Life of Charles Follen*.

Gallatin, James. Diary.

Gilbert, Amos. *Memoirs of Frances Wright, The Pioneer Woman in the Cause of Human Rights.* Cincinnati: 1855.

Gleason's *Pictorial Companion.*–"Sketch of Frances Wright," June 1854.

Gottschalk, Louis. Lafayette Collection. University of Chicago.

Jefferson, Thomas. Correspondence. Edited by W. C. Ford.

Keating. *History of Memphis.* Boston: 1916.

Lafayette. Correspondence. Vol VI.

Lamartine, A. *History of the Restoration of 1830.*

Lee, Elizabeth. "Frances Wright, the First Woman Lecturer," *Gentlemen's Magazine*, May, 1894, pp. 518-528.

Levasseur, A. *Lafayette in America in 1824-1825.*

Lockwood, G. B. *The New Harmony Movement.* New York: 1905.

Mackenzie, Charles. *Notes on Haiti.* London: 1830.

Morton, Samuel G. *Memoir of William Maclure.* Philadelphia: 1844.

Myers, Gustavus. *History of Tammany Hall.* 1901.

Nevins, Allan. *The Evening Post.* New York: 1922.

Nolte, Vincent. *Fifty Years in Both Hemispheres.*

Owen, Robert Dale. *Moral Physiology*, London: 1841. *Threading My Way*, New York: 1874. "An Earnest Sowing of Wild Oats," *Atlantic Monthly*, July, 1874.

Owen, William. "Diary of William Owen." *Indiana Historical Society Publications.* Vol. IX, No. 1. Indianapolis: 1906.

Pepe, G. *Memoirs et Correspondance.*

Podmore. *Life of Robert Owen.*

Saxe-Weimar, Bernard, Duke of: *Travels through North America during the Years 1825 and 1826.* 2 vols. Philadelphia: 1828.

Skidmore, Thomas. *The Rights of Man to Property: Being a proposition to make it equal among the Adults of the Present Generation; and to Provide for its Equal Transmission to Every Individual of Each Succeeding Generation, on arriving at the Age of Maturity.* New York: 1829.

Stephen, Leslie. *English Utilitarians.*

Stuart, James. *Three Years in North America.* 1833.

Tone, Theobald Wolfe. *The Life and Adventures of Theobald Wolfe Tone.* Glasgow (no date given). Written by himself, edited by his son, William Theobald Wolfe Tone. New York: 1883.

Trollope, Anthony. *Autobiography.*

Trollope, Francis Milton. *Domestic Manners of the Americans.* 2 vols. London: 1832.

Trollope, Thomas Adolphus. *What I Remember.* New York: 1888.

Waterman, W. R. *Frances Wright.* New York: 1924.

American Dictionary of National Biography.

GENERAL REFERENCES

Bradlaugh, Charles. *Biographies of Ancient and Modern Celebrated Free Thinkers*. Boston: 1877.

Commons, John R. *History of Labor in the United States*. 2 vols. New York: 1918.

Dictionary of National Biography. Edited by Leslie Stephen.

Encyclopedia of American Biography, 1887-1889. Edited by James Grant Wilson and John Fiske.

Fish, C. R. *Rise of the Common Man*.

MacDonald, William. *The Jacksonian Democracy*.

McMaster, John Bach. *History of the People of the United States*. New York: 1913.

Nordhoff, Charles. *Communistic Societies of the United States*. New York: 1875.

Noyes, John H. *History of American Socialisms*. Philadelphia: 1870.

Odell, G. C. *History of the American Stage*.

Index

THE AMERICAN UTOPIAN ADVENTURE

sources for the study of communitarian socialism in the
United States 1680–1880

Series One

Edward D. Andrews THE COMMUNITY INDUSTRIES OF THE SHAKERS (1932)

Adin Ballou HISTORY OF THE HOPEDALE COMMUNITY from its inception to its virtual submergence in the Hopedale Parish. Edited by W. S. Heywood (1897)

Paul Brown TWELVE MONTHS IN NEW HARMONY presenting a faithful account of the principal occurrences that have taken place there during that period; interspersed with remarks (1827)

John S. Duss THE HARMONISTS. A personal history (1943)

Frederick W. Evans AUTOBIOGRAPHY OF A SHAKER and revelation of the Apocalypse. With an appendix. Enlarged edition (1888)

Parke Godwin A POPULAR VIEW OF THE DOCTRINES OF CHARLES FOURIER (1844) DEMOCRACY, CONSTRUCTIVE AND PACIFIC (1844)

Walter C. Klein JOHANN CONRAD BEISSEL, MYSTIC AND MARTINET, 1690–1768 (1942)

William J. McNiff HEAVEN ON EARTH: A PLANNED MORMON SOCIETY (1940) With "Communism among the Mormons," by Hamilton Gardner

Michael A. Mikkelsen THE BISHOP HILL COLONY. A religious, communistic settlement in Henry County, Illinois (1892) With "Eric Janson and the Bishop Hill Colony," by Silvert Erdahl

Oneida Community BIBLE COMMUNISM. A compilation from the annual reports and other publications of the Oneida Association and its branches, presenting, in connection with their history, a summary view of their religious and social theories (1853)

Marianne (Dwight) Orvis LETTERS FROM BROOK FARM 1841–1847. Edited by Amy L. Reed (1928)

Robert A. Parker A YANKEE SAINT. John Humphrey Noyes and the Oneida Community (1935)

A. J. G. Perkins & Thersa Wolfson FRANCES WRIGHT: FREE ENQUIRER. The study of a temperament (1939)

Jules Prudhommeaux ICARIE ET SON FONDATEUR, ÉTIENNE CABET. Contribution à l'étude du socialisme expérimental (1907)

Albert Shaw ICARIA. A chapter in the history of communism (1884)